BY THE SAME AUTHOR:

ALBERT SCHWEITZER

DOROTHY L. SAYERS

DOROTHY L. SAYERS

*A
Biography
by*

JAMES BRABAZON

*With a Preface by
Anthony Fleming*

Foreword by P. D. JAMES

CHARLES SCRIBNER'S SONS
NEW YORK

Excerpts from letters of C. S. Lewis to Dorothy L.
Sayers are reprinted by permission of Harcourt
Brace Jovanovich, Inc. from *Letters of C. S. Lewis*
edited by W. H. Lewis, © 1966 by W. H. Lewis
and Executors of C. S. Lewis.

Library of Congress Cataloging in Publication Data

Brabazon, James.
  Dorothy L. Sayers: a biography.

  Bibliography: p.
  1. Sayers, Dorothy Leigh, 1893-1957—Biography.
2. Authors, English—20th century—Biography.
PR6037.A95Z62   823'.914 [B]   81-4831
ISBN 0-684-16864-2   AACR2

1 3 5 7 9 11 13 15 17 19   Y/C   20 18 16 14 12 10 8 6 4 2

Printed in the United States of America

CONTENTS

Acknowledgements ix

Preface by Anthony Fleming xi

Foreword by P. D. James xiii

Introduction xvii

Dorothy L. Sayers 1

Appendix: the *Bridgehead* series 278

Notes 283

Select Bibliography 297

Index 305

LIST OF ILLUSTRATIONS

Plates

Following page 44

Dorothy as a child

Dorothy with her parents and her cousin Ivy

Dorothy impersonating the Musketeer, Athos, in her 'teens

Dorothy with a friend at about the same period

Dorothy impersonating H. P. Allen (*photo Muriel St Clare Byrne, courtesy Bodleian Library*)

Cartoon originally captioned "Dr Allen puts his Bach in" (*courtesy Bodleian Library*)

Dorothy at Somerville (*courtesy Bodleian Library*)

École des Roches, Le Vallon

The photograph from Dorothy's Carte d'identité when she went to teach in France

The first degree ceremony for women at Oxford (*courtesy Muriel St Clare Byrne*)

Eric Whelpton

John Cournos (*courtesy Alfred Satterthwaite*)

The portrait by John Gilroy, 1929: Dorothy in a white wig (*courtesy J. Gilroy*)

The spiral staircase in Benson's office, featured in *Murder Must Advertise* (*courtesy Messrs Ogilvie, Benson & Mather Ltd*)

Drawing by John Gilroy, 1930 (*courtesy J. Gilroy*)

Aunt Amy with Anthony around 1928

Following page 220

Anthony as a schoolboy

Ivy's cottage at Westcott Barton, where Anthony grew up

Dorothy at around the time of her marriage

Mac

The house at Witham as it is in 1980 (*photo James Brabazon*)

Dorothy at work around 1950

With the Detection Club skull

All unacknowledged photographs are reproduced by courtesy of Anthony Fleming.

Illustrations in the Text

page

Three famous Guinness advertisements (*courtesy Messrs Ogilvie, Benson & Mather Ltd*)   136

Dorothy's handwriting: a page taken from a letter   230

ACKNOWLEDGEMENTS

My first acknowledgement must be to Mr Anthony Fleming for authorizing me to write this book about his mother and for allowing me unrestricted access to her private papers. To this I must add my thanks for his patient and enthusiastic pursuit of accuracy, both in delving through seemingly endless records and in exhaustive checking of the various drafts of the book. And I am particularly grateful that, when it came to a matter of judgement or comment, though we had a number of enjoyable discussions and some disagreements, he allowed me absolute freedom to write what I wished.

I would also like to thank Miss Muriel St Clare Byrne, literary executrix and life-long friend of Dorothy L. Sayers, for her unstinting help, both in regard to her own papers and memories, and in directing me towards other fruitful sources of information.

My other acknowledgements can only be placed in alphabetical order, for the contributions of so many helpful people cannot be evaluated, only gratefully recorded:

Col. John Beckett for information about the Cambridgeshire Fens; Sir Basil Blackwell; Miss Christianna Brand; Miss Joan de Saumarez Brock; Miss Margaret Burger; from Christchurch village: Mrs E. Bedford, Mrs Annie Beeston, Mr Bob Chapman, Mr C. R. Chapman, Mrs H. Cross, Mrs A. Russell and Mrs A. M. Stevens; Col. and Mrs R. L. Clarke of the Dorothy L. Sayers Historical and Literary Society; Dr J. G. Denholm; Mr William Everson for allowing me to see his print of the film *The Silent Passenger*; Mrs C. U. Frankenburg; Miss V. M. Fraser, present Headmistress of Godolphin School; Dr Trevor H. Hall; Mr G. Laurence Harbottle; Prof. Carolyn G. Heilbrun; Mr David Higham; Mr Anthony Hopkins; Dr Clyde Kilby of the Marion E. Wade Institute, Wheaton, Illinois; Miss Anne-Marie Køllgaard; Miss Norah Lambourne; Miss Margaret Lord; Mr Raymond Mander and Mr Joe Mitchenson for theatrical information; Mr Patrick McLaughlin; Mr Bartlett Mullins; Mrs N. Paton-Smith; Miss Ivy Phillips, contemporary of D.L.S. at Godolphin School and later Headmistress; Dr Barbara Reynolds; Miss Dorothy Rowe; Mr Alfred Satterthwaite for his help in connection with his step-father, John Cournos; Mr Julian Symons; Miss Doreen Wallace; from the village of Westcott Barton: Mr & Mrs Bauckham, Mrs

Monica Pratley and Miss Sullivan; Mr Eric Whelpton; Mr W. G. Williams.

I have also received valuable information and assistance from the following: the Bodleian Library, Oxford; Christ Church, Oxford; the Dorothy L. Sayers Historical and Literary Society, Witham, Essex; Durham University; Messrs Victor Gollancz Ltd; Messrs Arthur Guinness Ltd; the Houghton Library, Harvard University, Cambridge, Massachusetts; Lambeth Palace Library; the Marion E. Wade Collection, Wheaton College, Illinois; Messrs Ogilvie, Benson & Mather Ltd; Messrs Reckitt & Colman Ltd; the Principal and Fellows of Somerville College, Oxford; the Humanities Research Center, University of Texas, Austin, Texas.

And I would like to thank Mrs Carol Brand and Mrs Helen Dunphy for their care in typing the manuscript, and Mrs Sarah Hayes for preparing the typescript for press.

J.B.

PREFACE

by Anthony Fleming

WHEN IVY SHRIMPTON, her cousin and childhood friend, died in 1951, my mother, Dorothy L. Sayers, as her executrix and residuary legatee, asked me to wind up Ivy's estate on her behalf. She wrote: "I feel strongly that any letters or documents dealing with Ivy's charges should be destroyed immediately and, as far as possible, unread . . ."; and this was done. "Also, any old letters etc, from me should also be burnt – I will have no 'juvenilia' left about the world for journalists and biographers to unearth and publish . . .": but this instruction I was reluctant to follow for obvious reasons. So I had certain passages from her letters to Ivy typed, in case she should call me to execution; and I left it at that.

When Dorothy herself died in 1957, I found that she had kept not only all the letters she had ever written to her parents from her school-days onwards, but numerous exercise-books full of childhood poetry, drawings, plays and stories, often embellished with coloured drawings and fancy lettering, the earliest complete volume dating from early in 1908, when she was not yet fifteen years old – as devastating a collection of "juvenilia" as any established writer could hand down to posterity.

It can hardly have been through inattention that Dorothy had kept them. She would only have come on the letters – and possibly recovered the earlier exercise-books – when she went through her mother's papers on the latter's death in 1929; and that was the moment when it would have been easy and natural to destroy them if she had felt strongly about it. Moreover, since only a handful of letters to her mother from various other people have survived in an apparently accidental and quite unsystematic fashion, it seems that, unless her mother had been in the habit, unusual for the period, of destroying on receipt all other letters but those from her daughter, these must have been deliberately set aside by Dorothy herself, while practically everything else went into the fire. This discovery comforted me in my condition of disobedience and confirmed me in my intention to continue therein.

But the "juvenilia" motive put forward by Dorothy may have been an excuse; and its context in her letter to me rather suggests it. Dorothy had written to Ivy about one incident in her life – the incident of my birth –

which she had never revealed to her parents or anyone else; and she may have intended that I should thus destroy the only written evidence readily available on the subject, contained in her letters to Ivy. However, the essential facts of the matter have since been reconstructed and made public, as a result of independent research carried out without the aid of the letters.

Various accounts of Dorothy's life have already been published, without benefit of access to her private papers, and naturally therefore with varying degrees of accuracy. Had it not been for these, this book would not have been written, or at least not yet, in the light of Dorothy's expressed views on such a project. But it became clear that the only way to forestall the publication of further possible distortions of the truth was to put all the then available facts at the disposal of a competent and reliable biographer.

In addition to the evidence which was then available, other evidence has since come to light in the course of research, some of it of such a nature that, for my part, I could have wished that it had been destroyed long ago. But it exists, its existence is known to a limited few, it provides insights otherwise lacking into some parts of the rest of the story, and there could finally be no serious question of not taking it into account.

Responsibility for the publication of this book is mine, in the sense that James Brabazon was approached in this matter on my behalf; and that, with the accord of Miss Muriel St Clare Byrne, I put at his disposal all the material in my possession and signed authorizations enabling other people and bodies to give him access to any other material they might have. In this sense, the book is what is commonly known as an "authorized Life".

But, from the outset, it was understood that, quite unconditionally, it was to be, in the fullest sense, James Brabazon's book; and that, though he might, and did, discuss with me, and with many others, aspects of Dorothy's life on which he wanted their views, in the event of any difference of viewpoint or emphasis compatible with the facts, James Brabazon's judgement should prevail over mine or anyone else's.

Thus, if I refer to this book as an "authorized Life", it should in no sense be taken (as is sometimes supposed in such cases) that I in any sense 'inspired', or even necessarily endorse, any or every opinion, interpretation or hypothesis it contains – these are James's. But the facts, insofar as they have been drawn from documents which I already had or have since come by, I can vouch for without exception. And judgement is justified at the bar of fact.

FOREWORD

by P. D. James

THERE CAN BE few biographies more eagerly awaited by the writer or aficionado of detective fiction than this first authorized life of Dorothy L. Sayers. We can, I feel, be confident that she would have understood and approved the reasons for its premature publication. But would she, I wonder, have greeted with some surprise, disappointment or even chagrin the news that this Foreword was to be written, not by a mediaevalist, an academic, a translator or a theologian, but by a woman engaged in the craft of writing detective fiction. And yet the twenty-three years since her death have surely vindicated James Brabazon's verdict that, of all her work, it is the twelve detective novels that will last longest. It is a safe assumption that any reader, asked to name the six best writers or most famous heroes in the genre, will include the names of Dorothy L. Sayers and Peter Wimsey. Forty years after the publication of the last novel, readers in airport departure lounges all over the world reach for a Dorothy L. Sayers story to relieve the claustrophobic boredom and half-acknowledged terror of journeys whose modern horrors she was happily spared. Like all good writers she created a unique and instantly recognizable world into which we can still escape for our comfort, hearing again with relief and nostalgia her strongly individual, amused and confident voice.

Despite this enduring popularity, few writers in the genre have provoked such opposing responses from readers and critics. Those who are irritated by her, frequently focus their dislike on her aristocratic detective. She herself, in an address on the craft of the detective story, set down the basic qualities which an amateur sleuth, hero of a series, must necessarily possess and she created Lord Peter Wimsey in this image. He must, she wrote, be in a position to encounter murder and to be able to work with the police. Lord Peter's co-operation is almost servilely welcomed by the official force and his creator took the added precaution of giving him Inspector Charles Parker as friend and brother-in-law. He must have the versatility to tackle a variety of murderous means and methods if he is not to waste time seeking expert opinions on every detail. Lord Peter is a scholar in five or six languages, a fine natural cricketer, a connoisseur of food, wine and women, a virtuoso pianist who can move from Bach to Scarlatti without benefit of a score and a discerning bibliophile, and he is equally at home in an East End revivalist prayer meeting or a palace. He must be rich and leisured, free to drop his normal concerns at a moment's notice to pursue the elusive clue. Lord Peter is never hampered by time or money from buying the best advice, travelling freely, or chartering a plane to cross the Atlantic in search of a vital witness. He must have the physical equipment to tackle violent criminals. Lord Peter, although he laments his lack of inches, is an expert in physical combat, can control a recalcitrant horse and can seize the wrist of the younger and heavier Reggie Pomfret "in an iron grip". Miss Sayers' final requirement was that the character of the detective should be capable of gradual development and evolution through the series. This she certainly accomplished even if the change from the Wooster-like, monocled, man-about-Town of *Whose Body?* to the sensitive guilt-oppressed scholar sobbing in his wife's lap at the end of *Busman's Honeymoon* is less a development than a metamorphosis. It is little wonder that such an egregiously privileged and talented hero should attract criticism or that his detractors should proclaim Lord Peter and his creator snobbish, pretentious or intellectually arrogant. But the virulence of some of the criticism is a measure of her success. Other detective writers of her time go unscathed because Dorothy L. Sayers could write and most of them couldn't, because Lord Peter lives and their heroes are dead.

Although Dorothy L. Sayers did as much as any writer in the genre to develop the detective story from an ingenious but lifeless puzzle into an intellectually respectable branch of fiction with serious claims to be judged as a novel she was an innovator of style and intention not of form. She was content to work within the convention of a central mystery, a closed circle of suspects each with his or her motive for the crime, a superman amateur detective, superior in talent and intelligence to the professional police, and a solution which the reader could arrive at by logical deduction from clues planted with deceptive cunning but essential fairness. The novels, too, are very much of their age in the complexity and ingenuity of the methods of murder. Readers of the 1930s expected that the puzzle would be dominant and that the murderer would demonstrate in his villainy an almost supernatural cunning and skill. Those were not the days of the swift bash to the skull followed by 60,000 words of psychological insight. The murder methods she devised are, in fact, over-ingenious and at least two are doubtfully practicable. A healthy man is unlikely to be killed by noise alone, a lethal injection of air would surely require a suspiciously large hypodermic syringe, and the methods of murder in *Have His Carcase* and *Busman's Honeymoon* are unnecessarily complicated, particularly for the crude and brutal villains of these stories. But if she was sometimes wrong she was never wilfully careless and her papers bear witness to the scholarly trouble she took to get her details right. She was adept at the technical tricks of her trade: the manipulation of train timetables, the drawing of red herrings skilfully across trails, the devising of plots that depended on clocks, tides, secret codes and mysterious foreigners. But she used these ploys with a freshness, wit and panache which reinvigorated even the tritest of conventions.

She wrote, too, with a refreshing humour which is rare in detective fiction. There have been in the genre a number of notable farceurs, while other writers have adopted a facetiously hectic and juvenile humour in the face of fictional death. But few have achieved that underlying funniness which is born of a keen eye and a frank relish for the vagaries, inconsistencies and absurdities of life. No changes in fashion can diminish the humour of Mr Hankin's irruption into the office sweepstake in *Murder Must Advertise*, the Bohemian party in *Clouds of Witness*, the Village Inquest in *The Nine Tailors* or the literary cocktail chat about the Book of the Moment in *Gaudy Night*.

And how clearly the novels reflect their time. Perhaps because clue-making so often involves the routine and minutiae of ordinary life, the detective novel can tell us more about contemporary society than many a more pretentious literary form. In the Wimsey saga, the sounds, mood, speech, the very feel of the thirities seems to rise from the page: the resentful war-scarred heroes of the Bellona Club, the gallant or pathetic spinsters of Miss Climpson's agency, the ordered and hierarchical life of a fen village, now as obsolete as the vast rectories round which it revolved, the desperate gaiety of the bright young things, the fear of unemployment which underlay the cheerful camaraderie of office life in *Murder Must Advertise*. And what mystery plot today could depend on the certainty that the whole country would be still and silent for two minutes at the eleventh hour of the eleventh day of the eleventh month? Which character could emulate Lord Peter and casually park his car in Jermyn Street while he leisurely chose a ham or, like General Fentiman, could set out to spend a day at his club, buy lunch and pay for a taxi with an old ten shilling note? This period flavour extends to the fascinating sartorial details, although Harriet Vane's choice for picnicking in *Have His Carcase* of a skirt which waved tempestuously about her ankles, an oversized hat of which one side obscured her face while the other was turned back to reveal a bunch of black ringlets, high-heeled beige shoes, silk stockings and embroidered gloves seems a little outré even for a woman setting out to vamp a suspected murderer.

Henry James said of Edgar Allan Poe that to take him with more than a certain degree of seriousness betokened a lack of seriousness in oneself. Dorothy L. Sayers never took her detective stories with more than a certain degree of seriousness and she may have been amused by the weight of critical literature which has now accrued: the exploration of her treatment in the novels of the themes of justice, guilt, punishment and the imperatives of personal responsibility, the influence of Wilkie Collins, the moral basis of her plots, the unifying theme in all her work of the almost sacramental importance of man's creative activity. Much of this is important to our understanding of the novels and some of it is fascinating. But surely the enduring strength of the novels is that they were written to be, and are, superb entertainment. They were meant to be enjoyed and they, and their protagonist, have that creative vitality which alone ensures survival.

And, as James Brabazon shows, it is through the detective fiction that we can hear most clearly the echo of the author's own ebullient, pugnacious and gallant spirit. Many incidents, characters and snatches of dialogue which had always seemed to speak with a personal voice take on a deeper significance in the light of this work. That is why those of us who first enjoyed and were influenced by Dorothy L. Sayers in our youth, who still read her with something more than nostalgia, and who see new generations discovering her with pleasure are glad that we have not had to wait another 27 years for this perceptive and fascinating biography.

INTRODUCTION

DOROTHY LEIGH SAYERS published no autobiographical work. But thirty-three pages of undated manuscript do exist, entitled *My Edwardian Childhood*, which describe, in some detail, Dorothy's recollections of her first four years in Oxford before the family moved into the country. This is interesting enough in itself; but its real significance is that it corresponds, not word for word but event for event, with the beginning of another manuscript, also uncompleted but running to more than two hundred pages. This was to be the book which the *New York Times Book Review* announced on October 14 1934 as follows: "In leaving – one hopes only for a time – the field of detective fiction, Dorothy L. Sayers has adopted the pseudonym of 'Johanna Leigh'. That name will appear on the title page of her forthcoming *Cat o' Mary* (Gollancz)."

The correspondence between *My Edwardian Childhood* and the opening chapter of *Cat o' Mary*, and also the complete identification of the characters and incidents in the later chapters of *Cat o' Mary* with actual people and places in Dorothy's real life, establish beyond question that *Cat o' Mary*, at least up to the point at which the author abandoned it, was in fact a pseudonymous autobiography. Its importance to Dorothy was, of course, that it enabled her to reveal, under the guise of fiction, her true feelings about herself and her early years – feelings which in real life she took a great deal of trouble to conceal. And one reason she never finished the book may well have been that she was uneasy about making those feelings public even in this disguised form.

There are other possible explanations for the non-appearance of the book. According to the notes she left it is clear that in the later chapters the story of the heroine, Katherine Lammas, was to have diverged considerably from her own life. It is possible that she found it too difficult to make the transition from autobiography to plain fiction. Or it may be that the emotions that powered the revelation of her inner self were exhausted by those early chapters, making her lose interest in her heroine once the confessional section was off her chest. Certainly it seems likely that the story of *Gaudy Night*, which came to her about that time, enabled her to explore within the detective form ideas about women and work that she intended to include in the later chapters of *Cat o' Mary*; so she had a good excuse for not finishing it.

Be that as it may, in the early chapters of this book I have made considerable use of the manuscript of *Cat o' Mary*, having convinced myself that at all points it corresponds to Dorothy's own career. For any readers who may doubt the propriety of this procedure, I shall try to make it clear where I have made use of evidence from *Cat o' Mary* which is not paralleled in Dorothy's own letters and other writings. And all extracts from *Cat o' Mary* will be identified either in the text, or by footnotes, or both.

Dorothy Sayers told her literary executor, Muriel St Clare Byrne, that she wanted no biography written until fifty years after her death. By that time, she believed, the world would know whether or not her work was good enough to survive – only then did she think it right that somebody should record the facts of her life.

She has, in fact, been dead for less than half those fifty years; but various accounts of her life have already appeared, which, because their authors have been denied access to personal papers, have been incomplete or inaccurate or both.

Inevitably, speculation arose to fill the gaps. It became clear that in the absence of an authoritative account of her life, the field would be left to less reliable versions. In these circumstances Miss Byrne and Miss Sayers' son, Anthony Fleming, decided that a book should be written which incorporated the available facts, before those who knew her had died and the records had been scattered. Hence the present volume.

One further point: it is well known that she always insisted on being known professionally as Dorothy L. Sayers – for reasons which will be discussed later. I do not propose to be so formal. Dorothy L. Sayers was simply her professional name; and for the most part I shall refer to her simply as Dorothy – the name by which I knew her during the brief period when she and I were co-churchwardens for the parishes of St Thomas and St Anne, Soho.

DOROTHY L. SAYERS

CHAPTER ONE

I CAN'T GET the work I want, nor the money I want, nor consequently, the clothes I want, nor the holiday I want, nor the man I
want!! And then people tell me of girls who are oppressed and em-
barrassed by the possession of an income of £300 a year, and feel that
they ought not to have it and ought to be doing slum work and being
useful to society. I call that pure egotism and spiritual pride. How
thankfully would you or I support life under a load of similar em-
barrassments![1]

So wrote Dorothy Sayers to her parents in July 1921. She was twenty-
eight years old – a ripe age to be virgin and unemployed, particularly for
someone with a first-class honours degree and an unabashed interest in
the opposite sex.

The lack of a job is less surprising than the lack of a man. It was not
long after the ending of the First World War, and employment was
scarce enough for men; for women, only recently appearing in the job
market, it was next to impossible. But to have been unmated, in an age
that was just as obsessed with sex as our own and in a sphere of society
where that obsession was most volubly discussed, is less easily explained.

That letter was written at the lowest point of Dorothy's dishearten-
ment. Worse things were in store for her, not far ahead, but these were at
least to be positive experiences, not the long-drawn-out drag of nothing
happening. Within a year she had a job, she had found a man – though
she must often have wished she hadn't – and something else had
happened which put her on the road to becoming a household name.

In the same letter, Dorothy wrote of her friend Jim Jaeger (who, con-
fusingly, was a woman and whose real name was Muriel) that she was
"writing something mysterious which she won't say anything about to
anybody. I suspect her of a novel. Novels seem the thing to write
nowadays. I wish I had the application for it. Unfortunately, novels
seldom interest me, even to read, and the thought of grinding one out is
fearful."[2]

Just three months later a phrase leaps out of the middle of another
letter – "Lord Peter is almost ready to be typed."[3] The fearful thought
had been overcome, the grind had been undertaken. And when "Lord

Peter" was finally published, it was to the same Jim Jaeger that Dorothy dedicated it:

> Dear Jim, this book is your fault. If it had not been for your brutal insistence, Lord Peter would never have staggered through to the end of this enquiry. Pray consider that he thanks you with his accustomed suavity. Yours ever, D.L.S.

How ironical that it should be Muriel Jaeger, whose own books the world has forgotten, that we have to thank for the reluctant birth of one of the world's most popular detectives.

We, the public, know that book as *Whose Body?* But throughout the writing of it and during the long and dispiriting search for a publisher, Dorothy simply referred to the manuscript by the name of its hero, Lord Peter, the perfect gentleman who "walked in" to her mind at that crucial moment and saved the situation; and who was to accompany her faithfully through her encounters with the much less satisfactory males of flesh and blood. The contrast was perhaps not altogether a surprise to Dorothy who from the time she had first learned to read had found literature more satisfying, and indeed more real, than ordinary everyday life.

.   .   .   .   .

"I am a citizen of no mean city." So Dorothy L. Sayers chose to begin her only undisguised essay into autobiography, the unpublished fragment, *My Edwardian Childhood*. In those eight words she establishes both her life-long pride in the place of her birth and her equally life-long addiction to literary quotation – for the words are borrowed from St Paul.[4]

The corresponding passage in the crypto-autobiography, *Cat o' Mary*, runs:

> Katherine Lammas was born, very characteristically, at Oxford. All her life she remained exceedingly proud of this achievement, which was due to no exertion of her own, but merely to the fact that her father was headmaster of the Choir School at Wolsey College.

In real life the Choir School of which the Reverend Henry Sayers, M.A., was headmaster belonged to Christ Church College, and Dorothy was born on June 13 1893, in the old Choir House in Brewer Street, a narrow side street opening off St Aldate's nearly opposite the main entrance to Christ Church.

In addition to his headmastership, Henry Sayers held the post of chaplain to the college. By a unique historical accident, the chapel at

Christ Church was created a cathedral, and Dorothy thus was able to boast of another, equally unmerited, distinction – a cathedral christening. Having a taste for self-dramatization, she did not fail to exploit the fact when occasion arose.

The intellectual whirlwinds at that time disrupting the continental universities – the wild new ideas of Nietzsche, Marx and Freud that were to have so profound an effect on the intellectual, social and political life of the twentieth century – reached Oxford as little more than a mild breeze. Centuries of tradition and a preoccupation with eternal truths had taught the older universities how to absorb such shocks with the minimum of fuss, and few places could have been better insulated than Christ Church Choir School.

Not that Oxford was entirely untouched by the hand of time. Lord Nuffield had not yet established his motor car factory there, but a hint of things to come had already been provided by the successful onslaught of a few determined people on the hallowed principle that only men were worthy of a university education.

Fourteen years before Dorothy's birth, two small halls of residence had been set up for a few young ladies to stay in Oxford and study – though it was made clear at that stage that they must in no way be regarded as part of the University proper, nor could their studies ever lead to degrees. Lady Margaret Hall officially adhered to the Church of England. Somerville was non-denominational.

The enterprise had prospered. In the year of Dorothy's birth a new gatehouse was added to the two large halls which Somerville had already acquired, and Lady Margaret Hall was growing correspondingly. So when fate decreed that the first (and, as it turned out, only) child born to Henry and Helen Sayers should be a daughter, it was only natural that the ambitions of that academically-minded couple should immediately turn towards a university education; and certainly the idea seems to have been implanted very early in Dorothy.

The Sayers family came from County Tipperary in Ireland, where Dorothy's great grandfather (according to a chronicle found by Henry in the papers of his father, Robert) was "agent to one or two large properties", and "a man of singular piety and virtue, who was universally loved and revered". His grandmother, Robert proudly notes, was a cousin of William Hazlitt, the essayist.

Robert's mother, it appears, was as spotless as his father – "a godly woman, exemplary in all the relations of life", he wrote . . . "Never had son greater cause to revere the memory of his parents than I have." This filial piety sounds like a touch of Irish hyperbole, but the family may really have been like that, for Henry himself seems to have lived a life of untarnished perfection; unless you count dullness a flaw and suspect that he may have been virtuous partly through lack of the imagination to be anything else. Shortly after his death Dorothy wrote to her cousin Ivy about the way her mother was taking her loss – "He bored her to death for nearly forty years, and she always grumbled that he was no companion for her – and now she misses him dreadfully."[5]

Physically, Henry Sayers was:

a tall man – six foot two in those days before age stooped his shoulders – with a fine nose and forehead, the latter being the more noticeable because he was almost entirely bald at a very early age. The lower part of the face was less powerful than the upper, and his mouth I never really saw at any time, for he wore the rather full and drooping moustache of this period. His eyes, like those of all the Sayers family, were blue.

So Dorothy described him in *My Edwardian Childhood*. And in a telling phrase in *Cat o' Mary* she writes of his possessing "a certain mild stateliness" – a description which fits his photograph with a delightful accuracy.

He loved music – he wrote hymn-tunes for use in his church – and he loved books. His great ambition was to pass on these loves to his adored daughter, who remembered curling up on his knee in the evenings as he read her the Uncle Remus stories and, as soon as he thought her ready, *Alice in Wonderland*. But he was hardly a merry soul, and Mrs Cross, who was organist for him for fifteen years, found him "a very severe master"[6] and has no recollection of ever seeing him smile.

Helen Mary Sayers, *née* Leigh, was a much more spirited character. Dorothy describes her thus:

My mother . . . had an abundance of light brown hair and was a very vivacious and attractive woman. I suppose her long upper lip, strong nose and wide mouth made her face too decided for actual beauty, in a day when regularity of feature was more highly esteemed than it is now; but her broad, intelligent forehead, speaking eyes and liveliness of expression must have made her admired in any period. She was a woman of exceptional intellect, which unfortunately never got the education which it deserved. If she could have had the advantage of being her own daughter, she would undoubtedly have made remarkable use of the opportunities she would have given herself, and would probably have made her mark as a writer, for her letters show her to have had a great gift of humorous narration.[7]

Dorothy's educational precocity seems to have come less from the learned schoolmaster who was her father than from her largely self-taught, lively-minded mother.

Aunts, uncles and cousins from both sides of the family crossed and re-crossed her path throughout her life, with a preponderance of aunts, as often happened in those days. On the Sayers side she regarded her father as the best of the bunch, though Aunt Gertrude was commended as "a very entertaining aunt at all times" and in Dorothy's early years won favour by allowing her the run of her work basket; and she dutifully kept in touch with several others, notably Aunt Annie, who became a nun, and Cousin Gerald, who attained some eminence at the Colonial Office.

It was her mother's side of the family, however, that she much preferred. Although she deplored their tendency to take a pessimistic view of life (which she attributed to the fact that they were "everlastingly tied up inside or dosing themselves"[8]), and though her mother sometimes showed nervous symptoms that could often be depressing and were sometimes quite alarming, the Leighs were never dull.

Genealogically, too, they were much more impressive than the Sayers, with a pedigree traceable – so at least one of them claimed – twenty generations back to "Jacobi Ley or de Lygh, who held his lands in Land-ford, Wiltshire, by Knight's service of Aldrela de Boterell, in the reign of Henry III."

Helen herself was born in Shirley, near Southampton, where her father was a solicitor – besides being a considerable Latin scholar and a great believer in "muscular Christianity". On the nearby Isle of Wight, the Leighs had for several generations been one of the notable landed families; big fish in a not-very-big pond, and very much aware of their position in the community. It is not hard to guess how Dorothy first developed her taste for genealogies and family chronicles – the kind of thing she did so brilliantly for the fictitious Wimsey family in the years to come.

Dorothy's great-uncle Percival Leigh had been a noted contributor to *Punch*, and his educated style of humour ("Comic English Grammar" and "Comic Latin Grammar") might well have influenced his niece's gift of humorous narration and so passed to Dorothy, for it was very much up her street.

Her bias towards the Leighs is surely the true reason why Dorothy insisted on retaining the L in her professional name. In various letters in the 1940s she gave as her reason the fact that there was another Dorothy Sayers, a singer and dancer who appeared on the BBC and who, according to one letter, "is continually getting in trouble in police courts and divorce courts"[9] – a lady with whom she preferred not to be confused. The reason she gave to Muriel St Clare Byrne, her close friend from college days, was that "D.L.S." was an anagram of £.S.D.; and pounds, shillings and pence were a matter of urgent practical concern for many years. But though this would no doubt reinforce her liking for the "D.L.S." initials, appealing to her sense of fun, her use of the "L" goes back further still. The earliest poems and plays of her childhood are initialled D.L.S. And she even seems to have considered going further, and calling herself D. Leigh Sayers in professional matters. For that was the name under which she played the violin at a public concert in 1908. The pride that Helen Sayers felt in her family name is clear enough from the fact that she gave it to her daughter as a Christian name. Dorothy, to whom she passed on that pride, preserved the name in the cherished "L".

Shortly after Dorothy's birth it seems that the family moved along Brewer Street into a new Choir House – perhaps because the old one, a seventeenth-century house of no great size, could not cope with the new addition to the family.

The street was cobbled in those days, a circumstance which some people might find romantic, but which caused Dorothy to remark later, with her usual lack of sentimentality, that anyone who complained about the noise of traffic in the twentieth century had never heard metal-shod wheels rattling over cobble-stones.

Dorothy had only four years in which to pick up the flavour of Oxford before the family moved out into the country. But those four years left her with a few indelible recollections, as well as more numerous shadowy impressions. Nothing remained in her memory of the bronchial pneumonia she caught through being kept out in a November fog, except the cotton-wool jacket that somebody, when she was getting better, flung on the fire in defiance of the doctor's orders. A hearty spanking from her nurse was not forgotten.

Both in *My Edwardian Childhood* and in *Cat o' Mary* she writes of the entrancing vision of a mechanical set of false teeth which opened and closed ceaselessly in a local dentist's window. She remembered walks in Christ Church Meadow – that beautiful sweep of green which stretches from the great stone wall of the college to the tow-path where the rowing coaches cycle beside the Isis, urging their sweating crews to ever greater efforts. She remembered playing hide-and-seek behind the great elms that grew there, but which grow no longer since Dutch Elm disease has cut them down. She retained images, "viewed from a standpoint three feet from the ground",[10] of swans, deer, a goldfish in a shop window, and the Choir School sheepdog, Scrugs. And she remembered, smothering a college wall, sheets of small brown-leaved creeping ivy – a memory so vivid that whenever she saw the same ivy in after life it shrank her again, she said, to the pygmy size of those days, when she could walk between her father's legs and her parents called her Dossie.

The reason for the family's departure from Oxford was a matter of prudence. The living of Bluntisham-cum-Earith in Huntingdonshire was one of the richest in the gift of Christ Church, and it happened to fall vacant at a time when Henry Sayers was wondering how long he could stand up to the dual duties of headmaster and chaplain, with the demands made on his voice by having to sing regularly in the Cathedral services; besides which Dorothy had a suspicion that he was never entirely dedicated to the business of schoolmastering.

So the decision was made; and one January day, to the accompaniment of the usual turmoil, off the family trooped to a new life, parrot and all.

The change to a country rectory where he could retire to his study and browse among his books suited Henry Sayers well enough. For his wife, however, it was far from being a blessing. With her gregarious nature she was hardly likely to welcome the change from the active social life of Oxford to a village where most of the inhabitants were farmers or farm labourers, and where the nearest neighbours of the Sayers' class, in that class-ridden age, were the rectors and vicars of neighbouring parishes and their families.

H. Rider Haggard, famous as the author of *King Solomon's Mines*, is less well known for his two-volume report on the impoverishment of the English farming community at the turn of the century, *Rural England*. In the course of this herculean one-man survey of English agriculture, he stayed for a while in Bluntisham, probably a year or two after the Sayers family moved there. There is no record of their having met, though in such a small community the probability is that they did. At all events, his comments could scarcely be more pertinent:

> Cambridgeshire has but few resident gentlefolk, except, of course, the clergy. In the Fens, indeed, hardly anyone will live save those who are actively concerned in the management of the land, since here are to be found neither sport, scenery nor society.[11]

Bluntisham, on the Cambridgeshire borders, bore out this discouraging analysis. It boasted no squire and apparently no resident doctor, the only other families who would have normally been considered the rector's social equals.

The village sits on the southern edge of the Fens – that flat, marshy stretch of land extending south-westward from the Wash which man has only recently drained and made habitable. Until the middle of the seventeenth century this whole area, thirty miles square, was a swamp of waterlogged peat, only suitable for grazing, and then only in the summer months. Nearly all the traffic was by river, and the only routes across the Fen were wide tracks with drainage ditches on either side, known as "fen droves", since their sole function was for driving livestock to and from pasture.

Then a Dutch engineer named Cornelius Vermuyden was commissioned by a group of wealthy speculators to drain the land, protect it from further flooding and make it viable for agriculture. Vermuyden devised a system of long straight dykes, or drains, centring on the great Hundred Foot Drain and the River Delph. These flowed side by side to the sea, with an area of grazing land between them known as the Washes, which took the periodic overflow. At the northern end of these, at Denver, Vermuyden built big sluices to regulate the flow and to hold back the sea. The work was completed in 1652.

With minor setbacks and one major disaster in 1713 (on which Dorothy based her picture of the Fen flood in *The Nine Tailors*), the system worked and has continued to work to this day. As new forms of power have been invented they have been brought in to handle the constant pumping required. The safety of the inhabitants depends, as in Holland, on unceasing vigilance and hard work. Special clay, or gault, is brought from Ely to line the soft peat banks of the drains, and when Dorothy was a girl, the gault gangs – five men and a horse-drawn barge – were still to be seen against the skyline, making their plodding way along the endless ridges of the dykes. The gault is still needed, but its transportation is, of course, now mechanized.

Every Fen dweller lives in constant awareness of the threat of water, harnessed but never defeated. Each year of Dorothy's childhood the Washes had to be flooded, to absorb the excess water and protect the pastures beyond the dykes; and travellers by road or rail found themselves looking out at bright water stretching on all sides. Nothing as dramatically disastrous as Dorothy's fictional flood in *The Nine Tailors* has happened since 1713, but the waters can still get out of hand; and did so in 1937, only three years after the book was published, and again in 1947; sliding rather than thundering across the land, but menacing life and property none the less.

As a compensation, however, the soil is very rich and fertile; and

Rider Haggard found the Fenlands one of the least distressed farming communities that he visited. Though fever and ague still existed there, he wrote, and though property values had fallen by as much as fifty per cent in the previous twenty-five years, "still, as they are fertile, comparatively easy to work, and not liable to suffer from drought, even at the present price of corn, which is their principal crop, they remain much more valuable than the upland clays and chalks. . . ."[12]

The discomfort of the move to Bluntisham was somewhat alleviated by the fact that the entire staff of servants, after consulting together, elected to move with the family from the comparatively manageable Oxford house to the huge draughty rectory, with its two acres of garden, paddock, stables and cobbled yard. That the staff were prepared to consider the wilds of Huntingdonshire says a great deal for the charm and kindness of their mistress.

The size of the house had one advantage: the family could compensate to some extent for the loss of the social life of Oxford by creating a community within the rectory itself. They could no longer call round and visit Uncle Harry, Aunt Maud and Cousin Margaret, who had lived half a mile away in Holywell; but Grannie Sayers and Aunt Mabel Leigh could now come and live with them, and Aunt Gertrude Sayers could stay for extended visits.

From Dorothy's point of view, Aunt Gertrude and Aunt Mabel came into the category of "entertaining" aunts; perhaps it was the vigorous personalities of these spirited ladies that helped to persuade her at a very early age that the companionship of women could be just as enriching as that of men, if not more so. The aunts were very different: Aunt Mabel's technique with parish affairs was to leave them severely alone, exhibiting "an almost supernatural power of self-detachment from all forms of responsibility',[13] whereas Aunt Gertrude liked to involve herself in everything that was going on.

Grannie Sayers was even more inclined to poke her nose into things that might or might not concern her. She insisted on taking Sunday School, distributing the parish magazine and visiting the sick to an extent that finally necessitated a small showdown. Dorothy did not much care for Grannie, whose withered cheek, proffered for the obligatory kiss, and attempts at amusing Dorothy by exhibiting a gold tooth, only aroused in the little girl an insuperable physical revulsion which never entirely left her and which caused a combination of cruelty and guilt in her feelings towards the old lady.

Dorothy could hardly be said to have been a lonely child; her isolation came from the contrast in age between herself and her companions. And it was not an uncomfortable life, despite the winds that blew across the bleak wastes of the Fens, and the draughtiness of the long stone passages. A firm was imported from Oxford to decorate the rectory from top to bottom, and although water had to be pumped from a well in the garden, and taking a bath involved having the water heated in the kitchen, carried upstairs in cans and poured into a hip-bath in the bedroom, the family lived well. They dressed for dinner – at least when guests were present, which was not infrequently – and the staff consisted of a cook, the nurse, three maids and a manservant. When she was ill at school in her teens, the heroine of *Cat o' Mary* "felt that she must be well again if she could only get back to the cool green garden, with its ancient ivy-hung trees, to the seemly beauty of crystal and silver and fine starched linen".[14]

The wider political and economic problems of the area did not concern the Sayers family. The English middle classes of that time, and indeed until very recently, belonged to a non-political species; or to be more precise, their politics took the form of not believing in politics – by which they meant not believing in change. They were traditionalists who, being near the top of the social scale, found that scale very comfortable and reassuring; they held a deep-rooted conviction that God had ordered all things – their own situation in particular – and an almost total lack of the imagination to see things from any other angle.

It is important to remember, however, that in this part of the country the conservatism of the middle class was matched, and more than matched, by the conservatism of the farming community, a section of society which accepted and even enjoyed the status quo, in that they believed that this was how things were meant to be – a philosophy which has had to comfort the vast majority of mankind throughout history, and which thrives best in country surroundings, where the vagaries of nature teach a sturdy stoicism, and the rhythm of the seasons implants a deep sense of tradition and continuity. This was Dorothy's England, traditional, ordered, conventional, untouched by – indeed resentful of – the social disturbances of the Industrial Revolution and the intellectual excitements of the age; for East Anglia was then, as it still is, one of the last bastions of feudal conservatism in the British Isles.

Here Henry Sayers did his duty with kindness and devotion, for within his limitations he was a conscientious man. In a community like Bluntisham the Rector had to be his flock's adviser on all kinds of matters besides the strictly spiritual. As well as being the confidant and comforter of every man and woman in his parish, he had to be legal expert, letter-writer and, to some extent, political representative. At critical moments in his parishioners' lives he might be called upon to provide money, food, housing or transport – a pony and trap at first, later a

Model T Ford. His wife was the parish visitor, who kept in touch with every family and warned her husband when succour might be needed. Between them they provided all the social services that the villagers had in those days, administering the meagre provisions of the Poor Law and supplementing them from their own resources. There was a hot dinner every Sunday for an old man living on his own; and the official reward for having a baby was an egg custard pudding.

These tasks the Reverend and Mrs Sayers (assisted, whether they liked it or not, by Grannie) seem to have performed to the satisfaction of those who depended upon them. The portrait Dorothy draws of the vicar in *The Nine Tailors*, though she adds touches of fussiness and comedy behaviour that owe more to the stage stereotype of the country rector than to reality, has her father's qualities of gentle scholarliness and a readiness to set forth in all kinds of weather conditions and at all hours of day and night to help villagers in need.

Whatever Dorothy herself may have felt about the relative intelligence and liveliness of her parents, to the villagers it was the rector who was the impressive figure, with his domed forehead, his book-learning, and his insistence that villagers should touch their hat to him when they met him on the road. Beside him, Mrs Sayers seemed "a quiet, gentler little person, the complete opposite of her husband".[15] She evidently knew her place.

It was an orderly household. At 8.15 each morning the family assembled in the dining room, the servants filed in, and prayers were held. Then there was a pause, Mr Sayers looked sternly at his watch, and Dorothy left the grown-ups in the dining room and went for her breakfast to the nursery. For the rest of the day her life was, theoretically at least, separated from that of the adults. She did not visit them again till the evening, but spent the day with nurses, with servants, later with governesses and with the occasional visiting friend.

There are still some people who remember those days, at least from 1901 onwards, when Dorothy was eight. Mrs A. M. Stevens, then Annie Chapman, was the same age as Dorothy and used sometimes to have tea with her. John Chapman, her father, was Gardener to the rectory (the capital "G" establishing the dignity of the position). He also looked after the pony, Belinda, till she was sold at the coming of the motor car. His wife, Elizabeth, was cook and laundry-maid, and their son, Bob, was houseboy and helped his father in the garden.

The Chapmans moved on later with the Sayers family to Christchurch in Cambridgeshire, where Bob took over his father's job as gardener and Annie succeeded her mother and her sister Lilian as cook. The recollections of Bob and Annie, which have been gratefully used in this book, are of great interest in themselves – but they are also invaluable for another reason; they establish beyond question that the details of Katherine Lammas's life in *Cat o' Mary* are not merely similar to those of Dorothy Sayers in real life – they are identical. Setting the story of Katherine side by side with the letters that Dorothy herself wrote at that time, we have a picture in vivid perspective of those early years which, whether we like the fact or not (and Dorothy on the whole did not), make us what we are.

CHAPTER TWO

So DOROTHY GREW up, cut off from those of her own age by the barrier of class, and those of her own class by the barrier of age. This is not to say that she was unhappy. As children will, she took what she needed from what life provided. For friends she had her two toy monkeys, Jacko and Jocko, who, with a doll called Frenchman, made the dramatis personae of innumerable stories which she invented to amuse herself. (Jacko, Jocko and Frenchman, since they had no feelings to be hurt and no lawyers to bring libel suits, are the only real-life characters whose names appear unchanged in *Cat o' Mary*.)

For pretty dolls with frilly dresses she had no use. The attraction of Jacko, Jocko and Frenchman lay in their well-defined characters. Jacko was "puckish, mischievous, enterprising, always in disgrace, but enduringly beloved".[1] Jocko, whose "eyes beamed with red and black glass", was "utterly virtuous and amiable".[2] Frenchman was a rag doll, with a white face and black hair, who "was evidently intended by nature to play the villain's part".[3]

Other friends she had as well – dozens of them – who lived in books. The world of real relationships was largely closed to her, but the world of the imagination was hers to roam in to her heart's content. Of the few pages that we have of *My Edwardian Childhood*, she spends several analysing the particular sort of imagination that she was gifted with. Although she was physically extremely timid and always ready to envisage practical disasters and their painful consequences, she nevertheless "had a robust taste for literary horrors, pleading for the most murderous tales of ogres and the bloodiest parts of Robinson Crusoe".[4] Her mother had never allowed her nurses to terrify her with tales of hobgoblins and bogeymen and had impressed on her that none of the fearsome things in books could possibly happen to *her*. "Consequently" (and this, I believe, is a vital key to her personality and to her writing) "I was always readily able to distinguish between fact and fiction, and to thrill pleasantly with a purely literary horror . . . I dramatized myself, and have at all periods of my life continued to dramatize myself, into a great number of egotistical impersonations of a very common type, making myself the heroine (or more often the hero) of countless dramatic situations – but at all times with a perfect realization that I was the creator, not the subject, of these fantasies."[5]

Dorothy was well aware of the possible psycho-analytical implications of such self-dramatization, but was convinced that in her case these had no foundation and that "there was never at any moment any blurring of the conscious personality. . . . To me, a tree was a tree, a stone a stone, and I myself a child in a white pinafore with a big frill round the neck."[6]

It was obviously very important to Dorothy that she got this on to paper. It is equally important to us to take note of it, or much of her life and work can be misunderstood. Dorothy knew herself well: she was not a self-deceiver (though occasionally she may have rationalized her problems a little), and there is nothing in her life or her writing to make the reader doubt the accuracy of this insight of hers into the nature of her imagination.

In that house full of books her fantasies could roam and riot. Her vision of herself as hero was not discouraged by the presence of intelligent and literate adults who, even if they were not spoiling her, were always watching her, paying attention to her, making much of her – a single clever little girl surrounded by adoring and somewhat guilt-ridden parents, indulgent servants and devoted aunts with little else to do.

The immediate effect on her character was one which, when she looked back in her forties, she evidently disliked a good deal. The portrait she draws of herself in *Cat o' Mary*, under the alias of Katherine Lammas, is that of a spoilt, precocious little creature, all too aware of her power over the grown-ups and ruthless in using it; suggesting perhaps that her life-long lack of affection for children may have started with a frightening awareness of herself and of the complex mixture of conceit, deceit and fascination with life that was bred in her in those very artificial circumstances.

Certainly her self-awareness was extraordinary, and the clarity of her recollections is matched by the harshness with which she judged herself. Most people have forgotten how objectionable they were at times during their childhood – or, if they remember, can easily forgive themselves, on the grounds that they have grown out of all that. Dorothy, for some reason, seems to have needed to go back over it and lay it bare in some detail – even if in the end she spared herself the open confessional of publication.

There is no self-indulgence about the writing — no breast beating. The tone is objective, controlled, with a touch of humour and a definite air of observing life from a detached and objective vantage point. But the judgement is merciless:

If egotism, envy, greed, covetousness, cruelty and sloth are sins, then children possess that original sinfulness in a high degree. . . . When

Katherine in later years looked back on the childish figure that had been herself, it was with a hatred of anything so lacking in those common human virtues which were to be attained in after years at so much cost and with such desperate difficulty . . . Strangers rightly considered her a prig.[7]

"The Biography of a Prig" is, in fact, how Dorothy has subtitled *Cat o' Mary* on the handwritten title-page. And since the book is so clearly autobiographical, the word "prig" must in some sense represent Dorothy's judgement on herself. But its harshness is softened by the implications of the curious title, which is explained partly by the passage just quoted, and partly by some lines of verse, also written on the title-page:

The cats o' Mary seldom bother; they have inherited that good part;
But the cats o' Martha favour their mother of the anxious brow and
the troubled heart.

Beneath this, Dorothy has written "KIPLING, as adapted by Somebody". And in fact the principal adaptation is that where Dorothy has written "The cats o' Mary" and "the cats o' Martha", Kipling's original has "The sons of Mary" and "the sons of Martha". The only other differences are in the punctuation and in Dorothy's "anxious brow" where Kipling has "careful soul".[8]

It is evident that the cat image is important. In the manuscript children are described as being "secretive as cats", and, like cats, wild and capricious in their affections. "Everybody is flattered by the attentions of a cat or a child, knowing well enough that they are the fruit of a cold and calculating judgement."[9]

But the connection with the story of Martha and Mary means something more. It was Mary who sat and listened to Jesus while Martha rushed around worrying about the housework; Mary who had chosen, so Jesus told Martha, the one thing that was needful.[10] A cat o' Mary might thus be seen as a hard-hearted, unsentimental creature who yet has her priorities right; choosing, in the turmoil of the world, to sit quietly, listen, learn and ponder.

I do not think that in this case the "needful thing" necessarily indicates a desire to learn from Jesus; more simply, a desire for learning in itself. *Cat o' Mary* was to deal with a woman whose true life was bound up not with religion but with the intellect – as with Dorothy herself, in whom religion was an aspect of the intellect, not one of personal devotion.

A story in *Cat o' Mary* reveals the ambivalence in Dorothy's attitude to her heroine. It concerned a bed-time ritual which developed in the rectory. As a small child Dorothy had learnt to sing a little song that ran:

> Goodnight, Mamma, goodnight, Papa
> Goodnight to all the rest
> Goodnight, Mamma, goodnight, Papa
> I must love dolly best.

She would sing this each night on her way upstairs to bed, and as time went on she discovered what power she could wield by substituting for "dolly", in the last line, the name of whoever happened to be in favour with her at the time. Each night the grown-ups would stand around in the hall and wait for the last line, to hear who was to be loved best that night. The little girl would make use of this either to say thank you for a present or to crush by omission somebody who had displeased her. When she was nearly six, the real Dorothy wrote to her mother, who was visiting Uncle Harry's family in Oxford, that she missed her badly and "I'm going to love you best tonight".[11]

In *Cat o' Mary* "on one occasion Grannie, being unexpectedly promoted, was touched almost to tears".

Visitors were brought into the hall to watch the nightly performance:

> It became an extremely embarrassing business to Katherine, and very wearisome. It was however expected of her. Tedious as the duty became, it never occurred to Katherine to shirk it unless the evening had been a stormy one, and even then the rite would eventually be performed amid hiccups of distress, after suitable pressure had been applied.[12]

In this story we see "the self-dramatization, the self-importance, the deference to public opinion, the inability to say no, the pleasure in getting her own back, the occasional sentimentalities and the impatience with the outgrown"[13] that are characteristic of Katherine/Dorothy. In her eagerness to blame herself, it does not seem to occur to her how much of the blame attaches to the adults who egged her on, and who, after all, had the authority to stop the ritual and should have had the wisdom and experience to see its dangers and to guide the child in other directions.

The passage continues: "As time went on, Katherine developed all the faults and peculiarities of an only child whose entire life is spent among grown-up people. She was self-absorbed, egotistical, timid, priggish, and, in a mild sort of way, disobedient"[14] – though her disobedience was mostly of the passive kind, and stopped well short of real naughtiness.

Even her cleverness, she implies, was to some extent a matter of living up to what was expected of her. Clever she indeed was, but realizing from the flattery of adults that cleverness was her long suit, she proceeded to justify their expectations by adopting an air of knowledgeability that went a good deal further than her actual understanding warranted.

Most of her time was spent either reading or acting out endless dramas with Jacko and Jocko, playing every part herself – unless some willing grown-up could be found to carry out her very precise instructions as to how to perform some of the characters.

Spending more time, as she did, in the world of fiction than in the world of reality, she was perplexed to find that grown-ups did not behave in real life as they did in books. In some sentimental story she read of a little girl who stroked her mother's face sympathetically and remarked upon her poor thin cheeks. When she tried this on her own mother, the reaction was very different from the mother's in the story: "'Good gracious, it's enough to have other people telling me I look old and ill, without you starting.' . . . Katherine felt that Mrs Lammas had fluffed her lines."[15]

She knew that real life and book life were different, but their relationship was not so obvious as at first sight one might suppose. In *Cat o' Mary*, as in *My Edwardian Childhood*, Dorothy insists that she never confused her fantasy adventures with real life. But she did expect that the feelings and behaviour of people in books would correspond with those of real people – including herself. She was puzzled that she was unable to experience some of the emotions described so convincingly in books – or rather that she was able to experience them only as something existing in an imaginary world; and that conversely when something happened that demanded a real emotional response, such as a death, her experience of literary emotions left her feeling hypocritical, aware of her inability to produce an emotion that convinced even herself.

Reflecting on Dorothy's insight into the problems of her young mind, we cannot help wondering, as we survey the rest of her life, whether she ever fully overcame her difficulty with emotions; or whether it may not go some way to account for later developments in her life and the way she faced them.

About the emotions that could be aroused in her by words, however, Katherine/Dorothy had no doubts at all: "'The Assyrian came down like a wolf on the fold, His cohorts were gleaming with purple and gold' – If Katherine ever troubled to ask what a cohort was, she soon forgot it. The sound of the word was enough."[16] In church Dorothy fell in love with the phrase "Catholic and Apostolic Church". The ecstasy of great words and great phrases never deserted her. Many years later, though she had never brought up children nor associated with them for longer than she could help, she was nevertheless prepared to argue about the romance of words with people who had worked for years in the Children's Hour on BBC radio. She was convinced that all children could be trusted to revel, as she had, in grand, incomprehensible words without ever needing to know their meaning; and moreover that anyone who did not understand this knew nothing whatever about children.

For her education Dorothy was reliant on her parents, her aunts, and a series of governesses and mesdemoiselles, in a way that was normal in those days for any child of upper or middle class parents, out of reach of a private school. The village schools were primitive and the education they provided would have been unsuited to Dorothy's background and capabilities.

In the scholarly atmosphere of the rectory, and without the company of other children to instil the idea that learning was school and that school was tedious, Dorothy learned quickly. She could read by the age of four, and she moved rapidly on to Latin and to French as easily as another child might pick up hopscotch and lacrosse. In fact, given her physical timidity and lack of co-ordination, hopscotch and lacrosse would have been much more difficult.

With such a well-nourished opinion of her own cleverness, and a head full of bloodthirsty literary adventure, noble sentiments and high-sounding words, she was more or less bound to grow up with a sense of superiority to everyday life and the ordinary people around her. Typically, she puts it as uncharitably to herself as possible: "She liked correcting other people, but didn't like being corrected herself, and would argue a point with obstinacy. She had a great opinion of her own cleverness, and to be proved wrong was humiliating."[17] She quickly learned from her tutors as much as they could teach her, and at the same time kept on them, and on the visitors and villagers who made up her world, that cat-like stare, that unnervingly objective and appraising eye.

If her belief in her own intellectual superiority was virtually predetermined, it was even more certain that from an early age she should take to writing. The earliest efforts that survive, apart from a few childish notes to her mother on the occasion of the latter's visits to Oxford, are poems, the very first of which seems, from the handwriting, to have been composed when she was seven or eight.

It is no casual production. Dorothy's attention to detail, her sense of presentation, are already apparent. The paper is folded so as to make a front page which is elaborately decorated, and the title written in a careful, ornate handwriting:

Belle Series —

The Parliament

and

The Castle by the Sea

by

Le Papillon de Bluntisham

One can see why she looked back on herself as an intolerably blasé little creature. The naïve pretension with which she showed off her precocious command of French was surely quite innocent, but it was not a quality to endear her to others, nor to herself viewed from an older and wiser vantage point.

For all its grand exterior the poem hardly suggests early genius:

> The spider with his eight long legs was there
> The cricket and grasshopper fought for the chair
> The beetle and ladybird each took their seat
> The dragonflies came with the butterflies fleet
> The small tortoiseshell came with puss-moth his bride
> The clearwings also, their larvae beside.
> And then there swam in all the fish of the sea
> In company with the wasp, hornet and bee.
> When all was prepared they had nothing to say,
> So sullen and moody they all went away.

The couplet in which the fish unexpectedly arrive at a meeting otherwise wholly consisting of insects (presumably to provide a rhyme for "bee"), and in which the rhythm suddenly falls flat on its face as the wasp, hornet and bee have somehow to be squeezed in at the last moment, shows clear signs of an unequal struggle against technical difficulties.

Never again, however, were technical problems to show in her work. Between that poem and the next, the young writer had won her fight with the language, and could now express herself with the ease and wit that thereafter never failed her.

This poem is undated. But it was probably composed some time in her mid-teens:

The Gargoyle

The Gargoyle takes his giddy perch
On a Cathedral or a church.
There, mid ecclesiastic style
He smiles an early Gothic smile
And while the parson, full of pride,
Spouts at his weary flock inside,
The Gargoyle, from his lofty seat,
Spouts at the people in the street;
And like the parson, seems to say,
In accents doleful, 'Let us pray'.
I like the Gargoyle best. He plays
So cheerfully on rainy days –
While parsons, no-one can deny,
Are awful dampers when they're dry.

Neat, witty, with a pleasant acidity – Dorothy had found her style.

Mrs Sayers encouraged her daughter in her writing – this was exactly the sort of child she wanted. But she was a little distressed to find that Dorothy looked only to literature for her inspiration, never to the beauties of nature; as Dorothy disarmingly admits in *Cat o' Mary*:

[Katherine] wrote a poem about Dawn. Mrs Lammas said she had never seen the dawn, which was quite true, because Katherine didn't like getting up early. Her defence was to assert, quite untruly, that she *had* seen it. She had in fact only read about it, but what she read was to her always a little more real than what she experienced. . . .

This, however, the mature Dorothy did not regard as necessarily a weakness – "to start with invention is the mark of the fertile mind . . . and leads later to the interpretation of experience; to start with the reproduction of experience is the infallible index of a barren invention".[18] Her belief in the powers of invention sets her firmly in opposition to the current vogue for documentary writing; though to my mind her own writing was always at its strongest when it was based on personal experience, rather than wandering off into beloved realms of history and legend.

There were occasional ecstasies to compete with the thrills she could get from books: "a marvel of green light on the sea at Hunstanton"[19] seen during a holiday when she was about six, a sight which she listed forty-five years later as one of the three perfect moments of her life; and one winter, when there was a great frost and pack ice had jammed against the bridge at Bluntisham, "the redness of the setting sun on the black river and the crumpled white ice was a wild and poetic marvel".[20] These were among the rare, brief experiences when life contrived to be as dramatic as the story books.

When Dorothy was eight or nine two other children were invited to stay at the rectory to share her life and education, but the well-intentioned experiment was not a great success. It was hoped that the presence of these children – in *Cat o' Mary* called Charles and Gertrude – might encourage Dorothy to be less self-centred, but the expected improvement in her character did not occur – rather the opposite: "It did not suit her to be queen of her company. It only confirmed her in the belief that she was cleverer and more interesting than other people."[21]

At last, however, when she was twelve or thirteen, someone entered Dorothy's life whose mind was "cast from the same mould"[22] – someone who not only helped her through the critical years of adolescence but was to play an even more crucial role later in her life.

CHAPTER THREE

THE NAMES IN *Cat o' Mary* are mostly very thinly disguised. Bluntisham becomes Fentisham, Miss Wickes becomes Miss Weekes, Miss White turns to Green, and the original of the fictional Myrtle is easy to identify. Dorothy knew vast amounts of poetry, English and French, and must have had Milton's *Lycidas* by heart many years before she quoted the opening in her introduction to the third series of *Detection, Mystery and Horror*:

> Yet once more, oh ye Laurels, and once more,
> Ye Myrtles brown, with Ivy never sere . . .

The identification would be clear enough, even if we did not have a number of letters from Dorothy to her cousin, Ivy Shrimpton, which prove beyond doubt that Ivy was the original for Katherine Lammas's friend Myrtle.

Ivy was five years older than Dorothy, which made her "old enough to seem like a grown-up person, and young enough to be the real companion which Charles and Gertrude were temperamentally unfitted to be".[1] Her father, Henry Shrimpton, had tried farming in America for a while, but at this, as apparently at everything else, he was a failure, and the family had returned to England and settled in Oxford. Ivy's experience, however, had given her:

> . . . more wisdom of the rough and ready kind than any other person in Katherine's circle. . . . Her great merit was that she would discuss any question seriously and thoughtfully, and that if she did not know the answer, she said so. . . . Nor did she ever grow impatient with Katherine's conversation, which was apt to be too improving for the average adult.[2]

Improving certainly seems to be the mot juste. In a long letter written in December 1906, quite early in their friendship, Dorothy devoted a paragraph to criticizing the spelling of Ivy's previous letter as sternly as an old-fashioned schoolmistress. And in January, hearing that Ivy had been to see *A Midsummer Night's Dream*, she comments: "It's not at all one of my favourite plays, *as* a play, but I should think it must be charming, acted, and the scenery must be very pretty indeed."[3] She herself had recently written a play, which had been performed with, she says, great success by herself and her tutors – Dorothy casting herself as "a very young authoress who has just written a successful book";[4] so she clearly felt herself qualified to be condescending about Shakespeare.

The girls exchanged poems and short stories, and Dorothy kept Ivy informed of her varied activities – painting; classifying botanical specimens; playing the violin at village concerts; "sputtering" (a sort of pointilliste effect obtained by putting paint on to an old toothbrush and flicking it on to the paper with a comb); reading French novels and plays in the original ("why don't you work up your French a bit? You'd find it such a help, and some French books are very nice"[5]); and getting stuck on a country walk because of the flooding.

Then there were thoughts about religion to be passed on. Dorothy had already discussed with Ivy the need to enlighten "poor people" about the Creation, and not to allow them to go on imagining that it all happened in a week, as the Bible claimed; and she gave her father good marks for preaching a sermon on this subject on Septuagesima Sunday (January 26) 1907, "showing them how to reconcile science with the Bible . . . not that they'll think another word about it after today. At least I shouldn't think they would."[6] The second chapter of St Paul to the Romans (especially verses 14–16, and 26, 27) are recommended to Ivy as throwing light on the vexed question as to whether "savages and people who had never heard of God" would be given a second chance – "because of course God wouldn't punish them for disobeying laws they had never heard of. . . . Just read the whole chapter carefully . . . I love St Paul. He was such a fine little chap. . . ."[7]

Surprisingly enough, it seems that Dorothy, so far from being pumped full of Christianity by her parents, had to pick up her religious beliefs as she went along:

For a daughter of the parsonage Katherine was oddly uninstructed in Christian dogma. Mrs Lammas . . . shrank instinctively from doctrinal argument. . . . She had always eagerly begged that Katherine should not be "bothered" with these questions. Mr Lammas, actuated by God knows what sense of personal inadequacy or nervous dread of intimate personal contact, had sedulously refrained from giving any religious instruction to his daughter, beyond what she might pick up from regular weekly attendance at Morning and Evening Prayer. . . .[8]

There was little in the half-hearted, middle-of-the-road Church of

England theology of those days to stir any child with a mind of her own. Dorothy's speculations are simply part of her restless interest in everything that came her way. She was not a pious child. More than twenty years later, writing to Ivy about the education of her own son, she recalled that "when we had a fire in the kitchen beam at Bluntisham, I was pushed off to church – to church! – instead of being allowed to run round and help. I sometimes wish I'd been given the rough with the smooth more when I was a kid."[9]

One holiday – probably the summer of 1907, when Ivy was staying at the rectory – Dorothy hit upon a new game, "the last and most flamboyant of all Katherine's impersonations. The Three Musketeers took possession of the schoolroom, and life became a flutter of flags, an incrustation of jewelled baldricks, a sheen of swords."[10]

In fact it was not only the schoolroom that was taken over; everybody in the rectory was given a part. And when the holiday ended and Ivy went home, Dorothy took to heading her letters "le Chateau de Bragelonne" instead of "The Rectory, Bluntisham", and signing them "Athos"; for it was as Athos that she cast herself, the handsome devil-may-care nobleman incognito, with the tragic past and the melancholy smile. Her father was King Louis, her mother Cardinal Richelieu, a friend was the tubby Porthos and the governess d'Artagnan. Ivy, when she was there, was allowed to be Marie, Duchesse de Chevreuse, friend and confidante of the Queen. "Wigs of crepe hair, ruffled shirts, and boots made of buff-linen were constructed by the obliging Mrs Appleton" (there are photographs to prove it) "and French oaths of the most ferocious kind resounded about the house."[11] Dorothy began to write "Cavalier poems, with swaggering choruses",[12] and so deeply did she enter into the part that "the character of Athos was more real to her than her own".[13]

As ever, she lived more happily in fiction than in reality. In Dumas, blood and wine were spilt equally casually and in similar quantities, and shrugged off with a careless oath. But the death of Grannie in real life was one of those events when Dorothy "was not sure of being able to produce the gesture and speech suitable for such an occasion".[14] It was enough to give her a deep unease about the adequacy of her relations with other human beings.

The Musketeer period lasted for over a year. In the letters written in the autumn of 1907 the handwriting begins to change, becoming bolder, and freer – and so does the subject matter: the intellectual ideas still flow, but one whole letter is taken up with a meeting with a youth called Cyril Hutchinson, nicknamed for some reason "Dull Red" – "I have studied the matter and can tell you positively – his eyes are brown."[15]

At the same time, under cover of the masculine pseudonym Athos, we find her addressing Ivy as "My love" and "Belle Cousine", and writing "I do *wish* you were here, darling Duchess, to talk to".[16] Such endearments in many young girls might mean little, but Dorothy was, as we have observed, not a child of spontaneous feelings, "and exceedingly bad at aping an emotion that she did not really feel".[17] On May 2 1908 she sends a card addressed "à Madame la Duchesse de Chevreuse, c/o Mrs Shrimpton, 25 Stuart Road, Acton W", which consists simply of a three-verse love poem in French entitled "Stances à ma Maitresse", written over a drawing of a dancer and signed "Athos":

> Si je vous aime, c'est que je n'y puis rien
> Et que dans les heureux jours
> Du bonheur et des amours
> Votre cœur s'est emparé du mien . . .
>
> Si je vous aime, Marie, si je vous aime,
> Et vous éprouvez du chagrin
> Quand je meurs de votre main
> Ma mort est votre pénitence même.

(If I love you, it is because I have no choice, and because, in the happy days of contentment and love, your heart has taken hold of mine . . .

If I love you, Marie, if I love you, and if you should feel grief when I die for your sake, my death is your penance.)

Further impassioned communications followed in the succeeding months – "though thou and I were silent, though ages should sever and oceans divide us; though the tongue of one or both were forever made motionless in the grave, I should still be true, dear heart . . ."[18] And another neat little three-verse love-poem in French.

It would be absurd to imagine that any real passion lay behind these effusions. Dorothy was a fairly conventional girl, Ivy excessively so. Dorothy's passion was for passion itself, and in the character of Athos she could indulge it to the hilt. Ivy was soul-mate enough to be the recipient of her eloquent phrases, and would have known exactly how to take them. Her understanding enabled Dorothy to play the passion game, as adolescent girls love to do, without embarrassment. If anybody stirred Dorothy physically, it seems to have been "Dull Red", whose

impending arrival she notes with excitement – "I expect Cyril to propose
this year. He takes a long time to screw up his courage. By the bye,
shouldn't we all be flabbergasted if he did!!!!!"[19]

Though there is no evidence that Dorothy's sexual instincts were ever
anything but female, her character unquestionably displays certain
masculine elements. As a child she preferred beaten-up toy monkeys to
prettily dressed dolls; and she always chose to be a hero rather than a
heroine in her romantic fantasies. She also had an objective and
analytical turn of mind – and this is commoner (for whatever reason)
among men than among women.

Dorothy was mainly interested in her intellectual development: the
thing that stood out in her memory of the years of growing-up was not
a party or a relationship, but the moment when she realized that
Ahasuerus (who was Bible) was the same as Xerxes (who was History).[20]
She mentions this discovery both in her essay "A Vote of Thanks to
Cyrus" (reprinted in *Unpopular Opinions*) and in *Cat o' Mary*:

> The effect on Katherine was most extraordinary. It was like fitting
> together two pieces of a puzzle and hearing all the other pieces fall
> into place one after the other, locking and clicking. She felt as Coper-
> nicus must have done when he tried placing the sun in the centre of
> the solar system, and found that for a complicated variety of planetary
> aberrations he could now substitute a beautiful oneness of concentric
> circles. Now lessons ceased to be lessons; they were part of everything
> else. The Three Musketeers fitted into History and Poetry. Books had
> begun to make contact with life.[21]

When by using geometry (not one of her strong subjects), Dorothy unerringly found the post-holes and metal corners of the tennis court,
which had become so overgrown since the previous year that her father
had searched for them in vain, she felt that:

> . . . she had been brought face to face with beauty. It had risen up
> before her again – the lovely satisfying unity of things – the wedding of
> the thing learnt and the thing done – the great intellectual fulfilment.
> Nothing would ever quite wipe out the memory of that magnificent
> moment when the intersecting circles marched out of the Euclid book
> and met on the green grass in the sun-flecked shadow of the mulberry
> tree.[22]

This was where Dorothy found ecstasy – in the operations of the mind,
whether the solving of problems or the creating of verses. In a way they

were the same thing. They were a matter of discovering a pattern that worked. Dorothy's priorities are not shared by most girls, but nor, for that matter, are they shared by most boys. Intellectual passion crosses the border of sex as though it did not exist.

The abiding image we take away from this period is of an intent figure, bent over her work (which is also her play) accompanied only by some governess, some mademoiselle or Fräulein; her mind constantly absorbed in new interests, never at rest until it has mastered whatever it hits upon, whether it be a language, a rhyme-scheme, an astronomical phenomenon, a point of musical theory or the reason why it is more uncomfortable to fall on top of a bicycle than to have it fall on you.

These lonely delights brought their disadvantages. When other children in the neighbourhood held parties, they began now to leave Dorothy off the invitation list; they thought she was too grand and clever to appreciate such simple delights. Isolated already by circumstance, she now began to feel the extra isolation of being a social misfit, which led to an even greater concentration on study.

There was one other legacy from this period: a hatred of being "fussed". One form that this took in later years was a passionate dislike of being regarded as interesting for herself, rather than for her work. Her wish that no biography should appear until fifty years after her death is part and parcel of this feeling; and plenty of journalists who innocently sought a few personal notes to enliven an interview were amazed at the wrath this brought down upon them. The reason she gave for this fierce protection of her privacy was a vigorous semi-theological argument to the effect that the entire significance of writers was to be found in their writing, and the rest was dross and paperclips; a view that was hardly consistent with her own avowed relish for gossip and scandal about other people: "*All* the sordid details, please", she more than once requested with glee from a friend with a good story.

One explanation for her mild phobia about personal publicity is her awareness that her private life would not stand up to close investigation. But she did once suggest another reason:

> I can't altogether explain my violent dislike of personal interest, except that I connect it with the atmosphere of solicitude which surrounded me in childhood and of which I have been trying to rid myself ever since. So much so that I can't be civil if I am told that I am missed when I am away or welcomed when I return.[23]

That was written much later, in a mood of unaccustomed self-analysis. But in one of her letters to Ivy, we have the complaint new-minted:

I suppose you know that I have got a Fräulein here for the holidays. It really is perfectly *loathsome*. It isn't that she isn't nice – for she is, very nice indeed. But you see I *can not* get away from her . . . And I hate not being able to get away from a person. I can't make mother understand how I hate it. I can't do or make anything, you know, without being watched while I do it and asked what it is etc etc.[24]

Almost all artists have the problem of how to isolate themselves from the curiosity and helpfulness of friends and acquaintances. It does seem likely that Dorothy's vehement reactions against those who wanted to inspect the creative talent at work, rather than be content to enjoy the finished creation, stemmed from early formative days, however much they may have been aggravated by later experiences.

Apart from the insight into Dorothy's thoughts and character, and the confirmation of the autobiographical element of *Cat o' Mary*, Dorothy's letters to Ivy have another vital significance. They help to explain for the first time why it was Ivy to whom Dorothy, desperately in need of help sixteen years later, entrusted a secret that no one else in the world was allowed to share. The impression left by some accounts of Ivy as no more than an eccentric distant relative is deeply misleading. It makes much more sense of the vital role that Ivy played in Dorothy's later life when we see how close they were in adolescence.

A section of one of Dorothy's letters, written early in 1908, casts an extraordinary shadow forward to those later events. It is one of Dorothy's twenty-page epistles, each page decorated with painted flowers, devils and so forth. (C. S. Lewis was to call her one of the great letter-writers, and this was true of quantity as well as quality.)

The opening of the letter is ordinary enough. There is a long description of a village concert, at which Dorothy herself played three pieces and an encore on her violin; the platform consisted of springy planks laid across two trestles, so that "at every stroke of the bow the platform shook and danced and swung and sprang and jumped and rolled and tossed like a ship at sea".

Other participants are sketched with a few neat strokes, showing the budding novelist's maturing observation: the tenor "was a stout, grey-haired middle-aged person with a seal-ring and seraphic smile. Then there was an enormously fat lady with an endless double chin, vanishing away into her neck . . . she sang a sentimental song about the swallows. . . ."[25]

This is followed by some pages about a play she is writing; and then she begins to work towards the thing she has to say. She embarks on a discussion of the case of Ivy's cousin Freda, who was thinking of becoming a Roman Catholic. She warns Ivy against sneering at her cousin, as she has seen others sneering at people who changed their religious allegiance:

> I should never sneer at anyone or think the worse of him because he had changed his ideas . . . In the majority of cases (I speak as a fool) it probably requires a lot more courage to renounce one's faith and embrace another publicly than to march up to the cannon's mouth. . . . And above all don't try to argue. It never does any good, except to sharpen the tongue and the temper . . .[26]

After this sage advice, which in later years she herself frequently failed to remember, the letter continues:

> And now that I am writing about this, it seems to be an opportunity for me to say something that has been on my mind for some time, and which I have never liked to say for fear of offending you. . . . I think, old girl, that you are just a bit inclined to form a harsh judgement – or perhaps I ought to say a hard judgement, of other people. . . . I think you are a little apt to say, in effect, "What this man did was an offence against morality. It was therefore wrong and inexcusable. I do not care what excuse this person had – he did wrong. Therefore he is a wicked person and there is an end of it!" Dear old girl, get out of the way of thinking that. It is terribly closely allied to Pharisaism, which, you know, is the one thing our Lord was always so down upon. And I think that this attitude towards other people will make you have fewer friends, because they will be afraid of you. I shouldn't like to feel, Ivy, that suppose sometime I sinned a great sin, I should be afraid to come to you for help. Only, unless you would try to make allowances for me, I'm afraid I should. St Paul says, as you heard this morning, "Though I speak with the tongues of men and of angels, and have not charity, I am become as sounding brass or as a tinkling cymbal." And I think one phase of charity is making allowances for other people's mistakes . . . I have written all this in fear and trembling . . . Don't be angry. Try not . . . I don't want to lose my best friend . . . Write as soon as you can, please, and tell me whether I have or not . . .[27]

Dorothy did not lose her best friend. And when, almost as though fulfilling a prophecy, she did "sin a great sin", it was indeed to Ivy that she turned, and there seems to have been no lack of charity on Ivy's part. She had kept the letter. Did she remember Dorothy's admonitions, sixteen years later?

Intriguing though this is, the letter is even more important for the glimpse it gives us of the young Dorothy sorting out her priorities, and finding in the New Testament a morality which is above conventional ethics. Observing her at the age of fifteen as she reproves her twenty-year-old cousin, we see the budding of the woman who thirty years later (and with much less hesitation) was to attempt, almost single-handed, to put the Church of England back on course. By that time it was she who from time to time seems to have forgotten to make allowances. But I think we should remember that at the age of fifteen, though her mind was passionately occupied with ideas, with literature, with techniques of painting, writing and music (twenty pages of another letter were devoted to a treatise on minor scales),[28] the thing that really stirred her to protest was a lack of charity.

The time, however, of the Fräulein, the mademoiselle and the governess, the time of the lonely studies, the long letters and the Three Musketeers, was coming to an end. In one of Dorothy's extravagant epistles to Ivy she breaks the news:

> 'Twill out, I am leaving the Court and going far away. I am going to School! But and alas! for our noble company, the grand bond will be broken for ever after Christmas! for ever and for ever, and now no more shall the four Musketeers walk side by side in the garden or fight together for the King.[29]

The account in *Cat o' Mary* suggests rather a different reaction:

> "Shall you mind it very much?" asked her mother, delicately probing for some expression of regret at the prospect of leaving home for the first time on her own. "I think I should like to go to school. It would be a change. And I should like to know some other people. . . . When do I start? Next term?"[30]

CHAPTER FOUR

IT WAS NOT to be next term. A bout of chickenpox meant that Dorothy missed the autumn term and had to begin in January. Fate seemed to be contriving the most unpropitious way for her to start her schooling.

The school Mr and Mrs Sayers had chosen was the Godolphin School at Salisbury – a city of great beauty and antiquity, but perhaps a little stuffy. Dorothy was to write of it in her first novel that "the atmosphere of the Close pervades every nook and corner of Salisbury, and no food in that city but seems faintly flavoured with prayer-books."[1]

A London school had been discussed, but Mrs Sayers had been of the opinion that fresh air was a vital consideration and was not to be had in London. The notion of boarding schools was accepted for middle-class children in those days, but even so one must wonder that parents could so blithely transfer a treasured child from the insulation of a comfortable home into the turmoil of organized mass girlhood over a hundred miles away, with no intervening period of day schooling in which to get used to human beings in large numbers while still living at home.

The school had been built up by its headmistress, Miss Douglas, from small beginnings and now contained about a hundred boarding pupils and a similar number of day girls. Miss Douglas was one of that group of dauntless head-teachers who in the latter half of the nineteenth century became legends in their own time; and doubtless the Sayers parents felt that under such inspired guidance their talented daughter could only become wiser and happier.

Dorothy approached the new experience in a mood of rich and ecstatic melancholy, writing haunting poems about the break up of the Musketeers.

Tears of pure intoxication came into Katherine's eyes as she wrote:
What say the wailing trumpets as they
return from war?
They say that he is fallen, d'Artagnan
fights no more.[2]

She wrote to Ivy:
. . . my sky has been troubled, my beloved, very troubled by storms, wherefore I know not, save that such things come – whence no man

knows, borne by some homeless wind, to stay a little while and then to
depart towards their own place . . . Oh love, love! To see thee again!
To hold thee once more to my heart! I laid thy letter there, but I
would embrace thine own dear self. Oh, my adored one come, come,
come, come! To him who to the end of the world, must write himself,
here and hereafter, thy devoted lover, Athos. P.S. This invitation is
official.[3]

Her fantasies about the school itself were mixed – though in all of them
she held the central place. In some she was the centre of admiration – the
one girl who could quote by heart Shakespeare, Milton, even Molière
and Racine. In others she was sneered at by large clever girls who had
learnt their French in Paris, who were demons at hockey and who
despised her for never having been to school before. "She could never
be comfortably and ordinarily part of the herd. She would be either the
school star or the school butt. Which? She had not imagined that it was
perfectly possible to be both."[4]

Her introduction to the school was unfortunate. Not only was she
starting half-way through the school year, but there was a further embarrassment. Miss Douglas was noted for her legendary memory about
her pupils, but she had nevertheless unfortunately forgotten that the
new girl was not eight, like other new girls, but fifteen and a half; and
Dorothy suffered considerably from the confusion and hilarity which
ensued.

The humiliation and discomfort continued. She had no experience
whatever of the rhythm and discipline of group living, and was always in
the wrong place at the wrong time, clutching the wrong book; and there
was a smell which puzzled her till she realized that it was simply the smell
of human beings in bulk – something she had never encountered before
and did not much care for now she had.

She had her secret weapon, however, and bided her time till she could
bring it into play. The first French lesson came round. The teacher asked
the class, in French, who could tell her something about Molière.
Dorothy was shrewd enough to know that she must not open fire too
soon. But at last, when nobody else was able to offer any information,
she said her piece. In perfect French, with a flawless accent, she gave
Molière's dates, a brief summary of his career and a list of his major
works.

This "brought every head round with a jerk to stare at the strange
phenomenon in the back row. Miss Larotte, who had never before in her
life heard the subjunctive accurately and readily placed within the walls
of the lower fifth, reeled slightly from the shock."[5]

Such a display was hardly likely to endear her to her fellow pupils, but it was some consolation to her for her other failures, and there was little else to comfort her at Godolphin. Nevertheless, oddly enough, she did not feel homesick. Though unhappy, she was interested – and while she was interested she could never be totally miserable. There was, for example, the ravishing music which Fräulein Fehmer, for all her odd Germanic stiffness, conjured from the piano, so memorable that Dorothy, who in every other way did her level best to forget Godolphin, wrote a poem for the ageing Fräulein years later, when the British bombers were out over Germany, destroying city after city in 1944.

> . . . There is a particular Nocturne
> that I cannot hear to this day without thinking of her;
> when it is rendered
> by celebrated musicians over the aether
> I see the red-brick walls, the games trophies,
> the rush-bottomed chairs, the row of aspidistras
> that garnished the edge of the platform, and Fräulein Fehmer,
> gowned in an unbecoming dark-blue silk,
> lifting the song from the strings with a squaring of her strong
> shoulders;[6]

In her letters home she found it quite impossible to speak of her mental and physical distress. She knew that her parents would want her first of all to be happy at school, and secondly to look forward to the holidays. She could say neither of these things with any truth, but these are what her letters said. And to cover her lack of candour she filled them with factual information about where she kept her books, the names of the girls in her dormitory, her lessons and her progress with the detested compulsory games.

On the hockey field, she ran eagerly about, studying how to appear at home with a hockey stick, trying to look like the other girls, but all the while in mortal dread that the ball would actually come somewhere in her direction. If it did, she felt herself totally incapable of coping with it. Intellectual games were a passion with her; physical games she could never comprehend, and the easy co-ordination of other girls remained a bafflement and a source of bitterness.

She learnt to get by, as children have to in such circumstances, by a combination of slyness, defiance, and buffoonery. She knew she was disliked and despised by the other girls, but it came as a shock to find that the teachers too had a low opinion of her. The consensus in the common room was that she was a shirker, and the headmistress summoned her for a little talk about her character. She was informed that she did not like being criticized and that she made too many excuses; a school like this was for the formation of character and she must attempt to reform hers. As a result she became convinced that there was indeed something deeply and unalterably (but rather interestingly) wrong with her.

In this bleak time, however, there came to her occasional moments, unlooked for and inexplicable, of glorious exultation. Suddenly she would become conscious of an exhilarating sense of power – something within herself that was shared by nobody else at the school.

It had to do with words. To most of the girls the textual criticism of the French and English poets that they studied was dry and meaningless. But as Dorothy studied the placing of the words, the rhythm and sound of the syllables and the structure and rhyme-scheme of the lines, she came to have a physical feeling for the twisting together of language into a strong rope of meaning; and through this understanding there came to her word pictures:

> Le Roi Soleil, small, bewigged, superb, and with him all the people from the Viscomte de Bragelonne, rustling through the sun-drenched parterre to view the latest triumph of their court poet, that wandering player with his melancholy eyes, worn lungs and broken heart – the dying actor acting *Le Malade Imaginaire* – the darkening room and two nuns only to help him as he coughs out his soul. Black night and glimmering torches, and the corpse, huddled with maimed rites into the wormy earth.[7]

Here indeed was Dorothy's empire, unshared by the other girls – that seductive world where laden words transformed history into story. Here she ruled, and rejoiced in her dominance: "One day I will show them. I will set my feet on their heads, put the world in my hand like clay and I will build, build, build – something enormous – something they never even dreamed of. It is in me. It is not in them and I know it."[8]

An independent report tells of her announcement, about this time, that she had decided "to become famous, and that she would allow no one to stand in her way".[9] The story is at third or fourth hand, and far from sympathetic; and I think we may beg leave to feel that the line about letting no one stand in her way should not be taken too seriously in a self-dramatizing schoolgirl – even if accurate. But there must have been a germ of truth there. Under humiliation, Dorothy's ambition smouldered the hotter.

One thing which she found particularly alien was the form of religion practised at Godolphin – a low church pietism, drab and mealy-mouthed, which deeply offended her instinctive sense that if God mattered at all he was surely too robust to need to be treated with the hushed decorum and the wealth of prissy euphemisms that the teachers seemed to think appropriate.

In later years Dorothy wrote to a young theologian, John Wren-Lewis, that she might well have abandoned Christianity altogether at this time had it not been for the vigorous example of G. K. Chesterton, who saw the history of Christendom as "one whirling adventure . . . [in which] the heavenly chariot flies thundering through the ages, the dull heresies sprawling and prostrate, the wild truth reeling but erect".[10] To the lover of romantic images and luxuriant language this was irresistible.

The worst of it was that at the moment of her greatest need, her parents too abandoned her. It was hardly their fault, for Dorothy had never told them what she felt on the subject; but she resented it bitterly when they sent instructions that she was to be confirmed at Salisbury, along with a number of other girls, and it took four or five envenomed pages in Cat o' Mary to describe the incident and the effect it had on her:

> The awkward stutter and hush that accompanied the word "Gawd" was even more indissolubly attached to the words "communion" and "sacrament" . . . To these rites, which were held in secret, a strong flavour of the indecent seemed to cling. Like the central act of marriage . . . the central mysteries of religion were by common consent exceedingly sacred and beautiful, but on the other hand indelicate, and only to be mentioned in periphrastic whispers.[11]

Years later Dorothy looked back on this time in a letter to Ivy about the religious upbringing of her son Anthony:

> Being baptized against one's will is not nearly so harmful as being confirmed against one's will, which is what happened to me and gave me a resentment against religion which lasted a long time . . . the cultivation of religious emotion without philosophic basis is thoroughly pernicious – in my opinion.[12]

At the time of the confirmation, however, she said nothing about her true feelings, even to Ivy. She wrote to her, "it was a lovely day and it all went off beautifully. It was a huge ceremony, about two hundred and twenty candidates I think, and the Cathedral was simply *packed*."[13] She knew well enough what the world expected her to feel.

To her parents she wrote a similar letter – much longer and more detailed, with a PS.: "I never can write about my *feelings* – that's why I haven't."[14] She remembered that PS. when she came to write *Cat o' Mary*, though she had forgotten the exact wording: "She wrote in duty bound to her parents giving a detailed account of the ceremony. But that would not do by itself. She chewed her pen. 'I won't say anything about feelings,' she wrote. 'I can't express those very well.'"[15]

Dorothy's passionate condemnation of the hypocrisy of a ceremony that meant nothing to her seems to be almost the first instance in her life of a deep and unqualified emotion. She was considered insincere, shallow and unfeeling by her schoolfellows. The teachers regarded her as brilliant but superficial – an accusation that Dorothy strongly suspected of being accurate. She knew that she was expected to be simply herself, but the trouble was that she had little idea of what she truly was. When she tried to discover, she only became aware of layers and layers of self; below each layer of feeling another layer watching and mocking it. Nobody else seemed to have this problem, so once again Dorothy felt that the defect must be hers alone.

A case in point was the crush that she developed for Miss White, the French teacher. "I may be in love with Miss White – I probably am,"[16] she wrote uninhibitedly to her mother, fully aware that the girl with the adolescent crush was all an act:

> Katherine's pash ran its course with no more deviation from traditional lines than an L.C.C. tram. She suffered exquisite pangs and enjoyed herself enormously. Here she could dramatize life to her heart's content. The ridicule that she inevitably encountered she did not resent, for she was playing a chosen part, and the laughter of the audience was the world's tribute to the accomplished comedienne.[17]

Adopting a combination of calculated buffoonery and "a prickly assumption of independence", she forged for herself what she called "a corsage of defiance"[18] – the protection within which her mind and her heart could win time and space to come to terms with themselves.

Part of her trouble was that she was more aware of herself than most people, more troubled by the complex jumble of thoughts and emotions that she found in herself and by her inability to make sense of them. Her instinct was always to find a tidy pattern for things, and that included her own psyche. The turmoil of adolescence was worse for her because she was not prepared simply to live through it; she had to know what it all meant.

But there was unquestionably more to it than this. Dorothy's personality, apparently so direct, was in truth nothing of the kind. For her, the clear light of experience tended always to be refracted through the multicoloured prism of a literary intellect. Had she been able to do anything to alter her perception of reality, she would probably not have wished to do so, for this was where her strength and her joy lay. But the price she paid was that she felt no direct assurance even of the reality of her own personality.

This gave her, when she needed, the playwright's gift for inventing diverse characters and giving convincing speech and action to each of them. It enabled her to separate the compartments of her life, so that enormous secrets remained hidden from her closest friends. When, later, she entered into religious controversy, she was able to avoid the charge of insincerity by allying herself with tradition and the doctrine of the Church – a purely intellectual assent which demanded no personal stance. For the most part she made the best – and a very good best – of the cards life had dealt her. But from time to time throughout her life the problem reasserted itself and the weak spot – the lack of contact with reality – became apparent. On a very few occasions she was forced to acknowledge her weakness, but she never did so except in private correspondence; her need to be right was too powerful to permit that.

Cat o' Mary, the closest she ever came to exposing her private problems in public, was written when she had just weathered the worst tempests of her life; perhaps she needed to look back from a secure anchorage at perils past and at the course that had steered her to them. The sad thing about *Cat o' Mary*, in view of the fact that she never published it, is how well it is done: it is a story of self-criticism, uncertainty and humiliation – the precise opposite of the qualities Dorothy liked to adopt in public. Her preference for cheerful fiction is understandable, but has done less than justice to her potential stature as a writer.

The mental flux, the conflicting pressures that she suffered at school help to explain why she later settled for the security of intellectual certitudes and the pleasure that childhood had taught her of always knowing best. While it lasted, her turmoil of mind was most unpleasant and confusing. She wanted self-knowledge; she passionately wanted friends; even more she wanted approval; and most of all she wanted to attract attention. "She succeeded only too well in the last, and thereby probably lost both approval and friends."[19]

The struggle grew harder and harder: "She would wake in the morning with the heavy certainty that she could not get through the day. Something must happen . . . to relieve her of the burden of living."[20]

Something did indeed happen which very nearly succeeded in doing this. Having been "hammered" through a second Higher Certificate examination which included mathematics, so that she could qualify for Oxford – "her spiritual home, the holy city"[21] – she was preparing to work for her scholarship, when measles struck the school.

Miss Douglas was away when it happened, and the housemistress of the house in which the outbreak started decided sensibly to isolate girls who had been in contact with the disease. Miss Douglas, on her return, countermanded these orders and let the quarantined girls mix with the rest of the school, recommending a regime of fresh air, exercise and positive thinking. The result was that the whole school went down – Dorothy and one other girl catching the disease in an acute form and developing pneumonia.

Dorothy's mother came to nurse her and was allowed to stay by her bedside through her delirium. The illness was very serious, and something in Dorothy knew that death was not far off. For the first time, as she battled for life, she began to be homesick, and cried out for "the cool green garden, with its ancient ivy hung trees";[22] and the peach trees into which she used to throw her tennis racket because the only peaches she was allowed were the fallen ones.

The crisis came one night, and Mrs Sayers and a specialist were called to the bedside. The specialist failed to arrive. The school doctor decided to wait no longer, but to administer a saline injection – and Dorothy's life was saved.

She was not grateful to be brought back to the wearisome routine of school and the prospect of exams. She wished she had been allowed to die peacefully – and learnt from this experience that death is not so terrible, if one is ill enough not to care.

Inevitably, Mrs Sayers had discovered how the school preyed on Dorothy's mind, and she arranged for her daughter to be moved for her convalescence to a nursing home – where, to the doctor's suprise, the healing process was helped more by poetry than by the detective stories which he recommended.

All this happened in February and March of 1911; and at this point the manuscript of *Cat o' Mary* breaks off. We could have wished for more, but in a sense it has told us all that we need to know about the young Dorothy Sayers; we have clues as to what to ignore and what to take seriously in her subsequent letters and in the reports of people who knew her. We know how deeply she felt about some things, and how superficial was her superficiality. We know what to make of her buffoonery, and of her extravagant affectations of devotion; at least we know not to take them at face value – though Dorothy was perfectly capable of a double bluff which used a counterfeit emotion to conceal a true one. Above all we know that, however ambiguous her personal relationships were, about religion she had certain very clear and powerful feelings: she knew at least what she did not like.

In her notes for the continuation of *Cat o' Mary*, referring to the personal relationships of her heroine, Dorothy writes: "get in strongly the feeling about 'inside me I don't *really* care'." The problem that haunted Dorothy was not that she did not care, but that, unlike the female stereotype, she cared more about universal truths and abstract ideas than individual people. This, I believe, is the key to the accusations of insincerity. Despite her painful self-awareness and acute intelligence, she was nevertheless deeply enough conditioned to a conventional view of her sex to accept the accusations as valid.

Even today, when wave after wave of female emancipation has separated us from the age of Dorothy Sayers, the idea that a woman might find greater fulfilment in the intellect than in the emotions is still not fully accepted. *Cat o' Mary*, had it been completed and published, would have been years ahead of its time, and one wonders how it would have been received. What is certain is that anyone as aware as Dorothy of the contrast between the conventional idea of women and the truth about herself was in for a most uncomfortable life.

So modern an outlook on personal relationships goes in curious harness with Dorothy's delight in ancient words and ancient ways of thinking. Her attitude to religion was also an odd mixture of convention and free-thinking. The Christianity that G. K. Chesterton revealed to her was imbued with colour, adventure, humour, and unabashed vigour. It bore, apparently, no sort of relationship to the drab and apologetic thing that Christianity was at Godolphin.

Dorothy's principal reason for choosing Somerville College rather than Lady Margaret Hall was that Somerville was undenominational. It was of the greatest importance that she should be free from pressure, free to disentangle the conflicting patterns in her mind and find out which one was significant for her.

Dorothy did not go back to school till the beginning of the autumn term – a break of six months. There must have been much heart-searching before she went, for her parents knew, this time, what they were sending her back to and what she felt about it; and their trust in the school must have been considerably shaken by Miss Douglas's handling of the measles epidemic.

There was an additional horror: as a result of the illness and its attendant psychological wretchedness most of Dorothy's hair had fallen out, and she would have to face the mockery of her school-fellows at her near-baldness – or worse, a wig. Throughout her life, Dorothy's hair was to make her miserable. At best it was sparse and unappealing, and at moments of strain and crisis it tended to make matters worse by falling out.

However, she went back. She was a senior girl now, and was made House Prefect – a post which suited her bossy streak but which did nothing to make her more popular. It cannot have gone down well, for example, when she lectured members of the House about their untidiness – for tidiness was never one of her own more notable attributes. "A fish out of water",[23] her description of herself in those days, can only be seen as one of her rare understatements.

One or two events enlivened the latter half of the term: she went to the Albert Hall with the school orchestra, in which she played the violin; she was cast as Shylock in the school play (apparently her hair had by then grown enough for her to feel it was too thick on top to play the part without a wig); and Miss White kissed her unexpectedly when she was in bed with a cold.

There was a fine contretemps with Matron and another member of staff called Miss Parson about the proper treatment of actors. Some of the school had visited a theatre in Salisbury for a performance by a group of French players. One of these was a friend of one of Dorothy's aunts, and she had met him on a previous visit. The girls were not supposed to speak to the actors, but as they left the theatre Dorothy's acquaintance stood by the door and greeted her. She began to make a polite reply but was instantly dragged away by Miss Parson and, when she explained to Matron that the man had spoken first, was told that she should have ignored him.

Dorothy's fury was immense. Here was a chance for her to write openly to her parents about her scorn for some of the school staff: "The spirit of pride and contempt that buried the great Molière secretly at dead of night is still alive."[24] Fortunately, on this occasion Miss Douglas came up trumps and told Dorothy that she had acted perfectly rightly.

The incident may have appeased Dorothy's notions of justice, but it did nothing for her opinion of the religion taught at the school. She wrote a sonnet on the subject, in which the feeling was wholehearted:

> A hundred years and yet a hundred years
> Pass, and no change. How long, oh Lord, how long?
> We grow weary of the shame and wrong.
> Over our painted cheeks run bitter tears.
> Oh stainless Christians, how your Christ appears!
> What shall we call him who did sit among
> The publicans and sinners – wise, kind, strong? –

Him whom his Christendom nor heeds nor hears?
Nor have we sinned. We are thy servants still,
And they would take our service from us – yea,
God, they would take our very God away.
Hard is belief when Christians use so ill
Christ's prodigals. Just heaven, is this thy will?
We watch the dark. How slowly breaks the day![25]

A quarter of a century later she was to become a part of the theatrical world herself, and to get to know actors as friends and colleagues. The combination of professionalism and easy warmth that she found in that world was probably the greatest joy she ever knew, and this early sonnet is an appropriate salute to artists and craftsmen who were to give her so much.

Throughout the autumn term of 1911 Dorothy struggled to overcome her feelings about the school at least for long enough to complete her studies for the scholarship. The pale spires of Oxford beckoned, and all she had to do was endure.

It was too much for her. Some very compelling consideration – presumably some kind of nervous breakdown – induced her parents not to send her back after Christmas but to let her continue her studies at home. In February 1912 we find her writing to Ivy from Bluntisham about the work that she was doing for Miss White. Freed from the tensions of school life she could study to her heart's content; and in due course she emerged with her Gilchrist Scholarship to the place of her dreams, Somerville College, Oxford – the place which, unlike so many places of dreams, was not to disappoint her expectations.

CHAPTER FIVE

To go from school to university was to go from purgatory to paradise. For one thing, there were still relations in Oxford. Ivy and her family had moved to London in 1906, whence they were not to return till the outbreak of war in 1914; but this absence mattered much less to Dorothy than it might have done a few years earlier, for much of the intensity had now ebbed out of that friendship. Though Dorothy found her other aunts, uncles and cousins a little tiresome at times, relatives nevertheless offer a reliable, if intermittent, form of relationship, especially to an only child. Dorothy derived a good deal of pleasure from her duty visits to their homes and from the gossipy news she passed on to her parents in her weekly letters.

What really mattered, though, was the College. A story told by her friend Dorothy Rowe tells us a lot about Dorothy at that time – why she was so disliked at school and why, suddenly, she found herself at home at Somerville.

Several girls, among them Dorothy Rowe and Dorothy Sayers, were up at Somerville to take their scholarship examination. As they waited in a room together Dorothy Sayers began quoting from Rostand's *Cyrano de Bergerac* – in the original French. Dorothy Rowe took up the quotation; and immediately they were friends.

It isn't really done – reciting romantic French poetic drama among strangers. Does one describe it as lack of inhibition, or sheer showing off? Either way, Dorothy obviously did not care. She wanted to make an effect regardless of what the effect was. But more than that, she was displaying unashamedly a true passion for exciting words and the bold, swaggering panache of Cyrano.

"Panache" is a key word for Dorothy. It is a prime characteristic of the Three Musketeers, that arrogant refusal to be daunted by danger or disappointment, that flag of defiance waved in the face of the worst that life can do. It is at the worst moments that panache is most needed. And what often seems from the outside to be brashness and a lack of sensitivity, may in reality be simply a sign that the strain is telling, and has got to be expressed in some way.

What was new about Somerville for Dorothy was to find people responding to her at her own level. Well over half a century later, another writer, Marina Warner, described a similar experience:

When I first went up, the greatest pleasure of a women's college was, simply, the company of women . . . it was genuinely intoxicating to find oneself free to pass the day – sometimes the night – exploring, talking, discussing, befriending, learning, speculating, laughing, weeping, questioning in the midst of women who had come from a wide variety of backgrounds, cultural, geographical, intellectual. . . .
In all the unruliness, and eccentricity and effervescence, there was for all the royal road of self-discovery, of future expression.[1]

So it was for Dorothy – and more, for when Dorothy went up, the women's colleges were still on probation. Women still had to prove (though the battle was nearly won) that they were intellectually the equals of men, that they could exist as full members of the university, without resorting to feminine wiles, appeals to chivalry or pleas for special consideration.

Women of the 1980s have had half a century to get used to the idea that they have the right and the ability to seek fulfilment outside the home. In the second and third decades of the century it was very different. Women were advancing into unknown territory; and many of those in the forefront, aware of their exposed position, aware that the eyes of the world were on them, took great care not to jeopardize their progress by rash and scandalous behaviour.

Not that the Somerville girls associated themselves particularly with the Women's Movement: their battle was not on the political front but the intellectual. And the Somerville girls most aware of this were those most careful to conform to the rules of the University, and not be found climbing over a wall or wandering about the streets late at night.

Within its walls, Somerville was run with a decorum that would have done credit to a convent. The only men allowed in undergraduate's rooms were fathers, brothers, uncles and spiritual advisers. Chaperones were required for any event outside the College where there might be contact with the opposite sex. Dorothy herself was put into a considerable dilemma when she met a young man of her acquaintance in the queue for a Gilbert and Sullivan opera. Strictly speaking, she should have made sure that when they got inside, they sat in separate sections of the auditorium. But they chatted too long, the seats filled up around them and they found themselves together willy-nilly. The young man was the more alarmed of the two, at the thought that he might have compromised a lady's reputation – and was only pacified when Dorothy scrambled uncomfortably across the seats in the interval to where a senior student was sitting, and was laughingly reassured that the situation was not regarded as serious.

There were, of course, ways of getting round the problem. Had the authorities but known it, the visitor was often not one's own brother, but someone else's. And many of the girls had a surprising number of spiritual advisers. Certain chaperones, too, were known to be more sympathetic than others. But at all times it was essential to keep up appearances.

In her first few terms at Somerville, Dorothy had a friendship of mild intensity with the young man she met in the queue, whose name was Giles Dixey. They both wrote poems, which they showed each other; and discussed life in a serious and responsible manner. But the lasting relationships she made at that time were with a group of other first-year Somerville students who banded themselves into one of those coteries that flourish at universities, and called themselves the Mutual Admiration Society, or M.A.S.

It seems to have been Dorothy Rowe and Charis Barnett who founded the group, and Charis Barnett who devised its motto – "The best of what we are and do, just God forgive." It was Dorothy Sayers who gave the society its name – on the grounds that if they did not call themselves that, somebody else would.

The qualification for membership was a piece of original writing, which had to be read at one of the meetings. Contributions included playlets, sonnets, a soliloquy by Nero, a dissertation on Shakespeare's fairies, a discussion between Boswell and Johnson on adult suffrage (this was from Charis Barnett); and from Dorothy came a conversation between the Three Wise Men. She had thought of doing the conversation of the men inside the Trojan Horse – a more original notion – but the religious theme won the day.

Competition for entry into the Society was fierce. Though it had been formed by first-year girls, students in their second and third years vied to get in; but Charis Barnett (now Mrs Charis Frankenburg, to whom I am indebted for many of these details) remembers that they only elected "people we liked".

It was an exceptional group of girls, all of whom went on to distinguished careers in one way or another – in the theatre, in social service, in writing; and of them Dorothy Sayers was certainly the most brilliant. There were only seven members of the M.A.S. to start with. Muriel St Clare Byrne, two years younger than the rest, came up in January 1914 and was not admitted to the Society till May of that year. Some of the girls paired off, but Dorothy does not seem to have had a particular friend. They were all equally her friends, much appreciated in different ways for different qualities. Dorothy approached her friends

Right: Dorothy as a child

Below: Dorothy with her parents
and her cousin Ivy (on left)

Dorothy with a friend as about the same period

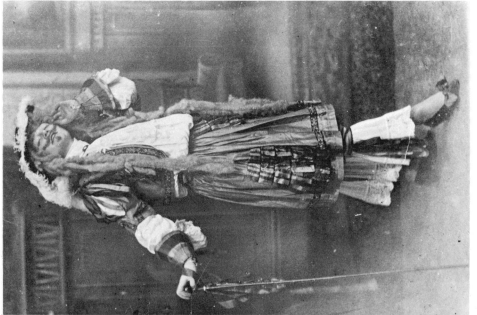

Dorothy impersonating the Musketeer, Athos, in her teens

Cartoon originally captioned "Dr Allen puts his Bach in"

Dorothy impersonating H. P. Allen

Left: Dorothy at Somerville

Below: École des Roches, Le Vallon: X marks Dorothy's window on the original postcard

Right: The photograph from Dorothy's Carte d'identité when she went to teach in France

Below: The first degree ceremony for women at Oxford; Dorothy is among the recipients on the right

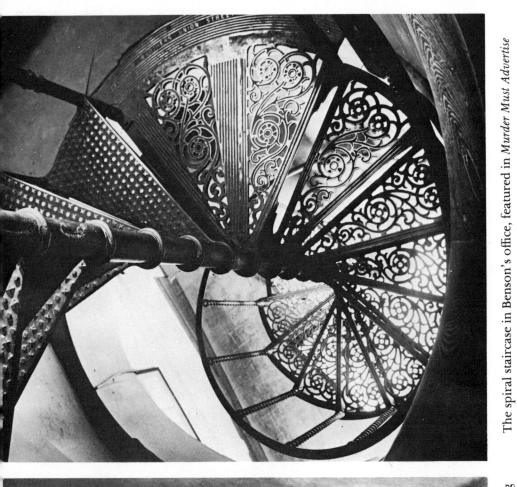

The spiral staircase in Benson's office, featured in *Murder Must Advertise*

The portrait by John Gilroy, 1929: Dorothy in a white wig

Drawing by John Gilroy, 1930

Aunt Amy with Anthony around 1928

with the same enthusiasm she showed towards every subject that came to her attention. As Dorothy Rowe put it, "Whenever she found anyone enjoying anything, she couldn't not join in."

The moment friendship turned to anything approaching love, Dorothy became uneasy. There had been the moment when her favourite, Miss White, at Godolphin School, had sat on her bedside when Dorothy had a cold and had asked delicately whether she might have a kiss. Though interesting, Dorothy found this somewhat "unseemly". Her enthusiasms could be passionate but they were not intimate, much less physical.

A curious ritual existed for establishing a close friendship: as a rule surnames were used however long one girl had known another, and the moment in a friendship when one of them suggested using Christian names was a crucial step known as "proposing". In Dorothy's case, it was a long time before the other M.A.S. members reached the proposal stage and ceased to call her D. Sayers.

This may have been to do with Dorothy's earnestness, for she did take things rather more seriously than most. On one occasion some of the brighter sparks had devised a spoof ghost – a spectral nun walking across the quadrangle with a baby in her arms. Dorothy was not amused when the hoax was revealed, because she had been carefully drawing a pentagram with the intention of exorcizing the spirit.

Dorothy's humour was of a different sort. She enjoyed observing human foibles and eccentricities; and she had a sort of hearty gusto, with a streak of coarseness in it, which appealed to some people but by no means to all. A silly jingle one day came into the head of Dorothy Rowe, and she told it to Dorothy Sayers:

> I killed my wife and children
> And was hanging them up to dry,
> When in came our new curate
> As he chanced to wander by.
> Said he "I hope I don't intrude",
> But all I could reply
> Was "I killed my wife and children
> And I'm hanging them up to dry."

Dorothy Sayers, with her energy, her ebullience and her need to make a spectacle of herself, immediately composed a suitable tune, grabbed several friends, and marched up and down the lawn chanting the silly poem. Small wonder that some of the more staid members of the

College felt that this behaviour was as likely in its own way to bring Somerville into disrepute as gadding around with men students and breaking bounds; and they did not care for it.

The only member of the M.A.S. who shared Dorothy's confidence more than others was Muriel Jaeger – the "Jim" to whom Dorothy was to dedicate her first detective novel. Muriel, more than any of the others, shared Dorothy's interest in religion.

Somerville did not even have a chapel at this time, so determinedly undenominational was it; though Dorothy's efforts to work out her own religious ideas must have been influenced by the fashion then prevalent at Oxford for Anglo-Catholicism. In her second term she wrote home that she had been thinking about Christ's disciples: "having read the two Gospels [no indication as to which two] with more attention than I had ever before given to the subject, I came to the conclusion that such a set of stupid, literal, pig-headed people never existed as Christ had to do with"[2] – an intriguing reaction from one who was to bring the Gospels so successfully to life for radio listeners thirty years later.

Dorothy was going through that uncomfortable stage of adolescence in which the delightful certainties of childhood are suddenly over-turned, and it is hard to understand how anybody can ever be sure of anything again. A year later she was writing:

It is difficult to make people see that what you have been taught counts for nothing, and that the only things worth having are things that you found out for yourself. . . . It isn't a case of "here is the Christian religion – the one respectable and authoritative rule of life, take it or leave it". It's, "here is a muddling affair called Life, and here are nineteen or twenty different explanations of it, all supported by people whose opinions are not to be sneezed at. Among them is the Christian religion in which you happen to have been brought up. Your friend so and so has been brought up in quite a different way of thinking. He is a perfectly splendid person and thoroughly happy. What are you going to do about it?" I am worrying it out quietly, and whatever I get hold of will be valuable because I will have found it for myself. But really, you know, the whole question is not as simple as it looks.[3]

Her method of worrying things out was probably not quite as quiet as she made out. In the summer vacation of 1913 she wrote from Blun-tisham to Muriel Jaeger that she was very frustrated at home, because her normal technique of "vehemently disagreeing with everybody"[4] did not arouse the response she hoped for, but merely resulted in people going rather quiet and polite. "Oh Jimmy, I miss our loud-voiced arguments . . . hang it all, what were tongues made for?"[5] All her life, Dorothy was a steam-roller in arguments and all her life she was to look for people who would stand up to her and give her back as good as they got.

Academically, Dorothy's brilliance was easy to recognize, especially in her chosen subject, French. The approval of her tutors was marred only by the fact that they wished she could be more attentive to subjects she was not interested in – particularly mathematics. Looking back in flippant mood fourteen years later she wrote:

> It cannot be literally true that I never did a stroke of work at Oxford, because my "schools" included a number of papers on Old French Morphology and Grammar which I certainly could not have dealt with by the light of self-generated "gas". It must, therefore, be a trick of memory that presents to me an Oxford day made up as follows. 9.30, breakfast – no later than 10, anyway, because the scouts started clearing away at that hour. 10, clean a pair of tennis-shoes and set them to dry in the quad. 10.30, gather with a party of friends in the lodge to await the arrival of the post: read letters. 11, coffee with friends. 12, cut a lecture, and write a sonnet for a literary society. Discuss Rupert Brooke – (it was in those days). Borrow a thermos, and go into the matter of the 2nd year play with the lender. 1.15, lunch. 2.15, punt on the Cher; the college expert harsh with me for failing to get the pole up in three; 4, tea with large and argumentative circle. 6.30, Canoe and dinner on the river. Early return to attend Bach Choir. 8, Bach Choir (very strenuous). 9.30, recruit exhausted nature with coffee and cakes in friend's room. 10.45, bath; reproved by Don for singing Bach in the bath-room. Midnight, bed (unless anybody happened to drop in).
>
> From time to time, of course, some unfortunate who had "got an Essay" – an affliction always referred to as though it were a kind of recurrent distemper, – was forced to go into retirement and write the thing. The masterpiece was usually concocted at the last possible moment, to be served up to a cynical tutor (who could not escape it) the following morning.[6]

Thirteen years after that piece, she wrote rather more seriously to her son: "At Oxford the only things I think I can say I was taught were the rudiments of old French grammar . . . and a general attitude to knowledge which I can only call a respect for intellectual integrity. And between you and me I doubt whether a liberal education can impart much more. . . ."[7] The most important thing she gained from Oxford was the mental discipline of a mind trained to tackle whatever problem was put before it; and this was something which in these early terms was still ahead of her.

Gaudy Night, the book in which she most completely expressed herself, explores the nature of the scholarly mind – the one essential characteristic of all the dons in Shrewsbury College, the fictional equivalent of Somerville. Muriel St Clare Byrne wished that in addition to this, Dorothy had been able to convey more of the dons' glorious eccentricity. Certainly one would not recognize the dignified Principal in *Gaudy Night* from Dorothy's description of Miss Penrose at a garden party in 1913: "frightfully nervous, in a huge black hat and making the silliest remarks in a very high nervy tone of voice. As for the famous grin, she never took it off, and was talking to her guests as if they were small children at a party. It was such fun to watch."[8]

Whatever their idiosyncrasies the dons were ladies to be respected and reckoned with. Their dedication to their cause was total, and so also, beneath the affectionate mockery, was the respect they inspired in their students, both for themselves and for the subjects they taught. To her work on Mediaeval French, in which she was specializing, Dorothy brought her passion for words, her love of the period and an exceptional breadth of reading; but it was the example and influence of her tutors that led her gradually from casual brilliance to the systematic thoroughness that she acquired as she moved towards her finals.

On one subject the dons were not so reliable – love. An article which Dorothy wrote in 1919, "Eros in Academe", complains with some bitterness of the total incompetence of the teaching staff to deal with a subject of such importance to the young ladies: "It cannot be accident that the conversation of all my friends revolves so unerringly about one only subject."[9]

Though this was written after she left the University, and though the post-war period was certainly more obsessed with sex than the years when Dorothy was a student, yet it is of student years that she is writing; and it would be a great mistake to suppose that during those years Dorothy was simply an academic frump, indifferent to young men. On the contrary she took a good deal of interest in clothes; and when she was invited to speak in a debate against Balliol College, she took as much care over the way she looked as over the way she spoke. "It is every woman's duty", she wrote to her parents, "to look as nice as she can, especially when brought under the eyes of undergraduates!"[10]

The photograph we have of her as a student shows that when she did take care she could be far from unattractive. But she had few illusions about her looks. In her last term at school she had written home: "How *very* kind of *dear* Mrs Wilde to say that I was good looking! ! ! ! She is completely mistaken – but that's quite beside the point. It's only that when I am properly dressed I give a sort of spurious impression of good looks – it's more a kind of smartness than anything else."[11]

She was tall and thin, with the long neck that gave her the nickname of "Swanny", and a face that required careful assessment. As Katherine Lammas she had made a thorough inventory of her appearance before going to school:

> She examined herself in a glass. A commanding height (when she remembered not to stoop). Blue eyes – but they might be bigger. A snub nose – dear, dear! A high forehead – very unfashionable. Dark hair, rather thin and soft. A long upper lip – and she had read somewhere that this was reckoned a defect. A wide but rather well-shaped mouth, with dimples at the corner. A good skin – when it wasn't afflicted with spots. And of course, pretty hands. Not a very good list of charms, but you never knew. This face must surely have character. It could not help being an interesting face – could it? – when it belonged to such an interesting person.[12]

Dorothy's taste in clothes was for the bold and dramatic rather than the delicate; the striking and statuesque rather than the subtle. She liked simple, vivid colours, long earrings, and dresses that showed off her arms. After the Balliol debate, for which she wore a black evening frock sent from home, Charis Barnett took the trouble to tell her she looked "ripping".

The motion debated at Balliol was "That the educated classes of the present day show a sad lack of enthusiasm". Her friends all remember that her speech was outstanding, and a great credit to Somerville. Her own comment in a letter home was that the debate was "very deadly. . . . But my speech went off all right, and the dress was a great success."[13] A month or two later her Aunt Maud took her to a dress shop (presumably for her birthday) with the intention of spending five and a half guineas on new clothes. The evening cloak which Dorothy chose was "really rather a magnificent affair . . . in red brocaded velvet, lined with silk in the same shade".[14] And about the same time "I made myself a most ravishing little cap to wear in New Coll. Chapel . . . executed in black ribbon and net".[15] She was also planning to take dancing lessons, little knowing that war was only a few months ahead and that all the young men she might have danced with would swiftly be sucked away into the mud of Flanders.

There was a particular reason why she wanted that evening cloak and that ravishing little cap: the Oxford Bach Choir (of which Dorothy was a member) was due to sing that summer in the Bach Festival under the baton of Sir Hugh Percy Allen, the New College organist.

One of the reasons for the popularity of the Oxford Bach Choir among the students of Somerville and Lady Margaret Hall was that it was a link with the University proper – of which, of course, they were still not fully members. For a choir, women were actually needed, not merely suffered as they were in other University activities such as debates. With her strong contralto and the knowledge of music that her father had instilled in her, Dorothy had no difficulty in getting a place.

Rehearsals were held in the stuffy, gas-lit Sheldonian and here Dorothy was first exposed to the personality of Hugh Percy Allen. Everything about him – his panache, his craftsmanship, his turn of phrase – was perfectly calculated to go straight to Dorothy's heart. When he died in 1946 Dorothy wrote to Cyril Bailey, who was gathering recollections about him for a memoir:

> In my Oxford days I rejoiced in H.P.'s eccentricities, exulted when he threw his baton at the tenors and performed his well-known strip tease act, beginning with his hat and scarf and ending, with miraculous timing, just at the end of the movement, when there seemed nothing but his trousers that he could take off.[16]

Dorothy was by no means the only young lady to develop a "crush" on Hugh Percy Allen. But in her usual fashion she dramatized it and made much of it: no one was allowed to remain unaware of Dorothy's enthusiasms. To say that her enthusiasm was not genuine, or serious, would not be true, but as with her Athos impersonation and her obligatory "pash" on Miss White, half the fun was in going through the motions, exploiting them for all they were worth.

Her admiration for "H.P." was not unqualified. Of his appearance on the podium she wrote: "He really does look terrible in a frock coat, with his hair plastered down – like a gentlemanly murderer with his portrait in the *Daily Mirror*. Also he had on a loathsome pale green waist-coat. Why do men make themselves so hideous in public?"[17] But she adored his comments during rehearsal: the entrance of the male voices at the beginning of the Verdi Requiem reminded him of old-fashioned black boot-lace liquorice; and of a held note by the sopranos which should have sounded like a single star on a clear night – "you make it sound like a damp firework".[18]

The festival for which the choir was preparing was an ambitious affair, lasting a week and featuring cantatas, motets, orchestral works, and finally a performance of the B Minor Mass. At the performance of one of the motets the choir disgraced itself by getting mass stage fright and totally failing to come in on a fortissimo entrance just off the beat. After a silence that lasted only an instant but seemed to Dorothy to go on for ever, everybody came in at once with any note that they could hit upon, and somehow the performance continued. Never, she said, had she suffered so much in one short moment.

But the Mass made up for it:

Nothing went wrong with it from beginning to end. It was more exciting than you can possibly imagine. I had never seen anything so hot, so tired, so excited, so breathless, or at the end so beaming as Dr Allen . . . I don't know what the audience was doing at the end but I know that the Choir went simply mad . . . I love being enthusiastic in a whole mass of people, don't you? . . . I will now stop Allenising, if possible.[19]

The academic year was ending, and there were garden parties, river parties, and interesting guest lecturers to listen to. One of these was G. K. Chesterton, whom Dorothy was agreeably surprised to find "much sounder than I had expected, and less fireworky";[20] and she was relieved that "his speaking had none of that aggressive and dogmatic quality which his writings are apt to assume when read aloud" – an interesting comment from one whose writings were, in their turn, to be noted for their aggressiveness and dogmatism. Bernard Shaw, on the other hand, she found disappointing – his humour cheap and his serious passages not particularly original.

But Hugh Percy Allen continued to occupy her thoughts. She bought a hatpin from a friend, made of an African teasel, with two "eyes" stuck in it to look like a bird, with a scarlet berry in its mouth. She called it Hugh Percy "because there is a kind of eager fanaticism in its eye, and because it appears to be devouring a human heart".[21] And for the Grand River Picnic organized by the M.A.S., she contributed "An Ode to Dr Allen", which, unhappily, does not survive.

1914 was not the wisest year in which to take a summer holiday in France. There had been threats and rumours of war for some time, and Dorothy had been aware of them. Nevertheless, plans had been made to go with two friends to Tours for the whole of August and half of September. And they went.

The danger was apparent immediately they reached France. Tours itself, she wrote, was in a state of siege. No one and nothing was travelling on the roads except military transport, and the trains from Paris were crowded with people escaping to the countryside. Dorothy appears to have been entirely unafraid, simply excited. "This thing is like a novel by H. G. Wells. The whole world is going to war. This has happened in two days."[22] She was full of admiration for the patriotism of the French, for the matter-of-fact way in which they accepted the threat and went about putting into effect a total mobilization. She notes a complete reversal of national stereotypes: "there seems to be more panic and excitement in England than here",[23] and she expresses doubts about all the rumours she hears of German wickedness and perfidy. She revels in the sense of drama, in being involved in something real and momentous, and in the opportunity it gives her for somewhat sententious comment.

Exactly how and when she got back to England is not on record, but it must have been hazardous and uncomfortable. All trains were commandeered until the middle of August, so presumably she and her friends had to stay until then, cut off from hope of return. Fortunately, her French was flawless, and, so her landlady in Tours told her, completely without English accent. At least she had not the normal foreigner's difficulty in such situations of making herself understood, and she arrived in good shape and with plenty of good tales to tell.

Oxford, when she returned, was already a very different city from the one she had left. Half the undergraduates had already volunteered for service, and in their place were large numbers of Belgian refugees, for some of whom Dorothy helped to find lodgings.

One feature that had not changed was Hugh Percy Allen, and Dorothy set herself to catch his eye. This she achieved by answering him back and refusing to be frightened of him; and in November he picked her out for the contralto part in a demonstration at one of his lectures. By the following term she was being invited into his organ loft. He was "a pet", and "such a big spoilt baby".[24] And though she goes often to New College chapel to pray that Oxford may be spared, "there is no praying done in the organ loft".[25]

At the end of January there was a party where everybody was supposed to go as shipwrecked mariners, but she made a sensation by going as Dr Allen, in borrowed clothes.[26] Dorothy's obsession was becoming the talk of Somerville.

Her letters to her parents are remarkably open about the Doctor, but it is not made entirely clear what did occur in the organ loft. "He seems inclined to add me to a long procession of little tame cats that have adorned his organ loft in succession. This is a nuisance because I do not want to be anybody's tame cat."[27] Whatever the frustrations, there were some bonuses to be had from the relationship; he agreed to come and lecture to the Literary and Philosophical Society, of which Dorothy was now secretary. To have hooked so big a fish was apparently "an awful achievement".[28]

In the spring vacation the College was taken over as a military hospital and the students were moved into Oriel College, now half empty. Finals were looming and, beyond them, the question of what to do next. Dorothy had considered going on to take a B.Litt., but that would mean fees and other expenses for her parents, so that was out. There were no jobs to be had in Oxford, and in any case the proper thing seemed to be to look for some post in France where she could help the war effort. Her friend Charis Barnett had already had a brother killed in the war, and, unable to face Oxford without him, had gone to France as a nurse.

The openings seemed to be either in nursing or relief work, and of the two Dorothy decided that she would prefer nursing: "Of course in one way I should hate nursing, hard labour and horrors, but I should be frightfully glad to have done it, and to have done something *real* for the first time in my life. And it's better than peasants and babies and local administration and inspecting drains, which is what one does in the other job."[29]

Her enthusiasm to do something real was possibly less wholehearted than she made out, for she wrote a little later to say that her age was against her for nursing. Charis Barnett, at the same age, had heard that the Quakers were asking for volunteers and had gone with them more or less straight to France; Had Dorothy's heart been in it, no doubt she could have done the same. Instead, she contented herself with complaining that the Red Cross was badly organized, and went to see the local hospital matron. "On the other hand," she wrote, "I believe many boys' schools are in great need of women teachers, in place of men who have gone to the war. Of course, if I thought I should be more use in that line than nursing I should not mind trying to teach for a year, say. But here again there is no organization, and one has to hear about things privately. . . ."[30]

Dorothy was finding it difficult to concentrate on academic work and, despite consistently good reports, had little confidence that she was going to do well in Schools – the final exams. "The war does make a great difference," she wrote, "it's no good saying it doesn't."[31] Her tutor, Miss Pope, comforted her by telling her that what one really came to Oxford to learn was how to work – an opinion that Dorothy herself was to report to her son many years later.

Dorothy *had* learned how to work: since the autumn of 1913 her reports had laid emphasis on the methodical way in which she tackled her work. The inclination to showiness rather than solidarity which her

tutors had noted in her first year (and which she had acknowledged in
Cat o' Mary) had been mastered, and at the end of the Michaelmas Term,
1913, Miss Pope had written:

> This term has shown quite unusual quality. She combines with a
> strong literary appreciation and considerable insight, a real, and
> rather rare, liking for thoroughness. She has tackled the linguistic side
> of her work with real competence, shirks no difficulties, and so laid
> the foundations of a scholarly knowledge of her subject. I emphasize
> this because, though I was expecting essay work of quality from her, I
> had been afraid that she might seek to avoid the less attractive
> philological work.[32]

Other dons noted the continuing streak of coarseness in her work: "At
her worst she runs off into rhetoric or journalistic slang or a pulpit
manner and spoils her style"[33] . . . "She is still lacking somewhat in self
restraint"[34] – thus criticizing the very traits that later enabled Dorothy to
earn her living in the big wide world, something she was to acknowledge
and defend twelve years later in a speech on "The Importance of Being
Vulgar".

Apart from these caveats, the reports in general indicated that
Dorothy was satisfactorily maintaining the standards of the college.
They were not ecstatic; a good steady Beta-plus is the average level –
"not yet quite first class".[35] But they were solid and consistent, and
represented a foundation that neither the nervous tension of the war nor
the excitement of Dr Allen's company was able to shake.

Not being sure of this herself, however, Dorothy tried to forewarn her
parents against disappointment: "even if I came out with a fourth, I
have learnt an enormous amount about people and things at Oxford – a
lot which I should have left unlearned if I had done nothing but
work".[36]

No doubt generations of students have sought to avert parental wrath
with some such consideration, but it is doubtful whether Mr and Mrs
Sayers would really have felt that Dorothy's experiences in the organ loft
were what she went to Oxford for. There were other places where she
might have learned that "it is much better fun to have all one's flirtations
with 'ineligibles'. Then there can be no possible disappointment on
either side."[37]

When she was still at school she decided that it was lucky she had not
been born beautiful – "I should have been an awful flirt".[38] And with Dr
Allen she was certainly getting some practice: "I can manage him pretty
well now, by the way. I can amuse him with fair ease and feel pretty

certain of being able to keep him where I want him."[39] When she felt that she was being taken for granted, she tested out her power by refusing one of his invitations into the organ loft; and discovered to her surprise and delight that this did not immediately stifle his interest. Her technique developed from the impertinent approach to the "womanly and sympathetic".[40] And within a very short time she had reached the patronizing stage:

> I should rather like to make a good job of H.P. while I am about it – finish him off neatly, and not hurry or spoil him with careless workmanship, so to speak. He is worth taking trouble for, both in himself and on the low ground that he is a useful person to know. (There is a mercenary strain in me somewhere. Where does it come from?)[41]

More important for our purposes, however, is a snatch of dialogue with Dr Allen which she reports with interest and pride. She had consulted him about the prospect of going to France as a nurse and he had given it as his opinion that she might be very suitable "because I don't get excited. So I said, 'Oh, but I do though!' He said, 'Well – if you do, you can control yourself' . . . As a testimony to character I value it highly, because it shows, doesn't it, that at least I have never made a fool of myself before him."[42]

Here is the paradox inherent in Dorothy's character – on one side, the flamboyance, the willingness to be mocked for her enthusiasms, and the total disregard of caution in laying bare at least some levels of her soul; on the other a determination never *really* to make a fool of herself in the eyes of anyone who mattered to her. Some instinct told her how far she could go in flaunting the very thing that she wanted to hide. Wearing the mask of the infatuated lover, she could be sure that no one could tell what was the real expression behind it. This was Dorothy's style, and to have it recognized by anyone so sensitive, so distinguished as her friend Hugh Percy Allen was a compliment indeed.

A few years later, when the friendship was renewed, but without that excitement that the first discovery of another person always brings with it, she wrote: "A strange man, symbolic of something enormous. The statue of a god, flawed in the smelting, poor dear."[43] A sad and rather chilly judgement on the man who had meant so much to her, who indeed had symbolized for her the splendour of sound, the glory of the precision of counterpoint; and certainly the man for whom, if for anyone, she had made that ravishing little cap, executed in black ribbon and net and designed to be worn in New College chapel.

CHAPTER SIX

DESPITE HER FEARS, Dorothy did get a first-class degree. That is to say, she passed examinations that would have given her a first-class degree if Oxford had been giving degrees to women at that time. It was, after all, no less than the truth that she wrote on her Curriculum Vitae ten years later when she described herself as "one of the most brilliant scholars of her year".

In fact she could have got her degree immediately, on her Oxford results, by going to Trinity College, Dublin; but, like most of her contemporaries, she decided to wait. It was quite clear from the mood of the University that the granting of degrees to women was only a matter of time, and nobody expected it to happen in the middle of a war.

In the space between the end of the exam and the end of term, Dorothy had a final tribute to pay to Hugh Percy Allen. It was a tradition that the students who had reached the end of their studies should present a Going-Down Play, and Dorothy and her friends were prominent in this year's offering. It was called *Pied Pipings or The Innocents Abroad*, and Dorothy was part author, musical director, and performer: she played the part of Dr H. P. Rallentando, the Pied Piper himself. The producer was Dorothy Rowe, who later built the Palace Court Theatre in Bournemouth and for fifty years ran it as one of Britain's most successful and distinguished amateur theatres.

Pied Pipings was presented in a complicated way at various entrances to the quadrangle, and the audiences had to move their seats between Act I ("Before Oriel College") and Act II ("The Never-Never Land"); it was a novel and ingenious notion – to save changing your settings by moving your audience – and apparently it worked "like a dream".

The story is of twenty sad students who can never catch up with all the new facts constantly being uncovered about famous people by assiduous researchers ("It has just been proved that the *Chanson de Roland* is of Icelandic origin" . . . "Mr Nichol Smith has just found a new letter from Pope to his washerwoman"); and who are transported by the Pied Piper to the Never-Never Land where they finally meet the famous face to face.

One of the three songs attributed to Dorothy in the credits is "The Song of the Bicycle Secretary", to the tune of "I've got him on the list" from Gilbert and Sullivan's *The Mikado*. The post of Bicycle Secretary

was one which Dorothy had filled herself at Somerville, and the first two
stanzas predictably castigate the evil-doings of bicycle owners:

It's well to be methodical where culprits are concerned,
  So I've made a little list, I've made a little list
Of members of this commonwealth who ought to be interned,
  And who never would be missed, who never would be missed.
The brutes who borrow bicycles without the owners' leave,
Who get their own in pound and come and ask for a reprieve.
Who take their breakfast on the Cher at half past six a.m.
And say they thought the general rule did not apply to them,
The people with excuses that you really can't resist,
I'm sure they won't be missed, I'm sure they won't be missed –

Chorus She's got 'em on the list, etc. . . . .

The third stanza, however, turns to rather more general criticism, some
of which seems aimed pretty accurately at Dorothy herself:

But these are not the only pests who poison College life,
  And I've made a little list, I've made a little list
Of those who wake the midnight air with dialectic strife
  And who never would be missed, who never would be missed.
The nymphs who stroll at breakfast time in nightgowns made of silk,
The people who remove your books, your matches and your milk,
The blighters who drop catalogues and whisper in the Bod.,
Or whistle Bach and Verdi as they walk across the Quad,
The superficial sceptic and the keen philanthropist,
They'll none of them be missed, they'll none of them be missed.

Term came at last to an end, and with it Dorothy's days of joy at Oxford;
but even then she managed to postpone the final breach by persuading
her parents to invite several members of the M.A.S. to come and stay at
Bluntisham. Muriel Jaeger, Dorothy Rowe and Catherine (otherwise
known as "Tony") Godfrey had a memorable weekend there in August
and found Mrs Sayers the ideal hostess, allowing them to sleep after
lunch sprawled on the drawing-room floor, and awake to a cream tea.
    They left, and Dorothy was alone with her parents, aunts, servants –
back in the world of her childhood. She seems to have abandoned her
attempts – never very vigorous – to find a nursing job, and was now concentrating on her second alternative, teaching. The life of a schoolmarm
was a little more suited to Dorothy's temperament than that of a nurse –

she did at least enjoy laying down the law – but she found small inspiration in either.

In truth, she did not know what she wanted: the war blighted every possibility. But the country needed women to fill the jobs of men who were fighting, and Dorothy had a powerful patriotic streak. Besides, the alternative to earning a living was staying at home, and that appealed least of all.

Life at home was hardly cheerful. Visitors included an uncle and a cousin, both recently returned from the front: "Both have nervous breakdowns – one has neuritis, the other has damaged his eyes gazing at aeroplanes. Jolly business, war! Both seem uncommonly gloomy over the prospects, but I don't know how far they can really judge."[1] Mrs Sayers' nervous constitution was not standing up well to the anxieties of the war, and she occasionally suffered acute nervous attacks that left her unable to speak or move – very frightening for all concerned.

Homesickness for Oxford was bad enough without all this, and Dorothy was deeply envious of Muriel Jaeger, who was going back for another year: "I wish I could be there, to have your company on my bed when you were in the dumps, and bring you a hot water bottle occasionally."[2]

In this mood she put together a collection of poems, some already written at Somerville, some new. Technically these are very impressive – varied, elaborate, ingenious and sometimes brilliant. In the set of poems entitled "The Last Castle", there is a series of nine songs, each attributed to a different stylistic school – "Pastoral School", "School of Sentiment", "School of Strong Simplicity" and so forth. The rhyme schemes fall naturally and seem effortless. The language is rich, mellow and romantic, like an augmented string orchestra. Nearly all the poems look to the past for their subject matter – to the world of Arthur and the Round Table, of Helen of Troy or of mediaeval theology; all share a tone of voice that harks back to the eighteenth century, but tinged with Victorian sentimentality in place of Augustan incisiveness; and all suffer from the sense that the creative impulse stems not from real emotional experience but from the ecstasy of being poetical:

> And those tall pillars, dim as amethyst,
>   Soaring like smoke incredibly aloof,
> Where, lift on high above the censer-mist,
>   Pale capitals glimmered in the golden roof –
> O marvellously, magically went
> Our music up among them, coldly kissed
>   From pipe and reed, or plucked in this consent
> By white, frail fingers of the lutenist.[3]

Dorothy had a true feeling for the sounds and rhythm of words, and their evocative power; but to modern ears, accustomed to a more astringent style, her over-ripe language smacks of self-indulgence, and a little goes a long way. She gives herself away by that self-consciously archaic "lift" instead of "lifted" in the third line, or by such absurdities as the phrase "girded queenliwise" in the song called "Wartime". We are still not far from poems of farewell to the Musketeers and the exquisite enjoyment of melancholy of which Dorothy was all too aware.

Her valediction to Oxford, however, which she put at the end of the book in which these poems were collected, is simple and effective. It is called "Last Morning in Oxford", and she prefaces it with a quotation from Hilaire Belloc: "The great poets . . . are not at the pains of devising careful endings. Thus, Homer ends with lines that might as well be in the middle of a passage." Taking her cue from this, Dorothy writes:

> I do not think that very much was said
> Of solemn requiem for the good years dead.

> Like Homer, with no thunderous rhapsody,
> I close the volume of my Odyssey.

> The thing that I remember most of all
> Is the white hemlock by the garden wall.

It was not until December that Dorothy had a serious reply to her enquiries about a teaching job. There was a vacancy for a teacher of Modern Languages at Hull High School for Girls, and she went to London for an interview with Miss Elliot, the headmistress. Everything seemed propitious, but the confirmation was a long time coming through. The days dragged on.

At the last moment the post was confirmed, and by the new year she was ensconced in lodgings at No. 86 Westbourne Avenue, Hull.

Like most people from the south of England, Dorothy had a vague notion that the north was a wilderness of poverty, barbarism and gloom – a notion which northerners themselves have been rather inclined to foster. So Dorothy was surprised to find, besides the anticipated dirt and smuts, plenty of cinemas, "at least one decent café and quite good shops".[4] And, better still, a great deal of laughter and good fellowship among the teachers.

The standard of teaching, however, was far lower than she had expected. Nothing in her experience had prepared her for the shock of facing a class full of girls whose sole idea of learning was repeating lessons by rote, without the least idea of the significance of what they

learnt or the least interest in finding out. Dorothy's vigorous views on
the uselessness of schools were now convincingly confirmed.

Hull was a way of earning a living – no more than that. Her heart was
still in Oxford. She wrote a poem "To Members of the Bach Choir on
Active Service":

> . . . Stuck waist deep in a slimy trench
> Your nostrils filled with the battle stench
> The reek of powder and smoke of shell,
> And poison fumes blowing straight from hell –
> Do your senses ache for another smell?
>
> For the smell of fossils and sticks and stones,
> Camphor and mummies and old dry bones,
> Of strenuous singers, and gas and heat –
> While you strove for a tone that was pure and sweet
> In air you could cut with a baton's beat? . . .

There were seven verses all told, and it was published in February in the
Oxford Magazine. Dorothy was delighted to hear from Muriel Jaeger that
Hugh Percy had laid down his baton in the middle of rehearsal and in
tones of great emotion adjured the choir to read it.

But the war was no longer only "over there", in the front line. Now it
came directly overhead. For eight hundred years no enemy from the
Continent had crossed the English Channel, and apart from the power
struggles within the British Isles the civilians of England had grown accustomed to the idea that war was something that happened a long way
away. Now, at the dead of night, the great shapes of Zeppelins floated
unopposed over the English countryside and dropped their bombs on
selected cities – a principal target being the port of Hull. Dorothy spent
miserable, cold, cramped and frightened nights in cellars, and her hair
began to fall out again. Her letters displayed an unchanged jauntiness –
danger brought out the Musketeer in her – but she did learn something
that Dumas never taught her about the effect of fear: "Believe me, it is
brutal, bestial and utterly degrading. I should say it was the one experience that is good for neither man nor beast."[5]

On the credit side, she heard in March that her selection of poems had
been accepted by Blackwell's for publication in their "Series of Young
Poets Unknown to Fame", called *Adventurers All*. She decided to call the
volume *Op I*. Had she gone on to give opus numbers to everything she
published thereafter, they would have added up to a goodly number.

Basil Blackwell, who was twenty-seven at the time and in the process of taking over the firm from his father, was publishing these young poets in the hope that Blackwell's would catch the new generation early. He was eminently successful at first; among those he caught were Aldous Huxley and all the Sitwells. What he omitted from his calculations was the lure of the big city. One by one all his young protégés were wooed away from him by London publishers with more prestige and more money. Acting as talent scout for other firms had never been part of the plan, and Blackwell's enthusiasm eventually waned; but in 1916 the project was still full of early hope.

Dorothy went on writing. The *Oxford Magazine* accepted several poems; and a journey to Oxford in June was financed by a three-guinea prize she won in a poetry competition in the *Saturday Westminster Review*. Dorothy's facility for pastiche was given full scope in her entry – fragments of an alleged unpublished poem by Robert Browning on the subject of Don Quixote, submitted under the pseudonym of H. P. Rallentando – the name under which she had guyed Hugh Percy Allen in the Going-Down Play.

Meanwhile she continued to practise the art of flirtation on the local curate, commenting that, though she did not find him exceptionally attractive, there was no one else around and he "must do for practice". One evening she would be "sprightly and rather coming on", the next "quiet, soberly but richly dressed (!) and rather religious"; on the principle that "variety is the spice of wife".[6] The effect on the unfortunate Mr Scott is, regrettably, not recorded.

These amusements helped to pass the time. But Hull gave Dorothy only minimal scope for her energies, and when in the summer she gravitated again to Oxford and had dinner at the Cadena Café with several old friends, the explosion of pent-up high spirits was such that observers supposed they were drunk.

Towards the end of 1916, two important events occurred. *Op I* appeared in print; and Dorothy's father went to see Basil Blackwell, to put forward a suggestion that his daughter should work for the firm. Whether or not Dorothy prompted this move we have no means of knowing, but it seems extremely likely. At all events, in January she received a letter from Blackwell suggesting an interview and discussing possible terms.

The proposed financial arrangement was that one hundred pounds should be paid to Blackwell's, which would be returned to Dorothy at two pounds a week for her living expenses while she was learning the job. To live on two pounds a week in London she thought would be impossible; in Oxford, easy.

Fortunately Mr Sayers was at the same time negotiating a move from

Bluntisham to Christchurch – an even smaller and more remote parish, deep in the Cambridgeshire Fens, but offering a small financial advantage which enabled him to put down the vital hundred pounds to launch Dorothy on a career in publishing.

By the end of January both moves were settled. Dorothy's job was "the learning of the whole business, from discount to the three-colour process";[7] and in the event of Basil Blackwell being called up (which was extremely unlikely, since he was Grade C3 in health and in addition was in a reserved occupation) she was to be ready to take charge of the firm! She immediately set about pestering the local printer in Hull to teach her the tricks of the trade – and so whiled away her last term of teaching.

The new arrangement was supposed to take effect from May 1, but we already find her on April 28 writing from Oxford about the joys of the new job as compared with the old. It was more relaxed, it was healthier, it was more interesting, and so far she could find no faults in her employer. In fact she found it positively sinful to be enjoying herself so much. With the war approaching its fourth year she might well have felt some pangs of conscience. Miss Penrose, whom she met in the street, did not hide the fact that she wished Dorothy had taken a job "of national importance".

Dorothy's room was at 17 Long Wall Street and cost her twelve shillings and sixpence a week – a sizeable proportion of the weekly two pounds. Not much was left for food and clothing. But what did that matter, when there was Oxford, there was the river, there were Hugh Percy Allen, Jim Jaeger, still completing her extra year, and Muriel St Clare Byrne, who had come up later than the rest of the M.A.S. and was about to take her finals?

To add to these joys Dorothy now received her first proposal. This seems to have been due less to the practice she had put in on the unfortunate curate in Hull than to the success of the poems in *Op I*, which inspired the admiration of the vice-principal of St Edmund Hall.

This gentleman, Leonard Hodgson, was a friend of Basil Blackwell and he had encountered Dorothy in the shop. A little later, when she had boldly picked up a couple of Australian airmen and invited them for an afternoon on the river, she remembered the vice-principal and asked him to make a fourth for the party. There were a few more meetings, and then, one evening when she was at Basil Blackwell's house, he suddenly arrived unannounced and, as soon as she was alone with him, made his avowal and his proposal.

Dorothy was totally unprepared, and all she could find to say was "Oh Lord!" – though she recovered herself sufficiently to remember the proper formula for such an occasion, explaining to him that she regarded him as a good friend and had never thought of him "in that way"; adding at the last moment the obligatory phrases about being deeply flattered and honoured. At this point, Basil Blackwell came into the room, and normality was restored.

Her suitor, however, would not take no for an answer. He continued to follow her and lay his life at her feet whenever the occasion presented itself. Had he known Dorothy better he would have realized that this was the worst possible approach. She wrote to her parents: "To have somebody devoted to me arouses all my worst feelings. I *loathe* being deferred to. I ABOMINATE being waited on. It <u>INFURIATES</u> me to feel that my words are numbered and my actions watched. I want somebody to fight with!"[8]

The unhappy man even joined the Bach Choir, presumably with the intention of showing her that he shared her interests. This gave her an opportunity of comparing him directly with Hugh Percy Allen, and was possibly his worst mistake. He was not even a good singer.

Despite her irritation, the episode must have done a great deal for Dorothy's morale; which was still further raised in July in even more unexpected circumstances. A sudden attack of appendicitis took her to Aclands Nursing Home, where the offending organ was removed by a surgeon named Whitelock. As soon as she began to recover Mr Whitelock grew flirtatious – and his technique, unlike that of her former swain, suited her down to the ground:

> I love having someone to fool with – meeting on entirely equal terms and seeing who can joke the other down. The moment either person begins to be even a trifle in earnest, the whole thing is spoilt. You remember Alice (in *Through the Looking Glass*). Her favourite game was "Nurse, let's pretend". The only game worth playing! I said all this to Basil Blackwell once . . . and he said, "But lovemaking isn't a game you know". And all I could say was "It is, to me".[9]

There were lingering doubts about her first conquest. Why should the touch of her unwelcome suitor have caused nausea: "Have I a physical horror of marriage, or just an aesthetic horror of him? I should so much like to know."[10] And she decided that the only way to find out was to embark upon a course of study based upon practical experience.

This of course was not so easy. The number of eligible young men was extremely limited. Conscription had been introduced the previous summer, and Oxford was a ghost town, haunted not only by the memories of the past but by fears of the future, for the war was going extremely badly. We are accustomed to remember the horrors of the trenches, but we tend to forget the very real fear of those at home that a German victory was imminent. The mood of Britain was that of a besieged city, keenly aware of the brevity of life. There was a determination to seek experience while the going was good, and Dorothy was certainly not going to miss it.

She was obviously not wholly unattractive. Those who knew her then are agreed that her charm was social rather than sexual – a necessary distinction in Dorothy's case. Her first suitor was doubtless fascinated by the depths of feeling and visions of romance that he found in her poetry, and looked to find them in her:

> Ah Helen! Helen! Helen! Thy white breast
> And gold hair heaped in shining bands, –
> Would I might lay me quietly to rest
> In thy enfolding hands,
>
> Lie still, and watch thine eyes grow dark with love,
> And feel thy kiss upon my brow,
> And think no more, nor ever stir nor move,
> Or count the time, as now.

How was the poor man to know that she was not writing about experience, but about a rich and voluptuous "let's pretend"?

Dorothy's second swain was attracted by her wit, her sauciness and style, the sheer fun of being with her. Both men were attracted by something in her which was not specifically sexual, but which, found in a woman, flowed over into sexual attraction and became indistinguishable from it.

She was still writing, of course. Nothing ever stopped her doing that. Several more poems appeared in the *Oxford Magazine*; and she was busy translating the *Tristan* of Thomas. Thomas was a poet who wrote in France in the twelfth century, and scattered fragments of his *Tristan* are all that remain of his output. One of the things that attracted Dorothy to him was the subtlety of his insight, given the period in which he lived, into the psychology of lost love. Technically the challenge of translating his octosyllabic couplets was irresistible. Translation always fascinated her; it offered the tantalizing prospect of a problem with a hundred different solutions, none of which could ever be wholly successful. Here in the *Tristan* was a fore-runner of the vast enterprise which ended Dorothy's working life – the translation of Dante's *Divine Comedy*.

Another rehearsal – an early draft, as it were, for a later work – is worth noticing. Muriel St Clare Byrne decided to produce a little magazine devoted to the writings of the M.A.S., which she called Blue Moon (a prophetic title, for there was only one issue); and Dorothy contributed a short story called "Who Calls the Tune?"

A millionaire has died, and the priest who has confessed him keeps vigil beside the body at night and falls asleep. In his dream, a seraph and a representative of the devil tot up the account of the millionaire's life and decide how many years' purgatory he is due. Some of the detail is delightful:

"Charities, various", said the angel, "valued at 100,000 years."

"One hundred thousand," said Mr Dowl, glancing over the papers, "yes, they seem generous and sensible. I think they will just about balance our account for ruined homes. It is a rather heavy one, Mr Seraphim, and has been running a long time."

"Ruined Homes?" exclaimed the angel, "my client's family life has always been . . ."

"Oh, not that kind," said Mr Dowl, "men with wives and children turned off the works under circumstances of peculiar uncharitableness. Here is the account."

"Yes, I see. Well, I have Kindness to Animals; subscriptions to anti-vivisection societies, two homes for lost pets, good treatment in my client's own stable and kennels, humanity while hunting and shooting etc., vegetable wool underclothing, etc., etc. Valued at 50,000 years."

"That's valuable stock nowadays," said the devil, making a note of it.

"Patriotism; financing a Liberal member; dinners, election expenses. £5,000 to various war-funds. Speeches to schoolboys on Empire Day. Valued at 50,000 years."

"Most of that's fancy stuff," said the devil, "we don't care about it at the office. I can't allow you more than 35,000 on it."

"Education: Women's college, and an undenominational school for the sons of publicans in Southwark: 50,000 years."

"All right," said the devil, "though, mind you, I think you over-value it. But it's the fashion, and it will pay us to take it."

"Encouragement of Art," pursued the angel, "establishment of a—"

"Nothing doing," interrupted the other, "no connection whatever with business. Can't take it. Nor Science."

The upshot is that the devil is entitled to take over the soul, mainly on account of an extremely high bill for "best double-distilled spirit of Pride." But the soul turns out to be a puny little thing, who pleads that it is not answerable, being only an infant. Body and mind have never let the soul grow up: "I was always kept in the nursery. In fact in the end I think they didn't remember I was there at all; they never gave me anything to eat; that's why I couldn't grow up, you know." The soul is not worth having, and the devil departs, thwarted – as he was to be thwarted by a similar form of divine legalistic trickery at the end of Dorothy's Faustus play, *The Devil To Pay*, written many years later.

The poetry Dorothy had contributed to the *Oxford Magazine* dealt mostly with war and death – subjects that could be expected to be much in the public mind. But she had also been preparing a new book of poems, all of them religious in background.

In this volume, *Catholic Tales and Christian Songs*, the plummy, romantic language is still there; but the poems show an increased mastery of metre and rhyme, a wide range of background, and a scholarly imagination that is able to portray Christ and Christianity in an astonishing variety of perspectives. She ranges from the satirical verse drama of "The Mocking of Christ" to the lyrical "Christus Dionysus", where Jesus is seen as the lord of laughter:

> Young Dionysus
>   Crowned with the thorn and vine;
> His feet and hands are red with blood,
>   His mouth is red with wine.

And from the uncharacteristically sentimental, "Christ the Companion":

> When my brain is too stiff for prayer, and too indolent for theory,
> Will you come and play with me, big Brother Christ?

to the final poem, "The House of the Soul, Lay", which is not only a technical tour-de-force but also, here and there, a genuine personal statement of originality and power.

As in *Op I*, the technical brilliance on the surface of these poems is almost too showy, the subject matter so swamped by verbal sauce that one is tempted again to suspect them of insincerity – of using the Christian faith as a series of pegs on which to hang a display of clever ideas. So many views of Christ are on show, but which of them is *hers* – if any? She seems to be playing with images borrowed from the past rather than searching her own heart for the words to express her own faith and feeling.

Doubts about the sincerity of her poems had troubled Dorothy since her school days. An English teacher there, to whom she had shown some of her work, had said something that made her realize how carefully she eliminated deep emotion from her poetry.

The passage in *Cat o' Mary* that describes these doubts is crucial:

> Why had she been so quick to forestall and repudiate any suggestion that her emotions were concerned in her writings? Surely it was deep emotion that gave value to all great literature – or so all the authorities agreed. She had spoken as if her emotions could not be genuine – but surely they were agonizing and genuine enough. Or weren't they? Did her instinctive certainty that they would somehow contaminate the verse mean that there was something wrong about them?

These questions are only a part of the much wider range of uncertainties that beset Dorothy during this period of her life. What *was* sincerity? If it meant being true to oneself, which of the many selves should she be true to? Even more vital – could emotion be trusted? Apparently it could "contaminate" the verse, it threatened to infect rather than illuminate the writing? Self-doubt could hardly go further. In her fear of being unable to distinguish between sentiment and sentimentality, Dorothy could only afford to trust words that were literature pure and simple, with every trace of personal involvement eliminated.

The passage continues:

> Twenty years later, . . . she wrote in a critical essay: "A man's fundamental beliefs are to be found, not in his expressed opinions, for to express an opinion is to admit that a contrary opinion may exist – but in his unexpressed assumptions. A thing really believed has passed beyond possibility of discussion and to say 'I believe' is to say 'I doubt'". When she had written that, she knew suddenly that the old teasing riddle was answered at last.[11]

Here we have a possible answer to the apparent insincerity of *Catholic Tales and Christian Songs*. If contaminating emotion has been eliminated, and if the poems are built only on belief, then it is clear that all kinds of literary games can be played without disturbing the bedrock conviction. To put Dorothy's point rather less extremely, it is only the insecure who have to be earnest about their faith.

At other times and in other places, Dorothy was to admit that religious emotion was not part of her experience. Intellectual conviction was. Basil Blackwell, himself an agnostic if not an atheist, remembers that she crossed herself before meals and had a crucifix on her desk. Doreen Wallace regretted that she was "so bloody religious". And she herself, warning her parents about the possible reactions to the yet un-published *Catholic Tales and Christian Songs*, wrote: "I can assure you that it is *intended*, at any rate, to be an expression of reverent belief; but some people find it hard to allow that faith, if lively, can be reverent."[12] For Dorothy there was no contradiction between this reverence and her note to Muriel Jaeger that the poems were "rather fun".[13]

Dorothy had hoped that G. K. Chesterton would accept the book for the *New Witness*, but this came to nothing and she fell back on Blackwell's. Before the book appeared, however, a scourge hit Europe which was to kill as many people as the War itself.

A measure of Dorothy's toughness – or insensitivity – is the way that she reacted to the Spanish Flu. In October 1918 she wrote:

> I have had to put off my All Hallows' party – that's been my chief grief. But one cannot give hilarious parties when people are dropping dead all round one! Lots and lots of people are dropping dead – they get pneumonia and are never seen alive again. It's like being in London when the plague was on. People are all right one minute and the next they fall down on the street and are carried away.[14]

Despite all of which, it appears from a subsequent letter that she did give the party after all.

Dorothy herself had had the flu early and mildly, which made her immune to the later and more virulent attacks. Naturally this made her somewhat complacent; but there is about her comment an inescapable air of unconcern, almost a sense that this, too, is "let's pretend". To Muriel Jaeger she relates the droll tale of the two Somerville students who were Christian Scientists and refused to have a doctor – "though they sufficiently acknowledged the objectivity of the disease to go to bed".[15] Miss Penrose insisted that if they would not have the doctor they were to be looked after by their mother, who duly arrived and im-mediately went down with the flu herself. But she also would not have the doctor. "Nothing like being prepared to die for one's creed!"[16] And later: "My dentist has been struck down in the midst of killing a nerve of mine. I don't know whether he is dead or alive (the dentist, I mean. The nerve is alive all right!)"[17] Here is the panache of a true Musketeer in the face of death; but this time the death is real. Though Dorothy claimed always to know the difference between fiction and reality, she still seems not quite able to find the right response to real-life situations.

In fact the dentist seems to have survived – unless it was another dentist – for she was once again in a dentist's chair when she heard the news of the armistice.

By this time *Catholic Tales and Christian Songs* had been published, and Dorothy was deep in a plot with Muriel Jaeger to stir up a little controversy about the theology of the poems and so increase their sales. Muriel was now in London working for the Ministry of Food, and was reasonably confident that she would be able to review the book for the *Church Times*. Dorothy immediately wrote with full instructions on how to handle the situation: "Don't slate it, because the C.T. is the organ of the High Church party, and I would as soon have them with me as against me. But having got it nicely reviewed there, you couldn't do better than send a furious letter from 'Pew-holder' or 'Via Media', wondering how they could possibly allow even the name of the vile publication to sully their pages." She adds, dutifully, "however you must, of course, follow your own inclination and conscience in the matter."[18]

This marked the beginning of an extensive hoax which Dorothy gleefully worked out with Muriel for use in the correspondence columns of *New Witness*. She had discovered that a Theodore Maynard was going to review the book unfavourably, on theological grounds, and she therefore suggested that Muriel should reply to the review under an assumed name; and indeed, if she felt so inclined, should reply to her own reply, and then reply to that under a number of other assumed names. Dorothy was ready with all the theological arguments, couched in the appropriate style of ecclesiastical indignation. She saw, she said, "a scrumptious row" impending. "It would be most exciting and make the book go like wildfire."[19]

Muriel joined in with a will, adding refinements of her own. But the most interesting thing about this unashamed attempt to serve God and Mammon at the same time is the discovery that Dorothy was already, at the age of twenty-six, totally informed about the traditional theology of the Roman Catholic Church. She accepted all its tenets save its rejection of the validity of Anglican Orders and its acceptance of the supremacy of the Pope. Though Dorothy never became a Roman Catholic, it is very noticeable in her correspondence that she accorded much more respect to Roman Catholic priests than to the clergy of the Church of England. "What I feel is this," she writes to Muriel at one point in the lengthy correspondence, "there is a real truth about everything, which (I believe) Catholicism has got hold of (as far as it is possible for us to grasp the truth about everything; we really couldn't grasp all of it unless we were omnipresent and eternal. That's how God sees it. Catholicism only gives us the whole truth as far as man is concerned)."[20]

The time of doubt and uncertainty was over. Dorothy had tested out the religion she had been brought up in and, having made a few

adjustments, was now satisfied with it. The letters to Muriel are almost
those of a teacher to a pupil. The shouted arguments have given way to
dogmatic assertion. Dorothy's new confidence could be alarming:
Doreen Wallace, who was a few years her junior, respected Dorothy
greatly for her mind and found her amusing as a companion, but said
she was "too positive for real liking". And her men friends still had to
meet the requirement of being "someone I can fight with". The men
about her at the time were far from measuring up to the required standard. Basil Blackwell was a perfect charmer, and certainly knew what he
was doing; but he was married, and totally devoted to his wife. Hugh
Percy Allen had the expertise she respected and the size of personality
she responded to; but he, apparently, was "flawed in the smelting".
There were those dashing young bloods, the Sitwell brothers, who awed
her with their sophistication and whom she helped to shepherd into
Basil Blackwell's fold. But there was little common ground between
them and Dorothy. They came once with Siegfried Sassoon to a meeting
of the Rhyme Club – a group consisting mostly of Dorothy, Doreen
Wallace and another friend called Eleanor Gietch, who amused
themselves by making up alternate lines of a poem. Sassoon was
suffering from a nervous breakdown, and the Sitwells were bored silly. It
was not their kind of game. For Sassoon, the poetry was "in the pity" –
the exact opposite of Dorothy's view. And the Sitwells were breaking
away into rhythms that reflected the twentieth century, not the Middle
Ages.

However, with the ending of the war, men were at last beginning to
drift back from the forces. Giles Dixey returned. So did Frank Brabant,
another of Dorothy's friends from her college years. And there was a
handsome young man called Eric Whelpton, who had been invalided
out of the army on account of polio.

Every silver lining has a cloud, and from Dorothy's point of view the
return of the undergraduates meant that her landlady, hitherto only too
delighted to have a lodger of some sort, now wanted the room to let to a
young gentleman of the University. Dorothy had to move.

At Christmas she had a rise of five shillings a week – hardly princely,
though it was in fact an increase of twelve and a half per cent. It enabled
her to move to rooms on the first floor of a house in a charming little
close called Bath Place. There was more space here than formerly, and
she set about making her rooms as attractive as possible, with the intention of having a little salon there, to entertain friends and potential
clients of Blackwell's.

The pale and interesting Eric Whelpton lived on the ground floor,
below her. Inevitably he was roped into her circle of friends and, by his

own account, much enjoyed her conversation and her company. He did not find her physically attractive, and in any case had little energy for that kind of thing since he was still suffering from the after-effects of his disease, and was subject to fainting fits and severe nervous attacks. In addition to all this he did have a lady friend elsewhere in the town.

The picture that has been drawn of Dorothy besottedly creeping around Oxford in the footsteps of Whelpton, making his life a misery with unexpected and unwelcome overtures, appears to have no foundation whatever. Even if Dorothy had been madly in love with him, the one thing she prided herself on was never making a fool of herself except in her own particular, calculating way. And Eric Whelpton himself, who was never one to underestimate his effect on young women, would surely have noticed and recorded so obvious an infatuation. In fact he had no idea of her devotion to him – for there was certainly some degree of devotion – until much later. What he does remember from that time was what most people remembered – Dorothy's noisy enthusiasm for Hugh Percy Allen.

Nevertheless, Doreen Wallace, whose memory is vigorous though her judgements are perhaps more enthusiastic than balanced, was once present when Eric Whelpton "fainted away in Dorothy's sitting room, and she nursed his head and cooed over him", in such a way that Doreen believed that he must have had some inkling of Dorothy's feelings toward him. Dorothy herself reports that Whelpton had described her as "a pillow"[21] – meaning someone on whom people reclined while they poured out sad stories of love affairs with other women. It would appear that the "womanly and sympathetic" technique that she had developed while dealing with Hugh Percy Allen, and which she also mentions as being useful in cases of shell-shock and nervous trouble, was now frequently in demand. Though hard to reconcile with what we know of her intellectual aggressiveness and her refusal to be sentimental, this facet of her temperament is confirmed by several sources; including Eric Whelpton himself, who in his autobiography *The Making of a European* describes her manner to him as "protective and almost maternal".[22]

Something in Dorothy prompted people – particularly men – to take her into their confidence. This is frequently the sad fate of girls who are not obviously sexually attractive: women whom men instinctively, but quite wrongly, assume to be therefore impervious to the sexual attractions of others. Because the plain girl is plain, they overlook the possibility that she too might like to have men weep over her for her beauty. The nearest thing such girls get to a sexual experience may be the maternal satisfaction of cooing over some stricken young man – stricken, that is, either physically, as was Eric Whelpton, or emotionally, as was the young Mr Clarke, who at about this time unburdened himself to Dorothy of a romantic tale of his woes, "full of stern parents and a hated rival".[23]

The male instinct to confide in plain girls is probably all the greater if the girl is notoriously brainy, and has interests outside and apart from the attracting of the opposite sex. Dorothy's emphasis, in the notes on *Cat o' Mary*, on the fact that her heroine simply did not care enough about personal relationships, finds an echo in the incident when her amorous surgeon called upon her, only to find her in "a brisk, un-kissable mood",[24] owing to the fact that she and a friend had spent an hour and a half practising a Beethoven violin sonata; the flirtation game, Dorothy found, "fades and palls when one has other ex-citements".[25] Doreen Wallace, who was well known as a breaker of hearts, surely knew enough about male vanity not to let a Beethoven sonata come between her and her prey.

Did Dorothy mind? Doreen Wallace, her friend (and, to some extent, her rival) at that time, is certain that she did. She remembers her as a passionate woman. Basil Blackwell, too, believes that she was highly sexed, and Eric Whelpton felt the same. Probably the characteristics that she gave to Peter Wimsey come near the mark – a nature "passionate and unsentimental".[26] And in her heroine, Harriet Vane, she was to paint a portrait of a woman with precisely the same problems – a woman of distinction, intelligence, and strong clear emotions, but without conventional beauty. In Harriet's difficulties in forming a satisfying relationship, Dorothy expressed her own problems; and in the later Peter Wimsey, she created the man who might have satisfied her and found her satisfying – the man she never found in real life.

If she had ever found a man who truly matched her spirit, as Peter Wimsey was fictionally to match the spirit of Harriet Vane, it seems likely that she would have dropped everything else for him. The romance that floods through her poetry, that carried away the heart of the unfor-tunate vice-principal of St Edmund Hall, probably did need expres-sion in real life – if only it could have found an object worthy of it. But the best men were gone. In the first years of the war, before conscription was introduced, the army consisted of volunteers. These were the brightest and bravest of their generation. They went into battle in bright uniforms and total ignorance of the kind of war this was going to be, and they were wiped out in their thousands. It may well be that Dorothy was robbed of her mate – the man who could have taken what she had to offer and given her back as good as she gave. She herself certainly believed it, at least in some moods – "If I could have found a man to my measure, I could have put a torch to the world."[27]

Perhaps she suffered also from a fear of sexuality. Very few middle-class Edwardian children grew up with any knowledge of sex. Again and again in autobiographies of the period, we find people totally incapable of visualizing their parents engaged in the act which created them. The children are doomed to start from scratch, without instruction or example. Often they feel that they are in some way different from, and inferior to, their parents. Love may be a proper subject for discussion. So may marriage, engagements, and all the external manifestations of pairing off, including flirtation, arguments, and partings. But the central act, the thing which, as Dorothy pointed out, is at one and the same time sacred and indelicate (and for both these reasons rather remote and unreal) was never mentioned between the generations. If Dorothy's father was unable to speak to her about religious doctrine, how much less possible must it have been for sex ever to be have become a subject for discussion. In religion she had at least a weekly service to chew upon, impersonal though it was; and she had the example of her parents, who did in their own way try to lead Christian lives. But we can be sure that nothing in their daily behaviour gave Dorothy any example of sexuality. Her mother no doubt instructed her, probably at the onset of menstruation, in the actual physiology of reproduction. But where other girls can share their puberty with schoolmates, Dorothy must have experienced her first period with no one of her own age to compare notes with. By the time she reached school, she was far too much the odd one out to exchange thoughts and information easily with the girls around her.

It must have been almost impossible for Dorothy to submit to the natural rhythm of growth. Everything had first to be experienced through literature, then carefully considered, and finally put into effect with deliberation and self-consciousness. Such people are not easy with others in a sexual situation, because they are not easy with themselves; and such unease is a blight on ripening affection.

Dorothy was a virgin until she was nearly thirty. A rarely revealing letter, in which pain has forced her to drop her sophisticated guard, reveals the vulnerable person that she really was: "I'd never been treated as a woman – only as a kind of literary freak – I wanted someone to want *me* to do things – not to have to ask. – I should have been – I was – terrified to try, because I never had lived a natural girl's life –"[28] To be Dorothy, with these inhibitions, in a society so full of sexual turmoil as Oxford – and indeed England – in 1919 must have been uncomfortable indeed. It is possible to regard her intellectual passion as sublimation: personally, I think it is far from being the whole story. But that intellectual passion – that wholehearted absorption in a Beethoven violin sonata, that insistence on the superior delight of creation and craftsmanship to which she was to adhere throughout her life – must surely have taken an added urgency from the anxiety, as she paddled in the waters of flirtation, that if she went a bit deeper she might not be able to swim.

For the most part, then, she remained on the bank, observing shrewdly but never plunging:

> Few friendships between women will stand the strain of being roman-tically considered – all those I've ever watched have ended in dead-sea apples [sic], and I avoid them like the plague. Men manage better I think, because most of them spend half their lives in Cloud-cuckooland in any case! Of course there is the amusing cock-and-hen friendship – but it is so very like a game of chess . . .[29]

Occasionally she was called upon to intervene, as when it fell to her to shatter the illusions of a Somerville student about a man who in fact did not want her. Both parties, wrote Dorothy, were behaving like perfect idiots, and she had to break the thing up. "The way of the third person," she complained, "is hard. Never mind!"[30]

The poems she wrote at this time are still so derivative and literary that it is impossible to say to what extent they express personal feeling. The only echo of her distresses that crept into her writing was in the article "Eros in Academe" that she wrote at this time for *Oxford Outlook*. There she complains that the learned women of her day are not also women of the world – unlike the learned women of the Court of Navarre:

> When I lived in Academe I should never have thought of going to one of its guardians for advice in any social difficulty. I should have feared, not unkindness or unwillingness to help, but just blank want of knowledge. "This kind of thing never happened to me" says the guide, philosopher and friend; "to a nice girl social difficulties do not occur." That is a cowardly lie. Things do happen; it is monstrous to pretend that they do not or ought not.

Harsh words about the academic ladies of Somerville, whom, years later, in *Gaudy Night*, she was to recreate with such sympathy and respect.

Later in the article she quotes a contemporary of hers as saying: " 'I am twenty-six, and I see now that I do not want an independent career; but I am unfit for marriage because I have been taught to demand too much, and I do not know how to give men what they want.' "

Dorothy was not happy. In January, after an attack of German measles, she spent a week in a religious retreat. To her parents she wrote that she was feeling spiritually musty; and to Muriel Jaeger simply, "Everything here is quite horrid."[31] The move to 5 Bath Place had obviously cheered things up in some ways, but in others it probably made matters worse, for though it satisfied her purely social ambitions, it stimulated her sexual awareness, and brought out into the open her sexual weaknesses. "Her other social life," says Doreen Wallace, "if only she had stopped thinking about men, could have been extremely full; and I think it perhaps was."

Eric Whelpton left for a job in France early in the spring. But the real blow was that Basil Blackwell no longer wanted her. She had always found the donkey-work in publishing very tedious; in an office she was, in Blackwell's judgement, "a racehorse harnessed to a cart". And now the firm was abandoning belles lettres and concentrating upon the publication of school books – a decision which was extremely wise from a commercial point of view, but which left Dorothy very little scope at Blackwell's, for she had concentrated most on the introduction and fostering of young poets. Writing to Muriel Jaeger she refers euphemistically to a "new arrangement"[32] with Basil Blackwell, whereby she was to do piecework for him (presumably reading and reporting on manuscripts), and supplement this with coaching and journalism. But in truth she had been gently sacked.

It was not difficult for her to get coaching work in French Language and Literature – and she was soon commissioned to do a weekly column or so for the *Oxford Chronicle*. But it was not what she wanted. In May she wrote home to say that she was feeling very depressed, though only "to do with little things" . . . "I feel that I have come to a blank wall, and I have lost grip."[33]

A little later she confessed that the problem was the lack of regular work – and moreover that her friends were very tired of her. Not, she says, the men; but most of the women. She was thinking of leaving Oxford. The holy city had failed her – or she it. "I want," she wrote, "a thorough change."[34]

Tentatively, in the next few weeks, she began to mention a new possibility: "Look here, should you mind awfully if I went to France for a bit?"[35] Eric Whelpton was already there – and something was stirring.

CHAPTER SEVEN

WHEN ONE FINDS Dorothy on the lookout for work in France, and Eric Whelpton deciding that he needs a French-speaking assistant in Normandy, one is bound to suspect collusion. One would be wrong: it seems to have been pure coincidence.

Dorothy's hints to her parents continued intermittently through June and the first half of July 1919, but she had nothing definite in mind. To Muriel Jaeger she wrote on June 27: "I am going down next week, maybe forever – I don't know! . . . At present all is confusion as regards plans, and I'd like to cut my throat."

But on July 22: "Last night I had to decide several things in a great hurry, and lost my head. France has materialized very suddenly. After our conversations of last Easter, you will be amused to know that I am going out to be Mr Whelpton's secretary. He is running a sort of Educational Bureau out there. . . ."

The school at which Eric Whelpton was teaching was L'École des Roches, in Verneuil sur Avre, about sixty miles west of Paris. It had been set up in flattering imitation of an English Public School, catering for the sons of many of the richest and noblest families in France; but it was far too high class ever to allow wealth or nobility actually to be mentioned.

Eric Whelpton taught English there, but he was also responsible for the bureau that Dorothy mentioned – an organization for the exchange of British and French schoolboys, to enrich their understanding of each other's language and culture. It was Whelpton himself for whom Dorothy would work, and who would pay her. She had no direct connection with the school.

Before she was permitted to accept the post, however, Eric Whelpton had to satisfy her parents as to his character and intentions. He was invited to spend a couple of nights at Christchurch, where he was scrutinized and pronounced worthy of being Dorothy's employer. They dressed for "an excellent dinner of five courses", and he noted that "Dorothy wore an evening frock to display her bare arms which were slim and well-shaped".[1]

There is no truth in the story that she cycled with Whelpton to the school. She did take her bicycle to France, and she did belong to the

Cyclists' Touring Club; but she made her way to the school by train, via Paris, in the normal manner – and Whelpton was not with her.

Term had not yet started when she arrived, and only twenty or so unhappy pupils were in residence, retaking failed examinations. Until term began Dorothy and Whelpton were allowed breakfast in bed as a treat – not, Dorothy hastened to reassure her parents, together. Indeed, the greatest decorum was observed, and when they sat opposite each other at table they took care to address each other as "Monsieur" and "Mademoiselle". As in an English Public School, the pupils were divided between several houses, and Dorothy slept in a different one from Whelpton.

She seems to have fallen surprisingly easily into the role of personal secretary – a sort of female Bunter to Eric Whelpton's Wimsey, making sure that his pen and ink were always at hand, that his newspaper was in its proper place each morning, that his coffee was hot and that he did not sit on the bar of chocolate that he had hidden under the cushion when visitors suddenly arrived.

The indulgent, motherly way in which Dorothy treated Whelpton was partly due to the fact that he was still a sick man. On one occasion he fell off his bicycle and fainted (or possibly fainted and then fell off his bicycle; afterwards, he could not remember which). In the fall he put his shoulder out, which led Dorothy to comment that it was like Bath Place all over again, except that she would much rather cope with a sprained shoulder than with the nameless nervous symptoms he had shown in Oxford. However there were "faints, and agues, and heart attacks, and all sorts"[2] to be coped with, and this she did with great cheerfulness and success. Twenty years after Dorothy's death, Eric Whelpton is still vigorously alive.

Her tasks included periodical ferrying of a group of boys from France to England – an onerous and responsible chore, but one that gave her experience and a chance to meet friends in London from time to time. Life at the school itself she found pleasant and amusing. Whelpton was good company, for he was something of a man of the world, and so were some of the other teachers. The French flair for delicate indelicacy was something that appealed to her greatly. Uncle Paul Delagardie, the wise old satyr in the Wimsey books who lived in France and supervised Peter Wimsey's amorous education, is a literary figure, as are all of Dorothy's creations. But the details of his character surely came from these months that she spent in France; and it is noticeable in all her books that a sane, practical and wholesomely sensual attitude to sex is invariably associated with the Continent and particularly with France.

Even in France, however, l'amour could not be relied upon always to remain neat and tidy. One of the staff became pregnant as the result of a liaison with a soldier (oddly enough, in view of Dorothy's own experience a few years later, he was a Russian Jew) – and Dorothy, perhaps with a touch of condescension, took it upon herself to straighten matters out.

She wrote home about it in some excitement. She and "E.R.W." were jointly going to organize the unfortunate girl's life. E.R.W. knew a number of people in Paris who might help the girl to start a new life, and this was why Dorothy had found it necessary to enlist his support. Together they would take responsibility for all that happened. Indeed the responsibility was heavy, for the girl had contemplated abortion, and Dorothy had persuaded her that this was a sin and a crime and that she must on no account go through with it. "I'm jolly well responsible for its existence, if anyone is,"[3] she wrote – and one cannot help feeling that she was getting considerable satisfaction from breaking out of her academic detachment and engaging actively in a real situation of life and death.

Whatever the final result may have been for the mother and the child, the immediate effect of the incident was to throw Dorothy and Eric Whelpton closer together than they had been before. Hitherto, Whelpton had taken pains to see that their relationship remained purely formal, concerned only with the running of the Bureau. Now they were involved in matters of deep emotion – abandonment, despair, birth; and this was the first moment, so he says, that Eric Whelpton became aware that Dorothy was definitely in love with him.

Dorothy's letters confirm that some change did indeed take place in their relationship at this time, though the way she puts it is somewhat guarded and her version, as one might expect, gives the incident a very different perspective from his. Dorothy's version goes like this:

On Wednesday I read him a lecture on his general behaviour, which first of all made him thoroughly ill, and has since produced a spasm of sentimentality. But he suddenly perceived this morning, of his own accord, that he was growing fatuous! So I hope for amendment. But generally speaking he behaves very well and is easy to get on with. . . .[4]

Later in the same letter, however, the image of a schoolmarm rapping a little boy over the knuckles is somewhat spoilt by a rather different mood:

. . . for the moment, Himself has taken a violent fancy to the black
jumper with the Tudor rose and the hair turned under. . . . You will
be interested also that I have:
pretty hands
nice neck
beautiful shoulders
good legs!
good ankles!! (at this point I began to think him really besotted. The
rest is true.)
a good temper and
a bit of the devil in me! . . .
I tell you all these absurdities because I know you trust me not to play
the fool, or do the lad any harm, and because it is only little secrets
that end badly, as I have had the opportunity of learning lately.
Besides, what is a man to do in a place like this? Such a set of frumps
you never did see. One has to let off steam somewhere. But you
understand that Doreen Wallace wouldn't do for this job.[5]

By the end of November the pregnant girl was safely installed in Paris, to
await her baby; and Dorothy took the opportunity for a little more
moralizing: "It's all a long and very silly story – that's the disheartening
thing – these stories always are so trivial – nothing at all inspiring about
them . . ."; and at the same time snatched a little credit for E.R.W. and
herself: "So you see we two irresponsible young people are resolutely
founding a family, in a morganatic kind of a way! However, we are not
going to have any crimes committed, that's the chief thing."[6]
The ambiguous involvement with Whelpton continued:

It was funny, all the time the above business was going on I had
E.R.W. in one of his worst "states of mind" – blethering, poor dear,
about his bad health and his blighted ambitions, and the girl who had
failed him, and how he didn't think he would ever be able to marry,
and how he was envious of the slackers all round who could knock
round and do things, and he tied by the leg here – and, finally, how he
had no business to be telling me all this, but I was the only person who
ever understood – with his head buried on my knees and making me
smell of brilliantine in the most compromising manner![7]

Two weeks after that letter, we find her admitting:

I don't know that my head is particularly well screwed on where
Captain Eric Whelpton is concerned, but I promise you that if I find I

am hurting him, I'll leave him like a shot. I didn't come over here to add to his burdens, but I think if it wasn't me it would be somebody else, and I'd rather it was me because I do mean well by him, and don't want to land him in difficulties or exploit his temperament to titillate my vanity, as some people might do who were thoughtless. . . . All this sounds very solemn doesn't it?[8]

It not only sounds solemn, it has a curious air of pompous naïvety about it. As Peter Wimsey was to remark in *Unnatural Death*, "You can't mistake real inexperience."[9] It is true that Dorothy was writing to her parents, and we might expect her therefore to put herself in the most flattering light possible; but she was on the whole very frank with them, and these laudable sentiments of hers were certainly not invented solely for their benefit. They may have been only a part of Dorothy's attitude to Eric Whelpton, but they were a genuine part.

She hoped to have a day in London "fooling around with Himself",[10] but the plans went awry, much to her disappointment – "he'd have known all the nice places."[11] One thing does seem certain about this relationship – that Eric Whelpton's belief that she "was certainly madly in love with me" was over-simple. In love she may have been, but at the same time she was greedily absorbing experience – the experience that her childhood had denied her. Clearly Whelpton found it hard to respond to Dorothy's conception of flirtation as a game, taking seriously her threat "that she was going to vamp me at one of my haunts in a neighbouring village by dressing up in a blonde wig and in complete disguise". Romance was something he took very seriously; and even when he gave her his regimental badge and "she told me that she had copied this crest on her underclothes", he had neither the sense of humour nor the knowledge of Dorothy's character to see this typical piece of comic excess for what it was. Here was Dorothy at twenty-six, highly sexed but still a virgin, thrown into contact with an attractive man in circumstances that inevitably led to thoughts of sex, and she relieved the tension, as she always did, by playing the buffoon. But Whelpton could never have been "a match for her", and it is not surprising to find her at the end of this episode in her life writing with considerable merriment about his "impressive pathos".[12]

All the while she kept in touch with her friends, and continued to send occasional pieces to the *Oxford Chronicle*. Some were poems; some, under the heading "From a French Eton", are cheerful pieces about the everyday life of the school, written under the pseudonym "Jill in Office".

Christmas she spent in Paris, with her pregnant protégée. And in the new year there was a fresh cause of emotional tension with Eric Whelpton. Hitherto, in her usual situation as confidante, she had had to listen to tales of his love for the girl in Oxford, ministering meantime to his ailments. Now, on one of his trips to London early in 1920, he sat next to a very beautiful woman in a theatre and was instantly head over heels in love again.

When he returned to Les Roches, large numbers of letters began to arrive addressed to him in a female handwriting. Dorothy, observing this, sulked for a while and then precipitated a crisis by demanding an explanation. The blow to her pride must have been considerable. To come second to one "distant beloved" may just be acceptable; but to find the first distant beloved supplanted by a second, while never being considered for the role oneself, is not at all flattering. There were scenes:

> Everything became so odd last fortnight that I thought I was becoming a nuisance, and offered to go, because I thought I was fighting a losing battle; however this morning it was made clear that whoever the fight was against, Eric and I are pulling on the same side, so that there is nothing to be ashamed of, if a lot to be coped with. We are both rather estimable people and the whole thing would be most heroic and pathetic if one didn't see the comic side of it. Anyway we both nobly shouldered our own share of the blame – in fact Eric claimed it all, but to tell the truth I have been partly responsible – and at present mutual admiration stands at par.[13]

Although the air was cleared and it was "all over now, and feeling better thanks",[14] the Bureau venture now began to go downhill. Whelpton could not earn enough money at Les Roches to keep his new beloved in the style he intended for her, and he spent an increasing amount of time in London, looking for better paid work. And in the following month Dorothy succumbed to the prevalent epidemic of mumps.

To while away the tedious time in bed, she embarked on a long and elaborate correspondence with Muriel Jaeger in which they subjected the works of Sexton Blake to a spoof historical analysis in the high scholarly style. It was the sort of joke at which Dorothy was unsurpassed – treating a fictional character as though he were a historical personage and giving him the full academic treatment. A whole society has grown up to do just this to Sherlock Holmes, treating his life and career as though they were those of a real man. It was inevitable that later in life Dorothy should make distinguished contributions to that corpus of bogus scholarship. But the Sexton Blake correspondence shows that she was already a mistress of the craft, with a wealth of delightful circumstantial detail at her fingertips – "I may now state, in short, that I do not hesitate to connect the legend of Sexton Blake not only with the Osiris mysteries and possibly with the Mithraic solar ritual, but also with the oriental Jesus cults whose solar origins have been so indisputably established by Drews and Robertson.",[15] etc., etc.

How serious was Dorothy's interest at this time in detective stories and thrillers? Certainly she had told Eric Whelpton that the detective story market was where the money lay, and had invited him to join a group including herself, Michael Sadleir and the Coles (G.D.H. and Margaret), who were planning to make a fortune in this way. But there is no evidence that this group had any formal existence. No doubt the scheme had been mentioned among them as something that might some day be fun to do – and, as on other occasions, Whelpton took Dorothy a little more seriously than he was intended to. Among her voluminous reading, however, she had certainly explored the available works of detective fiction, Sexton Blake's adventures included, and, being Dorothy, had not just skimmed through them but absorbed them thoroughly and studied the craft. It was after all a genre much after her own heart – full-bloodedly dramatic, and remote from any taint of what today would be called slice-of-life realism.

As she recovered from her mumps the future was far from clear. This uncertainty, combined with the after-effects of the illness and her emotional uneasiness with Whelpton, caused a recurrence of her hair trouble. She went to a specialist in Paris, who gave her "lots of lotions and ointments and smelly things"[16] and told her that there was no specific disease – the condition was due to a generally poor state of health.

One possibility for the future was that Dorothy would buy out Whelpton for the forty pounds which he had originally put into the Bureau, and continue to run it herself. But in the meantime she too was enquiring in London about other possibilities – particularly anything which would enable her to continue her Bureau work while living in London.

For London now was the goal of her endeavours. Oxford had failed her. France had been fun while it lasted, but L'École des Roches had never been likely to give scope for Dorothy's kind of ambitions, and once Eric Whelpton had gone there were few consolations. She was left with a memory of his yarns about the clubs and pubs and nightspots of the big city, inspiring in her the conviction that London was the place to be. This was where she would find kindred spirits. This was where she would find the variety that was lacking at the school, the sophistication that her upbringing had never taught her, the vulgarity that Oxford could not provide. Dorothy's nature demanded a rich and teeming social life, the chance to spread her wings, the chance to be a little outré without exciting adverse comment – and along with all of these a chance to earn her living. Somehow or other, London could surely satisfy all these demands.

CHAPTER EIGHT

IN THIS HOPEFUL mood began the five most difficult years of Dorothy's life. For a start, it took much longer than she expected to disentangle herself from the school. All through the summer of 1920 things remained uncertain, and it was not until September that the headmaster found somebody else to replace her there, and she was free to concentrate on a new kind of life.

In the meantime, on one of her trips to London, she had met and cultivated a film producer by the name of Mannering. He had suggested that she write a screen scenario of a book which had recently been translated into English and which was all the rage – *Blood and Sand*, by Vincent Blasco Ibañez.

Dorothy was delighted with the idea of earning her living as a writer: "I mean, supposing one could sell, say, £250 or £300 worth of scenarios per annum, one could live where one liked and go where one liked, when one liked. For instance, if London got too expensive, or too coal-less, one could make tracks, say, for Rome, where the lira is at present at 77."[1] But at the same time she was doubtful whether she could tackle this job alone, so she went into collaboration with Dorothy Rowe, the most dramatically-minded member of the M.A.S., who now lived on the south coast in Bournemouth. Dorothy paid several visits there to work on the scenario, and after some months took it to Mr Mannering, who expressed himself quite delighted – as indeed he had good cause to be, for it was professional and imaginative, with an excellent eye for visual effect and, considering Dorothy's predilection for words, shrewdly sparing in its use of dialogue. Now, said Mr Mannering, he must discover whether or not the rights to the book were free.

In her letters home there is no indication that Dorothy was paid; but she does not seem to have realized at this stage how casually she had been exploited. Never again, though, was she to be had for a sucker – her business sense grew sharper along with her other talents.

Soon after she had finally shaken off the dust of L'École des Roches, there was one glorious moment. Oxford had at last decided to grant full degrees to women students, and Dorothy was among those qualified to receive not only a B.A. but an M.A. She was determined to be "done" in the first batch, and she achieved this by a combination of persuasion and a ruthless assertion that the only date possible for her was the first one, October 14.

It was a curious and historic ceremony. Not only was it the first time that the Latin feminine, "domina", had been addressed to a graduate in those sanctified surroundings; there was also the unprecedented organization required for the processing of a whole group of graduates through the dual initiation of both Bachelor and Master of Arts.

In the event, the plan was simple and effective, if somewhat hilarious. A job lot of gowns and hoods was provided in a large basket and the lady bachelors, having arrayed themselves first in their B.A. hoods and lined up for ceremony number one, then returned to the basket and, after the briefest period of bachelorhood on record, exchanged their white-lined hoods for red-lined ones and formed up again for ceremony number two.

Fun though it all was, these academic splendours cut little ice with employers in London. Life became a succession of disappointments as one job after another failed to materialize, and one landlady after another proved unsympathetic to poverty. Dorothy lived for a little while in St George's Square, near Victoria, but soon after that she moved to Bloomsbury, an area which she never thereafter forsook, and which she used several times in her books. Her heroine, Harriet Vane, who shared so many other attributes with Dorothy, is living in that neighbourhood when she first makes her appearance in *Strong Poison*. And in the short story "The Vindictive Story of the Footsteps that Ran" Dorothy described the district as one "where people are always laying one another out" and where "births, and drunks and wife-beatings are pretty common".

At No. 44 Mecklenburgh Square, Dorothy had to do her own cooking for the first time in her life. She bought her first frying pan, and claimed that her success with it proved her contention that the academically trained mind could adapt itself to any new problem. "Food", she wrote, "is my most sinful extravagance."[2]

In fact, if she was to eat at all, she had to do without curtains. For at this time, apart from the occasional sale of a poem, a few temporary teaching jobs, filling in when other teachers went on holiday or fell sick, and some mysterious work she was doing on "Polish books", she was living off the charity of her parents. What exactly she was doing to or with the Polish books is not clear, but the work came through her father, and was presumably either translation or some sort of editing.

Despite the poverty and the anxiety, Dorothy desperately resisted the idea of going home. At all costs she must stay in the metropolis, where

86

DOROTHY L. SAYERS

there were theatres, parties, one or two men friends to take her to them
from time to time, and, of course, the hope, dwindling but persistent, of
a job more interesting than teaching.

Most of these men friends are mentioned by name in her letters home;
they came and they went, and they are of no importance in this story. But
there was one, who once or twice took her to tea at the Ritz, who
remained anonymous: "Guess who . . . No, you're quite wrong, it's
somebody you never saw or heard of . . . no, I won't tell you – it's so
nice to have a little mystery."[3] And the mystery remains.

Of Eric Whelpton she saw little. He was busy in Florence, where he
had taken a partnership in a firm of British house-agents. Dorothy's
view of his great love affair was rather different from his own. In her
opinion he had "more or less done for himself by giving his heart to a
dog to tear. He is marked out for misfortune, but he doesn't distinguish
between an honest woman and a dishonest one, so there is nothing to be
done for him."[4]

Her closest companion was Muriel Jaeger. There was talk at one time
of their sharing a flat together, but this came to nothing. Muriel had
landed a job as sub-editor of the newly founded *Time and Tide*, but the
job came to an end rather rapidly when she had a row with the management – a form of indiscretion to which she appears to have been rather
prone. Dorothy, though herself a talented and enthusiastic picker of
quarrels, did her best to warn her friend against such an injudicious
choice of foe, but to little effect. Muriel soon moved on to *Vogue*, where
she made the same mistake again; and this time there was no one to take
her in.

With time on her hands, Muriel plunged into the writing of a novel;
and so we come to July 1920, and the situation with which this story
began, with Dorothy lamenting her lack of job, money, clothes and
man, and protesting that she had not the application to grind out a book
herself. Soon after writing that letter, she went home to Christchurch for
a summer visit; and it seems highly probable that what finally spurred
her to the effort of grinding out a book was the simple fact that there was
nothing else to do. London was full of distractions; Christchurch could
offer none at all. Besides, home, for Dorothy, had always been a place
where she separated herself from the household and applied herself to
her creative concerns.

This was probably not the moment at which Lord Peter first "walked
in" to her imagination (as she was to describe the event); I shall suggest
later that he had already made a tentative supporting player's
appearance in another protagonist's story. But once given the starring
role he certainly developed fast, for by the middle of October not only

was he "nearly ready to be typed" but Dorothy was "feeling rather disgusted with him now that he is done".[5] The post-creative reaction can be as depressing as the post-coital and the post-natal.

And so, mysteriously, was born Lord Peter Death Bredon Wimsey, second son of the Duke of Denver; without whom Dorothy L. Sayers would surely never have made any discernible mark on the mind of the public at large.

The story he was given for his first performance was, of course, *Whose Body?* – though at this stage it was called, more in the convention of the period, *The Singular Adventure of the Man with the Golden Pince-Nez*. According to an interview she later gave to the *Daily Express*,[6] the germ of the story had been in Dorothy's mind since a party game at Oxford. And certainly it had come back to her some months before she began writing, for in January she had written to her mother: "Of course I have chosen this moment" (she was very busy teaching at the time) "to be visited with ideas for a detective story and a Grand Guignol play . . . my detective story begins brightly, with a fat lady found dead in her bath, with nothing on but her pince-nez. Now why did she wear pince-nez in her bath? If you can guess, you will be in a position to lay hands upon the murderer."[7]

That the naked body in the bath subsequently became male, and Jewish, does not rob this opening image of its instantly appealing vulgarity – indeed rather increases it, with the introduction of the subject of circumcision. (Dorothy seems to have shared with a number of other people the misconception that only Jewish males were circumcised.)

In the post-creative lull Dorothy, like most authors, had little, or at best intermittent, confidence in her offering. "I've written a silly book, but I don't suppose any publisher will take it."[8] And there was the typing to be considered, for which she had no money. So "Tootles" (her father) had to come to the rescue again to meet the bill. Then the typist was dilatory and it was some while before "Lord Peter", as Dorothy still called the book at this time, was ready to be submitted to a publisher. The "shaky investment",[9] as she described it, of her time and her father's money felt as though it had all the odds against it, as the days stretched into weeks and the weeks seemed like months. She had been "poverty-stricken and bothered for ever so long", she felt, and "I haven't the least confidence in the stuff, which is a pity because I really enjoy turning it out . . ."[10] though "it takes all one's time and energy to invent even bad sensational stories; but there is a market for detective literature if one can get in, and he [Lord Peter] might go some way towards providing bread and cheese."[11]

In November her landlady gave her notice to be out of her room by December 5. Pressures were piling up, and the prospect of an ignominious return home loomed larger.

Before the month's end, however, she was able to tell her parents that a publisher's reader was enthusiastic about Lord Peter and the publisher was showing interest. With this reprieve she took courage and sent the book to another publisher, for fear of being hustled into an unsatisfactory contract. Meantime Muriel Jaeger had found new accommodation for her in Great James Street, only a few hundred yards away from Mecklenburgh Square – three rooms ("quite small but very pretty"[12]) for little more than she had hitherto been paying for one.

Though the tide was turning, she was not to know how decisively. If she felt it at all, she only knew that it was very slow. She could not know that Lord Peter would bring her fame and financial security, that Great James Street would be her address for the next twenty years or so. What with the move, her teaching, and anxiety about Lord Peter, by Christmas she was tired and depressed: "Nobody can feel more acutely than I do the unsatisfactoriness of my financial position."[13] But she did know that she now had some prospect of repaying her parents for their support, some justification for staying on in London: "If you like I'll make a sporting offer – that if you can manage to help me to 'keep going' until next summer, then, if Lord Peter is still unsold I will chuck the whole thing, confess myself beaten and take a permanent teaching job."[14]

She badly needed those extra six months in London, for there was one thing she had not told her parents – or only half told them. It concerned a man who had entered her life at about the same time that Lord Peter had walked in. In contrast to Lord Peter, this other man was to bring her little but misery. His name was John Cournos.

CHAPTER NINE

So FAR AS her parents were concerned, John Cournos was just one of several young men who occasionally took Dorothy to dinner or a show. And we should be little wiser than they, had it not been for a bundle of her letters which Cournos kept, and which he deposited in conditions of great secrecy in the library of Harvard University before his death.

Thanks to the combined authority of Anthony Fleming and of Alfred Satterthwaite, stepson of John Cournos, it has been possible to see these letters for the purpose of writing this book. Without them, a vital side of Dorothy's life and personality would never have been revealed, even if it had been suspected. For here, as nowhere else in all that she wrote, or allowed in any way to be known about herself, we see Dorothy without her flippant, knowing pose, with her defences down and her human weakness exposed.

Some of her friends would wish that the human Dorothy had remained hidden for ever. For my part, it was with a feeling of great relief that I read those letters. It is not simply that they show that Dorothy shared the frailties of the rest of humanity; their passion and their pain also go a long way towards explaining the rigidity with which, once the affair was over, she protected her private self against further risk, and retreated into an invulnerability in which attack was her best means of defence.

John Cournos was a Russian Jew whose real name was Johann Gregorievitch Korshoon. He was born in Kiev in 1881, in the same week that Czar Alexander was assassinated. When he was five his father and mother were divorced, and his mother remarried a man named Cournos, a strict member of the sect known as the Hasidim.

Founded in the eighteenth century, the Hasidim "placed spirit above dogma and exaltation above cold formalities of knowledge";[1] and they taught that material things were an image of the deity. "With this in mind, man will always serve God, even in small matters."[2] As a result, Cournos senior believed, a new divine energy settled in men and added incentive and force to their creativity.

In his stepson John, unfortunately, this divine energy emerged in the form of pretentious self-importance and a self-pity of cosmic proportions. Not for him the normal process of coming into this world; he was conceived and born "by the blind will of my Nature".[3] He suffered, it is true, persecutions, both small and large, shared by many Jews during this period. As a child he was taunted by other children, who called him "Yid" and "Christ-killer"; and before long the anti-semitism in Russia grew so vicious that the family had to flee to America, where they settled in Philadelphia. A disturbed and sometimes terrifying life, indeed. But John seemed to find in everything some special significance for him – "Well, I have slain no albatross; not any that I know of; yet I have lived the life of one who, judging from his punishment, should have slain several."[4]

Cournos had come to England in 1912, to pursue the career of a writer and journalist. In 1921 he was in Oxford, which may have been where he and Dorothy met, for she was there also for a short time. While Dorothy was writing *Whose Body?* he too was at work on a book, *The Wall* – a much more intense affair. He was the kind of man, Dorothy wrote, "who spells Art with a capital A".[5]

He spent much of his time on the fringes of the literary world, pursuing and interviewing the famous – H. G. Wells, W. B. Yeats, John Masefield, G. K. Chesterton, D. H. Lawrence. And at this time he had an on-off engagement to someone called Dorothy whom he had met in the United States and who was his "first great love". This Dorothy, however, was not in England. Dorothy Sayers was.

There was much to draw the two of them together. Both were ex-troverts, to the point of exhibitionism. Both had a passion for life and both had a passion for literature; and although Dorothy would not agree with his dictum "there's surely too much literature in literature nowadays – and not enough life",[6] there would be plenty of raw material here for the passionate discussions which she so enjoyed. Furthermore, he was an inexhaustible source of those travellers' tales which were always her undoing, and his boundless self-pity would give full scope to her sympathetic streak. Above all, he was an idealist, with a large conception of life. Here, perhaps, was someone who could match her enthusiasm, her energy, her dogmatism – someone she could fight with.

She made no attempt to hide from her parents that she was interested in him. There was talk of her bringing him home to meet them at Christmas, but he was not living in London at the time, merely paying visits, and Dorothy explained that, though he would have liked to come, he was always too busy. One gets the impression that she doubted whether he would really have been much interested in her bourgeois family. In the same way she decisively evaded Aunt Gertrude's invitation to bring any of her men friends out to Putney, where she was now living. What, asked Dorothy, would they do with themselves there?

Early in 1922, when Cournos had started another book – *Babel* – and

Dorothy was beginning to think about following up *Whose Body?* with a second Lord Peter, she wrote briefly to her parents that he had turned up again and that "he and I have had a difference on a point of practical Christianity (to which he strongly objects!). And I may hear no more of him."[7]

She did hear more, though, for at the end of February she went to Bournemouth, to stay with Dorothy Rowe and get on with planning the new book, and she left John "to keep the flat warm in my absence".[8] Indeed, the relationship continued for another nine months – during which vital events occurred that must be related before we return to Cournos.

Though negotiations for the publication of *Whose Body?* still hung fire, in April Dorothy found herself an enthusiastic and hard-working agent, Andrew Dakers, who took that burden off her shoulders. She was still teaching here and there, still eking out her money and her time, when in May she heard at last that a job she had applied for in March was hers – at least for a trial period. It was a job she had particularly wanted, as a copywriter for one of London's largest and most progressive advertising agencies, Benson's; and it had the additional advantage that Benson's office, in Kingsway Hall, was about ten minutes' walk from Great James Street.

A month later the job was confirmed. She was told that she had "every quality which makes for success in advertising, and very few people have those qualities".[9] She wrote thanking her parents again and again for their patience and support. And she celebrated by inviting John Cournos to a slap-up dinner, as elaborate and costly as her purse could buy, for which we have the menu:

Wines and liqueurs
Vermouth – French Noilly Prat, Italian Martinazzi
Wine – Red Spanish Burgundy

Dinner
Hors d'oeuvre – Grapefruit refraichi on ice with whipped cream
Potage – Consommé au vermicelle
Roti – Beefsteak a l'Anglaise, potatoes and salad
Dessert – Fruit jelly with cream (natural fruit in calves foot orange jelly)
Savoury – Baked mushrooms en casserole
with coffee and Grand Marnier Cordon Rouge.

On which she comments: "Aren't I a little wonder? I do like cooking nice dinners."[10] One hopes that Cournos was not too wrapped up in his woes to appreciate it.

Whether or not Lord Peter sold was now irrelevant, so far as her offer to her parents to take a permanent teaching job was concerned. But in fact in July came an offer from the American publishers, Liveright. This caused Hutchinson, who had been humming and hawing for months on the British side of the Atlantic, to withdraw their offer; but Dakers and Dorothy were not sorry to be rid of them, and to be able to start again with the prestige of an American sale behind them.

Another month, and Benson's offered Dorothy a rise, from four pounds to five pounds a week. And before the end of the year Fisher Unwin had bought the British publishing rights, and the American serial rights had gone to the *People's Magazine*.

To all appearances, Dorothy had landed in clover. Nothing in the commercial world could have suited her better than the work she was doing for Benson's. She was in the company of craftsmen of various sorts – draughtsmen, designers and printers, as well as fellow writers; and she was earning her living by performing her favourite activity, playing with words. The enjoyment of one's own skill and craftsmanship is part of the fun of writing for any writer, and for Dorothy it was particularly so. Whether she was composing an advertisement for stockings or writing a sonnet or a villanelle, ideas still had to be fitted into a neat, predetermined form and expressed with the maximum possible impact. Dorothy loved problems like this, and to be paid for spending one's time solving them must at that juncture have seemed like heaven on earth.

Such were the triumphs of that year, 1923 – Dorothy's thirtieth. Never again was she to be short of food, money or recognition. How ironical it is that this long-awaited breakthrough should have been accompanied by such tribulations in her private life – tribulations that were to extend, by a sort of chain reaction, through the next four years, and whose results were to be with her for the rest of her life.

For Dorothy's belief that a trained mind will enable its owner to cope with any and every problem that may face it comes seriously unstuck when the problems concern the heart and loins. It was her other qualities – her courage and her self-control, not her education nor her intelligence – that enabled her to survive, with her career intact, through the storms that attended and followed her affair with John Cournos.

We only have Dorothy's side of the story, and that only after the event, in the form of those embittered letters written to Cournos three years after the affair was over; by which time she had supped full of miseries and was unlikely to be very objective. His letters have not survived and his *Autobiography*, written in 1935, skims rapidly over this period in its last chapter and never mentions Dorothy at all. We may search his other books, if we wish, and make guesses as to whether any of them throws light on this affair, but they would only be guesses.

The only indications we have as to his feelings are the marginal scribbles that he added to her letters, which have an unpleasantly contemptuous ring. For example, against her humble remark that "I'm not hard to companion, really. Bill filled the bill quite fairly well, you know", he wrote: "A clerk might!"[11]

That was later. These notes do not tell us anything of what Dorothy meant to him at the time, but even then it was probably not a great deal. The Cournos autobiography mentions his love of the other Dorothy, the American one, and of the woman he married in 1924, Helen Sybil Norton Cournos (the writer Sybil Norton). That he says nothing about Dorothy Sayers is surely significant in a man who recorded devotedly the slightest tremor of his emotions.

But the facts, as they emerge from Dorothy's letters, are clear enough, and bear out all too sadly what she had written a year or two earlier about the girl whom she and Eric Whelpton "rescued" at Les Roches: "These stories always are so trivial – nothing at all inspiring about them!"[12] Now she was to discover that the triviality is much less apparent when one is inside the story and living it, than observing it from outside.

In all its triviality, this is the synopsis of the story: she loved him. She wanted his children and would have married him. He wanted neither marriage nor children; he wanted to be "free to live and love naturally",[13] which of course involved contraception. This for her was the reverse of natural, and she would not have it. Deadlock.

This was the "difference on a point of practical Christianity" that Dorothy wrote of. But there was rather more to it than religious principle, as becomes clear from her letters. It must have come as something of a shock to Cournos, in view of Dorothy's penchant for bold language, her delight in "spicy" stories and her playing of the flirtation game, to discover that this sophisticated woman of twenty-eight was in fact "utterly inexperienced".[14]

It is possible that she even surprised herself. Flirtation, after all, is a sexual activity; after so many years of flirtatious game-playing, did she realize, any more than he did, that when passion came and intercourse was imminent, she would turn out to be the kind of woman who "longed to be overborne, like any Victorian fool"?[15]

"If only you knew", she wrote, "how pathetically ready I was to be moulded into any set of interests! . . . passionately wanting to be loved and to be faithful . . ."[16] What she wanted from sex was babies and "bodily comfort", decency, normality, social and physical "wholesomeness".[17]

> The fact is, I am afraid, that I am the person you are always talking about and don't like when you meet her – a really rather primitive woman. I mean, I really do feel (not think, certainly, but feel) it disgraceful to be barren . . . and I am disgustingly robust and happy-go-lucky about the actual process. And coarse and greedy like the woman in the comic medieval stories. And really quite shameless.[18]

It was a matter, really, of definitions. The primitive woman Cournos craved was that fantasy female of the male imagination, who responds ecstatically to his every sexual whim without reserve and without responsibility. Cournos, innocent that he was, imagined that he was some kind of monster of unique and unspeakable daring in expressing these desires, which were in fact the stock-in-trade of every trendy young man in the Bohemian belt. So far from being unconventional, Cournos was the epitome of the philosophers of the Bloomsbury bedsitters, trying their luck with pseudo-profundities about free love, and often enough getting away with it.

He believed his books too to be very shocking, but quite failed to shock Dorothy. "Why do men think themselves such devils?",[19] she asked her parents in an indulgent kind of way – managing at the same time, innocent that *she* was, to feel that Cournos "stood for something jolly fine".[20] "I suppose", she concluded later, "what I had for you was one of those abject hero-worships."[21]

One cannot help feeling a little sorry for him. He can hardly have expected to find Dorothy claiming that if a man was entitled to physical fulfilment, so too was a woman; and that for her, fulfilment consisted in bearing a child, not simply in sexual intercourse or orgasm. It is hard to tell to what extent this attitude stemmed from personal instinctive feelings and to what extent it was dictated by her fears or by her religion. There was widespread discussion about contraception at the time (Marie Stopes' first birth-control clinic opened, with great publicity, in March of the year they met), and in her letters to Cournos, Dorothy several times expressed her distaste for "the taint of the rubber shop",[22] and "the use of every dirty trick invented by civilization to avoid the natural result"[23] [of free love]. The Church was, of course, rigidly against interference with the natural processes of procreation, however unnatural the circumstances in which it took place, and no doubt this deeply influenced Dorothy. But there was nothing theological about her appreciation of her own body:

> . . . if you are implying that I cannot carry a child without being sick in the morning like any anaemic, nerve-wracked, constipated, suburban imbecile of a half-baked, undersexed, rotten-bodied, straight-corseted, flat-bellied, up-to-date semi-female degenerate, then you are offering an insult to my truly magnificent body, which, as I believe Sairey Gamp says somewhere, lambs could not pardon nor worms forget.[24]

By the time she wrote these letters, she had found the fulfilment she was asking for – at least the physical fulfilment, for the emotional fulfilment could only have come through bearing a child to the man she loved. She had discovered from experience that "the difference between the fruitful and the barren body is just that between conscious health and un-conscious – what shall I call it? – uneasiness, discomfort, something that isn't quite health."[25] She had also spent many nights of sleeplessness and tears ("I've been crying for about three years now"[26]), nights of such emotional tension and frustration that she had been "disgustingly sick".[27] ("I am always sick if I cry very much – especially if I've been physically worked up . . . passion *fulfilled* has no power to produce the phenomena, passion repressed, yes!"[28])

Looking back, both she and Cournos evidently felt that they might have managed things better:

> I dare say I wanted too much – I could not be content with less than your love and your children and our happy acknowledgement of each other to the world. You now say you would have given me all those, but at the time you went out of your way to insist you would give me none of them.[29]

At the beginning of this correspondence she had written, in a more con-ciliatory mood: "Both of us did what we swore we'd never do, you see"[30] – meaning that he had got married, when he had vowed never to do so, and that she had lost her virginity with somebody to whom she was not married, which she had refused to do with him. But the fact that he had married another woman, after telling Dorothy over and over again that he could not marry anyone, was still bound to be a sore point – "I believed everything you said to me in those days."[31]

Her devotion to game-playing had indeed deserted her now: "Well,

well, the prizes all go to the women who 'play their cards well' – but if
they can only be won that way, I would rather lose the game."[32] And
then, in a remark which seems to reveal her in all her surprising innocence: "But do you really believe that any woman gives herself to an
unmarried man *except* with the hope and intention of marrying him if
possible?"[33]

I think we may be grateful, on her behalf, that marriage did not
follow, and she probably realized it herself before long. Even the
courtship, such as it was, was a pretty dismal business:

> You drilled and sermonized [my wit] out of existence. I was really fond
> of you and afraid of you. You were a rotten companion for a poor
> girl . . .[34]

> You never asked me to go and do anything with you, or for you –
> never told me anything – I don't know now what your interests are,
> really . . . and how stupid you are! It wasn't that I wanted to dance – I
> wanted someone to think I was worth teaching to dance. I had never
> been treated as a woman – only as a kind of literary freak – I wanted
> somebody to want *me* to do things – not to have to ask – I should have
> been – I was – terrified to try, because I never had lived a natural girl's
> life – but of course I wanted to be persuaded – and in the bigger
> matter as well – I longed to be overborne, like any Victorian fool – so
> young, you'll say, I was – even at 28! . . .[35]

> Don't you offer me any more maxims . . . come off Sinai – I am
> damned if I'll be patronized any longer.[36]

Cournos left England in October of that eventful year, 1922. In
November she wrote to her parents that he had not sent her so much as a
postcard.

Now something had to be done to wipe out the memory of such a rejection – quite apart from satisfying the passions that had been aroused
but not fulfilled. And she lost no time. Two months after Cournos
disappeared from her life, she wrote home: "Dearest Mother, Don't
faint – I am coming home for Xmas on Saturday with a man and a motor
cycle."

The man who was cheerfully and casually to give Dorothy the physical
satisfaction she now craved for – including the child, though this was
not the intention – was not the patronizing sort. "It's a poor devil
whom I chummed up with one week-end, finding him left lonely. . . ." –
as, of course, was she. "He simply has not a red cent or a roof, and
his job has gone bankrupt for the moment – the job being motors . . .

the intellect isn't exactly his strong point – I mean, literary intellect –
he knows all about cars . . . in fact he's the last person you'd ever expect
me to bring home. . . ."[37]

Unless, of course, you realized what a relief he was after the pretensions of John Cournos. Dorothy had lowered her sights by now. This was
not a relationship involving emotional ideals, and, by a sad and self-
defeating irony, she was prepared to let the man she did not love use
"the products of the rubber shop" that might have saved her
relationship with the man that she did love. Her pregnancy, for which
she had besought Cournos and thus driven him away, was this time an
accident.

It is the wish of Dorothy's son, Anthony Fleming, that his father's
name should remain undisclosed, since it might conceivably be embarrassing or distressful to possible third parties directly or indirectly
implicated. During his brief appearance in this book, therefore, he will
be referred to simply as "Bill". Suffice it to state categorically, that the
name does not occur anywhere else in Dorothy's story, nor is it well
known in any other context.   Bill was a very different person from John
Cournos. He appealed to that aspect of Dorothy's character which was
stimulated by craftsmanship, by technical skill, by the satisfaction of
things well made that perform their function well.

Cournos – predictably, for he was the type whose self-esteem was supported by a large-scale disapproval of the civilization in which he found
himself – was against the internal combustion engine and in favour of
a return to horses. Dorothy queried the practicality of keeping a horse in
Bloomsbury, and since her nature responded to enthusiasm rather than
censoriousness, Bill soon taught her to delight in the sweet sound of a
smoothly-running engine, and how to service and repair one when
necessary. This knowledge provided her with the motoring background
for her short story "The Fantastic Horror of the Cat in the Bag", and for
the crucial clue of the air-lock in the motorcycle feed pipe in *Unnatural
Death*. Moreover, Bill was a good companion. He did not take a superior
view of her enthusiasms for crosswords and photography, and he was
eminently, as Cournos was not, a man on whose knee she could sit,
inventing rows of obscene limericks; for this she valued him. But finally
and all-importantly, Bill was the man who cut the cackle and acted. In
her letters to Cournos her name for Bill was "the Beast": "If you'd
wanted me, you'd have taken me", she wrote. "The Beast did, to do him
justice."[38]

Though Bill was for Dorothy a second best, she put all her considerable determination into making the best of a not-very-good job.
The couple were, on the face of it, badly mismatched, but I think we may

be sure that Dorothy was in earnest when she told John Cournos that she was ready to be moulded by a man she was attached to, and that she would have gone to great lengths to fulfil her side of the bargain.

Indeed one of the letters that she wrote home during the affair with Bill makes it clear that this was already beginning to happen. In February 1923, not long after Bill had performed the useful service of staining Dorothy's wooden sitting-room floor, the couple arranged to go dancing with two or three friends. One of the friends, like Dorothy, was no great dancer and was still having lessons; and the dance hall for which they were heading was no West End night spot but a much more modest establishment in the down-market purlieus of a northern suburb.

The day had been wet and foggy, and when Bill had washed off the grime of a day's work among cars and motorcycles, the couple had a quick meal and set off to pick up their friends. Arriving at the house, they found the friends

> . . . lounging round the fire in an atmosphere you could cut with a knife saying "Oh it was such a foggy evening, and the dance hall was so far, and they didn't want to go, and weren't dressed, and they'd quite decided in their own minds that we didn't want to go either. . . " And Howard roasting his posterior before the fire and looking all sleek and oily, saying in a haw-haw voice that it really was horrid out of doors – this to Bill, who had been testing motorcycles all day in fog and rain and inches deep in liquid mud. I was so angry I could hardly speak and I found afterwards that Bill was just as bad. And I told Howard not to try and come the heavy over me, and the whole lot of them that they were damned unsporting, and Bill and I slammed out of the house and went to the Hammersmith Palais de Danse alone.[39]

What a transformation we have here! It is not merely the fact that the awkward girl who eschewed physical activities like the plague is now setting forth through a wet, murky February night in search of an evening's dancing; not merely that the would-be sophisticate is seeking her pleasures in a West London dance-hall. Most remarkable are the value-judgements she lets fall – the scorn she feels for the well-warmed posterior, for the thick atmosphere, for the sleek and oily appearance of poor Howard and his haw-haw voice. Never before or after did Dorothy evince any preference for cold fresh air over warmth and fug, any objection to cosy evenings of conversation, any dislike of sleekness or upper-class voices. Her own accent was distinctly classy: she pronounced Sayers to rhyme with stairs, which is not quite "haw-haw", but well on the way. The whole passage reeks of the contempt of the man who works with his hands for the man who does not, the softie, the sissy, the talker. It is on Bill's behalf that Dorothy is indignant, it is through his eyes that she sees her erstwhile friends, even some of the words are surely his.

We do not know, of course, when they actually became lovers. Dorothy did not become pregnant until April 1923, but it is clear from the fact that she took him home for the Christmas of 1922 that she did not intend this to be a hole-and-corner affair – or, at least, not more so than was necessary to spare the feelings of her parents. She may well have been prepared to marry him on the terms she offered to Cournos – complete fidelity and devotion on her part, he to be free, if he wished, to have other women. For she recognized that this would be, for him, a marriage of friendship and convenience rather than of single-minded devotion; but that for her it would be, simply, the solution of her problem of what to do with those passionate feelings and that magnificent (if, according to her colleague John Gilroy, pear-shaped) body. With calculated efficiency, she had assessed the situation and worked out the future. She liked things to be orderly.

How long they would have remained orderly and static had the baby not intervened, is impossible to say. It is not totally beyond the bounds of credibility that she would have been able to adapt her personality to Bill's, and that the world would have seen quite a different Dorothy from the one that eventually emerged – a Dorothy who was indifferent to intellectual integrity and the claims of Christian theology – one indeed who thought such matters a load of highbrow nonsense.

However, it was not to be. By the end of May at the latest Dorothy must have been sure that she was pregnant, and the future had to be faced. Everything in her rebelled against the thought of an abortion – her religious beliefs, her upbringing, and the sense of physical outrage which is common to many women, but which seems to have been particularly strong in Dorothy, given her feeling for physical "wholesomeness".

On the other hand, the pregnancy was unquestionably a disaster. Though she had wanted a child by John Cournos, she had never much cared for children in general; and to be encumbered by a baby now could be seen only as a most unwelcome interruption of the career which she had so recently, and with such effort, got under way. Nor was it only the job that was in danger. Her relationship with Bill was also threatened, for he had no inclination whatever for fatherhood.

So whatever physical fulfilment her condition afforded her, Dorothy enjoyed none of the psychological satisfactions of a woman happily with child. She could talk about it to no one. To her lover it was a nuisance, and to her parents, with whom she had shared other problems so openly and blithely, it would have been a shock which they could not endure – or so she believed. That being the case, she decided that she could confide in nobody, for fear that the news might get back to them.

There was something else which Dorothy had to try to protect – her own status in her parents' eyes, her own reputation with them for "cleverness" and superiority to other people. There had been, without question, an element of patronization about the way in which she had spoken of the girl in a similar plight at Les Roches, and Dorothy had been the one who had descended from a great height to save and to succour. To confess now to being as vulnerable herself to the follies of the world would have been shattering.

The suggestion that she went back to Christchurch during her pregnancy is quite without foundation; her every effort was bent upon never allowing her parents to know what had happened. She wrote to them on May 22 saying that she was renting a small cottage in which to get on with the next Wimsey book; somewhere near enough to London for her to have access to her sources, which meant that she would not be able to come as far as Christchurch. A scribbled note, undated, and headed only "Kingsway Hall", begs them not to come to London to see her – "Look here – I'm awfully rushed and rather bothered. Don't come up till the Spring. I want to get things straightened out, and I can't do that till I get my accounts from America and England and have got my new book on to the Press both sides of the Atlantic. . . . Don't expect me at Xmas – At Easter I hope to see you with a settled scheme of things, but just at present I'm too 'hot and bothered' to cope . . ."[40]

In fact the progress of the new book – "associated with every sort of humiliation and misery"[41] – was pitifully slow, and it was not to be ready for the press for another two years. But the royalties from *Whose Body?* began to arrive, a timely bonus in view of the impending doctor's bills.

Dorothy had one other piece of good fortune. She had by now been earning for a year or so, and this had meant that she had been eating well. The tall bean-pole figure, which would have shown signs of pregnancy at a fairly early stage, was already filling out. Perhaps she was eating for consolation, on top of her natural love of good food; but certainly she was able to put her increasing girth down to straightforward calorie intake and get away with it – to such an extent that nobody in the office ever suspected the truth, and that when she returned to work (after an absence of only eight weeks) she was told, incredibly, that she had put on weight!

Throughout her pregnancy she went on hoping that Bill would

take his responsibilities seriously, marry her and acknowledge his fatherhood. Had this happened, Dorothy would undoubtedly have put up with the loss of her career and the fresh problems that that created. As we have seen, she had a strong sense of sin, and a sense of duty which would certainly have convinced her that it was right to take the consequences of her actions, had this been possible without giving her parents the shock that she dreaded.

Her hopes of bringing her lover round must have lasted until the very last moment; for it was not until two days before the birth that she finally took the other course that had been open to her from the beginning of the pregnancy.

Her cousin Ivy, whose father had died two years before, had been eking out a slender living with her mother Amy by taking in children who were orphaned or who, for whatever reason, could not be looked after by their parents. They were already caring for three – Isabel, Fluffie and Nellie, in their apartment in Oxford.

No doubt Dorothy's reluctance to go to her cousin was also aggravated by the damage it would do to her reputation with Ivy as a "know-all". But finally there was nothing else for it. On January 1 1924 she wrote:

Dearest Ivy,

Thank you very much indeed for your letter and the delightful pussy. I have been wanting for some time to write to you on a matter of business. There's an infant I'm very anxious you should have the charge of, and I hope very much indeed you'll be able to take it. It isn't actually there yet, but will be before many days are over. It won't have any legal father, poor little soul, but I know you would be all the more willing to help give it the best possible start in life on that account. The parents want to do the very best for it and will be ready and willing to pay whatever your usual terms are, and probably something over. They especially want it to have affection rather than pomp! I know that nobody could do better for it that way than you. I am very personally interested in the matter, and will tell you more about it later on, or when I see you as I hope to do before too long. The point is – what would be the earliest possible moment at which you could take it? At present everything depends on the girl's not losing her job. Everything has been most discreetly managed – her retirement from public life is accounted for by "illness" – but naturally she can't turn up back at work plus a baby – at least, not without letting stacks and stacks of people into the secret, which might then leak out. So you see, the sooner she could dump the infant on

you and clear [sic] back to work, the more chance there is of being
money to support it, as both parents are working and one of them alone
couldn't do much to support it. From the mother's history it *should* be
an extremely healthy child, having given not the slightest trouble or
bad time so far, and I understand the doctor thinks everything should
go easily. It will be a little gent (or lady as the case may be) on both
sides, and would probably be in your charge for some years – till circumstances enable the mother to take it herself. I think you would
find it a paying proposition and I do very much hope that you will be
able to help in the matter, as I feel that nobody could do better for it
than you. Indeed, I'd ask you to make a very special effort in the
matter – it is so great a relief to feel that somebody really trustworthy
will have the child, and its mother is counting much on my cousin!

   Please let me know by return of post whether you can manage it by
hook or by crook – and if so, the earliest moment at which you could
take it, and what your terms would be. I can guarantee the payments –
and you would be given an entirely free hand in such matters as
doctors, clothing, and necessaries of every kind. . . .

The handwriting is even and unhurried; there is nothing about the style
that suggests strain. Few writers of fiction would have dared to invent a
heroine who at such a time showed so little of the emotions that must
have possessed her, who so coolly covered her tracks. It is possible of
course that Dorothy did not expect the baby quite so early, but it must
have been sufficiently imminent to make her request for an immediate
reply something of an understatement.

   At the age of thirty Dorothy did not expect an easy birth, and she was
right. John Anthony was born, with some difficulty, in Tuckton Lodge, a
private nursing and maternity home in Southbourne, Hampshire, on
January 3. Southbourne is a seaside resort between Bournemouth and
Christchurch, Hampshire, where Anthony's birth was registered. The
fact that Bournemouth was the home of Dorothy Rowe, one of Dorothy
Sayers' great friends from Oxford, a member of the M.A.S. and
Dorothy's collaborator on *Blood and Sand*, has led many people to
believe that this other Dorothy was in on the secret. Why else would
Dorothy have chosen that part of the world? The answer to that question
is that we have no idea. Tuckton Lodge closed in 1958 and its records
cannot be traced. But certainly Dorothy Rowe knew nothing of the
event. It may simply have been that Dorothy wanted some part of
England where she was little known, far from Oxford and from her
parents in Christchurch, Cambridgeshire; but where she did not feel a
total stranger. She had visited Dorothy Rowe often enough to know her

way around Bournemouth, and she may have felt that should anything go wrong with the birth, there was a friend not far away.

That first letter to Ivy gave Great James Street as its address. Unfortunately, we do not possess the envelope, so we do not know where it was posted. Presumably it was from Southbourne; if not, there must have been a very anxious journey indeed from London to Southbourne – a matter of over a hundred miles – in the very nick of time. But it is more likely that the London address at the head of the letter was a blind.

The next letter is dated January 16 and this too is headed 24 Great James Street, which would quite certainly have been impossible. It says:

Dearest Ivy,
Excuse hasty note. Have been waiting to give you definite news. Your baby arrived on January 3rd – a sturdy little boy – and will be brought to you with all paraphernalia and particulars on or about January 30th. Terms quite satisfactory. Ever so glad you can take him. Will let you know further. Best love. Dorothy.

Then on January 27 comes another letter, this time headed Tuckton Lodge:

Dearest Ivy,
I am bringing the boy to you myself on Wednesday. Owing to the strike we shall probably have to come by road, so expect us at your door some time in the afternoon. As I shall try to get up to town by train the same night I may only be able to stay a minute or two, so am enclosing confidential particulars which I had intended to give by word of mouth. I know you are the most discreet woman in the world. Will you read them first yourself, and only tell Aunt Amy about it if, on consideration, you think fit. I trust your discretion absolutely. Yours affectionately. Dorothy.

The "confidential particulars" are, of course, the admission the baby was hers:

My dear, everything I told you about the boy is absolutely true – only I didn't tell you he was my own! I won't go into the whole story – think the best you can of me – I know it won't make you love the boy any the less. He is really a fine little chap – I can't feel too bad about him myself now, because it will be so jolly to have him later on. I am thirty now, and it didn't seem at all likely I should marry – I shall have something for my later age anyway. . . .

They know nothing about him at home, and they must know nothing. It would grieve them quite unnecessarily. You know, it's not the kind of ill-doing that Mother has any sympathy for. She isn't either a man lover or a baby worshipper – so I see no reason whatever for distressing her. So please, not a word of any kind to Christchurch. By the time I want the boy, they will be too old, if they are still alive, to worry much about anything, and they must have these last years in peace. . . .

The boy will have to be registered in my name of course, but I think he may as well be known by his father's, which is as non-commital and common as blackberries. . . .

There follows a page or so of discussion about feeding – Anthony had been breast fed for his first two weeks, on the doctor's advice – and Dorothy ends: "I'll tell you anything else there is time for when I see you. Goodbye till then, my dear – and be good to my son! Dorothy."

The very circumstances that Dorothy had imagined seventeen years earlier had now come about; she had committed what was to her "a great sin", and she was turning to her cousin for help, hoping that she would not be harshly judged.

Ivy seems to have come out of this test with honours. We do not have her side of the correspondence, but there is no suggestion in any of Dorothy's letters that Ivy made any comment whatever on the moral aspect of the situation, and Dorothy's trust seems to have been more than justified.

Thus the practical side of the problem was neatly disposed of. Emotions were another matter. Somehow, after the journey to Oxford, the hurried meeting with Ivy and the parting from her son, Dorothy had to manage a nonchalant reappearance at the office, with a convincing story for curious colleagues; and day after day thereafter the cheerful, unconcerned façade had to be kept up. She succeeded; and only the letters to Cournos tell us at what cost.

Now the training that she had had, at school and elsewhere, in hiding her true feelings was put to its greatest test. A tell-tale line in *Clouds of Witness* – the book she was now working on – speaks of someone "whose misfortune it was to become disagreeable when she was unhappy – perhaps the heaviest curse that can be laid on man, who is born to sorrow".[42] "I know it's very unattractive to be miserable", she wrote to Cournos, "and I've tried hard to be merry and bright and all that sort of thing"[43] . . . but even when she had been back at work a year the strain was still almost unendurable:

I hope Anthony and I don't come to the workhouse! but it's so hard to work. It frightens me to be so unhappy – I thought it would get better, but I think every day is worse than the last, and I'm always afraid they'll chuck me out of the office because I'm working so badly. And I haven't even the last resort of doing away with myself, because what would poor Anthony do then, poor thing? . . . I still want help, you don't know how badly . . . I'm afraid my nerve's gone a bit. . . .[44]

It was all a desperate drain on the gaiety and gallantry which Basil Blackwell had singled out as her principal characteristics; and there was no one but Ivy to admire her for them. That is when gallantry is gallant indeed.

But it would be a mistake to suppose that Dorothy expected this state of affairs to go on forever. She hoped, as anyone might in the same circumstances, that things would improve. Either Bill would gradually come to see the situation differently and enable Dorothy to give the baby a home; or at least a moment might somehow arrive when she would find it possible to talk to her parents about it – preferably when there were no aunts in the way. This was not a case of a bleak decision taken once and for all, but of that even more deadening thing – the slow fading of hope. In February she wrote to Ivy: "I must find out whether his father wants anything to do with him."[45] In April: "I saw the Christchurch people at Easter, and nearly told them, but Aunt M. makes everything very difficult. Better to wait – besides, things are being very rotten here for the time being."[46] And at the end of April she finally decided that nothing was to be expected from Bill and conclusively told him "to go to hell".[47] By December, she had the painful experience of seeing him with another woman, who must either have lived or worked near Dorothy, for she "plumped down at the table next to me in a restaurant, and while I was most tactfully not seeing her she accidentally flung an entire cup of tea into my lap and had to apologize, which must have been horrid for her, poor thing."[48]

Even when Bill was out of the picture, Dorothy still hoped to find some other man who would take on the responsibility of John Anthony, some way or other whereby she might in the end be able to live without this tremendous secret hanging between her and her parents.

It is all the more amazing, in view of the provisional and temporary nature of that secret as she then saw it, that in fact it was kept completely intact even after her parents were dead. Later on, Dorothy's secretaries knew about Anthony, for letters were exchanged and there were regular cheques to be sent. And some of the people in Witham, the little town where she then lived, seem to have picked up the secret. Schoolmasters, too, had to know. But outside the circle of those actually concerned with the boy, not one of Dorothy's friends knew about him until the day of her death.

In the uncompleted section of *Cat o' Mary*, the heroine's life was to diverge considerably from Dorothy's, according to the notes which she left. But the theme, that personal relationships are not to be relied on and that work and scholarship offer life's only security, was Dorothy's own.

Here and there in her notebooks, Dorothy wrote brief passages of dialogue, defining key thoughts and situations. Among these are two crucial lines, which give, as it were, the two possible ways of looking at her problem.

The first is this: "I have made a muck of all my emotional relationships and I hate being beaten, so I pretend not to care." A little later, however, she changes her mind: "It isn't that I've failed and pretend not to care. I don't care; and that is why I have failed."

Both of these judgements were probably true of Dorothy in some measure. She certainly cared a great deal at certain moments in her life; but her early life, while making it hard for her to establish relationships, had also inured her to the resultant loneliness. She did make a muck of things, she did care; but she cared less than others might, because she had other resources. She had her job to distract her day by day; and she had her writing. *Clouds of Witness*, the book she struggled with throughout this long, tense period, is concerned with sexual passion in a way that none of her other books is. The suspect, Peter Wimsey's brother, the Duke of Denver, is engaged in an adulterous affair which takes him across the moors for brief risky assignations with a sensational raven-haired beauty who is married to a brutal and violently jealous farmer. The criminal is the victim of a desperate passion for a Frenchwoman who plays with men's hearts – and his letter of farewell to her, written out at full length both in French and in English, is a melodramatic cry of pain and loss. There is a third case of seemingly hopeless love – that of the detective, Charles Parker, for Wimsey's sister Mary; and she too, like the other women, is described in terms of an almost impossible beauty. It is as though Dorothy is torturing herself with the vision of what some women can do to men, which she herself was unable to do; and at the same time letting the passion and despair, which she had to control, overwhelm at least one of her characters:

Goodbye, my dear – oh Simone, my darling, my darling, goodbye. Be happy with your new lover. Never mind me – what does it all matter?

My God – how I loved you, and how I still love you in spite of myself. It's all done with. You'll never break my heart again. I'm mad – mad with misery! Goodbye.[49]

Dorothy would have been ashamed to write such turgid, rhetorical stuff in real life. This harked back to the style of the Musketeer days, to the romanticism of the poems. But now, at last, she knew what she was writing about; and no doubt it did her good to write it.

CHAPTER TEN

THE ARRANGEMENT WITH Ivy was that Dorothy should pay her three pounds per month – which she dutifully did, increasing the sum as the cost of living rose, as John Anthony's requirements increased, and as her own financial situation made her more able.

At first she went to Oxford as frequently as she possibly could to see the baby; but after eight or nine months the visits grew gradually less frequent and the excuses for not managing to get to Oxford at that particular weekend more numerous. Dorothy was a lady with a positive turn of mind, and though she would never abandon her responsibilities, she would certainly not dwell on her failures or waste time on something in which she had perforce only an unsatisfactory and intermittent role. The bringing up of the boy had been entrusted to Ivy; Dorothy could only drop in from time to time, and coo and comment. There is nothing so frustrating as being half in, half out of an enterprise, having an interest but no responsibility; she had enough sense to know that there could be only one person who stood in the role of mother to the boy, and she was not the one.

Painful experiences, mercifully, do not occupy all our attention all the time. With her gift for keeping her emotional life in a separate compartment, Dorothy still managed to take a great interest in the world around her. Benson's alone gave her plenty to occupy her mind, and there was really very little fear of her being fired.

She could afford to eat well now, and that was a comfort; and she seems to have made no attempt to keep her weight down. She loved beer and pubs and pub songs and pub conversation, and wore the lapel badge of the Froth Blowers, the beer drinkers' union. Cournos was not the kind of man to be at home in a saloon bar, but Bill had been and so were some of her colleagues at the agency.

The silver wig was much in evidence, since her hair had contributed to her troubles by falling out again. But she made a virtue of the wig, and it does not seem to have cramped her social style. When the hair grew again there had been a merciful change of fashion and she was able to wear it short, which meant no more curlers at night. Dorothy was grateful. Affairs of the heart do not easily survive thin hair in curlers, and she knew that once in the bedroom the wig would become a liability.

Radio was the coming thing. Bill had taught her a certain amount about it and she wrote knowledgeably to her father about how to get Birmingham on his wireless set – "You should find it about 138° on each condenser. Couple up to about 60 or 70 when searching, and slack off if you get howling."[1] When crosswords came in, she fell upon them with eagerness and delight. This was a game that might have been devised especially for her, and she not only solved them by the dozen, but composed them too. Her short story, "The Problem of Uncle Meleager's Will", is based on a highly complicated and elaborate crossword, which naturally Peter Wimsey solves with as little difficulty as he wrestles, dives, plays cricket, or does anything else required of the super detective.

This was one of several short stories that Dorothy managed to produce while she was dragging herself out of her miseries and struggling to finish *Clouds of Witness*. Short story writing was never her strong point and she knew it. "A shockingly poor hand"[2] at it was how she described herself, giving the reason that, if she could think of an interestingly new method of murder, she would want to devote a full-length book to it. Dorothy never was an economical writer – whenever she took up her pen, she liked to spread herself, unless some strict poetic form forced her to harness what she had to say. So we find the short stories are based on wilder and flimsier fancies than the full-length novels. They are all plot and no character, and Wimsey himself is often forced to jump through the strangest hoops to make the stories work at all. These really are pot-boilers, and Dorothy brought no pretensions to bear on them whatever.

Whose Body? had sold reasonably well. Though it did not achieve any immediate startling success, the publishers were interested in seeing more of Wimsey, and Dorothy was glad to oblige. By the end of January 1925, *Clouds of Witness* and five short stories were ready for the publisher. It was hard work, after a day at the office, but just as Dorothy found Wimsey kept her mind occupied during her financial worries in 1921, so now he offered an escape from her other troubles, his perfections a welcome contrast to the inadequacies of the real men in her life. He had been created in order to pay the bills, but his importance was more than that by now. He was reliability; even, in a way, reality.

Dorothy's success in keeping her unhappiness to herself seems to have been complete. Whether or not some suspicions passed through the minds of her colleagues that Dorothy might have private problems, none of them ever remembered seeing her down-hearted, though she might have spent all night weeping, reaching such depths of despair and loneliness that she even considered suicide, the final sin in the eyes of the High Church Christian.

After such nights, she desperately needed the job and her colleagues to cling to. She had broken out of her shell, let down, at last, those defences of assumed sophistication and allowed her emotions to flood out into the open country of real life. It had brought her nothing but grief. "I am so terrified of emotion now," she wrote to Cournos, "and it makes me feel so ill and work so badly. . . ."[3] She would not risk it again. Now she would re-erect the barriers, put the romantic dreams back into the world of literature where she had kept them so long, and turn her passion in another direction – inward, to the intellect, and to that fierce belief of hers that it was work, and work alone, in a world of unstable personal relationships, that could offer enduring and reliable satisfaction.

Nevertheless, she did need a man – a steady, reliable one. Not a demon lover but a companion lover; or, better still, a husband. Several of her letters to John Cournos detail the kind of man and the kind of relationship she wants and does not want:

> The companion part is so necessary because, you see, it's such a lonely dreary job having a lover. One has to rely on him for companionship, because one's entirely cut off from one's friends . . . it's so dirty to be always telling lies, one just drops seeing them. One can't be open about it, because it would end by getting round to one's family somehow. . . .[4]

> A lover must be a companion, because he cuts one off from the world; a husband need only be a lover, because one then remains in touch with the world, and can get companionship from one's friends. . . . You were right in supposing that it is a husband that I really want, because I become impatient of the beastly restrictions which "free love" imposes. I have a careless rage for life, and secrecy tends to make me bad-tempered. . . . Give me a man that's human and careless and loves life, and one that can enjoy the rough and tumble of passion. I like to die spitting and swearing, you know, and I am no mean wrestler. But there again, precautionary measures cramp the style. Bah! If you had chosen, I would have given you three sons by now. . . .[5]

But there is one important proviso: "I say, for God's sake don't pick me out a highbrow. Marrying a highbrow (or living with one) would be like marrying one's own shop. Couldn't you make him a stockbroker, or an explorer, or an engineer or something?"[6]

She had tried the highbrow – Cournos. She had tried the lowbrow –

Anthony's father. From experience, she preferred the latter. Bill was an ordinary sensual man, and none too reliable in an emergency; but at least he had never pretended to be anything else. It was that kind of man she was after – a man who was unromantic, unpretentious, lustful, friendly, comfortable – and perhaps even willing to let her bring her child into their home.

This is perhaps the moment to lay to rest the suspicions sometimes voiced by those who knew her only slightly that Dorothy might have had lesbian tendencies; for this is the time in her life when such tendencies, had they existed, might well have emerged. Heterosexual encounters had proved sadly unsatisfactory. Male humanity had been found wanting. Surely now, if companionship was the first consideration, a relationship might have been sought with some intelligent, sympathetic woman. Dorothy knew many such.

Nothing of the sort was even considered. We must not be misled simply because Dorothy had a loud voice, tended in later years to wear tweed suits, and had a number of woman friends, some of whom had the same sort of characteristics. Women who like the company of other women do not necessarily go to bed with them, even today. In the early years of this century, there were many women to whom such an idea never occurred, even if there were touchings and tendernesses between them. There were others who knew all about the physical aspects of lesbianism, but whose liking for other women was based on something quite different; and I think that Dorothy was one of these. The little clan of the Mutual Admiration Society was held together by a pioneering spirit and a determination to compete with men at their own game and on their own level – and this was a bond strong enough to last most of them for a lifetime.

Some present-day campaigners for women's rights regard this kind of competing as a very crude method of asserting equality, since it assumes that men are better by the mere fact of attempting to equal them. But the M.A.S., as we have seen, was not consciously part of the Women's Movement – indeed they got a good deal of amusement from the views of the extreme suffragettes.

Some became excellent wives and mothers. Others did not. They observed the conventions to differing degrees and for different reasons. Dorothy and Muriel St Clare Byrne concluded that it was much more difficult to do a job properly if you had nothing to carry things about in but a lady's handbag. So they dispensed with handbags and opted, for purely logical and practical reasons, for sturdy suits with plenty of pockets. To do a man's job they needed a man's equipment, and there was no connection between this and what they did in bed.

To put it another way, the fact that they did not wish to be feminine does not mean that they were not female. Dorothy's interest in "the rough and tumble of passion" was certainly heterosexual – an interest which she enlarged on twenty years later in, of all places, a letter to Charles Williams about Dante, whom she adjudged, from the evidence of his poetry, to have been a passionate and satisfying lover:

> I am minded to write you a brief discourse upon
> BEDWORTHINESS.

After a preamble in which she threw out, among other things, the interesting suggestion that "on the strength of his literary output alone . . . any woman of sense would decline to tackle D. H. Lawrence at £1,000 a night", she got down to "the distinguishing marks of True Bedworthiness in the Male":

> I find them to consist in the presence of Three Grand Assumptions – and it is to be noted that they must be present *as* assumptions, and not as propositions, assertions, or boasts, for the Bedworthiness lies precisely in their being taken for granted by the Male in question and not painfully achieved or argued about. The Assumptions are:
> 1. That the primary aim and object of Bed is that a good time should be had *by all*.
> 2. That (other things being equal) it is the business of the Male to make it so.
> 3. That he knows his business.
> The first Assumption rules out at once all Satyromaniacs, sadists, connoisseurs in rape, egotists, and superstitious believers in female reluctance, as well as Catholic (replenish-the-earth) utilitarians and stockbreeders.
> The second Assumption rules out the hasty, the clumsy, the lazy, the inconsiderate, the peremptory, the untimely and (in most cases) the routinier – though one would not wish to be too hard on Mr Shandy, senior, since Mrs Shandy may have been as orderly-minded as himself and possibly preferred it that way – and those who have "l'Amour Triste" or are morose and unmannerly, or are without skill in the management of bed-furniture or wind the whole combination into toppling and insecure complications of pillows and blankets or (in extreme circumstances) bang their partner's head against the wall.
> The third Assumption rules out the tentative as well as the incompetent and inadequate. . . .[7]

That was written by a lady who certainly knew (by that time) what she was writing about, and enjoyed it. Bill had given her a taste for it, and she had no desire to relapse into a state of continence. It was at this juncture that Oswald Atherton Fleming came into her life.

Fleming was an archetypal Fleet Street man, whom Dorothy may well have met in the pubs shared by journalists and advertising people. Or he may have been a friend of Bill's, for both loved motor-racing and frequented Brooklands race-track.

As with Bill and John Cournos, the exact time and manner of Dorothy's meeting with him is unknown; but whether or not she had met him earlier in some casual way, the beginning of their friendship must surely have been after the letter in which she requested John Cournos to find her a companionable man – that is to say after August 1925.

Fleming had already been married and had two daughters, but the marriage had been going wrong since the end of the war and had ended in divorce that June. According to Ann Schreurs, his younger daughter by that marriage, the final break-up with his first wife took place about the time that Anthony was born. This causes her to speculate that Fleming may, in fact, have been Anthony's father – a theory more convenient than accurate.

What Mrs Schreurs is unfortunately unable to tell us is precisely why her parents' marriage collapsed. Her account draws a picture of an idyllic relationship, incomprehensibly shattered after the war; a view which is a little suspect, coming from a clearly embittered source, but all the same not impossible. World War I was not an experience out of which men came unchanged, and if Fleming emerged from it a different man, he was only one of very many.

He was a Scot, born in the Orkneys, where his father was working at the time as a Customs Officer. He was christened Oswald Arthur, but by the time Dorothy knew him he called himself Oswald Atherton – a touch of pretentiousness which goes with the fact that he liked to be called Major, whereas in fact he was only a captain. Dorothy herself was not over-impressed by the name, for she wrote to her parents, "He is called Mac to his friends and to you, because, of course, one could not call a person Atherton any more than Adolphus or Marmaduke."[8]

The self-important streak in Mac also led him to fantasize about the possibility that he was in actuality nothing less than the fourteenth Earl of Wigton. The Fleming family had owned lands at Biggar and Cumbernauld since the twelfth century. A Malcolm Fleming figures in Walter Scott's novel *Castle Dangerous* and his son, another Malcolm, was created Earl of Wigton by King David II of Scotland, son of Robert Bruce.

This earldom petered out with the death of the first earl's grandson, who died without issue. But it was re-created by James VI, who became James I of England when the kingdoms were united. Mac possessed two copies of a book on the history of the family: and a pencilled genealogical tree in his handwriting traces his claim to an earldom in the second line; though he must himself have been aware of the shakiness of his evidence (for his was by no means the only Fleming family in the British Isles), or he would surely have pressed his claim.

Mac (as I shall henceforward call him) was twelve years older than Dorothy. At the age of sixteen he joined the Fourth Battalion, Durham Light Infantry; but this was not an active service battalion, and the following year he got himself discharged from it in order to go to South Africa for active service with Rimington's Horse in the Boer War – during which he also acted, according to Dorothy, as Special War Correspondent to a magazine called *Black and White*.

In 1911 he married Winifred Meyrick. They lived first near Coventry, where he seems to have done publicity and other journalism for car manufacturers – particularly Daimler; and in 1914 they moved to Sussex.

He was commissioned in the Royal Army Service Corps as a second lieutenant in May 1915, and spent most of the war with the Twenty-Sixth Siege Brigade, Royal Artillery. Again he combined soldiering with journalism, this time as Special Correspondent to the *Daily Chronicle* and *Sunday Chronicle*.

He did not emerge unscathed. He was gassed and he was shell-shocked. The R.A.S.C. was very far from the easy option some believed it to be, as Mac showed in one uncharacteristically serious description in his book, *How to See the Battlefields*:

Roads vanished under a sea of mud, guns got bogged down when they were moved up into position, ammunition lorries got stuck and ammunition – heavy stuff, 8-inch and 9.2 – had to be man-handled in order to keep the howitzers supplied.

October was one long nightmare to anybody unfortunate enough to be in the Somme area. Many and many a time did we pray that our particular lot would be sent up to the comparative comfort of the "Salient" at Ypres. I wonder if any of my readers remember the road to Hebuterne? That road broke the heart of more than one man on the ammunition supply. How the batteries ever got ammunition at all beats me hollow. And yet there are people who still think that the A.S.C. (M.T.) had a soft job! Some of them had no doubt, at the bases, but what about the poor devils who – many times – worked forty-eight hours on end, at least half of the time under shell-fire, plunging and wallowing in and out of shell-holes, lorries heavily laden with shells and cartridges, well over the axles in mud, no lights, and very often no food, and not the slightest protection in the way of trench or dug-out when the road was under fire? . . . Try to imagine what it must have been like to work without lights at night – battery positions cannot be reached in the daytime except on certain occasions – and when the least error of judgement or sleepiness on the part of the drivers might precipitate both lorry and contents into some huge shell-hole or minecrater.[9]

Mac rose to be Acting Captain in September 1917, and Captain in May 1918; and was still a Captain when he left the army in January 1919. With characteristic bravado he forfeited his pension at the end of the war by discharging himself from military hospital – little knowing what the long-term effects of his physical and psychological injuries were going to be. For the moment he was perfectly capable of earning a living. He resumed his journalistic career, and swiftly cashed in on public interest by writing *How to See the Battlefields*, a combination of tourist guide and personal memoirs of the war.

His style was well suited to this kind of journalistic recollection: vigorous and forthright, if hardly refined. His attempts at fiction, however, exemplified in the bits of manuscript we possess, show a dreadful forced heartiness (a man scratching his head is described as "subduing his occipital irritation") that makes it obvious why he never succeeded in this field. This did not discourage him from writing *The Craft of the Short Story* in 1935 (albeit under the pseudonym of Maconochie, his mother's maiden name), in which he cheerfully recommended the kind of simplicity that his own work so notably lacked.

His journalism, however, prospered; and by the time he married Dorothy he was a correspondent of the *News of the World*, specializing in the reporting of motor-racing and crime – another interest that he and Dorothy shared.

There seem to have been other odd jobs on magazines and so forth at this time, but they were of such a casual nature that it is impossible to trace them. Mac was a man full of projects, some of which we know about, very few of which actually came to anything and most of which sank without trace.

Mac might not at first sight appear to be the ideal partner for Dorothy; in fact he combined a number of the characteristics which we have come to know appealed to her strongly. Like John Cournos, he had travelled widely and had stirring tales to tell of many parts of the world. Like Bill, and unlike John Cournos, he was a motoring enthusiast; and he had his fair share of panache – on one occasion, having run out of petrol, he is said to have driven his Daimler home on whisky. Also, rather unexpectedly, he was interested in, and knowledgeable about, good food – one of Dorothy's abiding interests. Though he was not by any means a first-rate writer, at least he appreciated the problems involved in writing, and as a crime reporter he could help Dorothy with her detective stories. He dabbled in painting, and he had an interest in photography. And on top of this, from every account of those who knew him in those early days, he was a charmer – a cheerful, down-to-earth, friendly, considerate man, amusing and unpretentious, with the ability to make a woman feel interesting and important. He offered that "decent kindliness" that Dorothy in her misery had begged for as a boon beyond price.

We may reasonably guess that he had one other virtue in Dorothy's eyes – that he was good in bed. We have no reason to suppose that she had anybody but Bill (briefly) and Mac (at leisure) to give her the understanding of lovemaking that she shows in her letter about Dante; and I think we are entitled to assume from her cheerfully knowledgeable tone that Mac passed muster.

The marriage was hardly likely to be popular at home. Dorothy had been christened in Christ Church Cathedral, Oxford, and confirmed in Salisbury Cathedral; and it was her father's dearest wish that she should also be married in a cathedral. She knew what a shock the news would be and, fighting her instinct for drama, contrived in her letter to play the thing down so effectively that it emerged as a kind of after-thought to her comments on the more exciting news that Uncle Cecil, twice married already, had been carrying on with a lady in the potting shed – "I feel inclined to congratulate him – at his time of life and with his infirmities I feel it argues a great deal of vitality of spirits." Then came, out of the blue, the thunderbolt:

In the meantime, I am getting married on Tuesday (weather permitting!) to a man named Fleming, who is at the moment motoring correspondent to the *News of the World* and otherwise engaged in journalism. No money, but a good job, forty-two [he was in fact forty-four] and otherwise eminently suitable and all that . . . I didn't mention this before, because it's our own business and I don't want an avalanche of interrogation from all sorts of people; so I thought I'd wait until Aunt G. and Aunt Maud had cleared off from Christchurch, as it might have been awkward for you to have them there and not tell them. . . . No flowers by request! – if all is well, we propose coming down to Christchurch at Whitsun and making an exhibition of ourselves then!

That letter was dated April 8 1926. We know, from villagers who remember the day it arrived, what distress it caused to Dorothy's parents; especially her father. But her mother managed to write back in just the terms that Dorothy had hoped, apparently taking matters in her stride. And on April 14 Dorothy wrote:

> Dear Mother, meant to send you a card last night, but nobody had any stamps and we had all overeaten and over-drunk ourselves. I understand that, the news having seeped out, the whole of Fleet Street, incapably drunk, decorated the bar of the Falstaff last night, and for all I know they are still there.
> We were "turned off" as the hangman says, in the salubrious purlieux of the registrar's office in the Clerkenwell Road.

And so, with a touch of characteristic panache, making the best of what life offered her, Dorothy embarked upon matrimony.

After all the emotional turmoil, she was no longer holding out for romance, or even for a proper church wedding – which would of course have been impossible in view of Mac's divorce. For a woman with Dorothy's love of ceremonial, of dressing-up and giving every occasion its full dramatic value, this was a sad admission of what circumstances had brought her to. But the triviality of the wedding must have seemed to her appropriate for such a shop-soiled couple.

Dorothy always insisted that the one doctrine of the Church of which she was emotionally as well as intellectually convinced was the doctrine of sin; and of course for a convinced Anglo-Catholic, her registry office marriage was not valid. In the eyes of the Church, she was living in sin with a man who was still married to his former wife. This awareness, added to the secret of her illegitimate child, must have nagged at her considerably – an intermittent spiritual sore, spoiling that wholesomeness and serenity of life that she longed for. In later years, when she so vehemently asserted the eternal and unbreakable truth of the Church's spiritual laws, it must have been particularly tiresome. She was not a lady to suffer excessively from remorse when she had done the best she could in the circumstances. But she could never again be in a true state of grace; for the Church's doctrine states that though any sin, however grievous, can be repented and pardoned, true repentance must involve abstaining from sin, and pardon can only follow upon true repentance. This may be the reason why, when she went home to Christchurch for weekends, it was noted by the villagers that as often as not she did not go to church. The vigour with which in later years she hammered the unbeliever was not so much that of the saved exulting over the damned, as of the soul in peril warning others of the dangers to be avoided.

The practical fact, however, was that Dorothy now had a man; a merciful God would no doubt take the circumstances into account. At last she could get on with life – and with writing. She and Wimsey were now established. Where did they go from here?

CHAPTER ELEVEN

DOROTHY HAD NO illusions about Lord Peter Wimsey. She had designed him as a breadwinner, not a figure of literary importance. For her own satisfaction she had decided to give him touches of class that would put him ahead of some of his rivals, but a breadwinner was what, first and foremost, he must continue to be.

Theories on the subject of Wimsey's origins have been many and varied. It is always entertaining to pin down some living person as the original of a fictitious character; and with many writers this is perfectly legitimate. Such writers deliberately take their models from life, and identifying them is part of the literary game of tracking down the intentions and the achievement of the author.

Dorothy was not like this. With the exception of her self-portraits in *Cat o' Mary* and to some extent elsewhere, her writing was of the other kind: the kind in which experience is absorbed and digested and transformed into something completely new and different before being released as fiction. Dorothy herself gave the process a great deal of thought and described it a number of times; one of her most interesting and original books deals entirely with the activity of the creative mind. So let us put together a number of her statements, and then we shall have an idea of the extent to which Lord Peter Wimsey was, and was not, Eric Whelpton, John Cournos, the chaplain of Balliol or any other claimant for the title of real-life original of one of the most memorable and enduring detectives in the whole who-dunnit range:

(1) The unscrupulous old ruffian inside one who does the actual writing doesn't care tuppence where he gets his actual raw material from – fantasy, memory, observation, odds and ends of reading and sheer invention are all grist to his mill, and he mixes everything up together regardless.[1]

(2) . . . what happens in the writer's mind is something like this. When making a character he in a manner separates and incarnates a part of his own living mind. He recognizes in himself a powerful emotion – let us say, jealousy. His activity then takes this form: supposing this emotion were to become so strong as to dominate my whole personality, how should I feel and how should I behave? In imagination

he becomes the jealous person and thinks and feels within that frame of experience. . . .[2]

(3) . . . there are two ways of creating a fictitious character; one, the more superficial perhaps, is to take observed behaviour and try to deduce from it the motives from which it springs. The other is to take some passing mood of one's own mind and say to oneself, if this fleeting mood were to become a dominant attitude of mind, what would my behaviour be under given circumstances? Putting aside the accidental attributes that an amateur detective must possess to get through his work without too much outside help – such, for example, as money, leisure, physical endurance, and the tricks of this or that trade – the essential Peter is seen to be the familiar figure of the inter- pretative artist, the romantic soul at war with a realistic brain.[3]

(4) I do not, as a matter of fact, remember inventing Lord Peter at all. My impression is that I was thinking about writing a detective story, and that he walked in, complete with spats, and applied in an airy don't-care-if-I-get-it way for the job of hero. The name "Peter Wimsey" was on his card all right, but I distinctly recall that at that time he was a mere Honourable, and said that his brother was the Earl of Denver. Later on, I decided to give the whole family a step up, ad- vancing the brother to a Dukedom, and giving Peter the courtesy title of a Duke's younger son. But for a long time I was haunted by the recollection of their former undistinguished position, and that is why, in *Clouds of Witness*, the Duke is twice referred to as "Lord Denver", which is all wrong.

At the first interview Wimsey informed me that he had a rather at- tractive mother, to whom he was much attached, and an immaculate "gentleman's gentleman", Bunter by name. Later on, I gathered more details about his personal tastes and habits. I also discovered that he was two years older than myself. This difference in age per- sisted, and we are looking forward to growing old together.

Lord Peter's large income (the source of which, by the way, I have never investigated) was a different matter. I deliberately gave him that. After all, it cost me nothing, and at the time I was particularly hard up, and it gave me pleasure to spend his fortune for him.[4]

Those quotations are spread over a number of years, and they vary in the seriousness with which they were written. But they all tell the same story; Lord Peter Wimsey was a purely literary figure, invented for a specific purpose out of all the bits and pieces of experience that Dorothy could bring to his creation. Since her experience was very largely literary, Wimsey's progenitors were mostly literary figures. The silly-ass aristocrat with the nerve of steel, who is he but Sir Percy Blakeney, the Scarlet Pimpernel himself? But being a modern silly-ass (in 1921), who does he take his cue from but Bertie Wooster? – who must of course be accompanied by his Jeeves, now transmogrified into Bunter.

As a blood-and-thunder addict from early days, Dorothy knew what the market wanted; and while she was prepared to let Wimsey mock at some of the absurdities of the fictional detective, she had no objection to using some of them herself if they suited her. So Wimsey was an all-purpose superman, and whatever the script required of him he was able to do effortlessly – if inexplicably. When, for example, did he find the time for the exercise to keep his wrists and fingers supple enough to play Scarlatti with the touch of a master, yet strong enough to grip the arms of strong men with a grip that they never forgot? We may believe that his discrimination in wine was finer than that of any other man in Europe, for he drank a great deal of it, and had the means to buy whatever he wanted. But we have no reason to suppose that he took any interest in swimming, except for the one occasion when, in a skin-tight harlequin's costume, he amazed the spectators by diving like an otter into a shallow pool from a great height. In short he was a fantasy figure, fun to read about and fun to write about. This is part of the game, but literature it is not.

Dorothy being the person she was, it is not surprising that Wimsey's intellectual wizardry is more convincing than his physical exploits. James Bond, a superman who shares with his distinguished ancestor a taste for all that is best in civilized living, is precisely the opposite. His physical adventures have a rich circumstantial detail, while his intellectual achievements are barely touched upon.

The main attribute Bond and Wimsey have in common is their sexual prowess. Dorothy was not averse to a little titillation, and she delicately but clearly gives us to understand that her hero, perfect in this respect as in all others, is also a flawless lover – courteous and understanding, but tigerish in bed.

Unlike James Bond, Wimsey learnt his amorous technique in France. All his early love-affairs were with Continental women – to such an extent indeed that when he finally wishes to make love to an Englishwoman he involuntarily lapses into French. It is not merely that French is conventionally the language of l'amour; for Dorothy the language conveys a whole outlook, a mode of life, first encountered at Les Roches, which the English language could not adequately describe; and which surely intrigued and fascinated her at the time, with her lack of physical experience, her long thin English body and her very English background.

For the reader, the fact that the sexy passages are all in French (and quite difficult French) makes them all the more succulent and tantalizing; just as the sly description of the illustration to the fourteenth-century manuscript which Wimsey is reading in *The Unpleasantness at the Bellona Club* as "extremely delicate in workmanship, and not always equally so in subject",[5] leaves so much to the imagination that nothing made of flesh and blood could possibly match the delicious debauchery conjured up in the mind's eye.

This of course was the style of the day – it is not peculiar to Dorothy. But she made wholehearted use of it, and we are left with a picture of Peter Wimsey's love life – until he encountered Harriet Vane, the figure based on Dorothy herself – as one of exquisitely controlled voluptuousness, undisturbed by unseemly or discordant situations such as afflicted his creator.

We have one curious side-light on the first appearance of Peter Wimsey. A pair of manuscripts, one in Dorothy's handwriting and one in Mac's, tell almost identical stories in synopsis, using almost identical words, and then, still in identical words, make a start on the story itself; the main difference being that in Dorothy's version, the heroes are Sexton Blake and his assistant, Tinker, whereas in Mac's, Sexton Blake has been transformed into Lincoln Brayle, Tinker becoming Tony Blenkinsop. Mac's synopsis also introduces the beautiful spy Olga Petrovsky and sundry other fine clichés that Dorothy omits.

One must certainly have copied from the other. And a comparison of the two shows that Mac's version is the later. Dorothy has changed her mind about some of the names that occur in the story – for example crossing out "The Green Park Robbery Affair" and changing it to "The Sullivan Hotel Poisoning Affair". It is the latter that Mac has copied, with no more than an alteration to "The Sullivan Hotel Poisoning Case" to establish his individuality.

At first sight we envisage Dorothy and Mac playing together with an idea which in the end did not work out; doubtless because she decided to use one of the devices of the tale – a mistake made by the criminal in the gender of the French definite article – in a quite different short story, "The Article in Question".

This theory however is totally dashed as soon as we reach page five of Dorothy's manuscript, which, beginning at the second line, reads thus:

"Well, Monsieur Briffault was living in a flat in Piccadilly, lent him by Lord Peter Wimsey."

"Who's Lord Peter Wimsey?"

"I looked him up in *Who's Who*. Younger son of the Duke of Peter-borough. Harmless sort of fellow, I think. Distinguished himself in the war. Rides his own horse in the Grand National. Authority on first editions. At present visiting the Duchess in Herts. I've seen his photo somewhere. Fair haired, big nose, aristocratic sort of man whose socks match his tie. No politics."

Now what is Peter Wimsey doing playing a subsidiary role in a Sexton Blake story? It seems evident that, when she wrote this, Dorothy intended to join the many contributors to the great Sexton Blake saga, and that Lord Peter Wimsey had "walked in, complete with spats" without immediately announcing that he intended to be the hero. The paragraph that describes his entry in *Who's Who* is an instant thumbnail sketch, which Dorothy might easily have dashed off in two minutes, out-lining an amusing secondary character to her story. He is already the younger son of a duke, but here it is the Duke of Peterborough, not of Denver. Otherwise, apart from the fact that never, in all the novels and short stories in which he was finally to figure, did he ride his own horse in a Grand National, this is already the Peter whom the world came to know and love.

Everything points to the conclusion that this manuscript was written before *Whose Body?* – five years before Dorothy met Mac – and that it is indeed Lord Peter Wimsey's first appearance on any page. In which case we must assume that Mac came across the manuscript years after Dorothy abandoned it, and decided either to adapt it as a story of his own or perhaps to use it as an exercise. But why did Dorothy abandon the story? Possibly because she wished to use the device of the French definite article elsewhere, but more probably because she realized that Lord Peter was much too good a character to be wasted in a Sexton Blake story – he must be given a starring role of his own.

The character of Wimsey, and various other elements in the books, have led to outraged accusations of snobbishness, anti-semitism, and intellectual arrogance. In fact this is not quite fair. Certainly Dorothy regarded the nobility as people "to love and laugh at",[6] as she admitted in her lecture on "The Importance of Being Vulgar" in 1936 – claiming that in this respect she was in tune with the common people. If this is snobbishness, it is a very mild form, hardly to be taken seriously. Had Dorothy been a true snob, she would have accepted without question all the goings-on in Wimsey's family. In fact her portrait of the Duke of Denver, Wimsey's brother, is of an amiable but fairly brainless fellow, with a boy-scout code of honour; and her delineation of Helen, his

Duchess, a genuine snob whose life is determined by class, rank and wealth, is savage in the extreme.

As to anti-semitism, Dorothy was as ready to criticize Jews as she was to criticize any other minority group. Moreover, she was not above drawing stereotyped characters, Jews among them; and she was prepared to allow the characters in her books to make anti-semitic remarks if this was appropriate to them. But her portrait of Sir Reuben Levy in her first book is not unsubtle, and is in some respects quite sympathetic.

The one characteristic of Dorothy's writing which might reasonably be considered offensive (and it is the connecting link between all the more specific sins of which she has been accused) is an air of rather patronizing superiority towards mankind in general. She patronizes the upper classes as much as the lower classes, and the Scotsman as much as the Jew. Today we are particularly sensitive to anything that smacks of anti-semitism or anything that seems to question the qualities of the "common man", and it is these particular areas of patronization that strike us, while others are passed by without question. Few of us can be absolved of some prejudice against someone, and when our prejudices coincide with those of the writer, we have no complaint. Indeed, it is rather satisfying and delightful to share a sense of superiority with the writer. For her day and age, Dorothy calculated her readership with great accuracy. A few protested at the time about her snobbishness, but a great many more rejoiced in the sense that they were being allowed to share in the author's elevated viewpoint. Throughout history, people have always preferred, when they step from reality into fiction, to move up a notch or two on the scale, whether it be social, athletic, intellectual or what-have-you. Whatever the subconscious process that produced Wimsey, he was the product as much of his public's weaknesses as his creator's.

One interesting aspect of Wimsey's character is its capacity for development: there is a considerable difference between the Wimsey of the early novels and the later. The description of him playing Scarlatti in *Whose Body?* is a piece of rather perfunctory character colouring, perhaps suggested by Sherlock Holmes's playing of the violin. But when in *Gaudy Night* he takes Harriet to hear the Bach Double Violin Concerto in a concert at Balliol, we are in a different world: "Peter, she felt sure, could hear the whole intricate pattern, every part separately and simultaneously, each independent and equal, separate but inseparable, moving over and under and through, ravishing heart and mind together."[7] A real man, in love with a real woman, is listening with true attention to marvellous music which symbolizes the kind of relationship he wants with her – a relationship not of placid and unadventurous harmony but of sharp counterpoint, each partner equal, neither subservient, yet both, whether going their separate ways or blending together, contributing their share towards a rich and satisfying result.

It is a mark of the soundness of Dorothy's original instinct that the later, mature Wimsey is all there in embryo in his earlier, sketchier self. The nervous agony that he undergoes at the end of the last novel, *Busman's Honeymoon*, is prepared for by his nightmares in the first, *Whose Body?* – nightmares brought on by his experience of being buried alive by an explosion during the First World War. The most noticeable change is that gradually, through the course of the novels, Wimsey drops the pose of the monocled silly-ass which Dorothy borrowed from P. G. Wodehouse's Bertie Wooster. For the rest, all that happened to Wimsey was that he grew up – or at any rate we all, Dorothy included, came to know him better.

Wimsey's arrival coincided with a crucial development in the field of crime writing – the point at which the formula detective began to take on humanity. The creature who previously existed only for his function in the plot, now begins to exist for his own sake, as a human being in his own right. We cannot, I am afraid, give Dorothy sole credit for this transformation. E. C. Bentley had already done it in *Trent's Last Case*, a book for which Dorothy publicly proclaimed her admiration in an article written on the occasion of its adaptation for radio. And privately, in a letter to Bentley himself, she acknowledged her debt: "I am always ashamed to admit how much my poor Peter owes to Trent, besides his habit of quotation."[8]

But even after we have added E. C. Bentley to all the other literary influences, there is still something in Peter Wimsey which is specifically Dorothy's contribution. That power of observation and analysis, both of herself and of others, which we find in the letters and writings of her adolescence, adds a special touch which is unmistakable. But more than this – her passionate intellectual curiosity and her fierce convictions about life, combined with her hard-won literary craftsmanship, ensure that Peter Wimsey is more than the sum of his parts. In Dorothy, the creative mind made its subconscious selection, marinated the ingredients, shook, stirred, simmered and let them settle – and a new creature emerged without Dorothy being aware where he had come from. So if Dorothy describes Peter Wimsey as looking "with his long, narrow face, like a melancholic adjutant stork",[9] and if we find that Eric Whelpton possessed a stork-like profile, that is not by any means to say that Eric Whelpton was Peter Wimsey, any more than a pinch of tarragon is a dish of Suprême de Volaille St Georges. But the dish would not be the same without the tarragon, and it may be that Peter Wimsey would not have been the same without Eric Whelpton. That is as much as one can say.

Though Dorothy clearly enjoyed Wimsey, and enjoyed writing the books, it is pleasing to find that she never became besotted with him, or complacent about him. She could hardly prevent him becoming an important part of her life, and she knew only too well that he was her passport to freedom from advertising and from the slavery of office hours. Nor had she any illusions about his artistic value. She liked writing about him, because she liked writing. But she had doubts about almost every book she wrote about him – "a silly book"[10] . . . "a disagreeable book"[11] . . . "rather a rotten story"[12] . . . "I hate it because it isn't the one I wanted to write"[13] . . . "not altogether satisfactory . . . it just wouldn't come right. . . ."[14]

She did not deceive herself, as some writers might have done (indeed as she did herself about some of her later works), that these books had some special value simply because she had written them. She always thought of herself as a poet rather than a prose writer, and contrary to general opinion, which assumed that the detective story writer was the "real" Dorothy L. Sayers and her transformation into a religious verse dramatist later in life was some inexplicable aberration, her own view of the matter was that Wimsey was the aberration, annoying but necessary, and that the real Dorothy Sayers lay dormant throughout the writing of those novels.

There is no place in this book for a critical analysis of the Wimsey novels. That has been done, excellently, elsewhere. But the story of her life must necessarily be reflected in her writing to some extent, and vice versa. And for my part I believe that the public's view of her work is more accurate in some ways than her own. Precisely because Dorothy did not regard the Wimsey novels as her "serious" work, she actually put into them more of herself and of her own fresh and personal observation of life than she ever did into the plays and poems, where one feels that Literature, Tradition and Scholarship lay a somewhat clammy hand on the brightness of the work.

The scholar in her had to come out, however, even in her detective work. She probably gave more thought and consideration to the nature and purpose of the detective novel than any other writer in that genre. Dorothy and Muriel Jaeger had already played their mock scholarly games with the Sexton Blake stories, and with her voracious appetite for such tales, her phenomenal memory and her analytical mind, she approached the subject as its foremost theorist as well as a practitioner.

In addition to her craftsmanship, her intelligence, and her joy in writing, Dorothy contributed a unique brand of cheerful vulgarity. Well aware of this trait, she defended herself fiercely in her lecture, already mentioned, on "The Importance of being Vulgar". A reviewer had accused her of being as vulgar as any author from *Peg's Paper*, and she eagerly embraced the charge:

> It is, of course, all too easy to be vulgar without being great; it is not nearly so easy to be great without being vulgar – indeed it is almost impossible in any activity which brings one into contact with one's fellow creatures. . . . The two great queens who have adorned our history were each the very embodiment of the common people of their time and that was the secret of their greatness as rulers. . . . I am quite sure that my own notion of a lord as something to love and laugh at is not due, as the reviewer thinks, to astuteness, but to my sheer unmitigated commonness. I like the common people and I heartily share their love of a lord because I am myself as common as mud in my likes and dislikes.[15]

This vulgarity, this loudness, this touch of bad taste, tastefully carried out – qualities that made her so successful in advertising – were also an essential element in the style that made her novels best-sellers. Her prose is fastidious; her images bold, melodramatic, often indelicate. The pince-nez on the naked body in the bath add a touch of absurd obscenity to the opening scene of her first book. In the second, *Clouds of Witness*, she embellishes a story of murderous passions and suicidal jealousies with the panoply of a trial in the House of Lords, and a last-minute flight across the Atlantic by Wimsey, carrying the vital clue through darkness and tempest – a pretty bold touch, for although a number of planes had made the crossing since 1919, it was still a very novel and hazardous business. The first solo crossing – Lindbergh's historic flight – did not take place till a year after the book appeared, and even the incomparable Lord Peter was not credited with piloting the plane himself.

In her next book, *Unnatural Death*, Dorothy presents her readers with a woman who is not only a ruthless killer but a mistress of disguise and a lesbian to boot, who tries to lure Wimsey to his death by seducing him first, but gives herself away to that experienced man of the bedroom by her inability to kiss with convincing heterosexual passion. Even in her most academic book of all, *Gaudy Night*, where the characters are mostly spinster dons in an Oxford women's college and the plot concerned with intellectual integrity, the clues consist of obscene drawings of the naked female form – a fine stroke of vulgarity in those surroundings, as well as being ripe with psychological possibilities.

Dorothy wrote only twelve detective novels. These appeared between 1923 and 1937 – an average of less than one a year. Only Agatha Christie, among her rivals, has survived half so well from that period; and she continued to write from that time almost up to her recent death in 1976, completing something like eighty books. Dorothy was not one of those writers who keep hold of their readers by producing new adventures ad infinitum. Her admirers go back to those few books time and again, because they offer more than simply a mystery which, once it is solved, leaves the reader's interest exhausted.

Oddly enough, though Wimsey is the central creation of the stories and the figure whom we all remember, he is not the one who best shows Dorothy's feeling for human qualities. We learn a great deal about how the world sees Wimsey – much less about how Wimsey sees the world. He is seen mainly from the outside, an object to admire rather than comprehend.

As one might suppose, it is through the eyes of a woman that Dorothy begins to show us a world of every-day human beings. Miss Climpson, to whom we are introduced in *Unnatural Death*, belongs to that group of people who were all too familiar to Dorothy Sayers – indeed to Europe in general in the years after the First World War – the army of ageing spinsters. For Dorothy, brought up among spinster aunts and barely escaping spinsterhood herself, Miss Climpson was someone she fully understood and sympathized with. Wimsey was fabricated for a purpose – Miss Climpson came from the heart.

Miss Climpson and her little Employment Bureau for unmarried ladies are financed by Wimsey partly for his own detection purposes, and partly from a recognition of the fact that great quantities of untapped intelligent woman-power could go to waste in a society which has found for these ladies no substitute for marriage. When occasion serves, Miss Climpson and her minions are sent out on fact-finding expeditions, acting on the assumption that no one is less likely to excite suspicion than an inquisitive gossipy spinster. Any community will yield up its secrets to a respectable maiden lady joining the local group of church helpers. Thus Dorothy made good use of her vicarage upbringing and her cat-like observation of that world where, beneath a veil of euphemism, nothing went unobserved or without comment, and the seemingly innocent were in fact sharply observant, extremely well-informed and virtually unshockable.

One of the more memorable features of the character of Miss Climpson is the style of the letters which she writes to Lord Peter about her progress with the investigation. All capital letters, underlinings and exclamation marks, the style was derived from Dorothy's Aunt Gertrude, and Dorothy, voluminous letter-writer that she was herself, clearly enjoyed this form of character-drawing and story-telling; so much so that a year or two after the invention of Miss Climpson, she decided to write a whole novel in the form of letters, reports, and other papers.

The form had been initiated by Samuel Richardson two hundred years before, in the very early years of the English novel. Dorothy had read Richardson and had commented that one of the characters in *Sir Charles Grandison* was remarkably like herself. There is even a theory that Lord Peter Wimsey was based on Sir Charles Grandison himself, but this I find totally unconvincing. Grandison was a humourless stick, quite lacking in Wimsey's irony and self-mockery, and without a trace of his facetious flippancy.

All the eight vast volumes of *Sir Charles Grandison* are written in the epistolary form. A much later example, and one nearer to her heart, was *The Moonstone*, by Dorothy's admired Wilkie Collins. Throughout her novel-writing career, Dorothy was for ever searching for variations of style and approach, and she must have welcomed the epistolary novel as a vehicle for one of her great skills.

To write fictional letters, one must inevitably enter into the minds of the writers; and it is an interesting confirmation of the view that Dorothy never got far inside the mind of Wimsey, to find that *The Documents in the Case* is the only crime novel she wrote in which Wimsey does not appear. It is essential to the mystique of the super-sleuth that he should keep much of his observation and deduction to himself until the ripe dramatic moment. He could have no place in a story about real people writing each other letters through which, little by little, the full situation is revealed.

The interesting point about *The Documents in the Case* is that it gave full scope to the dramatist in Dorothy. To create rounded characters, the dramatist has to see the situation from the point of view of all the participants, and give each of them a valid reaction to it. A novelist can get away with characters seen wholly from the outside – but not if the novel is written in the form of letters. Much of the fun, as well as the interest, in *The Documents in the Case* comes from the way in which Dorothy can quite brilliantly give us the thoughts and responses of one person, making them reasonable and justifiable, and then, through the eyes of another, show the reactions of the first as being irritating, egomaniacal, or

completely incomprehensible. More rewarding still is the instance when
Dorothy shows us a man who appears futile and insignificant to his wife
and even to himself, but in the eyes of one man who gets to know him
well is seen to have elements of true greatness and heroism.

Another of the great strengths of *The Documents in the Case* is its conclusion: the solution to the murder emerges from a religious and
philosophical discussion which shows at its best Dorothy's combination
of academic expertise and flair for dialogue and character drawing.

Dorothy often used some little-known scientific fact as the clue to the
method of murder – in *Unnatural Death*, for example, the murder is committed by injecting something totally undetectable into a vein – a bubble
of air. Interesting and ingenious – but Dorothy is not interested in the
philosophical implications of air in the blood stream, even supposing
that such implications existed. Peter Wimsey, prompted by an air lock in
the fuel system of a motorcycle, matches the murder's ingenuity with his
own, and there's an end of it. But in *The Documents in the Case* the clue has
to do with the very nature of life itself – the difference between an
organic and an inorganic substance.

The victim is a mushroom collector, and dies of a poison called
muscarine, found in the mushroom Amanita Muscaria. Muscarine,
however, can also be prepared synthetically – and there is only one
difference between the natural and the synthetic substance; one is optically active and the other optically inactive, and the only way to deter-
mine which is which is with a polariscope. If the victim can be proved to
have been poisoned by the synthetic rather than the natural substance,
murder is proved.

The Documents in the Case is the only book of Dorothy's in which she
shared the authorship with another writer – Robert Eustace, alias Dr
Eustace Barton. Barton had collaborated with one or two other crime
writers, and had also been responsible for some detective stories of his
own. As a medical man, he was able to supply technical backgrounds for
murders, but for *The Documents in the Case* he provided much more. He it
was who first suggested the plot, adding:

> . . . we can introduce some very deep and interesting questions into
> the mushroom story – the subtle difference between what is produced
> by life and that artificially produced by man. The molecular
> asymmetry of Organic Products marks the difference between the
> chemistry of dead matter and the chemistry of living matter, and this
> touches on the most fundamental problems of the phenomena of life
> itself.[16]

Barton also suggested the form of the end of the book, very much as

Dorothy finally wrote it, even to the image of the corpse-like faces clustered round the polariscope in the sodium flare.

Shortly after the book appeared, Barton was thrown into considerable alarm when a correspondent wrote to say that natural muscarine was not strictly speaking a protein, though closely related, and did not share with proteins the characteristic of being optically active. The polariscope would therefore show no difference between the natural and the synthetic muscarine, and the climax of the story was based on a scientific fallacy.

Dorothy was amused rather than perturbed by this revelation, judging, I think quite correctly, that the story stood up pretty well nevertheless. She always reckoned that, despite her best efforts, there were certain to be "howlers" in all her books, and the best way of dealing with them was to be philosophical about it.

Barton was deeply apologetic. He had considered this to be the best idea he had ever had, and an error of this magnitude would do no good to his credibility as a technical adviser. He went over the ground again, with great thoroughness, and a year after the book came out had to admit that he certainly seemed to have got it wrong.

Fortunately, the certainties of scientists can prove as frail as anything else in the mortal world; and a year later still he was able to write to Dorothy that further research showed that "although the *structure* of muscarine is still in dispute among these learned gentlemen, there is no doubt about its optical activity, and that is the whole point as far as we are concerned. It is very comforting after all the agonies and criticisms we had."[17]

The Documents in the Case gives the first indication that Dorothy might have become a significant novelist, had she been able to rid herself of Wimsey. We know that, at this stage in her career, this is precisely what she had in mind, and to this end Wimsey, almost from the moment that he next appears before the public, has undergone an important and far-reaching change. He is in love – and in love, it is hardly too much to say, with Dorothy Sayers.

The first two chapters of *Strong Poison* are an account of the trial of a young woman charged with murdering her lover. The woman, Harriet Vane, is a writer of detective novels and lives in a flat at No. 100 Doughty Street – just round the corner from where Dorothy had her own flat. She has, according to the dowager Duchess, Wimsey's mother, "a really remarkable face, though perhaps not strictly good-looking, and all the more interesting for that, because good-looking people are so often cows". She also has "a curious, deep voice" and "a steady gaze".[18] She is not the whole Dorothy Sayers, certainly, but she is very close to what Dorothy thought best about herself.

Peter's first meeting with Harriet is in prison, where he goes to offer his help in proving her innocence; and to ask her to marry him. He is a man with long experience of love affairs; he has come to believe that love is a myth and that friendly physical satisfaction is all that a man and a woman can give each other; he has only seen Harriet Vane for the time that she has been in the witness box; and yet he proposes marriage. So abrupt, even perfunctory, is his falling in love.

This, surely, is the moment for us to be taken inside the mind and heart of Wimsey; but Dorothy never even attempts it. We are given no idea what it is about Harriet that bowls him over so completely.

An article that Dorothy published in 1937 suggests the only possible answer. She was sick of Wimsey. She wanted to be rid of him. She wanted to move on towards the writing of proper novels, without the detective element. To this end she decided to get Wimsey married, and she was not too particular how she did it.

She did not, however, want his disappearance to be irreversible. She was sufficiently aware that Wimsey represented money in the bank for her; and she knew, of course, of the sad case of Conan Doyle who, having in the same way and for the same reasons killed off his hero, Sherlock Holmes, was forced to bring him back by a miraculous escape from the certain death that had apparently awaited him at the Reichenbach Falls. By marrying Peter off, she hoped to rid the world of him as a serious detective, while leaving open the possibility of bringing him back into service if she absolutely had to. At this stage, therefore, Harriet Vane was simply a means to this end, and rather an indulgent one. (It would be amusing, and not particularly surprising, to find Dorothy fully aware of this and acknowledging her own vanity in the name of her heroine.)

Had things gone according to plan, the indulgence would have been short-lived, for Harriet would no doubt have disappeared along with Peter. In *The Documents in the Case* Dorothy had tasted the joys of freedom from Wimsey, and *Strong Poison* was merely a matter of regularizing her divorce from him, clearing up a few loose ends and packing her bags.

Circumstances, however, were too much for her. To be able to live without Wimsey, she would have needed the security of some income from elsewhere, for in her writing she would have had to start wooing the public all over again. But by the time she wrote *Strong Poison*, with those treacherous thoughts in mind of palming Wimsey off on her alter ego, Harriet, and so whisking him off the bookstalls, such security had gone for ever. Much had happened to her, as well as to Wimsey, in the four years since she had married Mac.

CHAPTER TWELVE

YOUNG JOHN ANTHONY was still with Ivy. (Though later he was known as Anthony, at this stage he was always called John.) A crisis had threatened in April 1925, when Ivy's mother died and Mrs Sayers went to Oxford to stay with Ivy and help her over the shock; and of course met John Anthony.

Dorothy wrote to Ivy, honourably offering that "if things should become acutely difficult, you can always shove John off on to mother and tell her and I will come and explain"; adding, however, "but I think it would be rather a nuisance, what with Aunt Mabel and the Parish. I would rather like to wait until later. Tell me what mother thinks of him!"[1]

That situation was avoided; but it was not the only threat to their arrangements. Ivy's future came under discussion, and Helen Sayers advised her to give up the children altogether and seek other employment. Dorothy (not altogether disinterested) disagreed. She wrote both to Ivy and to her mother arguing that it would be hard for Ivy not to be her own mistress after so many years of independence; in any case she had not the qualifications for the kind of job that she might enjoy. And, fortunately for her and for John Anthony, this view prevailed.

About the same time, Ivy had a disagreement with her landlords, a couple whom she deemed socially inferior to herself, and with whose children she did not wish "her" children to mix. Dorothy, though she may have been something of a snob in her way, deplored this particular form of snobbishness.

Matters were straightened out, however: John Anthony stayed with Ivy and with Isabel, the older foster child (the other two having left), and Ivy stayed in Oxford – though she did begin to think about moving.

In the early years of her marriage Dorothy had high hopes that Mac would welcome John Anthony into the household. She had written to Ivy that Mac "seems quite satisfied to throw the eye of affection and responsibility over John Anthony in the future. This seems to settle the difficulty we felt as to his needing a boy's school and a firm hand in a month or two!"[2] She went on to say that the plan was not yet to have John Anthony actually living with them, since they were both continuing to work, and there would be no room in her London flat; but it is clear what she had in mind for the near future. Indeed she later claimed that

Mac had specifically agreed that sooner or later they would "adopt" the
boy and have him to live with them.

Financially, too, things were looking up. She had reported, in the
same letter that announced her imminent marriage, that *Clouds of
Witness*, which had been a constant burden for four miserable years, was
finally on the bookstalls and had had a remarkably good press. From
horizon to horizon the skies were clearing.

As we have seen, Dorothy was not much interested in politics, and the
General Strike of 1926 passed without more than a casual comment as to
its inconvenience, and to the fact that Mac spent most of the day in
headphones, listening to the news on the wireless.

Other matters were more important: the visits to Brooklands, where
Mac was not only a correspondent but on occasions an organizer of race
meetings; the virtues and vices of the "Ner-a-Car", a motorcycle-
sidecar combination that flourished and faded that summer; and the
purchase of a real motorcar, a Belsize Bradshaw 2/3 seater coupé, about
which Dorothy had serious misgivings – fully justified, as it turned out.
Then there was the shared delight in food, for Mac was an excellent
cook, and provided all the meals when Dorothy's parents came to stay
for a few days in London. Contributing a year or two later to a correspondence in the *Evening Standard* about perfect man-servants,
Dorothy wrote:

> I have a first-class, experienced male chef, capable of turning out a
> perfect dinner for any number of people, who not only demands no
> salary, but also contributes to the support of the household. I came
> across this paragon some years ago, and, having sampled his cooking
> and ascertained that he held sound opinions on veal (which I detest)
> and garlic (which I appreciate), married him. So far, the arrangement
> seems to work very well, and, since giving me notice would be a
> troublesome and expensive matter, I am hoping he will stay.[3]

It was a time of pride and happiness, marred only by a few early worries
about Mac's weak stomach, a legacy from the gas clouds of the war.

Clouds of Witness was selling reasonably well, and Dorothy was at work
on *Unnatural Death*. But her greatest success at this time, though
anonymous, was the work that she did for Benson's. Thundering down
the famous spiral staircase at Kingsway Hall, her beloved cloak floating
behind her (her office was at the top of the staircase, John Gilroy's at the
bottom), or striding about on her thick legs, flat heeled, with one hand
wielding her cigarette holder, the other stuck in the pocket of her little
black jacket, she was a memorable figure. Well able to flatten opposi-

tion, she was far from being in any danger of losing her job and might well in due course have become a director of Benson's had she had the inclination – or so John Gilroy believed.

Gilroy, who today is Sir John Gilroy and a highly distinguished portrait painter, was then a young artist supplementing his meagre fees from the Royal College of Art by designing for advertising agencies; and he and Dorothy worked closely together on several advertising campaigns which became classics of their kind. For Colman's they helped to invent the Mustard Club; and for Guinness they devised the Zoo advertisements, variations of which still appear today. Many people still remember Dorothy's original jingle that accompanied Gilroy's picture of the Toucan, his great bill poised over two glasses of Guinness:

> If he can say as you can
> Guinness is good for you
> How grand to be a Toucan
> Just think what Toucan do.

Dorothy's contribution to the campaigns did not stop at the words. It was often her rough scribbles which inspired designs which Gilroy then perfected and got credit for. "I adored this character – she was one of the great characters of my life," says Gilroy, placing her alongside Pope John, Lord Louis Mountbatten and Viscount Alexander.

He found her enormous fun – witty, entertaining and bawdy, (another of her colleagues remembers almost nothing about her except her love of dirty stories), besides being brilliant at her job, and not unattractive sexually – "terrific size – lovely fat fingers – lovely snub nose – lovely curly lips – a baby's face in a way" – a true painter's appreciation!

The portrait Gilroy painted of her and the two sketches he made, which are reproduced in this book, are the only records of how she looked at this vital period of her life. We have photographs of her as a child, we have photographs of her as a successful, middle-aged woman. But it is a great stroke of luck that a painter of such talent as Gilroy should have known and admired her at that moment of delicate balance when her career was beginning and her private life going through its greatest crisis.

Here, in Gilroy's portrait, is Dorothy as the world saw her – challenging, self-confident, amused; sporting without apology the silver wig that hid her thin and unreliable hair; and revealing an unmistakably come-hither look in the bright blue Sayers eyes.

Strangely enough, Dorothy still kept her private and her business life so rigorously apart that Gilroy never met Mac – though Mac in fact

Three of the famous Guinness advertisements which combined the talents of Dorothy Sayers and John Gilroy

contributed many of the recipes to the Recipe Book of the Mustard Club. Gilroy noticed that Dorothy never seemed to show any particular signs of affection towards Mac – nor indeed towards anyone. Her regard was reserved for those she respected and found efficient or amusing. And we know from others that Dorothy never indulged in warmer endearments towards Mac, nor he to her, than "old boy" and "old girl".

The Mustard Club was one of Benson's greatest successes, and it must have been a very special satisfaction to Dorothy, with her love of "the work", to see something that she and Mac had laboured and laughed over together becoming a household joke all over the country.

The campaign was an elaborate and wide-ranging affair, and gave plenty of rein to Dorothy's talent for punning, parody and pastiche. Exactly which bits she contributed no one can now remember. But her touch is everywhere. It is there in the names of the club's officers – Lord Bacon of Cookham, the Baron de Beef (president) and the secretary, Miss Di Gester. It is there in the spoof news item (a full page advertisement) of an action for libel brought by a restaurant against Miss Di Gester for writing to the papers stating that it was "a second class restaurant because the mustard was not freshly made". Counsel for the restaurant rashly based his case on the assertion that "in my client's restaurant the mustard is made freshly every week" – and the case was of course dismissed on the grounds that the remarks of Miss Di Gester were uttered in the public interest since every good restaurant should know that mustard should be freshly made every day. Rule number 5 of the Mustard Club was quoted – "Every member shall see that the mustard is freshly made, and no member shall tip a waiter who forgets to put mustard on the table."

Dorothy's hand is surely there too in the elaborate Prospectus of the Mustard Club (1926) Ltd (incorporated under the Health Act, BC 1000 to AD 1926), which announces that "the original Mustard Club was founded by Aesculapius, the god of medicine, in the days of Ham and Shem. One of the earliest members was Nebuchadnezzar, who found mustard a welcome addition to his diet of grass"; which states among the memoranda of association that "The responsibilities of directors are confined to taking their fees" (something that Dorothy seems rather to have felt about some of the directors of Benson's); and which names the auditors, "Glossit, Over and Hope".

The Mustard Club, with its claim that mustard aids digestion and health when added to practically any dish you care to name, featured in numbers of news items and cartoons of the time, and considerably stimulated the sales of a product that had little obvious glamour. And behind it we can detect Dorothy's enormous energy and enthusiasm, her

love of word games and the zest with which she would seize on an idea
that amused her and exploit it to its limits. Certainly she earned every
penny that Benson's paid her.

Whether she actually believed what she wrote is less certain. Her very
first advertisement had prompted her to comment: "It is all lies from
beginning to end – or at least a tissue of exaggeration";[4] though later
she was to qualify such strictures by a rationalization that placed a good
share of the blame on the public:

> It will be seen that the best defence against both suggestio falsi and
> suppressio veri is read advertisements carefully, observing both what
> is said and what is omitted. Those who prefer their English sloppy
> have only themselves to thank if the advertisement writer uses his
> mastery of vocabulary and syntax to mislead their weak minds. Caveat
> emptor.[5]

She did not at any point deny that there was plenty of suppression of
truth and false suggestion for the public to defend itself against. And in
later life she was to suggest that, in a modern Inferno on Dante's pattern,
advertisers would be among those found in the Lake of Ordure, the
place of the Flatterers.[6]

The doings of the Mustard Club were not the only excitements in
Dorothy's life at this period. Fate also provided her with a few good
moments of real life drama, something she loved. When Agatha Christie
disappeared in December 1926, one theory was that she had drowned in
the Silent Pool at Shere in Surrey, near which her abandoned car was
found. John Gilroy drove Dorothy down there. She gazed for a few
moments at that gloomily romantic stretch of water, and then briskly
announced: "She's not here". Not a particularly dramatic reaction,
perhaps, but at least accurate. A month or two later, Mac had to write a
piece in the *News of the World* about the death of his friend, the racing
driver, Parry Thomas, who died as dramatically and as horribly as
anyone in any of Dorothy's stories – he was decapitated by the broken
driving chain of his car, "Babs", while trying to establish a new speed
record at Pendine Sands.

The same month – March 1927 – saw Dorothy accompanying Mac to
Boulogne, where he was following up two sensational cases: the discovery of May Daniels, a London nurse who was found dead in a field
near the town with a hypodermic syringe beside her; and the arrest of
Lord Terrington on bankruptcy charges – a case made all the more
savoury for Mac's readers by the fact that his unfortunate Lordship was
accompanied by a lady who was not his wife and that, with a fine sense of

dramatic timing, he collapsed with a heart attack minutes after being arrested.

At this time, it is clear that Mac was not the penniless ne'er-do-well he has been painted, attracted to Dorothy by nothing but her earning power. In his own profession he was highly regarded, and neither he nor Dorothy had any reason to suppose that this state of affairs would not continue. It was rather Dorothy's career which seemed in something of a tangle at this point, for she very much wanted to leave her publisher, Ernest Benn, to join Benn's bright young employee, Victor Gollancz, who was leaving the firm and starting out on his own. It was Gollancz who had shown confidence in Dorothy, and given her confidence in herself, and it was to him that she felt allegiance, not to Benn himself. But Benn would not release her from her contract. So for a while she had to work for them both in tandem, writing her next two novels for Benn and only able to offer to Gollancz the short stories, in which she had little faith. However, he accepted these, and Dorothy wrote a few more to make up the twelve that appeared in the volume *Lord Peter Views the Body*. Thus, while she was still working out the term of her contract with Benn, there began a partnership between Dorothy and Victor which was fruitful, enjoyable and profitable for both parties, and which persisted to the day of her death.

It was probably Gollancz who encouraged her to embark on a project on which she toiled intermittently for the rest of her life, but never brought to fruition – a biography of Wilkie Collins. She honoured Collins as one of the fathers of the detective novel, and often preached a return to his use of character and background rather than events as a basis for plots. Dorothy collected a great deal of material about Collins over the years, and several chapters of manuscript exist and have been published – but she found herself hampered, as we have seen, by lack of information about his private life, and something more urgent always seemed to crop up to occupy her energies.

She now edited for Gollancz a volume entitled *Great Short Stories of Detection, Mystery and Horror*, writing an introduction that remains a classic summary of the subject – wide-ranging, erudite, witty and perceptive. From now on she was to be in steady demand as an authority on crime writing.

1928 was a productive year, with the publication of *Lord Peter Views the Body* and *Great Short Stories of Detection, Mystery and Horror* for Gollancz, and *The Unpleasantness at the Bellona Club* for Benn; for whom, as a break from detection, she also began a translation of *Tristan in Brittany* from the old French.

While the wrangle about publishers was in progress, Mac's health began to deteriorate and Dorothy became extremely worried. By the summer of 1928 he no longer had his job with the *News of the World*; he was now, as Dorothy explained to Ivy, "freelancing".[7] And they took a holiday in a quiet part of southern Scotland, Gatehouse of Fleet in Kirkudbrightshire, to help him recover. Here the warm water of the Gulf Stream comes closest to the land, and the climate is astonishingly mild and temperate; and here Mac picked up remarkably. Dorothy's affection for the place and the people was to emerge very strongly in the pages of her book *Five Red Herrings*, though it was for Mac's sake that she chiefly valued it.

It was fortunate that Dorothy's royalties were now beginning to come in more regularly and more copiously, for Mac's commissions were pretty sporadic. He did a cookery book for Crosse and Blackwell's in 1928, and was contributing cookery articles to the *Evening News*, but there was nothing substantial. At the same time it was becoming clear that the little flat at 24 Great James Street was too small to hold them both, and they were beginning to get on each other's nerves. Dorothy certainly cannot have been an easy person to live with, and Mac had a very quick temper. Neither was by any means "cosy". So a certain amount of space between and around them was very necessary for a peaceful life. This problem was solved when, in August, the flat above Dorothy's fell vacant. After much disruption, adaptation and redecoration, the couple had twice as much room to settle into – and twice as much rent to pay.

The extra space now raised the possibility of bringing John Anthony in to join the household, and Dorothy told Ivy that she was hoping to persuade Mac to agree. "Mac is getting quite interested in him," she wrote. "I haven't been shoving the kid at him, so to speak. I don't think small children appeal much to men (nor indeed to me), but I expect he will turn out to be quite fun in a little time."[8]

Ivy had moved from Oxford early that year to the village of Westcott Barton, about fifteen miles to the north west. Here she had rented a thatched cottage, with a large wild garden but with no modern amenities at all.

The cottage was of Cotswold stone, built in 1727, with oak-beamed ceilings and stone-flagged floors, and water had to be fetched from a single tap outside the back door. The cottage was known to the villagers as Cocksparrow Hall, a name which in that part of the country does not denote any particular grandeur; a big house there is known as a grange or a manor. Ivy, however, decided to change the name to The Sidelings, and there she devoted her life to bringing up the children in her care.

Ivy had her faults. Years of spinsterhood in her mother's company, years of struggling for a living, had left her with a more limited outlook than Dorothy's. She had her snobbish side, as Dorothy had noted, and she kept herself and the children very much to themselves. In the village she was regarded as something of an eccentric and a recluse – a reputation which is not hard to get in a village community. But there was undoubtedly something in it, for Ivy did regard herself as a cut above the rest, and did not wish the children to be sullied by contact with the village kids. We should remember perhaps that this kind of class consciousness was much more prevalent in those days than it is now; and Ivy was doing her very best, by her lights, to bring up her charges as the little lady and gentleman that their parents wished them to be. Whatever her failings, Ivy devoted every moment of her life to their welfare and their education.

Dorothy's attitude towards John Anthony was as brisk and business-like as her attitude to everything else. When he broke a collar bone, at the age of two and a half, she wrote: "I am glad the kid has pluck anyhow – maternal affection is by no means my strong point, I must say, but if there must be children, it is preferable they should have some guts."[9]

How hard did she really try to persuade Mac to let her bring John Anthony into the home? She seemed very ready to believe that men have no time for small children, and she appeared to regard this as a most reasonable attitude. It is hard to resist the conclusion that in fact it was to some extent her own view, and that her moves towards taking John Anthony under her wing were a matter of duty rather than strong feeling.

Before anything could come of it, however, a fresh crisis distracted her attention. In September 1928 her father died "very suddenly, peacefully and mercifully";[10] and as soon as the funeral was over and they had dealt with the other formal chores attendant on death, Dorothy and Mac had to set about finding somewhere for her mother to live, since the rectory at Christchurch was now required for the incoming rector.

Within a month, Mac had found a house. "10th October. Dearest mother, Mrs H. Sayers, Sunnyside, Newland Street, Witham, Essex – that is your new address. Get out the map – look up Witham. You will find it to be a pleasant, old fashioned town on the main road between Chelmsford and Colchester"[11] – and Dorothy, knowing her mother's nervous disposition, and the general disinclination of old ladies for change, spent several pages extolling the virtues of the new house and explaining that, in order to avoid estate duties, she (Dorothy) was actually going to buy the house and her mother would technically be the tenant. "You will grumble to me about the water butt, and the tap in the scullery. You will point out that outside repairs are my business, and say what a bad landlord I am."[12]

Some of the money for the purchase of the house was Mrs Sayers' own, and it was also helped by a legacy from Uncle Percy, who had recently died in Australia. But that Dorothy was able to think at all about buying a house shows that her finances were a good deal easier – especially since it appears from another note that Dorothy had also been paying off debts incurred by Mac, and had now wiped the slate clean.

As Dorothy had feared, her mother was far from grateful at first: "When mother went down with Mac the week before last to choose the papers etc, she couldn't seem to see anything but gloom and difficulties, and that depressed poor old Mac (who is suffering badly from nerves) till he almost had a breakdown."[13] But by Christmas things were much more cheerful. Mrs Sayers and Aunt Mabel had moved in, and Dorothy and Mac spent Christmas with them in the new house.

A few contented months followed. And then, almost as suddenly as her husband's, came the death of Helen Sayers. It was caused by an internal stoppage connected with a rupture of the bowel – no doubt aggravated by all the pills and potions that Dorothy had designated the vice of the Leigh family. She was buried in Christchurch cemetery, beside her husband; Dorothy firmly refusing on both occasions to allow any mournful hymns.

That was in August 1929. In the same month, Dorothy's financial situation took another step forward. Her reputation as a writer was now so secure that her new agent, David Higham, to whom she had recently gone on Victor Gollancz's recommendation, was able to get her a contract with an American publisher that secured her a regular income and meant that she did not have to wait for advances and royalties on individual books. This freed her to leave Benson's and concentrate entirely on writing. So the problem of what to do with her house in Witham was solved: for the rest of the year, until she finally shook the dust of Benson's off her feet, it would be a weekend cottage for Mac and herself, and thereafter it would be their principal dwelling place, with the flat in town kept on simply as a *pied-à-terre*. In Witham, Dorothy hoped to be able to work without interruption – and to be close enough to London to be able to get there quickly by train or bus when business required, but far enough to save her from casual callers and the temptations of the London social round.

She may not have realized, in releasing herself from the slavery of an office job, that in some ways the slavery of a freelance is worse. When there are no office hours, there is no time off. Office-goers may hate

Mondays, but only because they have had a free Saturday and Sunday. The freelance works a seven-day week, and the working day is as long as he can keep his eyes open. But this was the life that Dorothy had chosen, and for all its drawbacks she undoubtedly preferred it to the chore of trying to write her books while working at a full-time job in advertising.

It was certainly not for love of the country that she made the move – she had always said that she hated the country, and she never seems to have made any use of the countryside round Witham. She was no walker, gardener, animal lover or bird watcher; though as she grew older, the attractions of city life seem to have worn somewhat thin, and the success of the holidays in Scotland may have raised rural life a little in her estimation.

She never really entered into the life of the village. Witham never became a substitute for the community of Benson's, which, whatever its faults, had given her an outlet for her gregariousness. She was not to find that kind of enjoyment again until she began writing plays and experienced the camaraderie of the theatre.

Happily, just at the moment of her exile from London, from the company of kindred spirits, a new venture brought her for the first time into close contact with her fellow detection-story writers – a venture she was to support with fervent enthusiasm for the rest of her life.

The Detection Club emerged from a suggestion of Anthony Berkeley that writers of detective fiction should periodically dine together for the enjoyment of each other's company and for a little shop talk. The dinners proved such a success that the diners decided to form themselves into a Club – Dorothy being one of the most enthusiastic and energetic members.

Club premises were to be paid for, not by subscriptions but by collaborating in the writing of a joint detective story whose proceeds should belong to the Club. Dorothy contributed an episode to the first product of the Club's amalgamated talent – a radio serial called *Behind the Screen*, which was broadcast in June and July 1930 and subsequently printed in *The Listener*. It is a mark of her status among her colleagues that she was not only the organizer of the next one, *The Scoop*, but the writer of the opening and closing episodes. This appeared, also in *The Listener*, early the following year; her co-writers being Agatha Christie, Clemence Dane, E. C. Bentley, Anthony Berkeley and Freeman Wills Crofts.

Not long after this Dorothy organized a book along the same lines, called *The Floating Admiral*; and later, whenever the Club was short of funds, there were others of the same kind.

She also had a very considerable hand in the formulation of the rather bizarre initiation ceremonies of the Club. There exists a complete copy of "The Uncommon Order of Initiation of New Members of the Detection Club", and also of "The Order of SOLEMN INSTALLATION for a PRESIDENT of the DETECTION CLUB", both documents in Dorothy's writing, and both with crossings-out and alterations that suggest that she in fact drafted the Ceremonies.

The style is certainly hers:

The Company being Assembled, and the Lights Extinguished, the President (or the Ruler of the Feast appointed in his Room), shall proceed to the Place Designated for the Ceremony, with his Attendants & the Candidates in manner following.

THE ORDER OF THE PROCESSION
1. Two Torchbearers
2. Eric the Skull
   borne on a Black Cushion
3. The Secretary
4. The Candidates
5. The Sponsors
   bearing Torches
6. The President

Silence having been called by the Usher, then the President shall ask of the Secretary:–

President: "What mean these Lights, these Ceremonies, & this Reminder of our Mortality? . . ."

Later in the ceremony, the candidate being initiated is asked by the President:

"Do you promise that your Detectives shall well and truly detect the Crimes presented to them, using those wits which it may please you to bestow upon them and not placing reliance upon nor making use of Divine Revelation, Feminine Intuition, Mumbo Jumbo, Jiggery-Pokery, Coincidence or the Act of God?"

Answer: "I do."

The President: "Do you solemnly swear never to conceal a Vital Clue from the Reader?"

Answer: "I do."

The President: "Do you promise to observe a seemly moderation in the use of Gangs, Conspiracies, Death-Rays, Ghosts, Hypnotism, Trap-Doors, Chinamen, Super-Criminals and Lunatics,

and utterly and forever to forswear Mysterious Poisons unknown
to Science?"
Answer: "I do . . ."

And finally the President, in declaring the new member elected, utters
the following dread warning:

> . . . if you fail to keep your promises, may other Writers anticipate
> your Plots, may your Publishers do you down in your Contracts,
> may Total Strangers sue you for Libel, may your Pages swarm with
> Misprints and your Sales continually Diminish. Amen.

Whether Dorothy took all this quite as seriously in those early days as
she came to do later on, we shall, alas, never know. More recent
members, who knew her when she was herself President of the Club (a
post first held by G. K. Chesterton) found that she treated the whole
thing with such solemnity as to deprive it of much of its fun. Eric the
Skull, needing to be kept supplied with batteries for the light that glowed
from his eye-sockets, was, after all, hardly a symbol to be revered; but
Dorothy permitted no sign of frivolity or irreverence, and found it impossible to understand that any member could have engagements more
important than the monthly (later bi-monthly) meetings of the Club. As
to the divulging of the Club's secrets – the wording of the Ceremonies,
or the substance of the speeches – this was heinous, this was high
treason, a matter for solemn rebuke if not for excommunication.

It seems likely, however, that Dorothy took her fun less ponderously
in those early days. She was not yet a public figure, and had not learnt to
take herself too seriously.

Indeed, life persisted in reminding her of her fallibility, by working
out contrary to her hopes. Mac had been growing worse, not rapidly but
steadily, and only the holidays in Scotland seemed to do him any good.
Less and less could he be counted on to swell the household budget.
After the move to Witham, there was of course ample room to have John
Anthony with them, but Mac's sickliness had brought with it an increasing uncertainty of temper, which at the best of times had always
been capable of violence, and an increasing dependence on the bottle.
Dorothy had more or less given up hope of offering her son a happy
family home, though the reason she gave to Ivy, after the move to
Witham, was that Aunt Mabel was still with them and could prove an
embarrassment.

Both Anthony and Isabel knew her as "Cousin Dorothy", who visited

Ivy from time to time and brought presents, and remembered them on birthdays and at Christmas. Like Dorothy, Anthony did not go to any kind of primary school. Dorothy believed that so long as his mind was lively, so long as he was stimulated to continue learning for himself whatever he wanted to know, he was better under Ivy's private tuition than at any local school. Her experience at Hull and at other schools since had given her a scarifying insight into the general educational standards of the country at that time, and there is no doubt that she was perfectly right. But for Anthony, as for herself thirty years earlier, this led to an isolation from other children and from the community in general. The villagers of Westcott Barton were all too aware that they were not regarded as good enough for Anthony and Isabel to mix with; and though Anthony was regarded as a nice little boy, he tended to take his cue from the older Isabel, to whom a sense of superiority came naturally.

One thing on which Dorothy did feel called to comment was Anthony's baptism. She had left his religious education, like most other things, very much to Ivy's discretion. But the memory of her own parents' treachery about her confirmation was still strong, and when Ivy broached the subject of baptism, her reaction was fairly emphatic: "Personally, I'm all against making sacraments into conveniences, but if you feel strongly about it, do as you like." And then follows the remark already quoted – "Being baptized without one's will is certainly not so harmful as being confirmed against one's will, which is what happened to me . . ."[14]

For the most part, though, Anthony's problems could safely be left to Ivy. Mac was the real worry. Whatever else it was, her marriage to him had not been a matter of impetuosity. In the bad days at the end of her affair with Bill, when she was writing to John Cournos about her problems, she had made it very clear that she was looking in a pretty cold-blooded way for a particular kind of relationship. In Mac she had found it, and Dorothy was not the kind of woman to shirk the responsibility of her decisions. She had needed him, and in return would give him what he needed. If his war-time ailments made him difficult, she would endure the difficulty. If he was the kind of man – and he was — who demanded his meals on the table promptly at the same hour each day, she would see that he got them.

When he felt better, of course, he himself would do some of the cooking; and he also occupied himself by painting – something which Dorothy encouraged greatly, praising him considerably above his due. What she could share with him, she did: they both got plenty of fun from the parrot that Mac brought in one day in the summer of 1930; they argued about what to play on the gramophone, Mac favouring Chopin while Dorothy countered with Bach; and they shared an interest in the fortunes of Dorothy's various aunts, one or other of whom was generally staying, if not actually living, with them (and indeed sometimes dying with them).

What Dorothy would not do was to allow her private life to interfere with her professional life, with the result that of those who knew Dorothy Sayers, the writer, almost none had ever met Mac; and these people found it almost impossible to envisage Dorothy Sayers, the wife and housewife.

For Mac himself it cannot have been the happiest of solutions. Sickness and unemployment can isolate a man quite sufficiently from his fellow men: to see his wife busy about her affairs, meeting interesting people and becoming herself increasingly a celebrity, without being invited to share in these excitements, must have been an additional bitterness. Mac, the traveller, the man-about-town, everybody's buddy, was not the man to find it easy to be both housebound and dependent on a woman for his income.

One of the most painfully truthful scenes Dorothy ever wrote occurs in *The Unpleasantness at the Bellona Club*, between an out-of-work ex-soldier and his working wife. George Fentiman, still a sick man and unable to work as a result of being gassed during the war, bitterly resents his dependence on his wife Sheila, and his petty grumbling and irritable attempts to humiliate her ring uncomfortably true.

The book was written very early in Dorothy's marriage, when Mac was still working, and Dorothy had little reason to expect that her marriage would ever come to the same pitch. But such situations were far from uncommon in those post-war years, and there were already minor worries about Mac's "tummy"; Dorothy may have had fears which added conviction to her writing of the scene. And certainly it was not long before life in the Fleming household began to imitate art.

Everything combined to aggravate the problem. Had they still been in London, Mac could have visited his cronies in Fleet Street. Had Dorothy still been working at Benson's, she would have been out of the house all day. As it was, they were thrown together day and night, and the relationship grew more and more uncomfortable.

And as the first cheerful openness of the early years of the marriage began to dwindle, Wimsey, by contrast, filled out, grew more human, more in love, richer in character, more rounded. He was still the bread-winner – indeed he owed his survival to that fact – but now he had to become something more.

CHAPTER THIRTEEN

DOROTHY WAS NEARLY forty. The goals which had seemed so distant at thirty – financial security and a man of her own – were now achieved; both at the cost of compromise. The Wimsey books were all very well, but they were not the books she wanted to write. Mac, too, was all very well up to a point, but he was not the man she really wanted to marry.

It is unlikely that anyone with Dorothy's restless energy would have been satisfied to leave things as they were. Another woman might have set off into sexual adventures, and possibly even a change of partner. That was out of the question for Dorothy. She had written to John Cournos – "Absolute and utter faithfulness to the claims of lover or husband is a kind of fanaticism with me."[1] So she would have to look to her writing for variety and stimulus. She already tried to vary her approach with each new book – sometimes to the detriment of the book, for she embarked on *Five Red Herrings*, for example, one of the least successful of her books, simply because she felt (so she told Victor Gollancz) that she would like to try her hand at just one of the "pure puzzle" type of detective story. Now would have been the moment to break out of the detective-story field altogether, as she well knew. But the very circumstance that made her life wretched – Mac's illness – also meant that she was shackled to Wimsey, the provider. The best she could do to satisfy her own creative needs was to build into future Wimsey stories as much richness, as much of her own creative vision as she could, without jeopardizing the devotion of her public.

And, by pure chance, or by the grace of God, or by some unconscious movement of the creative mind, the means was already there, waiting to be used – Harriet Vane.

Technically speaking, the Harriet of *Strong Poison* had only two functions – to present Peter Wimsey with a crime to solve, and to lead him thereafter towards the altar and oblivion. Though Dorothy had amused herself by bestowing her own attributes on Harriet, she had not really exploited the similarities.

But now, what opportunities presented themselves! Here was a character who could express Dorothy's own vision of the world, whose thoughts could be Dorothy's thoughts, her perceptions Dorothy's perceptions, her emotions Dorothy's emotions.

Moreover, this paragon has already brought Wimsey to his knees. His fall might not have been so abrupt, so ill-prepared, had Dorothy fore-seen where it was to lead. In fact, by another happy chance, the way it happened was not, after all, likely to lead to wedlock – or at least not for a long while. Through no fault of his own, Wimsey's love is hopeless – the woman he has fallen in love with has been so bruised in her own emotional life that she is incapable of responding to him. Besides, she possesses such powerful emotional integrity that the last thing she will do is to marry a man who has saved her life. For a very long time she will be terrified of confusing gratitude with love, and will have to check and double check the reality of her feelings before allowing herself to believe in them. For perfectly valid reasons she will play a long game of hard-to-get, and Wimsey the invincible will be transformed to a humble suitor. He can be hurt. He can become fully human.

Dorothy did not do things by halves. Once she had allotted Harriet her new role, she gave her the whole first forty-seven pages of the next book, *Have His Carcase*, before Wimsey appeared at all.

Immediately there is a new breadth to the mystery, a new observation of detail, a new leisure to explore sensation. The description of Harriet's gradual discovery of the corpse on the rock is unlike anything in the previous books, because Dorothy is now entering into a character as never before. The plotting of *Have His Carcase* is not by any means Dorothy's best, but there is a new pleasure in the playfulness between Wimsey and Harriet as they unravel the clues together. That is part of the change in Wimsey. And though we are still not taken into his mind in any depth, we do see him in a new light, through the eyes of a woman who knows that he is in love with her and who is looking for his failings.

A look at the bookshelf reveals the most obvious result of this change. *Have His Carcase* and the books that come after it are considerably fatter than the earlier ones. Dorothy is not restricting herself to the plot, she is spreading herself; the bony structure of the murder mystery is still there, but (like Dorothy's own frame) it is increasingly covered, not to say smothered, by warm and sometimes unruly flesh.

Once Harriet had opened the windows of the detective story and let in the real world, however, she was not indispensable. In the next book she planned, Dorothy had other means of making a personal appearance.

Right from the start, *The Nine Tailors* was to be "a labour of love".[2] Dorothy had gone to considerable lengths to avoid having to go back to live at Christchurch, and she had regularly stated how much she disliked the country. But there was drama to be found in the countryside of her childhood. Moreover, it would give her a chance to say something about her belief in the old, traditional England that it represented. She could pay a debt in her own kind of way – a literary way – to the society that formed her, to the great churches that had given her her first glimpse of religion and, indeed, to the parents who had educated her, loved her, and supported her through the bad days until she found her feet.

Labour of love or not, *The Nine Tailors* gave Dorothy a lot of trouble. Another writer might have told the story without embarking on a thorough study of bell-ringing. So indeed might Dorothy, at an earlier stage in her career, but now she wanted to do the thing properly. So much so that for the first sixty-three pages of the book there is not even a corpse, not even a mystery; only the careful, detailed, loving building up of the portrait of a community. Wimsey appears briefly in the opening pages, but not as a detective – only as a snow-bound traveller, grateful for the hospitality of the vicar.

The village, Fenchurch St Paul, is no one village in the Fens, nor is its church based on any one real church. Dorothy loved inventing places, and drew elaborate maps to get the topography of her stories right. For *The Nine Tailors* she also had an architect friend design her a beautiful church. One can say that the angel roof, which Dorothy describes so glowingly, is borrowed from Upwell St Peter, a few miles from Christchurch; and that the general style of the church is much like many of the magnificent churches of the northern Fens – Walpole St Peter, for example, or Terrington St John. But Dorothy's church is an amalgamation, designed for Dorothy's own purposes. And similarly, the rector, though he may have some of Mr Sayers' characteristics, is not Mr Sayers – though there are villagers in Christchurch today who will tell you they recognize this neighbour or that among the minor characters.

The detail of *The Nine Tailors* took time to work out, especially the technical research into the mysteries of bell-ringing. Dorothy soon realized that she was not going to be able to finish the book in time to meet her obligations, and would have to put it aside while she got on with another one which she could polish off in a hurry. She looked around for an area of her experience that she had not yet exploited – and there was one very obvious one. This is how she came to write the one book of this period which does not feature Harriet Vane, a book which harks back to Dorothy's early days, when plot ruled supreme – *Murder Must Advertise*.

Her letters are full of complaints about the book. She thoroughly disliked it, and resented having to do it. And indeed, if one looks closely, it is a very artificial story, and the whole sub-plot which has to do with the Bright Young Things of the day, with their fancy-dress parties and drug taking, is hollow and unconvincing to a degree. What the reader enjoys and remembers – indeed what makes the story – is the detail of the advertising agency. With barely a touch of satire and with much warmth,

Dorothy draws an unforgettable picture of the kind of office in which she had worked for so many years, and once again triumphs by the sheer vigour of the writing and the enjoyment of life that she communicates to the reader.

Murder Must Advertise came out in February 1933, and by November she had finished *The Nine Tailors*. Another book of short stories, *Hangman's Holiday*, appeared the same year, and there had also been book reviews for the *Sunday Times*. When *The Nine Tailors* was finished, Dorothy's doctor ordered her to take a complete rest for three weeks.

She elected to spend the time motoring with Muriel St Clare Byrne. She needed time to be away from Mac and to think. This was the nearest she ever came to leaving him, and the holiday was spent quietly deciding whether or not to do so.

She had another bit of business to do on the same trip. Muriel remembers their calling, one dark winter's evening, at a cottage in a small village in Oxfordshire. Dorothy went in, leaving Muriel in the car outside for a few moments; and then came out to ask Muriel in. This was Muriel's first introduction to Anthony; though of course she had no idea, then or as long as Dorothy lived, of the nature of the relationship.

The real reason for the occasion was that Dorothy wanted to talk to Ivy about some form of "adoption" of Anthony, which would give her an official place in his life. It was not of course possible to adopt him in the legal sense, for to do this it would have been necessary to produce his birth certificate, on which Dorothy's name appeared, unconcealed, as the sole parent. (There are heavy penalties for falsification of such things.) So the adoption was an informal affair; but from now on Anthony was instructed to call Dorothy "mother" and refer to Mac as his father. He was also allowed to change the initial that he had carved on his ruler to J.A.F. – he was ready for school now, and Dorothy wanted him called Fleming when he went to school.

Dorothy came back from her trip with several things settled: she was not going to make the break with Mac – she would stand by him till death did them part; she had given up hope of bringing Anthony into the home, Mac being the way he was; and she had gone as far towards acknowledging Anthony as she possibly could in the circumstances, without actually letting the cat out of the bag. Personal matters thus being tied up, she was ready to write the book that would say, clearly and decisively, that in her opinion no trust could be placed in personal matters; that the only salvation came through work, through craftsmanship, through the creations of mind and of hand and through the intellectual passion that controlled those creations.

The brief fragment of *My Edwardian Childhood* had been written early in 1932. Now, two years later, she began work on *Cat o' Mary*, clearly using *My Edwardian Childhood* as a draft for the early chapters, transferring much of it word for word into the new manuscript, merely altering it from the first person to the third.

Then came the second transformation. Invited back to Somerville – one of their graduates who had achieved not only distinction but fame – to propose the toast to the college at that annual celebration known as a "Gaudy", Dorothy suddenly realized that she could say what she wanted to say without ever embarking on any kind of autobiography – in fact without even having to forswear the guaranteed royalties that the name of Wimsey would bring in. All the pieces fell into place – and the key piece, once more, was Harriet Vane.

Harriet was so nearly Dorothy that she could take the place of Katherine Lammas. Harriet had already suffered tribulations in her personal life, just as Dorothy had planned that Katherine should do. She had already rejected Wimsey's offer of marriage, for precisely the same kind of reasons for which Katherine was to renounce personal relationships – they were too hazardous, she had been too much hurt, she wanted something more secure. And here at Oxford was the precise place where Harriet could find that security, and could dedicate herself to work in the way that Katherine Lammas was to have done at the end of *Cat o' Mary*. Here, moreover, in the life of the intellect, she could be the equal of any man, including Wimsey. And only by meeting him as an equal, no longer as a woman in debt to him for her life, was there any chance of her meeting him as a lover.

So it is that in *Gaudy Night* Harriet finally moves up from the ranks of the supporting players and takes the centre of the stage. She it is who tries to solve the problem that is besetting her college, and only when she fails does she call on Wimsey. He does not appear till page two hundred and sixty-five. The theme of the book is the nature of intellectual integrity – the guiding light both of Harriet and of the college; and also, as it turns out, of Wimsey.

There is actually no real change in Wimsey. He has always been superlatively good at whatever the plot demanded – and this time it demands that he is a first-class scholar and the holder of one of the finest degrees of his year. Dorothy finally has her puppet on her own ground, Oxford, and it is not too hard for her to persuade us that this is what Wimsey has been all along – the serious scholar, the brilliant mind, the first-class academic, who has had to wear the mask of the silly ass and the man-about-town in order to be accepted among the common run of people. The only reasonable complaint readers might offer is that this is not quite what they had been led to expect from the Wimsey they had got to know in his earlier adventures.

Lovers of detective stories who like to know where they are with a book tend to find *Gaudy Night* one of the least satisfactory of Dorothy's stories. Others find it one of the richest and most satisfying. Both are right. As a conventional detective story, the book is not up to much. There is not even a murder in it – or at best a very remote one. And one can hardly defend Dorothy against the charge of smuggling in her own preoccupations while pretending that she was still merely trying to entertain the customers. But if one approaches it without preconceptions, there is a great deal to be admired and enjoyed.

At the end of *Gaudy Night*, it is intellectual integrity that has solved the mystery, and has also brought Peter and Harriet together; thus demonstrating Dorothy's thesis that adherence to the intellect is as necessary for the business of living as for scholarly study or the solving of detective problems. It is, I fear, rather a dubious panacea for love and happiness, as Dorothy herself knew too well. She had set up a very special couple of people, in a very special relationship, to make her point. But within the terms of the story she was telling, the point was made vividly and movingly.

Among those who were not happy about *Gaudy Night* were some who already detected and disliked the flavour of social snobbery in Dorothy's books, and who now found the offence double-dyed by the addition of intellectual elitism.

The most vicious attack came from Mrs Q. D. Leavis, a critic in her own right and wife of the eminent academic and literary critic F. R. Leavis. The burden of Mrs Leavis's complaint was not so much that Dorothy had written a bad book – though she did make a few telling, if overstated, points about Dorothy's academic literariness, and about the atmosphere of "a sort of female smoking room"[3] that pervades her "risqué" passages. What she really objected to was that others had praised it too highly, mistaking, Mrs Leavis claimed, literariness for literature. Moreover (and this was the charge that carried most venom in a pretty venomous and humourless article), she asserted that Dorothy had got it wrong about universities. They were not sanctuaries of integrity and disinterested scholarship; on the contrary, they were hotbeds of "literary glibness and spiritual illiteracy",[4] offering plenty of scope for personal aggrandizement and bogus scholarship.

The edge of Mrs Leavis's attack is a good deal blunted by the obvious personal grievances it reveals and by its total failure to take into account the simple fact that the book is enjoyably readable. But Dorothy was hurt. She had for once worn her heart tentatively on her sleeve, and for thanks had had it pecked at.

The public at large, however, did not have Mrs Leavis's preoccupations; nor did they seem troubled by the late arrival of Wimsey. And the other reviewers, on the whole, acknowledged how well Dorothy had brought off the grafting of high thinking on to the detective-story stock, even if some of them did think she had rather overdone the loyalty to Oxford.

Certainly *Gaudy Night* contains a good deal of what Mrs Leavis calls "rationalized nostalgia for her [Dorothy's] student days".[5] And Dorothy herself realized before long that the remoteness of academic concerns from the hurly-burly of outside life was not entirely a good thing. It has been said that some sort of feud developed between Dorothy and Somerville as a result of *Gaudy Night*, but this hardly squares with the fact that she was invited in the following year to become Chairman of the Somerville Association of Senior Members.

In this capacity she certainly raised the eyebrows of some of the staff, who found that she wanted to make too many changes too quickly, while Dorothy found them too settled and too slow; but this seems to have been the full extent of the feud – though obviously some members of the College felt more strongly on the subject than others.

With *Gaudy Night*, the long-drawn-out chase was over, and Peter had his Harriet. And, as Dorothy had foreseen, this very nearly meant the end of Peter as a detective. The one remaining Wimsey book would never have seen the light of day had it not been for Muriel St Clare Byrne, who was now teaching at the Royal Academy of Dramatic Art and had been deputed by Dorothy to read the various scripts that people regularly sent in to her in the hope of putting Wimsey on to the screen or stage.

Most of these Muriel had rejected as dreadful. And Dorothy herself had had a very unhappy experience with the film world, writing the story for a film called *The Silent Passenger*. This oddity, in which Dorothy's contribution was altered out of all recognition, and in which the actor playing Wimsey succeeded in making him look like a rather villainous Italian waiter, has one redeeming feature, and that was nothing whatever to do with Dorothy. The obligatory final chase of the villain – still the favoured way of ending a detective film – takes place in a railway engine shed, with the entertaining complication that someone accidentally starts one of the engines moving; and there are some exciting shots of the great steam-driven monster, like a mindless elephant, blundering slowly forward, crashing through huge doors, and finally pinning down the unfortunate villain.

It was the last time that Dorothy was to have anything to do with films:

I do not like the films and I do not want them. I do not need their publicity, which is likely to do me more harm than good. I do not need their money, for I can live very well without it. They have nothing to offer me which I would not very much rather be without. They will find it difficult to believe this, but it is a fact.[6]

The producer had promised her control over the dialogue and characterization, and had broken his promise – accordingly: "He is muck, and I don't want to be bothered with him."[7] She turned down an offer of ten thousand dollars from MGM for *Murder Must Advertise*, and when, later, a film was made of *Busman's Honeymoon*, with Robert Montgomery as Wimsey, she refused to go to see it, even though it was showing in the cinema next door to her house in Witham.

Busman's Honeymoon, which, besides being a play, was of course also the last Wimsey novel to appear, was the result of Muriel St Clare Byrne's persistence in nagging Dorothy to write a Wimsey story for the stage herself, since nobody else seemed able to do it. Dorothy, always a theatre lover, only gave in finally on condition that Muriel should guide her through the technical intricacies of the medium.

This was not Dorothy's first attempt at the dramatic form. She had of course written little playlets during those years at home before she went to school. It was one of her favourite occupations. And there does exist a particularly dire little manuscript, entitled "The Mouse Hole" which features Peter Wimsey, and may be best dismissed as a very early work. At all events, it shows clearly how badly Dorothy needed Muriel's guiding hand. And the work proceeded, with drafts flying to and fro by post, through most of 1935, while Dorothy was also working on *Gaudy Night* and *The Silent Passenger*.

It was while this was going on that Dorothy saw Peter Wimsey! She and Muriel had been keeping a look-out for someone suitable to play the part, but where was he to be found?

Dorothy's renewed contact with Oxford had led to further invitations to speak there, and it was on the occasion of a visit to speak on "Aristotle and the Art of Detective Fiction" (a classic example of her light-hearted and stimulating scholarly wit), that she saw *him*!: "My dear, my heart is BROKEN! I have seen the *perfect* Peter Wimsey. Height, voice, charm, smile, manner, outline of features, *everything* – and he is – THE CHAPLAIN OF BALLIOL!!! *What* is the use of anything?"[8]

The chaplain's name was Roy Ridley, and Dorothy and he became friends; though she later grew a little irritated by his exploitation of the

Wimsey label. Meantime, however, "Such waste – why couldn't he have been an actor?"

Devotees of *Gaudy Night* may be amused to know how that letter continues:

> In the meantime I have completed the love-scene, except for the infernal quotation, which won't come right. It is too, too shy-making for words, and kept on falling into blank verse in the most unfortunate manner. I expect it will have to be scrapped. . . . Two lines of blank verse ejected from the love-scene – did I invent them, or have I remembered them?
>
> > "We have come
> > To that still centre where the spinning world
> > Sleeps on its axis, – to the heart of rest."
>
> If I *did* invent them, they are rather good![9]

With Muriel's guidance and assistance, the play came on very well. Once finished, it encountered the usual pre-production vicissitudes, but the names of Sayers and Wimsey were assurance enough of public interest, and backing was not too hard to find. The play went into rehearsal in November 1936, with Denis Arundell as Peter Wimsey and Veronica Turleigh as Harriet; by which time Dorothy had already finished adapting it as a book.

With some accuracy, Dorothy described it on the fly leaf as "A love story with detective interruptions". The play does not range far from the necessities of the plot, and might be described as a detective story with romantic interruptions. But what interested Dorothy now was the relationship between her two principals. And in the book, the striking thing is the depth with which she explores the passionate, unsentimental, but richly rewarding progress of their love. As an analysis of what a woman of Dorothy's temperament and intellect required from marriage, it is fascinating and compelling. It reads with such conviction and such a sense of hard-won happiness that one is persuaded that she has experienced a relationship of this sort. But I fear very much that she never did; coming closest, perhaps, in a honeymoon year or so with Mac – and that was not very close at all.

The only glimpses that the fiction-reading public were to get of Wimsey after this came in two or three short stories published during the war. Dorothy's career was now to take a completely new turn. But for all her assertions at the time that Wimsey was no longer of any interest to her, there does exist a bulky manuscript, consisting of the first chapters of a novel called *Thrones, Dominations*.

From the evidence of those six chapters, one might suppose that this was to be a Wimsey book without any crime at all. The marriage of Wimsey and Harriet is contrasted with that of another couple, and the writing is saturated with an awareness of sex and its potency. Between Wimsey and Harriet the attraction is controlled, held in a state of tension and all the more powerful for that. Between Laurence and Rosamund Harlowe the passion spills out, it is visible to everyone, uncontrolled, violent and dangerous. Rosamund gets sexual excitement from a strangling scene in a play. She believes that "passion is cruel" and is prepared to use it cruelly. These two do not respect each other's integrity, they exploit and are exploited, and one can only suppose that as the story worked out they were due to come to a bad end.

In fact, from an odd sheet among Dorothy's papers, it is clear that she had not been able finally to relieve Wimsey of the burden of detection. An elaborate diagram of the development of the relationships builds to the capitalized word MURDER, rather less than half way through the story.

Apart from this excursion, Dorothy continued steadily in the direction set by *Busman's Honeymoon*, with its powerful and original vision of the ideal relationship between men and women. It is all the more disappointing that at this juncture, just when Wimsey was finally breaking free from his detective shackles, he was quietly allowed to die.

It may appear that I have used the word Wimsey as a kind of shorthand for all the writing that had made Dorothy famous during these pre-war years. But in truth it is not merely a shorthand. Wimsey it was who had attracted and held her public, even in novels in which he hardly figures at all. Among the short stories, Dorothy had published a dozen or so which did not feature Wimsey – some in which there was no detection element at all, and some in which she tried out an alternative detective, a travelling salesman named Montague Egg. We have observed that her short stories, even the Wimsey ones, never reveal the best of her writing; and I doubt very much whether the Egg stories or the others would ever have remained in print had not each of the collections in which they feature also contained at least two or three stories about Peter Wimsey.

Wimsey suited Dorothy as Philip Marlowe suited Raymond Chandler. And perhaps it is no surprise to find that, though she stopped writing books about him, he lived on in a dozen other forms. The last novel, *Busman's Honeymoon*, was published in 1937. That same year she wrote an essay on *Gaudy Night*, in which she traced the development of Wimsey in her writing; she also wrote a letter to *The Times* on "The Wimsey Chin"; and she wrote her "Account of Lord Mortimer Wimsey, Hermit of the Wash". This last was a pseudo-historical piece of high and excellent humour about one of Wimsey's eccentric ancestors, devised for a literary evening at Sidney Sussex College, Cambridge, at which other friends, Muriel St Clare Byrne, Helen Simpson and C. W. Scott-Giles contributed other humorous pieces, all of which were subsequently published. In addition she wrote a series of mock Elizabethan poems on "The Zodiack", allegedly by another ancestor, Roger Wimsey; for which, typically, she not only learnt how to write antique script but also how to cut her own quill pens and mix her own mediaeval ink. For fifteen years Wimsey had been her support and stay – the books having been translated into as many as eleven languages and having recently sold up to 36,000 copies in their first year alone. Now he was to be pensioned off to become her plaything, while her heart and soul were thrown into the theatre.

CHAPTER FOURTEEN

THE FIRST TIME I saw Dorothy Sayers she was talking about the theatre. It was 1943. I was part of her audience at a lecture in a series on Christianity and the arts; and she held us all enthralled as with intellectual passion, with humour, with warm human enthusiasm, she sold us her vision of the theatre as the place that offered the things that a church ought to offer, but rarely did. Inside a stage door, she said, you found comradeship, charity and, most of all, a sense of common dedication to a common purpose, each individual contributing selflessly to the final result. This was the revelation that had been vouchsafed to her through the production of *Busman's Honeymoon*, and, by the time she gave that lecture, several other plays – plays which she had not only written, but for which she had besieged managements, had involved herself in every aspect of production and had even taken out on tour, herself following them round the country. And this was the passion which she conveyed to at least one of her audience, and which pitched me irretrievably into a career in the theatre.

For fifteen years or so, the urgencies of earning a living and finding a mate had diverted Dorothy from the aesthetic and intellectual inclinations that had been formed in childhood and confirmed at Oxford. By 1937, with royalties steadily coming in from all her books and with her private life at least settled, if not satisfactory, she could at last ignore the compulsions that had forced her to invent and exploit Wimsey for the delectation of the public. She could afford to please herself.

She could never have anticipated the curious set of circumstances that were to lead her from Wimsey to the theatre, from the theatre back to theology, and from theology to a new career as the Church of England's multi-purpose champion, on subjects ranging from economics to the place of women in the modern world, and from education to the English character. This was a role which, though she often protested against it, in truth suited her well enough – possibly too well, for Dorothy was a woman with a strong streak of self-indulgence – in food and drink, probably in sex, and certainly in the intoxication of using rich, evocative language and in the delights of defeating other people in argument; she was to observe herself that being made an evangelist against one's will "fosters an irritable and domineering temper".[1]

The first step in the process came quickly. Plans and negotiations for a production of *Busman's Honeymoon* were still going on when a small conspiracy began to get Dorothy to write a play for the Canterbury Festival. Under the guidance of the Dean, George Bell, a prelate of unusual breadth of vision, a group calling themselves the Friends of Canterbury Cathedral had already commissioned and produced two festival plays – *Murder in the Cathedral* by T. S. Eliot in 1935, and *Thomas Cranmer of Canterbury* by Charles Williams in 1936.

According to the letter that Dorothy received in October 1936 from Miss Margaret Babington, Festival Manager for the Friends of Canterbury Cathedral, it was at the suggestion of Charles Williams that the request was made. But Harold Child, veteran contributor to *The Times* and the *Times Literary Supplement*, had already asked Muriel St Clare Byrne to sound her friend out on the subject and perhaps soften her up a little. It was clearly not easy to find dramatists who were competent, distinguished and Christian; and Dorothy, with her wide popularity and her new-found skill in theatrical affairs, must have seemed a heaven-sent recruit to somewhat meagre ranks.

Her initial reply was cautious, committing herself only to looking into the idea and researching possible subjects. It seems to have been Miss Babington's idea that she should use the story of the burning and rebuilding of the choir of the cathedral in the twelfth century; but once suggested, Dorothy immediately saw its possibilities: here was a chance to explore a theme she had already touched on in *Gaudy Night* – the relationship between a workman and his work.

It is almost accidental that *The Zeal of Thy House* is a religious play. It was a play commissioned for performance in a Christian cathedral, and inevitably it had a Christian theme. Dorothy, however, was more interested in it as a job than as a work of devotion. It allowed her to take another step along her new-found dramatic path; though of course it was a bonus that she was so completely at home with the ecclesiastical and theological aspects of the story.

The pressure of work was now intense. Dorothy still wrote all her letters and manuscripts in longhand – fortunately for the biographer a very readable longhand, for she poured her natural exuberance into her letters, rarely sitting down at her desk without covering at least four pages; and practically every one of her letters is worth reading. Now that she had added theatre production to her many other activities, the task of organizing her affairs became impossible. Muriel St Clare Byrne finally persuaded her to hire a secretary, who could at least impose some order on the mountainous piles of paper all over Dorothy's desk and look after the routine work, seeing that the bills got paid and that Anthony's cheque was regularly sent off.

On December 16 *Busman's Honeymoon* finally opened at the Comedy Theatre, to encouraging notices and good houses. Dorothy was in her element. In none of her letters, even to close friends and to her family, did she write as warmly as she did to her actor friends. High spirits, parties and celebrations were the order of the day. Wimsey had done his creator a final good turn.

Now there was the Canterbury play to get on with, and that took her to the end of February. Margaret Babington wrote that *The Zeal of Thy House* was far and away the best play that they had yet produced – a judgement that one might not agree with, but one that must have been most encouraging to Dorothy, who had been a little alarmed at having to follow the talent of T. S. Eliot and the odd genius of Charles Williams. Her play, as she warned Margaret Babington, was a much more down-to-earth affair than theirs, but at least she had the confidence of a West End success behind her.

With her usual thoroughness Dorothy had studied the intricacies of the dramatic form and had made sure that everything she wrote was thoroughly workable in production. *The Zeal of Thy House* was important to Dorothy, however, not for its stagecraft but for its theme. She claimed later that the theme was identical with that of *Gaudy Night*, and professed to be astonished that critics and the public saw "Zeal" as a completely new departure. There were in fact some significant differences. The stylistic ones were the most obvious – it was in verse, not prose; it was a play, not a novel; and it was "period", not contemporary, in its setting. These things were quite enough to disguise the similarity of theme. But more than this – a detective novel is inevitably felt to be not quite "serious". If it should by any chance have a message, then the message is assumed to be included only in order to further the plot or to strengthen the background against which the crime is worked out. As a detective-story writer, Dorothy did not expect to take responsibility for her themes. She played pretty fair in *Gaudy Night*, and gave the culprit a good chance to argue her case against the Dons – a case that rested on the argument that unqualified devotion to one's man is more important than any scholarly scruples. It was perfectly possible for the reader, not knowing Dorothy, to see Harriet and the Dons of Shrewsbury College as interesting and well-drawn characters who did not *necessarily* represent the viewpoint of their author.

It was a different matter when Dorothy stepped into religious drama. Here her protagonist was face to face with heaven, in the form of four massive and magnificent archangels. Statements made by the archangels, and by the hero himself in extremis, were evidently intended to be statements which Dorothy herself believed to be true. She had to take responsibility for them. Moreover, setting her play in the context of the cathedral, she raised the whole argument on to a metaphysical plane: what mattered now was not the intellectual or psychological bent of a human character – the play had taken its author into the realm of spiritual truth.

When the play was presented in Canterbury in June 1937, and then transferred to the Westminster Theatre in London, it is no wonder that Dorothy's devotees suddenly found themselves a little off balance; and Dorothy's professions of surprise were a typical example of how she sometimes allowed a specious logic to blind her to the ordinary reactions of human nature.

The story that Dorothy adapted to her purposes was that of a real man. William of Sens was a French architect, who in competition with other architects obtained the commission to rebuild part of the cathedral after a fire. He did magnificent work, and then was hurt in a fall from part of the scaffolding.

Dorothy's play, a variant on Ibsen's *The Master Builder*, sees William as a man of lusty appetites, who gives the monks the opportunity to debate the question as to whether it is better to employ a man who is impious and immoral but a good architect, or one whose life is blameless and whose work is second rate. The decision goes to the former, upholding Dorothy's belief that bad work can never be justified on the grounds that it is done by a Christian. The Christian, like any other man, is obliged to do the best he can; and in the end the work proclaims the worth of the workman. Private life is irrelevant.

Conversely, the legitimate pride that a craftsman may – and must – take in his work should never tip over into that pride which is the deadliest of sins because it places the self, instead of God, in the centre of the universe. This is the sin of William of Sens, who, exulting in his art, sets himself up as an equal with God in the process of creation. He is cut down in his pride by the archangel Michael and lives on as a cripple, unable to finish his work.

In a letter to Anthony a year or two after the play's production Dorothy wrote:

People are always imagining that if they get hold of the writer himself and, so to speak, shake him long enough and hard enough, something exciting and illuminating will drop out of him. But it doesn't. What's due to come out has come out, in the only form in which it ever can come out. All one gets by shaking is the odd paper clip and crumpled carbons from his wastepaper basket. . . . What we make is more important than what we are, particularly if making is our profession.

And she adds, as if in salutary warning to the present writer: "If you notice, the first thing that usually crops up out of people's biographies is the nonsense things about them, so that the general effect made is that the man wasn't so very remarkable after all."[2]

She finishes this section of the letter to Anthony by quoting her own lines from *The Zeal of Thy House*:

Now look, here I am trying to say this personally and rather badly at the end of a day's slogging, but I've said it – said it once and for all as well as I know how to say it:

> ". . . Let me lie deep in hell,
> Death gnaw upon me, purge my bones with fire,
> But let my work, all that was good in me,
> All that was God, stand up and live and grow.
> The work is sound, Lord God, no rottenness there –
> Only in me. Wipe out my name from men
> But not my work; to other men the glory
> And to Thy Name alone. But if to the damned
> Be any mercy at all, O send thy spirit
> To blow apart the sundering flames, that I
> After a thousand years of hell, may catch
> One glimpse, one only of the Church of Christ,
> The perfect work, finished, though not by me."

There, you see [she concludes] is the ultimate truth of the matter so far as I can tell anybody about it.[3]

The theme of *The Zeal of Thy House*, then, was a passionately held belief in the importance of creation, told in terms of historical characters but applicable with little or no effort to twentieth-century situations. In an attempt to avoid the "sham archaism and the fusty language which is too often expected and provided in plays of period",[4] Dorothy devised a style combining rather fruity blank verse, reminiscent of her Oxford poetry, with that slightly patronizing attempt at common speech which many plays and books of the period used for their working-class characters – "Well Simon, you made a nice mess of it. There, there, lad, I can see you're sorry. Don't 'ee lose heart, now. It's a bad business, but we must make the best of it."[5] The mixture of verse and prose was borrowed, of course, from Shakespeare; but where in Shakespeare the two types of rhythm work strongly and smoothly together, in Dorothy Sayers the two sit uneasily side by side, both of them rather literary and self-conscious and neither of them at home with the other – a considerable step backward, it seems to me, from the strong, fresh, original prose that she had developed for the later Wimsey novels.

The play did, however, bring to Canterbury Dorothy's vigour, clarity, craftsmanship and instinctive if rather unsubtle sense of drama; and certainly one must admire the way she used the space and background of the Cathedral, and came up with workable and effective answers to new dramatic problems. She interested herself in every side of the production, from the casting to the design and construction of the magnificent wings for the Archangels.

The response of the public was tremendous – at least, of that section of the public that would go to a Canterbury play in the first place. It has to be said that people who go to a play in a church or cathedral generally go looking for something quite different from the ordinary theatre-goer. They are seeking a spiritual experience, and the quality of the drama has very little to do with the fact that they often find one. Among the responses to the play, for example, was that of an Anglican priest who wrote: "I have been impressing on my people the desirability of going to see *The Zeal of Thy House* as a religious exercise."[6] And another correspondent wrote: "The writing is, of course, exquisite and the story enthralling, but it is the spiritual side that grips one so and leaves such a deep impression. Thank you for the *vision* you gave us all."[7]

Some of the Press reviews took rather the same line. The *Manchester Guardian* said it was "not to be missed by Church people" and the *British Weekly* felt that "everybody who feels that the theatre still has a contribution to make to our religious life should take an early opportunity of visiting it". Others were wider in their appreciation. The *Daily Telegraph* called it "a triumphant mixture of religious feeling, scholarship and plain humanity", and *The Times* said that it "reaches and encompasses in moving drama a crisis of profound spiritual significance".

One member of the audience went further: "The great scene between the Father Prior and the prostrate William struck me very forcibly . . . as the profoundest and most exalted, as well as the most superbly written scene that I have ever experienced, not excepting Shakespeare."[8] And Dorothy must particularly have appreciated a note which said: "Will you allow me to offer you a word of thanks for your understanding and appreciation of the architect –"[9]

Spiritual and exalted or not, Dorothy was not above helping along the box-office with a few professionally designed publicity hand-outs – as one might have expected, remembering her log-rolling efforts on behalf of *Catholic Tales and Christian Songs*. One of the items she included in the hand-out is amusing and revealing:

> Miss Sayers finds it much more entertaining to be a playwright than a novelist. "Because when a novel is written, it is finished, but with a play you have all the fun of putting it together on the stage – and sometimes the rare delight of seeing a part really brilliantly interpreted. I have been very fortunate with my actors in Zeal. Disappointments? They happen, naturally, from time to time, but no more often than in any other job of work. Of course, I am taking the view that it is the playwright's job to work *with* the actors all the time – not merely to criticize the finished performance. I am bound to admit" added Miss Sayers, with a twinkle, "that I am probably the most 'interfering' playwright in London. I shove my oar in at every rehearsal, and how my long-suffering producers put up with me I don't know" – In actual fact Miss Sayers is extremely popular with her cast, in spite (or perhaps because) of her "interference". Mr X – said (here quote anything amiable you can get Harcourt Williams, or Frank Napier or Fisher White to say about me!)

So the second vital step had been taken – Wimsey had gone on the stage, and the stage had yielded to "religious drama", without Dorothy's really noticing how critical a development this was. The next step, too, happened in the same unspectacular way. In a letter she wrote some years later she put the progression of events in that everyday perspective in which dramatic events do happen in our lives, when the drama is only seen in retrospect:

> One day, I was asked to write a play for Canterbury about William of Sens. I had just done one play and wanted to do another (being fascinated by the new technique) and I liked the story, which could be so handled as to deal with the "proper truth" of the artist – a thing on which I was then particularly keen . . . so I wrote the thing and enjoyed doing it. I never, so help me God, wanted to get entangled in religious apologetic, or to bear witness for Christ, or to proclaim my faith to the world, or anything of that kind. . . .
>
> When the show came to London, I couldn't escape the normal press interviews – one has to be fair to the show. And as a result of one of them, I wrote the article "The Greatest Drama Ever Staged" which eventually appeared in the *Sunday Times*. . . .

That did it. Apparently the spectacle of a middle-aged female detective-novelist admitting publicly that the judicial murder of God might compete in interest with the corpse in the coal hole was the sensation for which the Christian world was waiting.[10]

One thing led to another, and gradually the layers of anonymity were peeled from Dorothy and she found herself, quite without intending it, having to make personal statements about the Christian faith. She did her best to depersonalize the whole thing by scrupulously sticking to a restatement of Church doctrine, and refusing to be drawn at any time into "what Christ means to me" or any other form of personal avowal. Unfortunately the way in which she re-stated the Christian doctrines was so vigorous, so pugnacious, so stimulating – in short so personal and so unlike the normal clerical version – that there was no chance of her being able to get away with insisting that she was merely repeating what the Church was always saying. Orthodox theology it might be, but it bore little relation to what the man or woman in the pew heard, week after week, from the man in the pulpit.

Dorothy must have been well aware of the stir she would cause by describing the crucifixion as "the judicial murder of God". Good copy-writer that she was, she knew exactly how to create an effect – this was the same woman who had foreseen, stimulated and revelled in the "scrumptious row" about the theology of *Catholic Tales and Christian Songs*, and had written the blurb for *The Zeal of Thy House*. Indeed, as she says, the *Sunday Times* article was part of the publicity campaign for the play.

"The Greatest Drama Ever Staged" appeared in the *Sunday Times* in April 1938. It was an article of less than two thousand words, and its full title was "The Greatest Drama Ever Staged is the Official Creed of Christendom".

Its thesis was that it is not dogma that makes Christianity dull; it is precisely the neglect of dogma that has given Christianity the appearance of dullness. The sort of passage that made people sit up and take notice ran like this:

So that is the outline of the official story – the tale of the time when God was the under-dog and got beaten, when He submitted to the conditions He had laid down and became a man like the men He had made, and the men He had made broke Him and killed Him. This is the dogma we find so dull – this terrifying drama of which God is the victim and hero.

If this is dull, then what, in Heaven's name, is worthy to be called exciting? The people who hanged Christ never, to do them justice, accused Him of being a bore – on the contrary; they thought Him too dynamic to be safe. It has been left for later generations to muffle up that shattering personality and surround Him with an atmosphere of tedium. We have very efficiently pared the claws of the Lion of Judah, certified Him "meek and mild" and recommended Him as a fitting household pet for pale curates and pious old ladies. To those who knew Him, however, He in no way suggested a milk-and-water person; *they* objected to Him as a dangerous firebrand. True, He was tender to the unfortunate, patient with honest inquirers, and humble before Heaven; but He insulted respectable clergymen by calling them hypocrites; He referred to King Herod as "that fox"; He went to parties in disreputable company and was looked upon as a "gluttonous man and a wine-bibber, a friend of publicans and sinners"; He assaulted indignant tradesmen and threw them and their belongings out of the Temple; He drove a coach-and-horses through a number of sacrosanct and hoary regulations; He cured diseases by any means that came handy, with a shocking casualness in the matter of other people's pigs and property; He showed no proper deference for wealth or social position; when confronted with neat dialectical traps, He displayed a paradoxical humour that affronted serious-minded people, and He retorted by asking disagreeably searching questions that could not be answered by rule of thumb. He was emphatically not a dull man in His human lifetime, and if He was God, there can be nothing dull about God either. But He had "a daily beauty in His life that made us ugly", and officialdom felt that the established order of things would be more secure without Him. So they did away with God in the name of peace and quietness.[11]

The most widely diverse people have always managed to find in Christ a reflection of themselves. The meek and humble find their kind of Christ in the Sermon on the Mount. Revolutionaries can find theirs in the man crucified by the establishment. And somehow there is a touch of the Musketeer in the argumentative, unconventional figure, fond of good food and wine, that Dorothy emphasizes; a figure not entirely unlike Dorothy herself.

Unexciting churchmen were naturally delighted to be told that their God was such a vivid and romantic figure. And since Dorothy not only knew her theology backwards but continually emphasized the essential doctrinal point that Jesus was both God and man, with all the implications following from that paradox, she did indeed appear to be "the sensation for which the Christian world was waiting".

Despite the stir caused by this article and a similar one, "The Dogma is the Drama", which appeared at about the same time in the *St Martin's Review*, it was certainly not theology that, at this moment, most occupied Dorothy's mind. She was much more concerned about the fortunes of her plays.

Busman's Honeymoon had been transferred to the Victoria Palace with a new pair of leads, Basil Foster and Ethel Glendinning, and had then gone on tour. Dorothy had been pleased about the change of cast at first ("I can't help feeling it an advantage to an actor to have his *glands* in the right place"), but when the show went on the road the production apparently got out of hand (in the way of many touring shows), and we find Dorothy writing to a friend in Oxford advising her not to go to see it.

Undiscouraged, she continued her efforts at organizing a tour of *The Zeal of Thy House*. She was in her element – exercising her talent according to its "proper truth".

I shall try to discuss later what exactly this means, but what it meant for Dorothy at this time was simply that she was doing something that she loved, understood and felt at home with – something in which there was no dishonesty, as there had been a degree of dishonesty in advertising, and even in her detective stories, in as much as Peter Wimsey had been born of financial pressure, and forced by economic circumstances to live on beyond his allotted span.

When someone asked Dorothy to contribute to a book in which eminent people wrote about their childhood, she felt that this was not part of the proper truth of her job, and wrote back: "If there is anything more pernicious than chit chat about the early life and influences of important people, it is chit chat about the early life and influences of unimportant people"[12] – a line which she took frequently, and one which sorts ill with the detail and the psychological truth of the unfinished *Cat o' Mary*. The derogatory word "chit chat" begs the question entirely. We know that, had she wished, she could have contributed something of truth and importance about her early years; but now she asserted that "youthful faiths and hopes and fears are all, if you will excuse the expression, poppycock!"[13]

Similarly, when Rose Macaulay wrote asking her to write a religious play, she refused on the ground that it was not "in her line", and that it would use up more time than she had to spare from her legitimate work. But when Longman's approached her to know whether they might commission her to write a book about Christianity, her reasons for refusal were rather different:

I feel that lay persons such as myself can interfere in these matters much more successfully if they do not do it too often. To rise up once and lay about one is startling and effective. But when one makes a practice of it, the thing becomes official, and the public only say "Oh poor old Dorothy Sayers has gone religious", and pay no further attention.

Though she also added, more characteristically:

Also I feel that religious books at this moment should on no account be "personal". The thirst for reading other people's personal theories about religion is a bad symptom, I think. It is an aspect of that pulpit worship as opposed to altar worship which makes religion in this country and at this time so lacking in guts.[14]

Dorothy's concern for her "proper truth" and "the worth of the work" included, not unnaturally, a concern for the reward for the work. She did not believe in doing anything for nothing. One of her running battles with the BBC had to do with the size of the fees. And when Margaret Babington wrote from Canterbury to ask Dorothy for another play, her immediate reaction was to say that in the first place she was too busy, and in the second place she could hardly be expected to write the play for the thirty-guinea fee Canterbury was offering; the transaction was only acceptable if the production could be transferred to the West End, and plays that could be made to work both in Canterbury Cathedral and in Shaftesbury Avenue were not easy to devise. Not that a London production was any guarantee of income; she had actually lost money on *The Zeal of Thy House*. But at least in London royalties were a possibility – in Canterbury not so.

The challenge, however, was too tempting. Any playwright knows that one of the great incentives is the guarantee of a production – and where else would Dorothy find that except at Canterbury? However much the public loved Wimsey, the West End was always a gamble and a hazard.

Moreover, in Canterbury she ruled the roost. She was much dissatisfied with the acoustics, and one of the conditions upon which she agreed to do another play was that something should be done about them.

Her reluctance to embark on the writing of a second Canterbury play, with its dubious financial advantages, must have been aggravated by her experiences with the tour of *The Zeal of Thy House*. It opened in Norwich in October 1938, at the height of the war panic occasioned by Hitler's invasion of Czechoslovakia. It is likely that Dorothy's patriotism, her highly developed sense of honour and her instinctive bellicosity would have put her firmly on the side of those who condemned Chamberlain for his policy of appeasement, rather than those who praised him for peacemaking. But whatever her political reactions, the crisis also came home to her in a more personal way in the form of three financially disastrous performances at Norwich. This was followed a week or so later by an unprecedented gale and flood at Southport, which forced the leading man to roll up his trousers and wade to get into the theatre; and once again nobody came to see the play. Poor Dorothy was gaining her managerial experience against odds a Musketeer would have relished.

She was no absentee manager. At each new town that the company visited she would arrive on the Monday morning, "and receive a selection of her 'lambs', as she called us, at her hotel, where she would dispense coffee and quips and solve all our little problems".[15] Bartlett Mullins, to whom I am indebted for that recollection, thinks that "Dorothy was one of *the* happiest things that happened to me"[16] – just as being with actors was one of the happiest things that happened to her. Even to her closest non-theatrical friends, she never concluded her letters "With all love, Yours ever affectionately", as she did to Bartlett and many other actors and actresses – though even to them she would sign herself formally "Dorothy L. Sayers", rather than the informal "Dorothy".

"I am preoccupied with 'Zeal' to the exclusion of all memory and commonsense",[17] she had written to Ivy even before the play had opened in London; and such preoccupation was a drain on income (now about £3,500 a year) as well as time. She had contributed heavily to the funding of the tour, having tried and failed to persuade the ecclesiastical authorities to contribute some backing; and when the tour was threatened by the unkindness of the weather and the political situation, she was in some perplexity as to where to find extra cash.

She did manage to find another backer, which helped matters, but she also took a step which startled many of her fans and which, it must be admitted, seems rather incongruous in someone who had just been elected Chairman of the Modern Language Association. It even aroused quizzical comment in the leader columns of *The Times*. She lent her name to an advertisement for Horlicks Malted Milk.

Horlicks were running their famous series of "before-and-after" stories, and one of these was billed as: "TIGHT–ROPE. A true-life story by Dorothy L. Sayers, author of *The Five Red Herrings, The Nine Tailors,* and part author of the recent West End success *Busman's Honeymoon*". (No mention of *The Zeal of Thy House*.)

The story concerns one, Bob Brown, whose prospects of becoming manager are slipping away as a result of "this everlasting tiredness". The doctor diagnoses Night-Starvation, and two months later Bob is back on the road to success. There is, in fact, not a trace of difference between Dorothy's story and the dozens of others put out by Horlicks.

The Times, tongue in cheek, regretted only that Lord Peter Wimsey had not been involved. "Noblemen, so far as is known, are not immune from night-starvation, and often wake up tired",[18] they pointed out. Dorothy responded by explaining the reasons for which she had contributed to the series, and reminded the editor of The Times that this was not the first time that either Peter Wimsey or she had been connected with the advertising profession. She added:

> I heartily agree that the style of the advertisement in question is not up to Peter's standard or mine – but then the advertisers refused to make use of the elegant copy I prepared for them and rewrote it according to their own notion of what was fitting. This is what invariably happens to copy-writers.[19]

While all this was going on, Dorothy had also broken her own embargo on writing religious plays, to the extent of doing a radio nativity play for the BBC children's programme. In He That Should Come she was able to put into practice, in a small way, her thesis that the story of Jesus was "the greatest drama ever staged"; and it was of course to lead to the massive radio serial, covering the whole of Christ's life – The Man Born to be King.

Dorothy's particular blend of scholarship, imagination, vigour and homely realism was a revelation to radio listeners. Here was the sacred story springing to life in a way they had never heard before. If it had a weakness it was over-thoroughness: it lacked that refinement of art which lies in concealing the craft. It is a little too apparent how careful Dorothy was to see that every level of society should have a representative, every viewpoint a spokesman. That apart, her re-creation of the society of the day was masterly, every character being historically accurate yet immediately recognizable as a perennial type.

Once again she had a winner. Produced with understanding and imagination by Val Gielgud (brother of John Gielgud, one of London's leading actors) the play was received with rapture. The few who thought there was irreverence in it were overwhelmed by the many who sensed that truth to life could never be irreverent:

> We quickly felt the wild, unruly, unfriendly atmosphere of the inn and as the play progressed the whole scene became amazingly vivid, and the people "came alive". None of us realized before how much we

had just *accepted* the story without properly visualizing it. It gave us a new vision of it all and the tiny infant's cry brought home to us as never before the *real* humanity of Jesus. . . .[20]

For the first time it was possible to "place" the Story against a "real" background without "groping" with one's imagination. For much blind groping, especially for the everyday details of long-past times, rather tends to prevent one from yielding fully to atmosphere. The sincerity and beauty of your Nativity Play are so free from sentimentality. Moreover, many references to politics and serious questions of those times might apply equally well to today. . . .[21]

For the first time for years I listened to a broadcast play, and thoroughly enjoyed *He That Should Come*. So, you may be interested to know, did my "pub audience", roughly speaking the older generation of the village. As one of them put it, "it's nice to think that people in the Bible were folks like us".[22]

In the meantime, the authorities at Canterbury had agreed to take the necessary steps about the acoustics in the Chapter House; upon which Dorothy set herself to a task that would daunt the most experienced dramatist – a new version of the Faust legend.

The Zeal of Thy House had been based on a true story about a real man, and it did – this is perhaps its greatest virtue – make a personal and original statement. *The Devil to Pay* was a different matter. It was not, of course, a simple restatement of the Faust legend; like any good writer who takes on the story, Dorothy had something of her own to add. But basically it was a retelling of the traditional tale, and the point that Dorothy made in it was not anything specific to her – it was simply an aspect of traditional Christian theology.

Part of the fun of it, part of the challenge from Dorothy's point of view, lay simply in the problems of style and staging which it presented; and her introduction to the play, with her analysis of these problems, reads much more interestingly and convincingly than the play itself. With her usual scholarly precision, she distinguishes the three types of devil in traditional literature – the fallen angel of Milton and of orthodox theology; the personification of total evil; and the comic demon, beloved of mediaeval crowds. She also describes the different possible outcomes of Faust's bargain with the Devil, and the different possible reasons why, in any given age, an intelligent man might make such a bargain. In the middle of the twentieth century, she reckoned, the intellectual temptation would be a desire for immediate and unconditional social change – the dream (though she does not say so) of the socialist revolutionary. Here she sees the sort of temptation that would delude a man of intelligence and honour with visions of unreality, and lead him into paths of evil for the sake of a future good.

The device by which the devil is tricked of his due is the same one that Dorothy used in her short story *Who Calls the Tune*, written nearly twenty years before. The soul which is finally handed over to the devil is so shrivelled as to be not worth having; in fact, when Mephistopheles opens the bag in which the soul is concealed, all that emerges is a black dog – a trick which, as Dorothy says in her introduction, would have delighted the mediaeval mind. And in fact Faust, by accepting the justice of his punishment and by calling on Christ even at this last moment, ensures that his hell will really only be purgatory, the place of cleansing, and that in the end Christ will be able to lift him out of it.

All this, as foreshadowed in the preface, seems likely to be interesting, effective and, within its mediaeval terms, logical. One sets about reading the play full of anticipation. Unfortunately, the anticipation is not fulfilled. The execution of the drama is so simplified as to rob it of all serious tension. The characters have no human reality and exist only as mouthpieces for a kind of diagrammatic laying out of the story. And the weakest of all are the "good" characters, Faust's servants, Lisa and Wagner. The latter is supposed to be a comic simpleton, but the simplicity of his comedy is not child-like so much as childish, not simple so much as inane.

Dorothy would no doubt have pointed out that the mediaeval models that she was following, and the mediaeval events that she was celebrating, reflected a much simpler and more naïve society than today's; and that the simplicity was part of its strength. She herself, however, knew well enough that one cannot go back in history, and she should have known better than to try to do so in literature. But the temptation was too great; the mediaeval, ecclesiastical world was the world of her childhood imagination, and it had not lost its hold.

Sealed off in a separate compartment of her life, Dorothy's domestic concerns demanded their share of time and attention. Anthony had won a scholarship to Malvern College; which, even allowing for his inherited intelligence, says much for Ivy's care and skill in his upbringing. Dorothy was full of appreciation, and took as active a part as she could in the preparations for his departure to the school in October.

He and she had often met at the beginnings and ends of terms when he was on his way through London to his preparatory school in Kent, or on shopping expeditions for school clothes and other requisites. Dorothy had thoughtfully seen to it that he was equipped with such vital items, desirable in a schoolboy's eyes for prestige purposes, as a reliable watch, a fountain pen and a stout pen-knife with all the proper accessories. And her letters to him were friendly, funny, unpatronizing, sensible and, in short, what any boy might be delighted to receive from a parent.

Though Anthony was never told that she was his true mother, it was no great shock or surprise to him when, needing a passport after the war, he sought out his birth certificate and discovered that the big energetic woman who had been signing herself "Mother" was just that. If there was any surprise it was not unwelcome, for she had established a firm sense of trust and affection between them; and the only resentment he felt was that others had known so much more about him than he had been allowed to know himself.

Mac was a different matter. He was in frequent pain with rheumatism, he had taken to the bottle and he was often very bloody-minded. In 1934 a letter from Ivy had gone astray and had been discovered, several weeks later, under a pile of books in Mac's bedroom. Dorothy wrote to Ivy: "Mac is getting so queer and unreliable that it is not safe to trust him to do anything at all, and if he is told that he has forgotten anything, he goes into such a frightful fit of rage that one gets really alarmed. The doctors say that he *is* getting definitely queer – but there doesn't seem to be much that one can do about it." All the doctors could say about it was that it was "due to some kind of germ or disease or shock or something – probably the result of the War".[23]

Quite apart from this vague "queerness", however, one can understand Mac's feelings. It had been bad enough to be married to a successful detective-story writer, but at least she could be expected to work most of the time at home. It was another thing when she began spending long periods with theatrical folk, running around the country to touring theatres and throwing cheerful parties to which he was not invited – the problem being that when he was invited, he could behave so dreadfully that nobody wanted to invite him again.

When she was at home, Dorothy put up with his moods as cheerfully as possible, trying to make up for her absences by being the model wife, letting him dictate the times of meals and writing late into the night after he was in bed, so as not to aggravate his sense of jealous inferiority. What redeemed this sour situation was that each felt a deep underlying affection for the other; and on her side there was, in addition, a sympathetic understanding of his troubles, on his real respect for her qualities and a pride in her achievements. In spite of all the aggravation, the affection held.

The peace that Chamberlain had bought was a frail thing. It was very soon apparent to anyone who thought about it at all that war was on the way. Early in May the Incorporated Society of Authors, Playwrights and Composers sent round a questionnaire to its members, at the suggestion of the Ministry of Labour, asking for a list of their credits and qualifications, "in order that the fullest use may be made, should an emergency arise, of the special abilities of authors."

Dorothy, who was busy with the run-up to a London production of *The Devil to Pay*, wrote back, rather flippantly, saying that she could hardly be expected to have kept count of all the articles and short stories she had written, and for her part she intended to offer her services to the Ministry of Propaganda, where she felt her gifts might be properly used. In fact she had already written on May 9 to Sir Frank Newnes, who put her in touch with Major General Ian Hay Beith. He was not only Director of Public Relations for the War Office but also, using the name Ian Hay, a most successful writer of light comedies for both page and stage. (An intriguing side-light on this incident is that John Cournos was already in the same sub-section as Ian Hay Beith, on account of his special knowledge of the Soviet Union. Whether Dorothy was still in touch with him – whether indeed the idea had come from him in the first place – we do not know; but the coincidence is curious.)

The result of Dorothy's approach was a letter in July from A. P. Waterfield, asking her to be on the Authors' Planning Committee of the Ministry of Information – the purpose of the committee being to advise how best various authors could be used in case of war.

Dorothy, increasingly able to pick a quarrel almost anywhere, wrote back to say that the Ministry ought not to presume to tell writers how and what to write; and only after she had been assured that there was no such intention did she agree to join the committee.

Even then she wrote cheerfully to Anthony that she suspected that her ideas might prove a bit too good for the Government; and immediately sent to Waterfield what he described as "a most interesting and comprehensive scheme of propaganda"[24] – in fact a scheme for organizing the entire work of the Ministry, complete with charts illustrating the man-power structure. It was, of course, not what she had been asked for, and Waterfield acknowledged it politely and set it on one side.

The committee duly met at the end of July, other members including R. H. S. Crossman, A. P. Herbert, L. A. G. Strong, and Professor John Hilton, with A. D. Peters, the literary agent, as Secretary. Shortly after this Dorothy was appointed to an advisory sub-committee, "to examine and advise upon scripts referred to the Authors' Committee by any branch of the Ministry"; and at the beginning of September, just as the war began, she did indeed report on a couple of secret pamphlets: "The

Economic Position of Germany" and "Why are we fighting Germany?"

By the end of the month, however, she was writing to a fellow author: "At the moment I feel there is nothing to be done with the Ministry of Information. I have tried myself to get them to exercise a little sense, and to make proper use of trained writers. But they are in a hopeless muddle, and will never get anything done until they have carried out a ruthless purge of parasites."[25]

In fact, some kind of power struggle had been going on in the Ministry, and a new panel had been set up to take the place of the com-mittee – a panel whose composition and function were discussed in long memoranda for a couple of months, during which Dorothy's name still survived on it. But in a memo from Waterfield (now Deputy Director General of the Ministry) dated November 22, there is a cross against her name, with the words "Very difficult and loquacious"; and a week later, she has disappeared from the list altogether.

A few months elapsed, and then Professor John Hilton, who had evidently suffered an eclipse during the "muddles" of the autumn, wrote to Dorothy to say that things had now straightened themselves out and he would like her back again; but by this time Dorothy had had enough.

There will never be much love lost between ministries and people like Dorothy, and it is not surprising that the Civil Service found it impossible to deal with her difficult and loquacious opinions. She had anticipated her rejection, but it was all the same a considerable blow. She deter-mined henceforward to give the Ministry the cold shoulder, and temper her avowed loyalty to the powers that be with a very sharp eye for their follies and their incompetence.

It was a disappointment – but there were other things to do. On the whole Dorothy met the war with exultation. Within the bulky frame of this upper middle-class Englishwoman there still lived the Musketeer soul. Dorothy's patriotism, her sense of history and her sense of romance, deep-rooted qualities all three of them, responded to the image, romantic and yet for once real, of the little peaceable island standing as a bulwark against tyranny; and not only tyranny, in Dorothy's eyes – heresy was involved as well.

For Germany had committed the final unforgivable sin – the sin against the Holy Ghost. Her rulers had chosen to see evil as good, and good as evil. They had deliberately cut out of their philosophy all respect for the individual human soul. For Dorothy (as for many other thinking Christians) this was not merely a political or economic struggle, it was a religious one.

Six days after the war began, Victor Gollancz asked Dorothy whether she would care to think about writing a Christmas message to the nation, for him to publish. He probably had in mind something of about the same length as "The Greatest Drama ever Staged" – a twenty-page pamphlet that could be printed and distributed in a hurry. But Dorothy got the bit between her teeth, and wrote him a book of a hundred and sixty pages.

She called it *Begin Here*; and its argument was that people should not regard war as a time for ceasing to think about the problems of peace and of a right way to live – on the contrary they should welcome the opportunity to throw away all the old assumptions, the habits of thought that were being torn up by the impact of war, and use the time to think afresh.

The particular fresh thoughts that she wished to set before her readers concerned a return to spirituality and individuality, and she pleaded especially for a transformation in people's attitude to work. Human beings live by work. They spend most of their lives at it. If they do not enjoy it and make something creative of it, they have thrown away a great part of life. Dorothy's plea was that all work should be made worth doing, and that the point of working should be for the satisfaction of doing the job, not for the financial reward – a corollary of the ideas she had put forward in *Gaudy Night* and *The Zeal of Thy House* about the need for the worker to serve the purity of the work.

In the interests of making her point, Dorothy embarked upon a summary of the different theories of the nature of man from the Renaissance onwards. Before the Renaissance, she claimed, man had been seen as a whole being. The doctrine of the Church had been that body and spirit were both real and both good. For all the failures of the Church to put this ideal into practice, the ideal itself, she believed, was the only adequate one, since it provided for a complete fulfilment of man, in relation to himself, his society, his natural surroundings and his God. This she called theological man.

Theological man was followed by humanist man, who was man complete in himself but without a relationship to God. He in turn was followed by rational man, the embodied intelligence of the eighteenth century. Then followed biological man, ushered in by Darwin and his followers; sociological man, the member of the herd; psychological man, the response to environment; and finally economic man, man seen simply as the response to the means of livelihood.

This whole process, Dorothy suggested, represented the gradual whittling away of the essential wholeness and dignity of man; and since it was not possible to return to the Church-made vision of theological man, a new conception of man was now needed to rescue him from this spiritual impoverishment – this was to be creative man.

In this book it becomes clear that Dorothy's essential conservatism has nothing to do with capitalism. She has often been criticized for her right-wing attitudes, and it is true that she had little sympathy with or understanding of the left. But her arguments show a profundity that her critics do not often realize; for Dorothy, both capitalism and the sort of socialism that is only interested in economic equality are tarred with the same brush – both put ultimate value on money. To see life solely in terms of the haves and have-nots begs the question as to whether the thing they have or do not have is really the only thing worth having.

It is not even quite fair to say that she was simply a traditionalist. There is no doubt she instinctively harked back to the old ways and the old days; and her theory of the theological man of the Middle Ages, though she realized how rarely her ideal was achieved in practice, still betrays the romantic in her. Despite this, and despite the fact that later, in a correspondence with a friendly but critical monk, she acknowledged that the book was full of errors and faults and she hoped that it would be forgotten, *Begin Here* is not a backward-looking book. It has flashes of insight, a stimulating freshness of approach and a fair measure of Dorothy's argumentative punch. Not many people had the ability to probe as deeply or as shrewdly into the very basis of our everyday assumptions. Her solutions may have been impractical, but her questions were very much to the point and she surely pointed in the right direction.

Apart from a few minor articles, *Begin Here* was the furthest that Dorothy was ever tempted out of her depth and out of that proper sphere of work that she so believed in. But it established her more firmly than ever in the eyes of Churchmen as a spokesman for liberal Christianity, capable of walking into enemy country and taking on the foe on his own terms. She had a way of putting a very accurate finger on the essential weaknesses of other people's arguments, in a way that the clergy lamentably failed to do. And it established something else: at a time when Churchmen were desperately wondering how to tackle this great new disaster, the war, Dorothy waded in with a cheerful assurance that it was an excellent thing to have happened to the Church. Here were régimes, she pointed out, that had been defying the divine law as preached by the Church, and now the catastrophic results could be clearly seen. What were the clergy waiting for? Their justification was all around them. Let them rise up and hammer home their points!

Another type of Christian might have mourned the folly of man, the loss of life, the break-up of homes, the fear and misery and boredom and disruption that the war would surely bring. Not Dorothy. Providence had given her a powerful case to argue, and nothing could suit her better. The work of Christ and His Church was, after all, to bring good out of evil. Christians were right and pagans were wrong; and what harm was there in a little short-lived suffering, a little destruction, if it gave her the chance to prove it?

CHAPTER FIFTEEN

WRITING BOOKS WAS not Dorothy's only contribution to winning the war. She organized a group of lectures for the Workers' Educational Association, and herself toured the factories speaking on "The Great Economic Obsession" – a subject in which she had no qualifications apart from a strong sense that the emphasis on economic progress in both capitalist and marxist countries was a serious obstacle to the coming of Creative Man. She began knitting a great many socks and sweaters for trawlermen, her own personal trawler being H.M.T. *Varanis*; and this led her, almost inevitably, into a long and acrimonious correspondence with the Ministry of Supply about their inefficiency and lack of imagination in organizing the supply of knitting wool. She dragged Peter Wimsey back to life for a series of articles in the *Spectator* about the war: Wimsey was now occupied in work of vital importance to the nation "somewhere in Europe", and the articles consisted of family letters to him, about him and from him. The eleven pieces, mostly fairly light-hearted, gave Dorothy a chance to trot out most of her hobby-horses. She must have got considerable satisfaction from sending Wimsey's sister-in-law, the objectionable Helen, to the Ministry of Instruction and Morale, a transparent disguise for the hated Ministry of Information: "What *she* can possibly have to instruct anyone about I don't know, but as the place is packed with everybody's wives and nephews and all the real jobs seem to have been handed over to other departments it's as good a spot as any to intern the nation's trouble-makers . . ."[1]

The last letter, however, is suddenly serious – a short extract from a letter from Wimsey to Harriet:

> It's not enough to rouse up the Government to do this and that. You must rouse the people. You must make them understand that their salvation is in themselves and in each separate man and woman among them. If it's only a local committee or amateur theatricals or the avoiding being run over in the blackout, the important thing is each man's *personal responsibility*. They must not look to the State for guidance – they must learn to guide the State. Somehow you must contrive to tell them this. It is the only thing that matters.[2]

There speaks Dorothy, loud and clear.

Other preoccupations included accommodation for the Detection Club, of which she was now Hon. Secretary; Anthony's education (and she was none too complimentary about the senior universities at this time, finding them much too remote from life); the ever-present problem of Mac; and the endless chore of running her household. The kind of scene is set in a letter to Muriel St Clare Byrne in October 1939, while Dorothy was working on her ideas for *Begin Here*:

Well, dash it, if it comes to that, how about A Day in the Life of an Inoffensive Citizen, anxious only to toil for the nation's good.

8.30 – Breakfast – 2 letters from persons applying about the situation.

9.30 – Invent new kind of batten [for her model theatre], while waiting for husband to vacate bath.

9.40 – Bath and dress.

10.10 – Secretary arrives, dizzy with anti-cholera inoculation.

10.15 – Cook says another young person has called about situation.

10.17 – Interview young person.

10.25 – Send Secretary to buy screws to mend cigarette-box broken by outgoing housemaid. Order meals.

10.30 – Ring M.S.B. about W.E.A.

10.45 – Start on letter to Sec. of W.E.A.

10.50 – Stop to mend cigarette-box – unsuccessful.

11.00 – Continue letter to W.E.A. Sec.

11.10 – Listen to Secretary's symptoms and say she had better go home after lunch.

11.20 – Continue letter to W.E.A. Sec.

11.30 – Irritated by failure of cigarette-box to function. Mend it again (one of the automatic kind, made in Japan, with interior like intoxicated spider). Successful.

11.50 – Draft letter to W.E.A. Sec. and further letter to Sec. of C.S.U. at Newnham, offering to lecture on Nov. 9.

12.30 – Feel it is too late to start on Christmas Message to Nation. Saw batten preparatory to experiment with new idea. (Mem. Husband has borrowed best saw.)

1.00 – Lunch. Remind Cook prospective housemaid arriving 2.15 and will she meet her at station.

1.30 – Present housemaid says, can I tell Cook name of prospective housemaid. Tell her Dora Wybrook.

1.35 – Suddenly recollect, not Wybrook but Wymark. Convey correction to Cook.

1.40 – Feel disintegrated. Cut out and hem grey border.

2.00 – Front-door bell rings. Nobody to answer it. Cook at station, housemaid changing.

2.5 – Call housemaid down to answer door.

2.6 – Caller turns out to be Dora Wymark, train having arrived 15 mins earlier than Passenger Enquiries (L'pool St) said it would, so that Cook missed her at station.

2.8 – Explanations. Take D.W. to kitchen and leave her there.

2.10 – Uneasy feeling of expectation. Sew border.

2.30 – Hearing Cook return, apologize for error in information. Sew border. Cook and D.W. exploring avenues, & the house.

3.00 – D.W. returns. Interview. Says she would like to come.

3.5 – Interview Cook separately. She is willing.

3.10 – Engage D.W.

3.12 – Hunt house for change to pay D.W.'s fare.

3.20 – Return to library. Secretary says she is feeling better.

3.25 – Telephone. Mysterious caller for husband. Fetch husband.

3.30 – Husband says message is from local baker, asking why we have changed to rival baker. Did not know we had. Refer husband to Cook.

3.35 – Return to library. Sign letters, and try to understand where everything is.

3.40 – Ring Bun, and tell her must urge Ed. Spectator make up his mind about Wimsey letters and must soothe Gollancz about blurb. Bun says Hodder & Stoughton interested in booklets provided they are a) religious or educational & b) edited under my supervision; hopes of really embracing scheme for getting stuff out. Say, Excellent – perfectly ready to edit anything provided others do most of the work.

3.45 – Return to library. Dismiss Secretary with good wishes and wedding-present.

3.55 – Try to think about Christmas message to nation.

4.10 – Local joiner arrives to ask what it was I wanted done about battens & fly-gallery. Explain model theatre to him and work the curtains. Place order. Ask about spot lights and cleats. Local joiner says he has friend with diploma for making models of things, but he is in R.A.F. Reserve & may go any minute – also he is "busy courting".

4.40 – Try to think about Christmas message to nation. Disintegrated.

4.45 – Disintegrated.

4.50 – Abandon message to nation. Try to put batten together.

4.57 – Joiner's friend arrives unexpectedly.

5.00 – Tea-bell rings. Tell husband I am engaged with joiner's friend. Explain too hurriedly and have to explain again.

5.05 – Joiner's friend very intelligent and voluble. Says he will explore avenues.

5.20 – Tea (cold).

5.50 – Come up to library and write letter to M.S.B.

So there you are. At any rate, I have engaged the housemaid.[3]

Cook, incidentally, was no more permanent a feature than the housemaid, and often enough Dorothy had to do the cooking herself. What with one thing and another, in fact, the first two years of the war were the busiest, as well as the most varied and prolific, of Dorothy's life. The spring of 1940 saw many seeds being sown, of which some fell on stony ground but others, sooner or later, bore plentiful fruit. In February, for example, came a proposal from Canterbury Cathedral to revive *The Zeal of Thy House* in the summer – little knowing that by summer the German army would be less than forty miles from Canterbury, poised for invasion. So that idea was to come to nothing. But the same month a letter came from Dr J.W. Welch, Director of Religious Broadcasting at the BBC, suggesting "a series of short plays about the life of Our Lord". And that was the start of one of Dorothy's great triumphs, *The Man Born to be King*.

There was also a letter from Patrick McLaughlin, then an Anglican priest, about the launching of a magazine to be called *Christendom* – which was to lead to Dorothy's long connection with St Anne's House, a religious discussion centre of which McLaughlin was one of the directors. And in April Dorothy was corresponding with E.V. Rieu about a series of books under the title of *Bridgeheads*, to be edited by herself, Muriel St Clare Byrne and another great friend, Helen Simpson (who was to die, suddenly and tragically, soon after).

The prospectus of the series was evidently written by Dorothy, and deserves quoting in full, for it sums up, as concisely as she was able, the sort of concerns that she had at heart; and it expresses the basic philosophy that underlies all her public pronouncements. It may be found reproduced as an Appendix, on page 278.

What is remarkable is the hugely ambitious range of subjects on which Dorothy was prepared to lay down the law, regardless of whether or not she had any real knowledge of them. She still suffered from the all-knowingness that she had confessed to in *Cat o'Mary*; but now she could justify it by the view that theology, known in the Middle Ages as the queen of the sciences, was able to pronounce, in principle at least, on any area of human life or knowledge. Thus she could confidently discuss not only the inexorable operation of the moral and spiritual law when unredeemed by Grace ("justice is what happens to you if you reject salvation"), but also the proper place of work in society, the ideal system of education, the disastrous flaws in capitalism, the folly of supposing that peace would bring stability or permanence (since all human institutions carried within themselves the seeds of their own corruption), and the idiocy of expecting that the people could be financially helped by the Government, since the Government could only find money by taking it from the people.

The aim of *Bridgeheads* was "in general, to help any man to discover for himself the nature and extent of that creative power which constitutes his real claim to humanity"; and it started from "the assumption that no social structure can be satisfactory that is not based upon a satisfactory philosophy of man's true nature and needs".[4] The projected authors were Dorothy herself, Muriel, the surgeon Denis Brown (Helen Simpson's husband), Una Ellis-Fermor and Dr G. W. Pailthorpe; and the hope was that the bridgeheads which they established would be used by "the remakers of civilization" to "throw forward their pioneering works".[5]

Like many such enterprises, *Bridgeheads* did not get very far, because, despite its high ambitions, the editors had neither the time nor the spare energy to give the project the concentrated attention it required. Only two books actually appeared. But the first of these alone, Dorothy's own *The Mind of the Maker*, was enough to justify the idea – and the association with Rieu was to lead, five years on, to even greater things.

The Mind of the Maker deserves fuller appreciation, and will receive it in the following chapter. For the moment let us consider the range of Dorothy's less weighty occupations in that same vigorous month: joining the executive committee of the Religious Drama Society; publishing an article (written in association with Muriel St Clare Byrne), on a congenial theme, "The Contempt of Learning in Twentieth Century England"; considering and finally rejecting a request to write a book for the *Christian Newsletter*, a publication which she had assisted in founding in 1939; and busily helping with the production of her stage comedy, *Love All*.

Love All had been written at least a year earlier, and a production had been planned for May or June of 1939, but abandoned for reasons we can only guess at. Now, in that odd and unreal period between the declaration of war and the beginning of the real fighting that came to be called the phony war, the play finally reached the stage.

In a light-hearted manner, this play tells us almost as much about the way Dorothy saw herself and her life as *Cat o' Mary* or Harriet Vane. And one might find some significance in the continuation of the "cat" theme in the play's original title, which was "Cat's Cradle".

It was presented at the Torch Theatre in Knightsbridge in April. The occasion can hardly have been scintillating – the Torch Theatre was a tiny, uncomfortable place known to its habitués as the Torture Theatre, accommodating a hundred people at most and generally holding about twenty. It was one of several such little theatres that existed (rather than flourished) in London at the time, offering a limited run of two or three weeks, often in the hope of a transfer to the West End.

Love All was clearly aimed at a West End audience. It is a craftsman-like light comedy in three acts, very much of its period and replete with crashing coincidences and conversations violently wrenched off-course to provide the next twist in the plot.

The story starts in Venice. Dorothy had been there for a brief holiday just before the war, thus providing herself with a new literary background. She had used up on the Wimsey books nearly all the places that she knew well – her childhood home, her college, her place of work in advertising, the countryside of her holidays in Scotland, and the semi-bohemian artistic world of Bloomsbury and the West End. Indeed, the only background which she might have exploited but never did was Les Roches, the school where she had worked with Eric Whelpton eighteen years earlier.

Act One of *Love All* concerns Godfrey, a writer of popular romantic novels who is living in an apartment in Venice overlooking the Grand Canal with his mistress, Lydia, an actress who has abandoned her career to run away with him. They are awaiting a divorce from his nice but boring and unglamorous wife, from whom nothing had been heard for several months. Now, they too are bored – with Venice and the heat, but in truth somewhat with each other. Each of them separately decides to return to London without telling the other – he to see his wife, ostensibly to hasten the divorce but secretly with the thought that he might want to return to her – she to see if she can get a part in a West End play written by a strikingly successful new authoress.

It comes as no very great surprise, when Act Two opens, to find that the authoress is one and the same as Godfrey's unglamorous wife; and that the reason she has been too busy to see about the divorce has been her preoccupation with her new career. Equally unsurprising is the fact that the authoress, Janet Reed, is Dorothy to the life, revelling in an unending series of visits and telephone calls from actors, theatre managers and journalists unsuccessfully demanding personal stories. She has "irregular but intelligent features", and "she obviously feels that she is on top of the world, and animation makes her almost goodlooking".[6] This time the self-portrait is neither sourly self-critical, like Katherine Lammas, nor interestingly haunted by tragedy, like Harriet Vane. Here she disports herself in her element; and the once uninteresting woman has now become strikingly fascinating – all because she now has an activity which interests and absorbs her.

When Godfrey arrives, half in mind to offer to return, she points out, kindly but firmly, that this would not be any sort of a favour. He is presented as a bumbling, unimaginative fellow, who can only see his wife's playwriting as a means of occupying and distracting herself from her true longing – to return to domesticity with him.

The scene is a good one. Indeed the whole act is entertaining, peopled with theatrical types that are nicely observed and only very slightly overdrawn, and every page proclaims Dorothy's exhilaration with the theatre and her delighted involvement in it. And, contrived though it may be, she makes us look forward to the second-act curtain, which is bound to be, and is, the arrival of Lydia, asking for the leading part.

Most of Act Three consists of a long dialogue between Janet and Lydia, during which they find that what unites them is much stronger than what separates them, and that their principal concern is to do "whatever is best for Godfrey's writing".[7] Godfrey's secretary turns up and explains that she thinks that neither of them has made the slightest difference to Godfrey's writing – neither Janet's housewifery nor Lydia's glamorous inspiration has affected him at all. And they realize that sacrificing themselves for him is really a waste of time; they must get on with their own careers: "Every great man has a woman behind him. . . . And every great woman has some man or other in front of her, tripping her up."[8]

The play is something of a give-away: Dorothy's high claims for the integrity of the artist wilt a little when they are seen in the context of writing light-weight West End comedies. For despite some good lines and an entertaining exposition of the case for taking women seriously as individuals, the play can hardly be said to contribute any profound insights into the human condition. Its failure, in theatrical terms, is not that it is too serious or original, but that its structure and style are too conventional.

In accordance with Dorothy's usual theatrical bad luck, the show opened on April 9 1940, the day that the German army invaded Norway – an advance warning of the end of the phony war and the beginning of real war. The reviews were friendly enough. *The Times* wrote: "Miss Dorothy Sayers manages to poke some agreeable fun at a number of conventions, sentimental, literary and theatrical";[9] and *Time and Tide* (admittedly somewhat partisan, since Lady Rhondda, its proprietor, was

a Christian and a friend of Dorothy's) called it a "well written, excellently handled comedy".[10] But history saw to it that there was no
transfer to the West End.

The German advance through Holland and Belgium began on May
10, and by May 25 the British Expeditionary Force had been driven back
through Belgium to the Dunkirk beaches; France fell at the end of June;
suddenly everything in England was very different, very frightening –
and, in a way, very exciting.

Three years later, when the war had swung against Germany, Dorothy
looked back at the romance of it: "Hitler scooped up Norway,
swallowed Denmark alive, bombed and blazed his way across Holland,
battered Belgium to a mummy, tossed the British Army into the sea,
blew France to fragments and smashed through to the Channel Ports.
The world stood still. And Britain [was] stripped naked in the arena to
await the pounce of the beast."[11]

At the time, she wrote to Anthony: "England is back now in the centre
stream of her tradition. She is where she was in 1588 and in 1815. Spain
held all Europe. France held all Europe. They broke themselves upon
England. We have got to see that the same thing happens to Germany."[12] And the same sentiment rings through a poem that she wrote a
month or so later; a poem which Noël Coward, on one of his tours to
entertain the troops, picked up one day in a house occupied by General
Wavell and read in his concert that evening:

> Praise God, now, for an English war –
>   The grey tide and the sullen coast,
> The menace of the urgent hour
> The single island, like a tower,
>   Ringed with an angry host.
>
> This is the war that England knows,
>   When all the world holds but one man –
> King Philip of the galleons
> Louis, whose light outshone the sun's,
>   The conquering Corsican . . .[13]

However, it was not only the Germans, in Dorothy's view, who
threatened the English people – there was also that other old enemy, the
Ministry of Information, who provoked Dorothy into battle over an
anti-rumour campaign mounted jointly by the Ministry and the BBC in
July.

The campaign exhorted the public not to be "chatterbugs" and "jay-talkers" – thus insulting, Dorothy felt, the honour, dignity and common-sense of "the commons of England" . . . "Civil Servants are servants of the English civitas. We of the common people, we are England. We will not endure this insolence in the servants' hall."[14] And she wrote to Sir Richard Maconochie, Controller of Home Services at the BBC, suggesting instead that they stir people's pride and sense of responsibility with slogans such as: "Let them say at the end of this war – it was won by the self-control of the British people, who did much and said nothing."[15] The Ministry did in fact abandon the campaign, though whether Dorothy was in any degree responsible for the change of plan is impossible to say. Certainly her alternative suggestions were never taken up.

At a more active level, she accepted an invitation from the University of London's Regional Committee for Education among His Majesty's Forces to join a panel of lecturers performing at depots and camps within the extra-mural area of the University; and soon after was enlisted by the even more cumbersomely-named "Church's Committee for Work among Men Serving with H.M. Forces" – her brief being "to go about and instruct the serving soldier in the Christian Faith".[16] "I feel", she wrote to a friend who was himself in the Forces, "that to be harangued about religion by a middle-aged female must add very greatly to the horrors of war for these helpless and unhappy young men." Nevertheless, she did it, on the grounds that if she did not, the young men might be faced by "perambulating parsons talking straight-from-the-shoulder religion and exhorting them to be good boys. And what *is* the good of that, if they aren't given any idea what it's all about?"[17] And we may safely assume that her audiences found her a great deal more entertaining than most of their other lecturers.

A very different kind of assembly harangued by the middle-aged female was the Archbishop of York's Conference on "The life of the Church and the Order of Society". Archbishop William Temple (later an outstanding Archbishop of Canterbury) was one of Dorothy's keenest admirers: "How magnificent Dorothy Sayers is!"[18] he had written the previous winter to Dr J. H. Oldham, editor of the *Christian Newsletter*. With rare imagination he chose the majority of the speakers at his conference from among lay-people: Dorothy being paired (rather uncomfortably) with Donald McKinnon, the brilliant and eccentric professor from Keble College, Oxford.

The fear of invasion that summer and autumn, though it did not deter the Archbishop, forced him to postpone the conference by a month or two and move it a couple of hundred miles westward to Malvern –

where, it will be remembered, Anthony was at school – and there it finally took place in January 1941.

Dorothy may have believed that writing plays was her "proper job" and that lecturing to clergymen was an improper deviation, but it is one of the ironies of her life that *Love All* is a rather undistinguished light comedy, but this lecture (like, indeed, most of her lectures) is outstanding.

Her subject was the Church's place in society. How closely should it identify itself with the society it found itself in at any given time? At one extreme there was the view that the role of the Church was to isolate itself from corrupting contacts with society's secular concerns. At the opposite end of the scale were those who felt that it should involve itself so closely with the secular authority that ecclesiastical law becomes the law of the community. The first approach she compared to the theatre, which she never tired of praising for its unity and its purpose. The second she compared to Nazi Germany, where every aspect of society was dominated by party dogma.

How convenient it would be if Christians could go about their own concerns, as theatre people did within their enclosed community, without worrying about the far-from-perfect world around them! Or, on the other hand, how glorious the world might be made if only the Church, guided by the Holy Spirit, could have the running of it!

The second, however, was ruled out because all human institutions, political parties and dogmas, are fallible and short-lived; and the Church, the keeper of eternal truth, could never afford to lend its name and its authority to anything flawed and temporary. The first was rejected because the Church acknowledged that its master was a God who had become man. He had sanctified material life by his material existence, and for the Church to stand aside from everyday human life would be to betray its own origins. As in all things, the balance must be held between the two extreme viewpoints, the two heresies. The Church must concern itself with social and political matters, must study them and pronounce upon them and make its voice heard in every area of human concern; but it must never identify itself wholly with any organization or policy, however noble the aim, however desperate the circumstances. Only by remaining detached could the Church's authority be maintained.

The lecture stimulated yet more demands on Dorothy for further contributions towards the popularizing of Christianity. And having got herself in so deep, it became more and more difficult for her to extricate herself. From this time on an increasing irritability enters into Dorothy's correspondence with enquirers – the irritability of someone who knows, or at least suspects, that she has allowed herself to be put into a false position, and is furious as much with herself as with those who led her into it.

However, in addition to all the multifarious activities in which she was engaged in these first two years of the war, which would have been quite enough in themselves for anyone of normal energy, she was occupied with not just one major work, but two – one dramatic and one theological. These were unquestionably part of the "proper job", and between them did more for the Church than any number of lectures and articles. It may be for Peter Wimsey that Dorothy is most widely remembered; it may even be that she put more of herself, more original writing, into the Wimsey novels than into anything else she did. But the work that went deepest, and made the deepest impression, was surely the work she wrote during these two years: *The Mind of the Maker* and *The Man Born to be King*.

CHAPTER SIXTEEN

BOTH *The Man Born to be King* and *The Mind of the Maker* were in a sense expansions of something Dorothy had written before. She was always at her best when she had plenty of elbow room. Novel length suited her much better than the short-story form, and she was never happier than when spinning out an idea and exploring all its possibilities. It is a mark of the energy and freshness of her mind that a writer so much in love with words should so rarely become verbose or tedious, and that almost anything that one picks up at random, either from her published works, her letters or her unfinished manuscripts, is striking enough to make one want to read on.

The Mind of the Maker was a working-out in detail of the idea that Dorothy had expressed at the end of *The Zeal of Thy House* – the idea that the most godlike thing in man, the attribute that gives us our best chance of grasping, however imperfectly, the nature of the Divine Mind, is our ability to create. And *The Man Born to be King* is a natural, though vast, successor to *He That Should Come*.

Dorothy was immediately tempted by James Welch's suggestion in February 1940 that she should consider writing a dramatized life of Christ in half-hour episodes. From those Godolphin days when she had reacted so bitterly against the mealy-mouthed pietism of the school's official religion, up to her recent entry into the fray with "The Greatest Drama ever Staged", Dorothy had always had something to say about Christianity. Here was an unparalleled chance to demonstrate what the Church (and Dorothy) believed about the True God and True Man who was the Way, the Truth and the Life.

The plays were to be broadcast, as *He That Should Come* had been, on the Children's Hour programme. Dorothy immediately laid down the conditions under which she was prepared to start the work. She was not interested in talking down to the children. Children, in her view, were perfectly capable of understanding a great deal more than adults gave them credit for. Remembering her own childhood, and the joy she had found in the great words of the Christian creeds and affirmations long before she understood their proper significance, she laid it down as a principle that she should be allowed to give other children the same sort of joy. She wanted them to understand with their emotion and intuition things which they could not possibly yet understand with their intellect.

The people at the BBC agreed wholeheartedly; it seemed that this was what they had always said themselves. And Dorothy began to write.

As so often in creative matters, agreement in principle is a good deal easier than co-operation in practice. Words turn out to mean different things to different people, when those people are face to face with the actual thing that the words were supposed to describe. Unfortunately Dorothy's former producer at the BBC, Val Gielgud, had been promoted to Head of Radio Drama and was not available for the project. In the absence of her new producer, Derek McCulloch, it fell to his assistant, Miss May E. Jenkin, to write and say that she and her colleagues felt that certain speeches in Dorothy's first script were "right over the heads of children" and "rather difficult for our audience". "Though we agree with you that it is not necessary for them to understand everything they hear", she wrote, "yet when there is no spectacle to help them and they depend upon their ears alone, it is essential that difficulties of thought and language should not be too great."[1]

The speeches that Miss Jenkin quoted were: "Jove himself, the imperial star, was smitten and afflicted between the sun and moon in the constellation of the virgin"; and "I knew that I stood in the presence of the Mortal-Immortal, which is the last secret of the Universe." She also added one or two technical points to do with making it clear where a scene took place, and a suggestion that here and there Dorothy's dialogue had "dropped into too modern an idiom". But the main burden of the letter that contained these criticisms was one of enormous enthusiasm and warm congratulation, and the criticisms themselves were to be seen, Miss Jenkin wrote, as mere "spots in the sun".[2]

Whether or not Miss Jenkin was artistically justified in her comments, and in her request that either Dorothy should re-think these passages or allow the BBC personnel to edit them, is a matter of opinion; but certainly her letter, which Dorothy was later to describe as impertinent and tactless, was gentle, sensitive and reasonable. "We wonder if you would allow us discreetly to edit!" she wrote. "If you would prefer to make these small alterations yourself, I will send you the play back, but we are anxious not to delay having the copy duplicated, as the posts are so slow at the moment. We would, of course, get your O.K. for every change before the broadcast."[3]

Dorothy's response was less moderate. She began by saying: "I shall now proceed to be autocratic, as anyone has a right to be who is doing a hundred pounds' worth of work for twelve guineas"; a curious justification, one might think, for taking a high line on artistic integrity (even though her income had dropped 20% in the past year). She continues:

I don't think you need trouble yourselves too much about certain passages being "over the heads of the audience". They will be over the heads of the adults, and the adults will write and complain. Pay no attention; you are supposed to be playing to children – the only audience perhaps in the country whose minds are still open and sensitive to the spell of poetic speech . . . it is the language that stirs and excites . . . I will swear that no child has ever heard unmoved "when this corruptible shall have put on incorruption and this mortal shall have put on immortality" . . . I knew how *you* would react to those passages. It is my business to know. But it is also my business to know how my *real* audience will react, and yours to trust me to know it. . . .[4]

She goes on to discuss the question of dialect. Miss Jenkin had raised the point that some of the speeches of the more countrified characters were inconsistent in their dialect and Dorothy's reply is:

This is entirely a matter for the actor. That is why I never give more than the very slightest hint of dialect. . . . If he decides on a touch of Yorkshire, for instance, he will not say "it do be", but use some other form. When he has settled this, *then* if he finds that "conduct you to your tent" is too formal for the speech he is using, he can say "see you to your tent" or "bring ye to your tent" . . . this is a matter for rehearsal, and you must learn to consult the actor.[5]

There was a good deal more in the same vein, from a woman who had written four plays to a woman who had produced ten times as many. When Derek McCulloch returned from Scotland and found Dorothy's letter he wrote – accurately enough – "You have wielded a huge bludgeon",[6] and politely asked her if she would come to Bristol to meet the staff of Children's Hour and discuss the whole thing face to face.

To this not unreasonable request from her producer, Dorothy's letter begins:

Dear Mr McCulloch, Oh no you don't, my poppet! You won't get me to do three days of exhausting travel to Bristol in order to argue about my plays with the committee. What goes into the play, and the language in which it is written, is the author's business. If the management don't like it, they reject the play, and there is an end of the contract. If travelling is at all possible, I am ready to meet the producer and the actors *in rehearsal*. Then, if there is any line or speech which *in rehearsal* I can hear to be wrong, or ineffective, or impossible to speak

aloud, I will alter it, if I think the objection to be justified . . .
anything that has to be done with the *production* I am always ready to
modify . . . you are the producer. Where production is concerned, I
will respect your authority. This is not a matter of production. It falls
within the sphere of *my* authority, and you must respect mine.[7]

Anyone who has had anything to do with writers will recognize
Dorothy's stance immediately; and will know that more often than not it
is to be found in people whose talent is not quite so overwhelming as
they suppose. Any kind of dramatic enterprise is a co-operative effort
between a number of people, and it is quite impossible to maintain strict
dividing lines between the writer, the producer, and the actors. Their
functions interrelate totally, and though each must have the final word
in their particular sphere, a courteous exchange of views – or for that
matter passionate argument – is an essential part of the process.

Dorothy should have known this. Indeed with people she knew,
people who had already won her professional confidence, she was quite
capable of co-operation. Poor Mr McCulloch might well have doubted
it:

You are, I know, bound to back up your colleagues and subordinates,
but you must allow me to tell you that this kind of thing, phrased as it
is phrased in Miss Jenkin's letter, is a blazing impertinence. If I am
asked to write a play for you it is because I have the reputation of
being able to write. Do you think I should have that reputation if I had
allowed my style to be dictated to me by little bodies of unliterary
critics?[8]

Having despatched his assistants, she now turned on McCulloch
himself:

I must also make it plain to you that I am concerned with you as
producer for my play. In that capacity you are not called upon to
mirror other aspects of your work at the BBC; you are called upon to
mirror me. If you prefer to act as the director of a committee of
management, well and good; but in that case you cannot also exercise
the functions of a producer. You can reject the play, in which case the
matter is closed; or you can accept it, in which case you must find me
another producer with whom I can deal on the usual terms, which are
perfectly well understood by all the people with proper theatrical experience. I am sorry to speak so bluntly, but I am a professional
playwright and I must deal with professional people who understand

where their proper spheres of action begin and end. I am writing to Dr Welch, to make the position clear to him, and shall suspend all further work on succeeding plays until the matter has been put on a more satisfactory footing. Yours sincerely.[9]

The bludgeon whose blows Mr McCulloch had hoped to soften in the approved professional manner of discussion and mutual give-and-take had descended with redoubled force on his own head. Dorothy's letter to Dr Welch went over much the same ground, at much the same length. She described Miss Jenkin's letter as "excessively tactless" and added that Derek McCulloch seemed "to think it part of his business to teach me how to write. This will not do."[10]

One of the points she had made to Derek McCulloch was that:

if I am asked by the BBC to do a play for you, it is because they think I can supply a quality of some kind which they cannot get from their staff. That is why outside writers of standing are asked to do things. This always involves the risk that the outside writer may do something which is different from the routine thing which the staff is accustomed to do – and *this difference is the thing for which the outside writer is engaged and paid*. If the writer's authority is not to be absolute in his own sphere, there is no sense in approaching him; he is approached because of his authority, and for no other reason.

Now she went on to claim that "In a case like this, there are only three authorities to which an author must be ready to submit", and these were (a) the Church, (b) the State, and (c) the producer – and then only if he could show good technical or other practical reasons why a certain passage of the script would not work.

This, for Dorothy, was what it meant to be professional; and she flung far and wide her accusations of lack of professionalism in the BBC – the only person exempt, apparently, being Val Gielgud.

Get me Val, and I will go to Bristol or Manchester or anywhere, and work twenty hours a day with the actors, but I must have a producer who is a professional producer and nothing else, and who can talk the language of the theatre. If there is any more nonsense, there is an end of the plays and of the contract. . . . The brutal fact is this, that I consented to do these plays, representing about a hundred pounds' worth of my work apiece, for a derisory sum, merely because I so much liked the idea that I felt it would be a pleasure to do them. If I cannot do them in my own way, it will no longer be a pleasure. And I may say that if the pay were more adequate I should still refuse to do them except along the lines I felt would be artistically right. . . . My reply to Miss Jenkin was not conciliatory, I admit, but I knew that I had come to the point where to cede an inch was to cede the whole territory.[11]

She also took the occasion to deliver a short homily on what was wrong with the BBC (too much bureaucracy, as with the Ministry of Information), which one might think was rather less her business than her writing was the business of her producer. And she concluded by pointing out that the reason why dictators have to lock up artists is because of the latter's insistence on their freedom of artistic judgement – which was presumably what she felt was threatened by the gentle suggestions of Miss Jenkin.

Welch's reply was conciliatory in the extreme. He had spoken to McCulloch and the Children's Hour team at Bristol; they all felt, he wrote, that personalities were less important than the project, and were prepared to back down for the good of the show. Derek McCulloch even offered to stand down as producer, if that was going to help matters. Would Dorothy consider meeting him in London, she as writer and he as producer, and starting from scratch?

Dorothy, mollified, wrote at some length that she would: and went again into all the pros and cons of the situation. She forgave Derek McCulloch, on the grounds that he had merely been doing the proper Civil Service thing and backing up a tactless and misguided colleague:

I am quite prepared to believe that Miss Jenkin has had great experience in the Children's Hour, but when you entrusted the job to me you were taking the adventurous step of cutting out the juvenile experts and trying a new experiment – that of giving the children professional theatre. I think we must stick to the terms of that experiment and deal with the thing on professional theatre lines. "If we fail, we fail", but we must try it out properly and not mess about with it. . . . By all means let us pretend that Miss Jenkin never happened, and return to the starting point.[12]

Welch was delighted. He was sure all would now go smoothly. McCulloch was, he pointed out, a professional radio producer of many years' experience, and moreover had had considerable experience of the theatre and of working with actors. Indeed, he had actually produced more plays than Val Gielgud – though this point would not have cut much ice with Dorothy, who was after quality, not quantity.

All seemed set fair for an auspicious new start, when the maligned

Miss Jenkin decided that she was not prepared to allow Dorothy's slanders to go unanswered; and wrote to Dorothy in reply to "the charges of impertinence, tactlessness and literary ignorance that you have levelled against me".[13] It was perhaps not the wisest thing to do, but it was very understandable, for it does no one any good to have an enemy of Dorothy's reputation flinging irresponsible accusations around the organization for which one works.

That Miss Jenkin, consigned to oblivion, should actually dare to defend herself was too much for Dorothy. The furious comments that she scrawled in the margin of the letter make it quite clear that, at this stage at least, Dorothy's reaction was no calculated piece of political manoeuvring, no throwing of a deliberate temperament in order to get out of a situation she did not care for, as she was later to suggest, but a vehement personal rancour.

Miss Jenkin's main concern was to establish that she had competence in the sphere of radio drama, and that this competence entitled her to comment on the script. She had produced fifty or sixty radio plays for Children's Hour, and in addition had "handled tens of thousands of letters from children commenting on our programmes . . . I therefore can claim to know something of radio drama and something of children's taste in it."[14] She made the point that she had written on behalf of Mr McCulloch and not merely in her own person – "He did and does agree with every word of my letter."[15]

On these points Dorothy makes no comment. But when Miss Jenkin writes: "I gather you do not object on occasion to letting your actors rewrite their parts",[16] the scribble in the margin reads: "If you gathered that from my letter you cannot read." That is savage and not entirely fair: certainly the passage in Dorothy's letter that allows variations of dialect to an actor could be read to mean that she consented to a certain amount of rewriting of a part. Dorothy is on stronger ground when Miss Jenkin writes: "Had your play been written for the stage, I should never have suggested altering any lines on the score of difficulty. But a play over a loud-speaker is an entirely different pair of shoes."[17] In capital letters Dorothy writes: "BALLS! – How would a stage set make the 'mortal-immortal' passage easier?"

This is good knock-about stuff. The real issue comes in Miss Jenkin's penultimate paragraph – "The responsibility for the Children's Hour programmes rests firstly with Mr McCulloch and in his absence with me. Therefore we cannot possibly delegate to any author, however distinguished, the right to say what shall or shall not be broadcast in a Children's Hour play."[18] Against which the marginal scrawl reads: "But the author can refuse to write".

Dorothy had in fact accepted a contract to write for the programme, and she cannot have been unaware that radio programmes, like newspaper articles and indeed books, are subject to editing and comment by those appointed for the purpose. She had rewritten her own books, at least at an earlier stage in her career, at the behest of her publishers; and she could hardly pretend to be so experienced a radio writer as to have complete immunity from the normal editing processes.

Her own claim, to which she returned several times in the course of the correspondence, was that her "standing" as a playwright in the theatre entitled her to such immunity; and that the BBC, having brought her in as an "outside expert", had thereby forfeited all right to have any say in what she wrote for them. But in fact scripts are always discussed between writer and producer, and often between writer and editor, before rehearsal, so that points of disagreement or misunderstanding do not have to be thrashed out in front of the actors. Dorothy's reiterated complaint that she did not wish to have her work mauled by a committee could hardly be justified when all that had happened was that the thoughts of her producer had been passed on to her by his deputy in his absence.

Why did she over-react so violently? It is clear that she sensed danger for her project: she felt some doubt and insecurity about the ability of the Children's Hour team to achieve what she had in mind. For all their protestations, she had certainly found in them something of that unctuous piety that she had come to detest so much at school. She may well have felt trapped by her commitment, and instinctively fought back like a cornered animal. But it needs more than this, I feel, to account for her venom.

The trouble with Dorothy had always been that she had to be right, she had to be above questioning. At any suggestion of criticism, her hackles rose; and it was simply intolerable that a distant authority whom she did not particularly respect should have the right to question her judgement. Allied to this, perhaps, was a residue of that hatred she had felt for the governess who was forever looking over her shoulder as she worked. Perhaps in the careful phrases of Miss Jenkin's letter she had heard echoes of the gentle but inescapable comments of those ladies whose job it had been to shadow her every move in the rectory at Bluntisham. At all events, she tore her contract into small pieces and wrote to James Welch saying that the whole thing was off.

Welch was not going to let her go so easily. He would like, he wrote, to hold the series in abeyance for some while, to see what could be done with it later. He felt that it was wrong for anyone to stand on their rights in such a project, in which it was a privilege to be involved; and though he thought that some of Dorothy's comments were "unnecessarily fierce", he had always felt that "in the writing of these plays the spirit of God would be working through you".[19]

Many a Christian writer might have found it hard to resist such an appeal to the Divine. Not so Dorothy. It must have been yet another shock to the good man to find his appeal to her Christian feelings treated as some sort of religious blackmail. "Dear Dr Welch, I do not greatly care about arguing a business contract on a religious basis. It is difficult to avoid the appearance of making unwarranted claims for oneself, but you have appealed over the head of Caesar, and I will take you to the higher court if you insist. . . ."[20]

In the higher court, that original simple claim of hers that "if I cannot do them in my own way it will no longer be a pleasure" was transposed by theology into something rather different:

I am bound to tell you this – that the writer's duty to God is his duty to the work, and that he may not submit to any dictate of authority which he does not sincerely believe to be to the good of the work. . . . Above all, he may not listen to the specious temptation that suggests that God finds his work so indispensable that he would rather have it falsified than not have it at all. The writer is about his Father's business, and it does not matter who is inconvenienced, or how much he has to hate his father or his mother. To be false to his work is to be false to the truth. "All the truth of the craftsman is in his craft". . . . There is no law of God or man that can be invoked to make a writer tamper with his conscience.[21]

The claims that Dorothy made in *The Mind of the Maker* and elsewhere on behalf of "the worth of the work" never quite encompassed the infallibility of the worker; nor did they suggest quite so close a parallel between the work of the writer and the work of Christ himself. Dorothy had always disclaimed any personal involvement with these propositions: now she was applying them very distinctly to her own situation.

The theological issue having been dealt with, Dorothy turned to the legal argument. Since the BBC did not provide what she regarded as adequate and proper contracts, her agent had insisted upon clauses which stated that she had the right of approval of the producer, and that nobody was to alter her lines except with her consent; such consent not to be unreasonably withheld. Miss Jenkin had, so Dorothy claimed, "instructed" her to alter certain lines, and had informed her that, should anything happen to Derek McCulloch, she herself would become the producer. Dorothy maintained that the BBC was therefore in breach of contract and that consequently the agreement was null and void. There followed a lecture on the nature of contract law and the impossibility of dealing with the BBC, who were such amateurs that they did not understand this law; and Dorothy concluded by saying that she would only consent to continue with the play if she could have "*one* management, *one* producer who is not a secondary management and *one* responsible contracting party who understands the nature of contractual obligation".[22]

And it worked. The BBC capitulated. They moved heaven and earth (or, more accurately, their religious department and their drama department); they took the plays out of the hands of the Children's Hour team, and, as Dorothy had wanted all along, found a way of making Val Gielgud available to produce them.

If it is true that the end justifies the means, then Dorothy was justified to the hilt: it is doubtful whether a Children's Hour producer would really have done justice to the plays. But it was after all with the Children's Hour department that Dorothy had originally entered into an agreement – an agreement from which she only managed to free herself by considerable wrenching of the facts, slandering of an innocent and reasonably competent executive and finally by pulverizing a rather fragile nut with theological and legal sledge-hammers. And since the law of reciprocity – the law that says that with what measure ye mete it shall be meted to you again – is as valid and inexorable a spiritual law as any of those which Dorothy administered with such evident satisfaction, let it be said now, by someone who has been a professional in the theatrical business for almost thirty years, as actor, writer, editor, director and producer, that in this matter, whatever the outcome, it was the staff of the BBC who behaved like professionals, and Dorothy who behaved like a spoilt and hysterical amateur, reinforcing her tantrums by an extremely dubious application of religious doctrine.

Once the deed was done, however, and she was back (professionally speaking) in the familiar arms of Val Gielgud, she was a different woman. Witty as ever, revealing that warmth she reserved for theatrical people she knew and liked, she was quickly making plans to meet and discuss the production. And so through 1941 she toiled at the plays; wearing out a Greek Testament in her determination that the modern speech she was to give to her characters would be a truthful translation of the Greek; and amassing a large theological library as she consulted with all the great religious minds of Christendom in her search for an interpretation of the events of Christ's life that would be historically valid, theologically sound and psychologically convincing. The six radio talks she gave that year on "God the Son" were, as it were, a by-product of all this study.

The Gospels are a rag-bag of anecdotes, and ever since scholars at the end of the eighteenth century began to dare to ask the question, "What really happened in the days of Jesus?", there has been fairly passionate disagreement on the subject. So the telling of the story was by no means a straightforward affair; and by the mere act of deciding how to tell the story, Dorothy was making a theological judgement.

She found that theology, psychology and story-telling all fitted together.

> Any theology that will stand the rigorous pulling and hauling of the dramatist is pretty tough in its texture. Having subjected Catholic theology to this treatment, I am bound to bear witness that it is very tough indeed. . . . I can only affirm that at no point have I yet found artistic truth and theological truth at variance.[23]

There remained great problems, however – perhaps the greatest being that of the character of Judas:

> What *did* the man imagine he was doing? He is an insoluble riddle. He can't have been awful from the start, or Christ would never have called him; I mean one can't suppose that He deliberately chose a traitor in order to get Himself betrayed – that savours too much of the agent provocateur, and isn't the kind of thing one would expect any decent man, let alone any decent God, to do.[24]

The solution she hit upon was new, convincing, ingenious and in no way at variance with any theological doctrine. The trouble with Judas, she decided, was that he was *too* eager. Like her Faustus in *The Devil to Pay*, he was deeply aware of social injustice and political corruption, and he wanted reform and revolution all at once. Believing that Jesus would bring this about, he followed him. When it became apparent that this was not Jesus's intention, he felt betrayed; and so the way was left open for him to betray Jesus.

Dorothy revelled in problems like this. Or this: ". . . Herod has to explain, in words of one syllable, the extremely complicated situation in Judaea, and to rage characteristically in language suitable for the nursery!"[25] as she wrote to Archbishop Temple in the course of explaining why she had no time to write a play for his diocese. And such phrases litter her letters to her ever-increasing circle of correspondents throughout her nine months' travail from March to December 1941.

After such a stormy conception, James Welch no doubt had hopes that the series would have an untroubled birth. The BBC's Central Religious Advisory Committee, representing every major Christian denomination in the country, was astonishingly and admirably united in support of *The Man Born to be King*. The thoroughness of Dorothy's research, and her scrupulous adherence to the basic doctrines of Christianity, had ensured that what she had written was acceptable to every shade of Christian belief represented on the committee. If you stick to the Gospels and the Creeds, she used to say, you can't go far wrong; and she refused to be drawn into arguments about the Virgin Birth, the infallibility of the Pope or the Transubstantiation of the Bread and Wine.

Such caution, however, was not enough. Beyond the wide spectrum of Christian thought represented on the committee, there lay the outer fringes of religion and pseudo-religion, whose spokesmen had strong views and loud voices. Dorothy had this at least in common with Jesus, that she brought not peace but a sword.

It all began at a press conference at the Berners Hotel on December 10. Dr Welch spoke, and so did Dorothy. Welch pointed out that Christ had not been represented on the British stage since the Middle Ages; and Dorothy brought out that striking phrase of hers about "The judicial murder of God". The press scented a good story – as they were intended to do. The very idea of a "real" Christ – as it were a documentary version – written by a newsworthy crime novelist who was already describing the crucifixion in terms appropriate to a crime story, was certainly worth a few paragraphs. And on the whole they were prepared to be sympathetic.

But there was better to come. Nothing makes such good copy as a nice row. And the newshounds who were looking for a row did not have far to seek.

It was predictable that objections would come from the Protestant strongholds of Wales and Presbyterian Scotland, where religious controversy is – or was then – a way of life, and an air of scandalized outrage was all too often the outward and visible sign of a sincere Christian soul. But nearer home as well, the watchdogs of the Protestant Truth Society and the Lord's Day Observance Society were on the alert. Mr J. A. Kensit and the Reverend H. H. Martin were doughty champions of the proposition that the life of Jesus should remain decently obscured behind the veils of tradition and the language of the King James version of the Bible.

The charge that came from the Lord's Day Observance Society was that "For sinful man to personify the Deity is approaching blasphemy".[26] It was a contravention of the Third Commandment, in that it took the Lord's name in vain. But this somewhat academic argument got lost in the excitement about the style of the language. The point seized upon by a reporter from the *Daily Mail*, and headlined by his editor with a shrewd appreciation of the reaction of the more conservative English churchgoer, was Dorothy's use of contemporary speech – "BBC 'Life of Christ' play in US slang"[27] said the headline.

This of course was the ultimate crime. It was not enough that Dorothy was abandoning the Authorized Version and using her own translation of the words of the Gospels; nor even that she was putting into the mouths of the Apostles words which were not to be found in the Gospels at all. She was actually giving them slang to talk, as though they were ordinary humble working folk; and, the ultimate horror, it was American slang.

Or so the *Daily Mail* would have its readers believe. In point of fact, the reporter had seized upon a single line in one of the scenes which Dorothy had read at the press conference – the opening scene of Part Four – in which Matthew, the one-time tax gatherer, is trying to teach Philip, the treasurer of the group, something about the handling of money. Philip has allowed himself to be cheated in the market, and Matthew says: "Fact is, Philip my boy, you've been had for a sucker". It is not the only line of the speech, but it is the only one which could remotely be considered American. Matthew goes on to say: "Let him ring the changes on you proper. You ought to keep your eyes skinned, you did really. If I was to tell you the dodges these fellows have up their sleeves, you'd be surprised."

Dorothy's character sketch of Matthew described him as "As vulgar a little commercial Jew as ever walked Whitechapel, and I should play him with a frank Cockney accent."[28] Though it is hard to ignore the snobbish overtones of this, it is worth noting that the character sketch ends with the words "Jesus loves him very much". The point, however, to remark here is that a character such as she describes would certainly have been using Americanisms among the Cockney slang, and there is nothing out of character in the phrase "had for a sucker".

At that time, however, English insularity was putting up a stiff fight against the importation of Americanisms, especially those emanating from Hollywood. This particular form of elitism was one which the press was safe in playing on, and the idea of the author of the first Gospel speaking American English was much more dreadful than speaking with any kind of regional accent. The Bishop of Winchester, chairman of the Central Religious Advisory Committee, was moved to suggest that the offensive sentence be deleted.

Meanwhile the Lord's Day Observance Society and the Protestant Truth Society were both still gathering their forces, and Mr Martin was reported as being prepared to spend twelve hundred pounds on the campaign to have the series banned. A question was asked in Parliament two days before the first play was due to go out: the member for Devizes "asked the Minister of Information if he was taking steps to revise the script of the series of plays on the life of Jesus, which were announced to be broadcast by the British Broadcasting Corporation from December 21, in the Children's Hour, so as to avoid offence to Christian feeling". In his reply, the Parliamentary Secretary to the Ministry made no reference to the singular audacity with which the member claimed to speak for Christian feeling as though every Christian in the world must inevitably agree with him, and contented himself with replying that it was no business of the Ministry to tell the BBC how to do its job. He did say, however, that the BBC had been asked to refer the plays once again to its Advisory Committee.

The committee was not due to meet until after the transmission of the first play, which was duly broadcast as scheduled. And the worst of the furore immediately died away. It is true that the voice of Christ was not heard in this episode, nor did the famous Americanism occur in it. But it became clear that nothing sensational or blasphemous was going on; and indeed a correspondent from the *Church of England Newspaper* noted that the four people who had listened to it in his home were neither particularly shocked nor yet particularly thrilled by it.

But the overwhelming reaction of the public was favourable; the Lord's Day Observance Society and its allies had done the series a very good turn (which Dorothy acknowledged with ironic thanks) by providing a great deal of free publicity, and their indignation was seen to be hysterical nonsense. A large number of clerics from the Advisory Committee alarmed Val Gielgud and his actors by attending a rehearsal of Episode Two, but as a result they unanimously endorsed the decision of the BBC to proceed, and the series went steadily ahead.

There were minor hurdles still to surmount. The Bishop of Winchester continued to worry about the American slang in the fourth play, and was only persuaded to change his mind when Dorothy pointed out that if they now changed a phrase which had had so much publicity, it would set a precedent of appeasement that critics would surely exploit in the future; and that in any case the suggestion that American was in some way inappropriate for our Lord's disciples was one that might well be taken amiss by our transatlantic friends – was the Bishop prepared to accept the political consequences of the suggested climb-down? Her point was shrewdly made, and the line stayed in.

There can be no doubt of the importance or success of the series.

Nobody else has tackled such a project – probably nobody else could. Such a combination of first-rate scholar, first-rate theologian and highly competent dramatist is rare enough in itself; but this enterprise demanded something more – and got it: Dorothy's unique, zealous, pugnacious spirit, the ability to override obstacles and hammer her project home.

Such was the excitement roused and the arguments provoked about the pros and cons of doing the series at all that little attention was paid to the question of how well it was really done. In one sense Dorothy was on to a certain winner: the story itself, with all its connotations, overwhelmed all normal standards of criticism. Only here and there in the reviews, among all the superlatives of approval and disapproval, is one brought up sharp by some criticism of a purely practical nature, some mundane suggestion that there are too many voices to identify, too little clarification as to who is talking to whom, and where.

Such criticisms are an indication of the technical difficulty of encompassing a story which, had it been fiction, would certainly have been trimmed of some of its cast and locations. An editor would no doubt have suggested that twelve disciples were too many – six would be much more manageable. And would it not have been much more satisfactory artistically to simplify the story by eliminating the complicated relationship between the religious and civil authorities, and between the Jewish leaders and their Roman overlords? But Dorothy had no choice, and this particular carp is not a fair one.

Nor perhaps is it fair to complain that Dorothy failed to transcend the radio techniques of her time. As an honest craftsman, she studied the way things were done and she did them that way, with care and competence. But reading the plays now, one cannot help wishing that, in addition to all the qualities she did bring to them, she could also have provided a touch of flair, a spark of inspiration that went beyond the boundaries of a rather predictable technique and matched the greatness of the story with a little more magic in its telling.

The achievement was there, however. She had brought alive the man-God for millions of people for whom he had long been buried by his church; and she had justified her obstinacy about the production.

Let us leave her there then, for the moment, with one triumph, and look at her other one – *The Mind of the Maker*; the book which, more than any of her other scholarly or religious works, deserves to last.

It deserves to last not only because it is Dorothy's only really original book, but because her achievement in this book is a very rare one indeed: she has managed, without any intellectual cheating, to bring God and man closer together.

In *The Man Born to be King* she achieved this by making humanly comprehensible the historical figure of Jesus. In *The Mind of the Maker* she did something much more remarkable – she took a baffling theological proposition and proved that it was a matter of everyday experience. She demonstrated that the doctrine of the Trinity is not a piece of intellectual hair-splitting, but a diagram of what happens every time a human being uses mind and hand to create something.

It is not, of course, in any way a "proof" of the doctrine of the Trinity. But to me, at least, and to many others to whom I have talked, it offers something remarkable and marvellous: a sense that there are some real intellectual grounds for perceiving a connection between human and divine. For those who, like Dorothy, have no intuitive apprehension of the presence of God, here is a demonstration that the concept of man made in the image of God need not be born out of emotional need, nor does it involve any kind of anthropomorphic picture of an old man on a cloud. It does not even involve the highly contentious notion that God is love – a notion forever challenged by the fact of human suffering.

Briefly, Dorothy's vision is this: that the creative act consists of three stages, and that these three stages correspond with the three Persons of the Godhead, the Father, the Son and the Holy Spirit. The speech of the Archangel Michael at the end of *The Zeal of Thy House* states the germinal idea from which the whole book grew and flowered:

> Praise Him that He hath made man in His own image, a maker and craftsman like Himself, a little mirror of His triune majesty.
> For every work of creation is threefold, an earthly trinity to match the heavenly.
> First: there is the Creative Idea; passionless, timeless, beholding the whole work complete at once, the end in the beginning; and this is the image of the Father.
> Second: there is the Creative Energy, begotten of that Idea, working in time from the beginning to the end, with sweat and passion, being incarnate in the bonds of matter; and this is the image of the Word.
> Third: there is the Creative Power, the meaning of the work and its response in the lively soul; and this is the image of the indwelling Spirit.
> And these three are one, each equally in itself the whole work, whereof none can exist without other; and this is the image of the Trinity.

The Father, then, is that first vivid moment in which the artist – and for this purpose the artist is every man or woman at a creative moment – sees in a flash of inspiration the whole overall vision of the thing he or she intends to create. There is no detail in it, but in its essentials it is all there, a thing which fills the creator with joy, anticipation, and a powerful desire for the work that will bring it into existence.

The Son, in Dorothy's vision, is the process of incarnating that grand vision. By craftsmanship, by toil, by sweat and frustration, by the application of technical skill, little by little there arrives on earth something that approximates the image the creator first saw in his mind. The greater the artist, the more nearly will his creation reflect the original image, awakening in the mind of the beholder the same sense of joy and power that first drove the artist on.

That sense of joy and power, communicated from one to the other, is the third person of the Trinity, the Holy Spirit. And these three aspects – the original conception, the physical creation and the joyful power that breathes through both, though they can be separated in theory, can never really be separated in fact. All of them are aspects of the same creative act, just as, in the doctrine of the Trinity, there are three persons but only one God.

Part of the delight of the book is the way in which Dorothy works out the details of this imaginative idea. She discusses, in terms of actual works of art, what happens when one or other of the three persons of the Trinity is stronger or weaker than others. In some writers or artists, for example, it is obvious that the original idea was a noble and powerful one, but the technique is insufficient to convey it. In others, the technique is flawless but they have nothing much to say. There are yet others – sentimental popular writers, for example, who have neither anything much to say nor any particular skill in saying it, but who have a special knack of communicating with large numbers of people on a superficial level. Here the Spirit is more powerful than either Father or Son.

These imbalances correspond to the heresies of Christianity, all of which are cases of an over-emphasis on one or other aspect of Christian truth at the expense of others; the Church's job being to hold the balance right.

Dorothy discusses a thousand aspects of writing: the difference between imagination and fantasy, that distinction that so preoccupied her in the opening pages of *My Edwardian Childhood*; what happens when a writer falls in love with one of his own characters; why propagandist literature is always feeble and thin; the distortions that arise when a character is forced by his creator to behave in a way contrary to his true nature (the equivalent to God denying the free will of his creatures); and the State of Grace when plot and character, each developing "in conformity with its proper nature, . . . arrive of their own accord at a point of unity, which will be the same unity that pre-existed in the original idea".[29]

The book is rewarding enough simply as a brilliant analysis of the mysterious act of creative writing, disregarding the theological parallels altogether. For practical insight into the ways in which writing can go wrong it is well worth study by aspiring story-tellers. But the really great achievement is Dorothy's demonstration that this act, mysterious in theory yet familiar in practice, can match, point by point, freely and without forcing, the equally mysterious central doctrine of Christianity; so that we become convinced that that mystery too may represent something familiar, whose truth can be tested by experience.

CHAPTER SEVENTEEN

WHEN PEOPLE ASKED Dorothy for a brief biography to go with one of her publications or one of her lectures, she used to say that her life was far too humdrum to be worth writing about at all. And so indeed it must have seemed. Whatever writing she was engaged in, whatever battles she might have on hand, the daily routine at Witham offered little variety.

She was a late riser, and liked to read while she took her bath, her book laid on a rack across the tub. In those war years, sometimes she had servants and a secretary, sometimes not. Mac never did any cooking any more, even when the household was without a cook; but he still demanded his meals on the table with the utmost punctuality. He tended to retire early, and it was only after he had gone to bed that Dorothy could really concentrate on her writing, without the fear of interruption and mockery.

Some idea of their life together can be gleaned from Dorothy's letters to Muriel St Clare Byrne. In the winter of 1941, for example, when the car transporting Dorothy back from a speaking engagement at an army camp near Norwich broke down and kept breaking down, so that she did not reach home till after midnight, she wrote that she arrived "very cold and empty . . . Mac said I had been on the binge with the soldiers, and that I was drunk and a liar. So I threw my boots at him, and so to bed."[1]

About a year after this, she was late again – only an hour this time, the Chairman at a W.E.A. one-day school having misread his watch. "Mac would listen to no explanations, and punished himself by refusing to eat his dinner – a kind of behaviour which I think, and always have thought, quite silly."[2]

Besides Mac, Dorothy was looking after Aunt Maud, widow of Uncle Harry Leigh; a responsibility that proved to be something of a blessing, for Mac liked Aunt Maud and she tended to take him off Dorothy's hands. For two years an evacuee boy from London was billeted in the house, and his mother wrote gratefully to Dorothy when the boy returned home:

It is with great sorrow that I approach you in a spirit of gratitude for your care and kindness to my son. It was a great blow to him when he was recalled. He was quite sad about it, saying he had spent two happy years with you, though I and my girls are quite sure he would never convey to you half the nice things he's said about you and the Major. . . .[3]

There were also several cats, whose owners had prevailed on Dorothy to accept them as refugees from the bombing in London. And there was the pig – or rather several successive pigs, for Francis Bacon reached his prime and was eaten (his raison d'être, in fact), and Fatima and others succeeded him; but his was a cheerful life while it lasted, and Dorothy was an indulgent, even fond mistress, laughing when the creature got entangled in the knitting wool and only cursing at the number of forms she had to fill in for the Ministry of Food before she was allowed to kill him.

The early years of the war had at least brought some excitement, but soon Dorothy, like most people, was to find that its most noticeable hardship was tedium, the restriction and constriction of life, the queueing, the shortages, the difficulty of travel, the blackout. She was never one, however, to let circumstances subdue her spirits. She had learnt resilience long ago, and her enthusiasm for life, if it could find nothing better to work on, was perfectly capable of making do with the common domestic round. To her cooks, her cats, her pigs and her cactuses (these last had become a hobby of hers since Muriel Byrne had given her a plant at the end of the run of *Busman's Honeymoon*) she gave the same lively, alert, amused attention that she gave to everything else.

In a casual moment she devised a couple of pages of "Economy Recipes for British Households" which are barely distinguishable from the real thing and give a fair idea of Dorothy's opinion of the kind of household hints that filled the newspapers of the day:

It is a great mistake to suppose that the dishes you see mentioned on fashionable menus need always be expensive and troublesome to prepare. By the exercise of a little goodwill and ingenuity wonders can be done with the odds and ends found in any ordinary household, at the cost of a few pence:

Tripe and Onions: Procure $\frac{1}{2}$ yard white flannelette and a new dishcloth (the kind made of string). Cut into strips and boil with the onions until indigestible. Flavour, drain, cover with White Sauce (see below) and serve in a luke warm dish.

White Sauce à la Billsticker's Paste: Mix flour and water and boil till lumpy.

Welsh Rabbit: Procure a mustard plaster. Boil till limp and serve on buttered toast.[4]

Despite her enforced domesticity she determined not to give up her outside interests. She regularly exercised one or other of her hobby-horses, either in print or in speech, and she added one or two more to her stable. Her patriotism had already led her, during the early months of the war, to write an article in the form of an open letter to Americans ("My dear cousins"), explaining the reasons for the British involvement, and recalling the historic links between the nations: ". . . Go back another hundred years, and you were with us. . . . Spain was lord of the world and the year was 1587. Men of Devon, men of Dorset, men of Hampshire, men of Sussex, men of Kent, think back. It was you that hurried to your posts, each man for his own county, each man for his own roof-tree, and looked across the narrow seas to watch for the Spanish galleons. . . ."[5] Now it was for the safety of America and the whole Western world that Britain kept watch.

Nobody wanted the article in 1939, and Dorothy had felt rather snubbed; when an enthusiastic Anglophile named Eric Underwood had written from New York in March 1940, asking for her help in his efforts to persuade the American people that it was their war, her reply was far from gracious.

In August 1941, however, she was moved to respond to a friendly speech and broadcast by Herbert Agar, an Anglophile American writer who had lived for many years in Britain and had some influence with the American Embassy. She felt she should explain to him certain things about the English that she felt were unique and extraordinary and impossible for any foreigner to comprehend, so that he might pass these on to his people and save them from making embarrassing mistakes.

"The English are consumed by a pride that would startle Lucifer", she wrote, in the unmistakable tones of a Musketeer bragging of romantic sins, apparent confession failing to mask a deep complacency: ". . . it would please our pride if we could win the war with the tools you provide. But it would not please us if, having provided nothing but the tools, America were to dictate the peace and arrange Europe to her economic liking, as though her money gave her a better right to speak than our blood."[6]

The tone is similar to that found in lectures such as "The Mysterious English", delivered the previous year, and "The Gulf Stream and the Channel" and "They Tried to be Good", which came towards the end of the war, in 1943; a heady mixture of shrewd insight, historical perspective, fine rhetorical flow and passionately partisan special pleading. Her view of the Irish situation, for example, is characteristically wilful: "We knew in our hearts we had wronged Ireland; therefore we gave her back not only the freedom she now uses to harbour our enemies, but also the Irish ports – for which gesture we are paying now in the wreck of English ships and the bones of drowned sailors."[7] Centuries of oppression and insensitivity are tossed aside in the first clause, becoming simply the prelude to the story of hard-done-by virtue in the rest of the passage.

As with so many of Dorothy's ebullient outpourings, it is hard to know whether to regard these forays into Anglo-American relations with admiration, irritation or both. She is so persuasively enthusiastic, so well-read, so clever, so full of astute observation, that the reader is almost ready to be carried away on an agreeable wave of assent. At the same time he is all too aware of what is left out, of the insensitivity behind many of the bold assertions; and the boldness itself begins to seem crass and superficial. All that eloquence about "our blood" and "the bones of drowned sailors" comes in fact from a paper tiger who rather obviously steered clear of going to the front in the First World War, and in the second was only prepared to lecture within a limited distance from home because of the discomforts of war-time travel.

A favourite bone of contention during this period concerned what has come to be called the personality cult. Worthy societies of various sorts would write asking if Dorothy would address them. Politely she would enquire on what subject they would be interested to hear her views. Equally politely, as it seemed to them, they would reply that any subject would be fine – she herself was the real attraction.

If this was an attempt at flattery, it failed totally, and instead provoked that exasperation that welled up in Dorothy all too readily – the exasperation with which she greeted anything that smacked to her of stupidity. For stupidity was actually a sin in Dorothy's book: "Stupidity is the sin of Sloth," she wrote, "nourished and maintained by a furious spiritual Pride that leaves intellectual Pride nowhere in the race to destruction."[8] And she thought it extremely stupid to regard her person as being more important than the eternal truths that she had to utter. She did not like lecturing. Her only reason for abandoning her "proper job" and doing it was to make people think; and if her efforts to do this merely made them want to collect her autograph, what hope was there for them?

As the war went on, the savagery with which she expressed her exasperation became progressively more noticeable. A brief example must serve for many.

A Wesleyan minister from Tunbridge Wells wrote to her several times, recommending her to read various books on the virtues of abstinence and asking for her aid in fighting the demon drink. Her response at first was a fairly mild sarcasm:

> It must be a great grief to you that Our Lord should have been so ill-informed, or so lacking in common moral and Christian sense, as to use [wine] both for His Sacrament and for His pleasure. What a pity he had not the advantage of being able to study Miss Baker's pamphlet on the subject. However, since I am a Christian and not a Mohammedan, I shall make so bold as to follow His example, despite any claims made on behalf of the Free Churches to know better than God Almighty. . . .[9]

Her correspondent was unwise enough to pursue the matter, and then Dorothy let rip:

> I will put to you two questions, and will trouble you to answer them in two words or not at all.
>
> (1) "The Son of Man came eating and drinking and ye say 'Behold a gluttonous man and a wine-bibber'." Do you agree with this criticism, yes or no?
>
> (2) If the answer to the above is yes, then please state in one word whether you consider that Our Lord, in drinking wine, showed himself to be: (a) wicked or (b) ignorant. . . .
>
> If you believe that Jesus was wholly God, then to condemn his conduct is presumptuous. If you believe that he was not wholly God, but only partly or in some respects divine, you are a heretic. If you think he was not God at all, you are an infidel.
>
> Yours faithfully . . .[10]

Even to the distinguished writer Helen Waddell, she could not forbear ending a dissertation on the distinction between justice and mercy with the severe little admonition – "Nothing is gained by confusion of mind and the use of inaccurate language."[11]

It was not until some years later that she admitted to that "irritable and domineering spirit"; and by that time she had largely shaken it off. No doubt it was due, at least in part, to the reason she gave – that she had found herself caught up against her will in the evangelization business. But there were several other possible causes, or at least aggravating factors: the strain of the war; her heroic struggle (and it was heroic) to subdue, day by day, her reaction to the behaviour of Mac; and perhaps the painful awareness that can easily afflict those who seek to improve the lives or minds of their fellow men, that for all their efforts the world is continuing on its foolish and unregenerate way.

For many of the letters Dorothy received were from such desperately ignorant and bewildered people that she must sometimes have wondered whether the world was full of madmen. Often she would reply to the crazed logic of these letters with a furious, icy reason; apparently unaware that such people were in the grip of a neurosis so extreme that no amount of reasoned argument could possibly have any meaning for them. To find that the people most anxious to follow up her arguments, even in her support, were often cranks and religious maniacs, must have been deeply depressing. What Dorothy liked was a proper fight, not an unequal struggle with handicapped opponents.

Despite her intolerance, Dorothy must inwardly have been far from secure. I have suggested earlier that her uncompromising attacks on heresy and error were not launched from the commanding heights of a flawless conscience, but rather from an embattled position into which she had been forced by the complications and compromises involved in achieving a tolerable emotional equilibrium. To prove or disprove this suggestion is impossible in a woman who was so successful at hiding her deeper feelings, but there are one or two pointers. One is Dorothy's admission that the only aspect of religious truth which she knew by personal conviction and experience was the existence of sin – all the rest being a matter of the intellect. Another is the curious episode of the Lambeth Degree.

A Lambeth Degree is a rare honour. It is bestowed by the Archbishop of Canterbury and can be in any subject. Dorothy's old fan William Temple had been elevated from York to Canterbury in 1942, and now he was offering her a Doctorate of Divinity. The honour was the greater in that Dorothy was only the second woman ever to have been proposed for a Lambeth Degree, and since the previous proposal had not gone through, Dorothy would have been the first woman to receive the Degree – had she accepted it.

The offer was made in September 1943, "in recognition of what I regard as the great value of your work, especially *The Man Born to be King* and *The Mind of the Maker*".[12] Unfortunately we do not know what exactly were Dorothy's reasons for refusing the honour, because her letters are not being released by Lambeth Palace Library. But it is evident from the Archbishop's letters that she felt some scruples about her suitability for the honour. "I do not think there is the least harm in a Doctor of Divinity writing detective stories or any similar literature",[13] he wrote in reply to her first protests; and a few days later, ". . . it would be a great mistake to suppose that a D.D. is to be regarded as anything like a certificate of sanctity. . . ."[14]

His persuasions were unsuccessful. His next letter began: "I am so sorry to have put you all in a flutter!";[15] and finally he capitulated – "I think I do fully understand the situation; indeed you have persuaded me that if I were in your position I should have reached your conclusion."[16]

For the moment, alas, we can only guess what the situation was that the Archbishop fully understood. Dorothy was not normally one to refuse honours and dignities, and she delighted in pomp and ceremony. She was extremely proud of the Honorary Degree bestowed on her by Durham University in 1950, and academic distinction was more important to her than to most people. So her reasons for declining, and continuing to decline, this rather special honour, in face of considerable persuasion by the Archbishop, must have been weighty indeed in her eyes. Three possibilities seem to present themselves: first, she may have feared that if she were so singled out by the Church authorities she might find herself irretrievably bound up with the ecclesiastical propaganda machine that she felt was not her "proper job". Second, that she was too deeply aware of a personal sinfulness ever to be comfortable with such a label, despite the Archbishop's reassurances. And third, that at the back of her mind there may have lain the ever-present possibility that some enquiring reporter might one day ferret out the secret of Anthony's existence; from which it would only have been a step to looking up his birth certificate in Somerset House and finding out that he was actually her son. This, she might have felt, could throw discredit in the public mind on the Church that had honoured her.

A subject which inevitably cropped up with some regularity in Dorothy's correspondence, in view of her championship of the Church and her known views on women's intellectual equality with men, was the ordination of women. One after another, enthusiasts would seek to enlist her support for a cause that, on the face of it, would have appeared likely to appeal to her very strongly.

To all of them, Dorothy's reply was the same – there was a prior job to be done, namely to convince the world in general that women had a right to be taken seriously as individual human beings, and not simply as members of a sex. She had made the point very prettily in an address she gave in 1938, "Are Women Human?":

When the pioneers of university training for women demanded that women should be admitted to the universities, the cry went up at once: "Why should women want to know about Aristotle?" The

answer is NOT that *all* women would be the better for knowing about
Aristotle . . . but simply: "What women want as a class is irrelevant. *I*
want to know about Aristotle. It is true that many women care
nothing about him, and a great many male undergraduates turn pale
and faint at the thought of him – but I, eccentric individual that I am,
do want to know about Aristotle, and I submit that there is nothing in
my shape or bodily functions which need prevent my knowing about
him."[17]

Once that battle was won, and a proper distinction made between functions in which women really were different from men and those in which
there was no possible need for discrimination to be made between the
sexes, *then* would be the time to talk about admitting women to the
priesthood. Besides which, at a time when attempts were being made to
bridge the gap between the Protestant and Roman Catholic com-
munions, the idea of ordaining women could only aggravate matters,
since the Catholics could not by any stretch of the imagination be
expected to accept such a revolutionary step.

That was her rational and stated attitude. But Dorothy had such a
profound and instinctive respect for Catholic tradition that she may in
fact have had some sympathy with the traditional view that, Christ
having been a man, there was something essentially male about the
function of celebrating the mysteries of His Body and Blood.

A few months before the offer of the Lambeth Degree, Dorothy
received a rather different salute to her propagandist skills. It came in
the form of a letter from General Sir Wyndham Deedes, asking for her
support for, of all things, the cause of Zionism. Dorothy was a surprising
choice in view of the fact that public comment had already been made
about alleged anti-Semitic feeling in her writing.

The letter arrived in April 1943, and was followed a couple of months
later by another, similar approach, this time from a Miss L. M.
Livingstone, who was deeply involved in the effort to combat the wave of
anti-Semitism which was passing through England at the time.

Dorothy's reply to both was that she felt she was not a suitable person
to take up the cudgels on behalf of the Jews, because (a) she knew comparatively little about the problem, and (b) she feared that anyone who
tried to present an objective and impartial view of the situation would
end up by offending Jews and Christians alike.

Typically, her main concern was not for the Jews but for her beloved
English. If they were taking to anti-Semitism ("poor dears") it was
because they had been driven past endurance by "bombs, black-out,
restrictions, rations, coal-targets, bread-targets, clothes-coupons, call-

ups, income-tax, lack of domestic help and general bedevilment";[18] and an influx of people with alien culture and alien standards was one imposition too many. For she believed that anti-Semitism, however horrifying its manifestations in Nazi Germany and elsewhere, was not always a matter of mindless wickedness, but was based on certain very definite incompatibilities between the Jews and their host nations; and that unless these incompatibilities were acknowledged and faced realistically, no real progress could be made.

Though the incompatibilities could be shown to have all sorts of historical sources – chiefly the inevitable division of loyalty in the majority of Jews between their host nation and the international race-religion of Jewry – the level at which they were beginning to be felt was no longer that of a generalized suspicion of foreigners, she wrote, but in what she called the "trifles of daily life experienced among the inhabitants of Hampstead and Whitechapel":

the British Jewesses in 1939 dashing to the bank and announcing in loud tones: "Of course, we're sending all our money to America"; the children who cannot learn the common school code of honour; the Jewish evacuee offering his landlady double the rent she asked in order to secure the rooms and then informing against her to the billetting authorities; the inhabitants of a London street complaining bitterly that everybody, from the high-class publishers' staff at one end to the little rookery of prostitutes at the other, eagerly did their turn of fire-watching – all except the houseful of Jews in the middle. They word it in different ways; but it all really boils down to the same thing: "bad citizens".[19]

Since this was how Dorothy saw the situation, the solution could not in her view be found in the proposal that people should meet the Jews and get to know them, in the hope that they would then drop their prejudices; for the dislike began precisely when the Jews moved in next door.

Dorothy made it clear that she knew of many instances that totally contradicted these generalizations – individual Jews who were deeply aware of the debt they owed to the land they lived in and who would be excellent citizens of any country in the world. Nonetheless, nothing could alter the "otherness" of Jews, which indeed they themselves fostered and took pride in. Having fostered it, she maintained, they could hardly object if it was commented on and sometimes resented.

Given Dorothy's cast of mind, it was probably inevitable that she should trace back this "otherness" to the great watershed of Jewish and Christian history, the life of Christ. To a Mr J. J. Lynx, who wrote asking for her views on the subject, she replied in June 1943: "I cannot, you see, bring myself to approach the question as though Christ had made no difference to history. *I* think, you see, that He was the turning-point of history, and the Jewish people, whose religion and nation are closely bound up with the course of history, missed that turning-point and got stranded: so that all the subsequent course of their history has to be looked upon in the light of that frustration."

"Naturally", she added, "I cannot expect Jewish people to sympathize with this point of view, but I do find it rather difficult to discuss a problem if I have to leave out what appears to me to be the major factor."[20]

Dorothy's doubt whether this kind of contribution would really be welcome is more than understandable. A friend of hers, who had taught for several years at a school with a large number of Jewish pupils, had recently written an article dealing with some of the characteristics which she considered made it difficult for these pupils to be assimilated into the school community. The editor of the journal for whom she had written the article, himself Jewish, had refused to print it, claiming that it was based on lies and prejudice. In Dorothy's next letter to Mr Lynx she quoted the experience of her friend and pointed out that "It doesn't seem worth while trying to explain the difficulties from our point of view if one isn't allowed to say plainly what those difficulties are, does it?"[21]

Despite these discouragements, both Miss Livingstone and Mr Lynx persisted. Miss Livingstone invited Dorothy and a friend to a discussion group that included both Jews and Christians, assuring her that here she would find nothing but reason and peaceful discourse. It seems not to have been a great success, and Dorothy wrote that she had "aroused a small storm, not so much among the Jews as among the pro-semitic Christians".[22]

This seems to have been the end of Miss Livingstone's efforts, but Mr Lynx's determination was not shaken. He wanted an article from her for a symposium on "The Future of the Jews" – the only condition being that it should be *constructive*.

Dorothy felt that it was time to go to bedrock – by which she meant of course religious and historical roots. And when in March 1944 she finally sent in her manuscript, it no longer dealt with any of the contemporary complications that she and her friends had observed at first hand, but had become a theological dissertation of twenty-six typed pages on the coming of Christ as the mystical central point of all history, and the misfortunes of the Jews as the sad but inevitable consequence of their failure to recognize their Messiah when he came. Few people, Gentile or Jew, and whether or not they shared Dorothy's view of the significance of Christ's coming, could possibly find much practical relevance in this elaborately argued thesis.

Had the article been published, its remoteness would almost certainly have ensured that it was either discounted or ignored. A few cranks might have seized upon it as some kind of divine sanction for their prejudices, but on moderate modern minds the only likely effect would have been the revelation of a frighteningly eccentric seam in Dorothy's own form of Christianity.

Unfortunately, a number of Jewish contributors to the symposium played straight into Dorothy's hands. Already suspicious of her attitudes, they first demanded to see what she had written, and then, having read it, refused to have their contributions printed in the same volume. The publishers wrote to Dorothy, pointing out their dilemma and virtually asking her to withdraw her article – and Dorothy triumphantly did so, her original warnings justified to the hilt:

In this country, where self-criticism and the toleration of criticism are practised almost to excess, nothing can so alienate sympathy from the Jewish cause as the policy at present pursued by a certain section of its apologists. And indeed neither goodwill nor co-operation is possible when the expression of opinion by one party is resented or stifled by the other. I beg these people, Christians and Jews alike, not to stir up anger in this country against the Jewish nation by continuing in this deplorable attitude of mind. They may succeed in silencing criticism, but it is when the English are silent that they begin to think."[23]

Regarding the degree of anti-Semitic prejudice that this story displays, two points should be borne in mind: first, that the word prejudice means the prejudging of a question before studying the facts; and second, that awareness of others' faults is not the same as hostility. Whether or not Dorothy's criticisms are judged to be valid, they were carefully considered and honest.

Religious controversy was not, of course (and thank heaven), Dorothy's whole life. She was developing, as we have seen, a serious interest in economics. She had frequently aired her views on the subject in a general kind of way, but she was honest enough to realize that her understanding was severely limited; and she now looked for instruction to anyone among her growing circle of acquaintances and correspondents who might have practical experience.

Her approach, she wrote much later to Maurice Reckitt, was that of the Village Idiot, whose job it is "to see that from time to time the *right questions* are asked, and to go on asking them in a loud bleating voice till somebody takes notice. The error (if I may say so) of many eminent ecclesiastics is that instead of just saying 'This is WRONG; put it right', they commit themselves to advising HOW it should be put right. Then all the experts fall on them and chew them up.''[24]

In her role as Village Idiot, she then goes back to basics, demonstrating the kind of right questions she has in mind – though being a positive kind of lady, her questions rapidly seem to become statements: "I do not understand what MONEY is. But I seem to distinguish five kinds of it, some less incomprehensible than others."[25] And she proceeds to outline these five with that wit and shrewdness that is particularly apparent when she is writing to someone she likes and respects and who will appreciate her. I shall not quote the entire summary of each kind of money, but only the first few lines; which is not fair to her powers of argument, but will give an idea of her approach and the evident fun she had with it:

1. *Payment for Work* I understand this to mean that other people are willing to give me some of their work (beds, boots, buns etc.) in return for my work (ideas, and the manual labour of writing them down). . . . "Money" in this sense I understand to be a convenient token for work and real goods – handier, for instance, than receiving part of a live elephant from an elephant-hunter who wants to read *The Man Born to be King*. . . . It is a kind of barter, and it is "real" money. . . .

2. *Profit* This appears to be an arrangement for getting more work and goods out of a business than you put into it. I am never quite clear where payment ends and profit begins. . . .

3. *Usury or Investment* I understand this to mean that when I have in hand £100 of real money which I might expend in [*sic*] buns, I am persuaded to forgo the buns and lend the money to a man who wants to start manufacturing bedpans. . . . I see that it is not unreasonable for the manufacturer to pay me for the use of my money – otherwise, why should I give it to him?. . . . He takes the money, and gives me the equivalent of so many bedpans every year while he is using it, and I buy buns with that. . . . As things usually are, most investments seem to me to produce money which isn't a payment for anything, and so is "unreal". . . . It is *irresponsible* money.

4. *Gambling or Insurance* This is comparatively straightforward: I bet the Insurance Company (or the State, or whoever is the layer) that I will die (or suffer some other catastrophe) before they have time to collect from me the full amount of their stake. They bet I shall linger on long enough to pay all that and a bit more. . . .

5. *Fairy-Money, or Speculation* By this I mean money that seems to come from nowhere and corresponds to no ideas, beds, boots, buns,

Right: Anthony as a schoolboy

Below: Ivy's cottage at Westcott Barton,
where Anthony grew up

Mac

Dorothy at around the time of her marriage

The house at Witham as it is in 1980

Left: Dorothy at work around 1950

Below: With the Detection Club skull

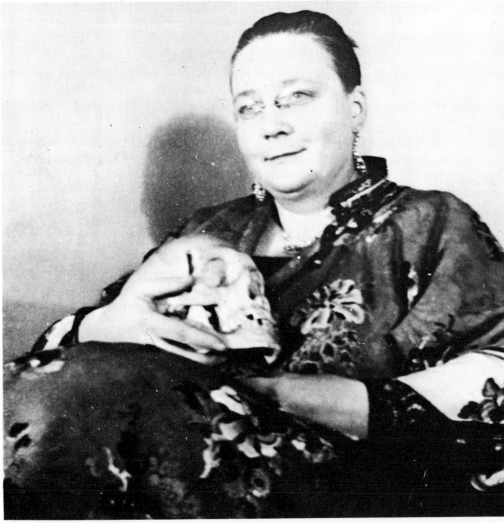

or labour. It includes company-promoting, and buying and selling shares and buying and selling "money". You do no work for it and produce no goods for it. . . .

Of these sorts of money, 1 & 4 seem "real", 2 & 3 trembling on the verge of unreality, and 5 completely chimerical. . . .[26]

So Dorothy works her way round to a position much like that of the mediaeval Church, which condemned usury as a mortal sin because it represented nothing real. It is ironic that the "unreal" activities of investment and speculation have become the very ground on which the City of London has built much of the prosperity of Dorothy's beloved England in the past two centuries.

As the war ground on, much of its romance for Dorothy ebbed away. No longer did Britain stand alone against overwhelming odds. By October 1943 the Eighth Army had driven the Germans out of north Africa, the Americans had joined the fight, and the drone of aircraft over southern England was not that of enemy raiders but of thousands of Allied bombers on their way to demolish German cities. But there was still a long way to go. Panache had given way to dogged endurance, and Dorothy could no longer write the kind of poetry with which she had greeted the heady days of the Battle of Britain. The style of *An English War* was barely distinguishable from the indulgent stuff she had written in her twenties about the First World War. Now, at last, she began to write in the rhymeless, a-rhythmical manner that had been fashionable for twenty years but which she had hitherto spurned:

Yes – it's marvellous how they take these photographs – marvellous –
what does the explanation say?
The white splotches are blast
and the black blobs are craters,
and the little speckly bits
are sunlight shining through windows upon the floor inside,
showing that the roof's off –
yes, quite –
the power house has been hit,
it doesn't look much of a hole,
but doubtless the bomb exploded and damaged something important
that one can't see. . . .

Oh, look!
look!
but I *know* this picture –

that's real,
something that means something,
that I can interpret for myself
without any arrows and diagrams,
something that I have seen,
and known from a child,
standing on the Seven Holes Bridge at Earith
looking across the washes
to the Isle of Ely
over the drowned fen stretched out sullen and silent
in the last redness of a level sun . . .

Well, I must say,
those are wonderful pictures,
I am delighted to have seen them –
let me have the paper back when you have finished with it,
I want to look again,
and go on looking,
because I recognize this,
because I know what it means, and understand it,
because I can see exactly what we have done –
we have blown up the dams,
burst the sluices,
unshackled the waters.[27]

The irony and the pity are a very welcome gain for the loss of the old poeticism, and the change seems to correspond with a profound, and much more general, softening and moderation in Dorothy's personality. The tirades grew less frequent and less severe. People writing to her for advice were less likely to meet with a theological left hook, and often encountered gentle and sympathetic help. The energy was still there, but now began to give off warmth as well as light.

In another woman the mellowing might have come from age or weariness. But Dorothy was a woman of enthusiasms. As she told the film producer Michael Powell after the war, when he wanted permission to make a film of *The Nine Tailors* and claimed to have sensed in her a veiled enthusiasm, a willingness to be persuaded: "If you were ever to see me really enthusiastic about anything, it would be about as unmistakable as a tank going into action."[28] And it was from the last great enthusiasm of her life that the change in her seems to have resulted – an enthusiasm that was to keep her happy and occupied until the day she died.

CHAPTER EIGHTEEN

IN 1943 A new book about Dante had appeared, written by Charles Williams and called *The Figure of Beatrice*. Some account must be given of this book, and also of Williams himself; for though it was in Dante that Dorothy was to find the most perfect artistic and intellectual satisfaction of her life, the way was pointed for her by *The Figure of Beatrice* and by Charles Williams' extraordinary insight, ecstatic yet matter-of-fact, into Dante's mind and heart and into the whole spiritual world charted by *The Divine Comedy*.

Of the little group of Christian lay-people who exerted such a strong influence on the Church of England at that time – C. S. Lewis, T. S. Eliot, Charles Williams and Dorothy herself – Williams was the least widely known, but far and away the most extraordinary in the originality of his vision and style. Comparing him with C. S. Lewis, Dorothy wrote: "Lewis is a writer of highly disciplined talent; Williams was a really profound and original mind, with the authentic mark of genius."[1]

To many people, the originality of Charles Williams seemed merely eccentricity. As Dorothy herself wrote in a review of his novel *Many Dimensions*:

> To read only one work of Charles Williams is to find oneself in the presence of a riddle – a riddle fascinating by its romantic colour, its strangeness, its hints of a rich and intricate unknown world just outside the barriers of consciousness; but to read all is to become a free citizen of that world and to find in it a penetrating and illuminating interpretation of the world we know.[2]

That was true chiefly of Williams' poetry and his works of fiction. His critical works are less obscure – though even they demand constant adjustment to novel, yet often strikingly obvious, ideas. In *The Figure of Beatrice* the novelty lies in Charles Williams' refusal to see in Dante a "period" author, and his insistence on treating him as a man like other men, who, for all his different intellectual background, had feelings that we can recognize and identify with: "We have looked everywhere for enlightenment on Dante," he wrote, "except in our lives and our love-affairs."[3]

Beatrice, the Florentine girl with whom Dante fell in love in his youth and who died soon after, was transformed in *The Divine Comedy*, written years later, into the radiant creature who leads him into the very courts of heaven in the third book of the poem, the *Paradiso*. Instead of dismissing that first staggering shock of young love as insignificant infatuation, Dante saw in it a true foretaste of the eternal bliss of Paradise. The youthful worship he felt for the face and the body of the laughing girl, which made him ready instantly to forgive his enemies, desperate to perfect himself in order to be worthy of her perfection, was not for him romantic illusion; it was a genuine ray of the eternal light that every perfected soul reflects, untarnished, back to the Creative Light that is the Lord of the Universe.

Charles Williams also believed in the validity of romantic love; he believed that that first, undisillusioned vision that a lover (of either sex) has of the beloved is a vision of something real – the unfallen state of man, the thing that, but for sin, we could all be; moreover he believed that what Dante felt for Beatrice was by no means unusual, but was felt by multitudes in every generation. For him therefore the *Commedia* was not a piece of "classical literature", but a permanently and universally relevant story of man's heart and soul.

This is only a part of the general principle Williams calls "the Affirmation of Images" – the belief that the eternal is all the time revealed in everyday life, and that the smallest decisions we make have momentous implications, all of them leading in the end either to the pit of the Inferno or the glories of the Paradiso. Of this principle he wrote with a sort of intoxicated radiance that was as irritating to some as it was illuminating to others. Its effect on Dorothy was mixed, but the illumination far outweighed the irritation.

They make an odd pair, Williams and Dorothy, their similarities as striking as their differences: his knowledge and love of literature were as wide and as deep as hers (he had been on the editorial staff of the Oxford University Press since 1908, and lectured at Oxford on English Language and Literature); he too wrote novels when he would rather have been writing poetry, because novels sold better; and his imagination, like hers, throve in a romantic version of a past period – in his case the days of Camelot and the Arthurian legend. Like Dorothy, he had written a play for the Canterbury Festival; and like her he believed and rejoiced in the great intellectual design of Catholic theology.

There the resemblances ended. Where Dorothy loved to argue for the sake of demolishing the foe, Williams "argued", in the words of the poet and critic Anne Ridler, "to discover, not to vanquish".[4] Where Dorothy was really more stirred by the wrongness of pagans than the rightness of Christians, Williams responded most vividly to the beauty of holiness.

Where she instinctively hated the idea of self-sacrifice, his conception of "co-inherence" (one of the special words that he used for his own special meanings) involved the indivisibility of all experience, suffering included, and the belief that all human beings could, and should, share in Christ's work and help, quite literally, to bear one another's burdens and ease one another's pain by offering their own pain in a mystical exchange.

At the heart of all these contrasts was one fundamental difference: that where Dorothy expounded the laws of the spiritual world like an exceptionally brilliant law-student, Williams seemed actually to inhabit that world, and to understand in his blood and bones the truths of which the laws were merely man-made formulations. And where the only religious conviction that she could speak of from personal experience was the conviction of sin, he was aware of it all, from the depths of damnation to the height of salvation and all the highways and byways between. "I can enter into Charles's type of mind to some extent, by imagination," she wrote, "and look through its windows, as it were, into places where I cannot myself walk. He was, up to a certain point, I think, a practising mystic; from that point of view I am a complete moron, being almost wholly without intuitions of any kind. I can only apprehend intellectually what the mystics grasp directly."[5]

Nevertheless, their interests lay so close together that it would have been surprising if they had not corresponded from time to time. In fact, he had written ecstatically to Victor Gollancz as early as 1933, about *The Nine Tailors*: "Your Dorothy Sayers . . . ! Present her sometime with my profoundest compliments. It's a marvellous book; it is high imagination. . . . The end is insurpassable. (I dare say I exaggerate, but I've only just finished it and I'm all shaken.)"[6]

They had met not long after, and in 1937 he had bounced on his chair with excitement in Simpson's restaurant as he read aloud from *The Zeal of Thy House*, crying "Of course, you know, it's all quite true", and "Ah now, it really is blasphemy!" – much, Dorothy claimed to her embarrassment,[7] though she herself was quite capable of similar behaviour. Certainly she was considerably flattered.

Thereafter they had met or written intermittently about his books and about hers, as occasion arose. It was inevitable that after *The Figure of Beatrice* the subject of Dante should crop up in the correspondence sooner or later. In fact it did not happen till August 1944. But before that there had been a couple of brief passages in his letters to her that cannot be passed over, so profoundly did they threaten her most cherished attitudes.

Exactly what prompted his remarks is not certain. The letters from

Dorothy to which he is replying are missing. But it seems evident from the context that Dorothy had been expatiating on her two favourite arguments – the importance of the dogmatic pattern in Christianity; and the comparative values of the work and the worker, the writing and the writer. In August 1943, Williams wrote:

> Moved by a sentence in your letter which you will remember I permit myself to say again that I feel that this matter which we were discussing is very serious indeed. There is a point at which you and I will no longer be able to get away with an explanation of how admirable we think the pattern is, and I think that point is very near for both of us. I know as well as you do of the byways of the literary mind, but I do not feel they are going to be much excuse. There are awful moments when I think that perhaps it is precisely people like us, who are enthralled by the idea and stop there, who are really responsible for a great deal of the incapacity and the harm.[8]

And the following June he came back to the subject: ". . . I darkly suspected that you and I were both dangerously near coming under judgement. The temptation of thinking that the business of writing frees one from everything else is very profound . . ."[9]

Few people could have got away with suggesting to Dorothy that the byways of the literary mind were an "excuse"; or that people enthralled by the pattern and the idea could possibly be responsible for any harm. The byways of the literary mind were her life. She had defended them again and again under the twin banners of intellectual and artistic integrity. They were her "proper job", which it was near sacrilege to question. The clear implication that she herself, the human person, mattered more than these great abstractions, and that when she thought she was upholding them she was in reality hiding behind them, must have been most frightening. Worse: Williams was saying that the hiding had to stop; and she had no way of pretending that he did not know what he was talking about, for he very clearly did; and moreover, with the courtesy that he both praised and practised, he included himself in the accusation – thus in one way softening the blow, but in another making it far harder for her to defend herself.

Even if – as is possible – Dorothy herself had "darkly suspected" something of this sort already (for she was honest and no fool) confirmation of one's own self-suspicions is often a worse jolt than a totally unexpected accusation.

If only we had her replies! But there is no direct evidence of any reaction. We can only observe that it was from about this time that she became noticeably less given to arrogant certitudes, less dismissive of the doubts of the weaker or less intellectual brethren. Her letters become a good deal more agreeable to read, and in point of fact more convincing – though perhaps rather less entertaining, for it is never quite such fun when the champion starts pulling his punches.

Whether or not I am right in seeing a connection between those critical remarks of Charles Williams and the mellowing of Dorothy, it is quite certain that he rendered her another service – a more palpable one, and one which very probably had the same effect, for there is nothing like being contented in one's work to keep one in a good humour.

On August 16 1944, Dorothy wrote to Charles Williams:

I have embarked upon an arduous enterprise for which you are entirely responsible. Having read *The Figure of Beatrice* and coped with *Lewis on Milton* and actually re-read the greater part of *Paradise Lost* in consequence, I cheerfully remarked to a friend that Milton was a thunderingly great writer of religious epic, provided it did not occur to you to compare him with Dante. My friend, with mild countenance and disarming honesty, replied that she had never read Dante. I then became aware that I had never read Dante either, but only quoted bits of him and looked at Doré's illustrations to the Inferno. . . . It then came to my mind that I had better read Dante, or else I might find myself condemned to toddle round for ever among the Hypocrites . . . so I resolutely hunted out Dante (finding him, for some reason which I cannot explain, upon that shelf of my library which is devoted to English poets of the 19th century) and addressed myself to the task of really reading Dante, "tu duca, tu signore, e tu maestro".[10]

Her reason for never having read the *Commedia*, she says, is that she knows virtually no Italian; but fortunately her copy has the Italian on one side, the English on the other, and so, "by slipping and scrambling between the original and the crib, and spelling out the Italian, as one who with two fingers executes a complicated passage of music upon the pianoforte, [I have] travelled in five days through the Centre to the Antipodes. . . ."[11]

In other words, she has finished the *Inferno*. Much to her surprise, her strongest impressions were excitement about the story and admiration at Dante's skill in keeping the excitement going. This was the last thing she had expected. Noble poetry, yes. Grim imagery, yes. But swift story-telling, suspense, tenderness – even humour – in the midst of the horror, and verse which could range from the profound to the conversational in a couple of lines – these were totally unexpected. She felt that no commentary or translation that she had come across had ever prepared her for the real thing. And for page after page she let her excitement pour out, excusing herself on page nine with "My dear Charles, nobody can possibly have written a more boring letter to anybody. Unfortunately I have nobody to talk to here (my husband's comment would only be, 'What on earth do you want to read that stuff for?').''[12]

The excuse that she had no one to talk to was not entirely accurate. The friend who had confessed that she had never read Dante was Marjorie Barber, and Muriel St Clare Byrne and she were both staying at Witham for the summer vacation; Dorothy having insisted that their London house was too dangerous at that time, because of Hitler's secret weapon, the flying bomb or "doodlebug".

There was some slight danger in Witham, too, for these mindless aerial monsters rumbled over any part of England within a hundred and fifty miles of the Pas de Calais; and when the sirens sounded, Mac, playing the protective male, would herd his household into the shelter he had built in the garden, himself keeping watch outside like the captain on the bridge.

These alerts were rare and short-lived and Dorothy did not take them very seriously. Even in London one got used to the fact that they were no danger until the engine of the machine cut out – and then one had fifteen seconds to take cover. The suggestion has been made that Dorothy (of all people) spent hours in the shelter, terrified of the bombs, and there got to know Dante, but this hardly fits the facts.

At all events, by the end of the month she had got through the *Purgatorio* and the *Paradiso*, and two more ecstatic letters had been despatched to Charles Williams, pouring out her joy and her amazement, and the thousand and one ideas, insights, queries, connections and delights that had welled up in her as she read.

Perhaps the most astonishing thing was that it had not happened earlier. Everything about Dante made him the perfect writer for Dorothy – his period, his clarity of mind, his range of interests, his theology, his humanity and the brilliance of his writing. He was a soulmate, and at the same time a master; a man, at last, to her measure, to whom she happily gave the rest of her life. Yet she met him, properly, for the first time at the age of fifty.

The reason for the omission was simply the commentators. Until she read *The Figure of Beatrice*, Dorothy had never come across anyone who led her to suppose that Dante's writing might hold any excitement or delight for her. "His religious doctrine and mystical experience are never examined in the light of a living faith. He is left to bombinate in a vacuum. In the midst of this sterilized wasteland, the Italian scholars sit in a compact ring, with their backs turned to the outside world, industriously chewing chaff."[13]

So she was very much aware of her debt to Charles Williams:

> I'm very glad I didn't try to read the *Commedia* till I had your book as a guide; because the usual sort of notes and comments don't seem to help much. . . . One would really never guess from them that the whole thing is a poem about something happening inside Dante. They say . . . "Beatrice in the Purgatorio stands for Divine Philosophy and in the Paradiso for Divine Wisdom" – no doubt she does, but if she *isn't* anybody and only "stands for" these abstractions, the situation as regards Dante seems to lack poignancy. All this business of the Images is very important, and you are about the only person who seems to bother about the relation of the Image to what it images.[14]

Though Dorothy was to publish, with her translation of the *Commedia*, notes and comments on Dante's world which are unsurpassed in scholarship, clarity and vigour, and though she was to lecture widely and brilliantly about him, nothing that she ever actually published was quite so fresh and compelling as these letters to Charles Williams, written in the first happy flush of infatuation: "Top marks for that passage, Charles – alpha plus with star"[15] . . . "It is no small achievement to have made a person [she is referring to Virgil] consistently good, kind and wise, through two long epic books, in which he is *never once* tedious or pompous or patronizing or superior"[16] . . . "The colour of the opening Cantos of the Purgatorio is a sort of miracle"[17] . . . "One of Dante's nicest traits is his readiness to make fun of himself"[18] . . . "Was there ever a heaven so full of nods and becks and wreathed smiles? So gay and so dancing? Or where the most abstract and intellectual kind of beatitude was so merrily expressed? . . . Surely nobody ever so passionately *wanted* a place where everybody was kind, and courteous, and carried happiness so lightly."[19] And, finally and above all: "What a writer! God's body and bones, what a writer!"[20]

And Charles Williams, whose own enthusiasm had helped to create hers, was so delighted with her letters that he wrote in reply one of his few long letters, asking if he might publish hers – "or at least something like them", perhaps an open letter to him, or extracts to be selected by him and approved by her. "I do very much want people to get all you say about the laughter and lightness and fun – even – of Dante. We want to

2

ta sudden Domestic reassurance, "no fear lest dinner cool" is bound to give one a slight shock, as if sitting down suddenly on a kitchen chair. But the style which carries one along & can practise the necessary art of sinking in verse is the style which can pass at will from the magnificent to the familiar without any jolt & without startling one into anything more than a delighted chuckle. Could anything be more absurd & endearing than the picture of Dante trotting eagerly along while Virgil & Statius talk over his head, and making no notions of beginning to speak & then losing courage, like a baby stork flopping about on the edge of the nest? I mean, damn it, Charles, a style that can do that and do the "per ch'io te sopra te corono e mitrio" can do anything. Nothing in the world is impossible to it. Incidentally, that line, coming as & where it does knocks one out quite flat. It is at the same time totally unexpected & dead right — I couldn't believe my eyes when I saw it. (Yes, of course it is in your book, but I hadn't, as it were, noticed it — which shows either that I am your most inattentive reader or that the actual placing of the line has something to do with the spell).

Having said this, I find I am starting Purgatory at the wrong end. However, there I am — & disposed to brood, a little sadly, over the fact that not even Dante has been able quite to escape the dreadful tendency of sympathetic characters to run away with the play. Satan is the hero of <u>Paradise Lost</u>, Judas has to be forcibly restrained from collaring all the "fat" of Passion-plays, the killing-off of any charming person at the end of Act <u>II</u> makes it highly probable that the audience will spend Act <u>III</u> in the bar — & it's a bit of a strain on Beatrice, poor girl, to take over from Virgil. It cannot be helped. I do not say that we do not get over Satie eventually, but it is a perilous passage. Like Mr Lewis's Ransom who, faced with a brand-new world full of green ladies & eldils, uttered a regretful sigh for the "old furry

Dorothy's handwriting

break up the hideous monstrosity of the Catholic mystical poet which they envisage as part of their solemn culture . . . Oh do, do!"[21]

Whether or not this would ever have come to anything is hard to say. Her response is half-hearted: she wants to go on writing to him as the fancy takes her, with no thought of a public, for that would inhibit her and make her try to organize her thoughts; nonetheless, if he wants to make something of her ramblings, that is up to him. But Charles Williams died, suddenly and unexpectedly, in May of the following year, and with him died any plans for publishing the Dante letters.

In the meanwhile, however, she went on writing to him; long disorganized letters in which one can see the seeds of many of her most interesting observations and insights. She was suffering, as she freely admitted, from Dante-mania, cheerfully inflicting her obsession on all her friends; and the letters to Charles Williams range over every kind of topic, whether the historical background of the poem, its theology, its style, its humanity, or the character and personality of Dante himself.

It is in that last connection that she bursts out into her dissertation, already quoted, on Bedworthiness. The passage that prompts these reflections is not part of the *Commedia* at all, but an earlier poem, an ode known as the "Aspro Parlar", addressed to a lady quite other than Beatrice; and Dorothy is discussing the man Dante in a much wider context than the *Commedia* alone. Oddly enough, shortly after writing that section of the letter she came across a book called *Dante Vivo*, in which the author, Giovanni Papini, accused Dante of "savage fantasy" and "atrocious desires" – in short, of sadism – on the strength of some lines in this ode in which Dante dreams of the fierce love he would make to the lady if only she would burn for him as he does for her. Dorothy's scornful reply is contained in her article "The 'Terrible' Ode", published after her death.[22] The case she makes for her hero as a passionate but perfectly normal lover is not only convincing in itself but also strong evidence, as I have suggested earlier, as to where her own sexual preferences and sympathies lay.

Dorothy's great strength as an interpreter of Dante lies precisely in this – that in addition to all the critical apparatus of an academic, she approaches him with the experience of a practising writer and dramatist. She is accustomed to study not only what is written but how it is written, and why, and by what kind of person in what state of mind. Given this approach, it was unlikely to be long before she was seized by the old irresistible urge to translate.

In her earlier years it was French, which she knew well. Now it was Italian, which she had only just begun to learn – and perhaps the most difficult Italian that could possibly be attempted, demanding faithful attention at one and the same time to the precision of its thought, the exactness of its imagery, the range of its effects, the clear delicacy of its beauty and the relentless demands of its rhyme scheme.

The greater the difficulty, the greater the challenge. She seems to have begun a few tentative stanzas some time before Christmas, but without telling anybody but her close friends. By that time she had presumably gone over in her own mind all the arguments that she was later to rehearse in letters to her publisher, E. V. Rieu, and in her lecture "On Translating the Divina Commedia", as to the most suitable form in which to cast her translation – whether prose, blank verse, heroic couplets or, most difficult of all but in the end, she found, unavoidable, Dante's own terza rima, with its overlapping triple rhymes that lead the verse onward in an unbroken, plaited cord of sound, pausing every nine or twelve lines but never faltering or flagging.

There was an additional difficulty for her. Her own verse writing still tended to suffer, unless she was careful, from that verbal overloading under which it had laboured in her early years. Dante had been called a miser with words. He told his story swiftly and made his effects with the utmost economy and simplicity. What he had to say was often complex, but the way he said it was limpidly clear, even childlike. He wanted the man and woman in the street to understand what he had to say. Dorothy quoted Marjorie Barber (who had caught the Dante contagion from her) as remarking: " 'From the things said *about* Dante, you expect something tremendously solemn in the "Sing, heavenly Muse" vein; and instead, it's like someone sitting there in an armchair and telling you a story'."[23] In seeking a style to match his, Dorothy had to pare down her own romantic rhetoric to a spare classical clarity – an exercise which she undertook gladly, such was her admiration for her master, and which certainly did her writing nothing but good.

Looking at other translations, she wrote:

> I think that the trouble with all of them is that they have far, far too much reverence for their author. They are afraid to be funny, afraid to be undignified; they insist on being noble and they end by being prim. But prim is the one thing Dante never is . . . one can get away with roughness, awkwardness, inaccuracy, archaism, anachronism, baldness or excess of ornament, but one prim line kills the whole thing stone dead.[24]

This un-primness was what Dorothy had to contribute. This, she felt, was what justified her, in face of so many existing translations, in starting on another one. The shock of finding that Dante was rough and coarse and funny and above all lively was the one that she wanted to pass on to other people. And so she embarked on a labour that was still un-completed when she died thirteen years later.

Even with all her enthusiasm, the thing might never have gone ahead but for the lucky chance that E. V. Rieu, who had backed the *Bridgeheads* series and had published several of Dorothy's articles as pamphlets for Methuen, was now also the editor of the Penguin Classics; and it so happened that he very much wanted a new translation of Dante.

When they lunched together in December 1944, she made no mention of the fact that she was working on the opening Cantos, being still very unsure of her ability to carry through such an immense task. And it was not until March of the following year that Muriel St Clare Byrne told Rieu what Dorothy was up to.

He immediately wrote, protesting about her reticence. "I have devoted more thought and work to the problem of getting Dante 'across' than any other author in my long Penguin list except Homer"[25] – and he asked to see what Dorothy had done.

He actually had in mind a prose translation (such as his own version of Homer), believing that the difficulties and disadvantages of verse were far too great. Dorothy acknowledged that this might well be true, and that a wholly satisfactory verse translation was certainly impossible; but she believed that it was even less possible to convey the spirit of the original without the swing of the verse; and her long, comprehensive letter, surveying all the possible methods and metres of translation, their pros and their cons, at least convinced Rieu sufficiently to persuade him to invite her to come and read him the stanzas she had already com-pleted.

As with *The Man Born to be King*, she brought to the task a combination of qualities that was probably unique. Rieu was not to know of the dozens of metrically ingenious poems she had written in her teens and twenties, nor of the extreme fluency and facility with words that she had developed at that time. Had it not been for that facility, his doubts about a verse translation would have been justified, however convincingly she argued her case and however thoroughly she understood Dante's mind and world. As it was, he was able to write to her on April 8, having heard her extract read and then having read it himself:

It is full of fire, swift movement, poetry and vigour, and, above all, for my purposes, it is clear. It would be foolish of me to cavil at the general style, when the result is so excellent, or to complain that you have achieved it at the cost of that modernity which I am aiming at . . .

I have great pleasure therefore in accepting your offer to translate the Divine Comedy for my series of Penguin Classics . . . May I tell them that you could deliver Inferno by January 1, 1946, Purgatorio by January 1, 1947, and Paradiso by January 1, 1948?

As for the Introduction, I had much rather have one by you than by Charles Williams, having heard you talking about Dante as you did. I feel you could tell people just what they should know when they start in on their reading.[26]

Dorothy asked for four years, rather than three, to complete the whole work. In fact, it was four years before even the *Inferno* came out (though this was largely due to printing delays), another six before the publication of the *Purgatorio*, and the *Paradiso* she never finished; it was completed by her friend Barbara Reynolds after her death.

However, the great journey was under way. From now on, Dante was with her, even if only in the background, morning, noon and night. She left instructions with Mr E. Seligman, dealer in rare books in Cecil Court, off Charing Cross Road, to keep his eye open for any books about or in any way relevant to the *Commedia*. The majority of lectures that she gave henceforward had some connection with Dante or his world. A rapturous welcome awaited any fellow-Dantist. Her thoughts, even about matters quite unconnected with Dante, began arriving willy-nilly in terza rima. Peeling potatoes or washing up the dishes she would find herself brooding over difficult or favourite passages; and sometimes would awake to find that in the night her subconscious had presented her with whole sections ready translated, every word inevitably and satisfyingly in its right place.

CHAPTER NINETEEN

BESIDES CHARLES WILLIAMS, Dorothy was of course in touch with the other two members of that quartet of High Church writers, T. S. Eliot and C. S. Lewis; and it is not surprising that there were differences of opinion between the four. Eliot was the most aloof of them, and Dorothy's letters to him were stiff and formal in comparison with her usual chatty style, suggesting that she stood in some awe of him; they seem to have met only very occasionally, mostly as members of the Advisory Council of St Anne's House, of which more later.

Between Dorothy, Williams and Lewis there was much more in common, Lewis, too, being an Oxford man and one who combined scholarship and a passion for theology with the writing of popular novels. One of the first letters that we have from Lewis to Dorothy contains the plaintive passage: "Oh Eliot! How can a man who is neither a knave nor a fool write so like both? Well, he can't complain that I haven't done my best to put him right. I hardly ever write a book without showing him one of his errors – still he doesn't mend. I call it ungrateful."[1]

The criticism was not entirely one-sided. I myself remember hearing Eliot, on one occasion, mildly wondering whether God really required the strenuous efforts of Dr Lewis to push him back on to his throne.

Between Lewis and Williams there were no such difficulties. They knew each other well, both being members of a group calling themselves "The Inklings" – a title with the double meaning that they were all in the writing business and also that they all shared a sense that they had caught glimpses, but no more, of the Divine Plan. J. R. R. Tolkien, author of *The Lord of the Rings*, was also a member, so that between them they made a formidable bunch of fable-makers. Dorothy herself was not actually one of them, since the group was confined to men and was exclusively Oxford-based. But she had so much in common with them that had she herself lived in Oxford, it would have been interesting to see whether they would have waived the men-only rule in her favour. She could certainly have put up an extremely good case for being admitted, since the group was exclusively concerned with matters of the mind which, as she was fond of pointing out, transcend sexual differences; but some of the group were singularly lacking in experience of women (C. S. Lewis in particular – Dorothy was very dubious about his views on sex), and might have been disturbed by the inclusion even of Dorothy's transsexual mind and not-very-stimulating body.

The correspondence between Dorothy and C. S. Lewis was almost wholly concerned with literary matters and is not, perhaps, of much general interest. But two points are worth mentioning, the first being Lewis's opinion, touched upon earlier, of Dorothy's letter-writing: "Although you have so little time to write letters, you are one of the great English letter-writers. (Awful vision for you – 'It is often forgotten that Miss Sayers was known in her own day as an author. We who have been familiar from childhood with the letters can hardly realize . . .')"[2] Lewis was undoubtedly right; and if anyone should one day set about editing the letters, it would be an immense but most rewarding labour.

The second of C. S. Lewis's points was less complimentary; it had to do with her doctrine of "the proper job". He had written asking if she would contribute to a series of short booklets which should be "a sort of library of Christian knowledge for young people in top forms at school".[3] Her reply was predictable, questioning whether this was the "right" thing for her to do. But Lewis was unconvinced:

> Yes, I see your point only too well. I also am haunted at times by the feeling that I oughtn't to be doing this kind of thing. But as the voice, when interrogated, can never give a good reason, I doubt if it comes from above. How is one to decide? If by what other people say – well, your "Six Other Deadly Sins" is about as good as it could be. And if you wrote a book on Sin for this series, it would certainly be a good one. Against it stands your artistic conscience. I wish I knew what place artistic consciences will hold a moment after death. It might be – then it might be exactly the reverse. . . .[4] Of course one mustn't do *dishonest* work. But you seem to take as the criterion of honest work the sensible *desire* to write – the itch. That seems to me precious like making "being in love" the only reason for going on with a marriage. In my experience the *desire* has no constant ratio to the value of the work done. My own frequent uneasiness comes from another source – the fact that apologetic work is so dangerous to one's own faith. A doctrine never seems dimmer to me than when I have just successfully defended it.[5]

Dorothy's answer is simply to state that she knows as much as anybody about the sinful pride of the craftsman; and she quotes bits of *The Zeal of Thy House* to prove it. But this is really not Lewis's point; and to the simple but trenchant accusation that she seems to confuse what she ought to do with what she feels like doing, she appears to have no convincing reply.

She could have pointed out, with truth, that no really good work could ever be done without a sense of enjoyment. But perhaps she lacked the spiritual subtlety of Charles Williams, who knew precisely how to distinguish between enjoyment and indulgence; and knew too that the distinction, delicate though it is, is vital.

How vital it was for Dorothy can clearly be seen, I believe, if one compares her translation of the *Inferno* with the play she was working on at the same time, *The Just Vengeance*. For the *Commedia*, she had the natural and inevitable discipline of following the original, which forced upon her Dante's own simplicity and directness. For her own play, steeped though it was both in Dante and Charles Williams, she had no such curb; and the result, though some of the speeches are very fine in themselves, was wordy, didactic and dramatically cumbersome.

The Just Vengeance was commissioned in April 1945 (the same month as the commissioning of the translation of the *Commedia*) for performance at the 750th anniversary celebrations of Lichfield Cathedral in the summer of 1946. Looking back after it was all over, she thought it the best thing she had ever done.

Immediately after finishing it, however, she was not so sure. "I was afraid it was getting very static and abstract," she wrote to Muriel St Clare Byrne, "pleasing to theologians rather than to actors. . . . It's a different technique from my other things, and I feel that with more experience I could have handled it better."[6] In extenuation she explained that the speeches had to be formal and incantatory rather than casual, in order to allow for the necessarily static nature of a Cathedral production, and to cope with the acoustics. Besides, "it is deliberately built to feature the music – I mean the literal music, so that the sung choruses should be an integral part of the thing, and not just 'incidental music' ".[7]

The argument that religious plays require incantation was one which she had vigorously opposed when she first started work on *The Zeal of Thy House* for Canterbury. Then, she was campaigning against churchiness and the pulpit sound, and in favour of natural dramatic effects. But at Canterbury the plays were performed in the Chapter House; and even there she had to demand improvements in the acoustics before she would undertake a second play for them. Here, in the immensity of the Cathedral itself, the acoustics were far worse.

In fact it was not only the technique that was different from anything that she had done before. The thing that most vividly strikes any reader of this play who is familiar with the writing of Charles Williams is how completely she has succumbed to his influence. She has taken over his images, such as the City as the image of society; she has taken over his ideas, such as the emphasis on the timeless moment after death, when choices made while living are seen in the light of eternal reality (images and ideas which Williams in turn had adapted from Dante); and in addition she has borrowed his verse rhythms and even his diction.

Perhaps in doing so she also borrowed some of his faults. Eight years before, commenting in a letter about one of Williams' own plays, *Seed of Adam*, she had written perceptively to the producer:

> I feel that Mr Williams has really packed his lines too full of a number of different and difficult thoughts, which go by before the ear can grasp them. And they are too often handed over to the chorus to relate, instead of being dramatically shown in a conflict of personalities. . . . It is not really a drama but a mimed poem, and really more suited to be read and studied thoughtfully than shown in action on the stage. . . .[8]

With slight adjustments, the same criticism could apply equally to *The Just Vengeance*. To make matters worse, she had added at that time: "It is clear that you may have felt this, since you have discovered the necessity for a preliminary explanation, both by word of mouth and in a programme. But a play ought to explain itself."[9] Yet now we find her blithely remarking:

> I think I shall have to write a warning preface, indicating that "nobody can give an intelligent opinion of this play without having undergone the tremendous intellectual discipline of reading *The Divine Comedy*," so that they won't ever be sure whether they are falling foul of me or of an elder and better poet! Anyhow, nearly all the argument and most of the best lines are Dante's – I shall say so, and leave them to entangle themselves.[10]

When she was writing *The Mind of the Maker*, she would have poured scorn on anyone who so neglected the duty of plain communication as to make the reading of Dante a pre-requisite of understanding their own work. But now, infatuated as she was, how could she fail to think this the best thing she had done, having modelled it so closely on her mentors?

In fact, the modelling was not as close as she had hoped. Where both Dante and Charles Williams had contrived to fuse the natural and supernatural levels of life in such a way that there seems to be no barrier between them, Dorothy's attempt to do the same thing was, as she suspected, a failure. Her central character, a dead airman shot down in combat and confusedly finding himself faced first by the history of his own city, Lichfield, and finally by the redemptive grace of Christ himself, is a contrivance that one has to work hard to accept. Dorothy knew well enough that the supernatural world was not her territory, and it is odd that she decided to venture into it. Dante and Charles Williams achieved the fusion simply because the fusion already existed in their own consciousness. In Dorothy's, it was a theoretical proposition – and no amount of technique could turn that into an experience that could be communicated with theatrical power.

Even more surprising, in view of Dorothy's incisive understanding of literary and dramatic technique, is that she seems to have forgotten that a crucial factor in making such a conglomeration of heterogeneous elements work is a simple, naturalistic storyline upon which to hang them. And she has, in addition, allowed her weakness for long didactic speeches to get totally out of hand. It is in a way endearing and reassuring to find that Dorothy's vaunted objectivity about her own work can be overthrown by a new love; that her passion for Dante, intellectual though it might be, was as capable as any other passion of leading her astray.

It would be an overstatement, however, to suggest that she had now lost interest in everything else. The Detection Club was reawakened from its war-time sleep at the end of 1946, thanks largely to Dorothy's efforts. The tedium of the routine administrative details that she undertook was more than compensated for by her enjoyment of the meetings, the initiations and the dinners, where the distinguished guests ranged from Bertrand Russell to the Coroner of St Pancras Court. And she continued to write the occasional review, and the odd article or poem; or to spring to arms in some cause that attracted her attention.

Besides all this, there was St Anne's House, Soho. Reluctant as ever to associate herself with any specific religious group or organization, she nevertheless gave unstinted time to this redoubtable, if confused, enterprise.

St Anne's is in Dean Street, in the heart of that golden square mile which is London's theatreland as well as being a centre of good eating, prostitution, and mild gang warfare – not to mention the home and workplace of dozens of small traders and craftsmen of all kinds. The house itself – the actual building – was the clergy house belonging to the once fashionable eighteenth-century church. The church had been demolished by a landmine in 1942, leaving the solid, ugly, uncomfortable clergy house still standing. Also left standing was the tower, a distinctive Soho landmark, its clock now stopped permanently at the hour of destruction. Where the church had stood was a barren wasteland of rubble, covered with willowherb.

Towards the end of 1942, the Rev. Patrick McLaughlin and the Rev. Gilbert Shaw had approached the Bishop of London for permission to use the house as a sort of mission centre for thinking pagans. Both were highly intelligent Anglo-Catholics; but they had, unfortunately but perhaps inevitably, rather different ideas as to what they personally would prefer to do with the opportunity presented by the empty house. It would be only a slight oversimplification to say that they represented respectively the Negative Way and the Affirmative Way. Fr Shaw's interests lay in the deeper regions of the spiritual life – the mysteries of ascetic practice, the life of prayer and meditation, the realms of white and black magic, and the exorcism of evil spirits. Fr McLaughlin was concerned with the relationship between the Church and society, the exploration of the social environment and the discovery of religious significance therein.

It is obvious which would appeal more to Dorothy, with her love of good things to eat and drink; especially after she came under the influence of Charles Williams and his celebration of the Way of Affirmation of Images; though Gilbert Shaw contributed expert advice on the subject and history of magic and sorcery when she came to tackle the place of the sorcerers in the eighth circle of the *Inferno*. In her letters to anyone asking her for spiritual guidance, it was to "the people at St Anne's" that she directed them, though with special recommendation to Fr McLaughlin; often going out of her way to mention that there were few other clergymen of the Church of England in whom she could place much confidence.

In addition to its internal divisions, St Anne's House was early threatened by the Diocesan Reorganization Committee, which wanted to abandon the whole experiment and sell the site of the church for a very large sum of money; the theory being that Central London was either not worth saving or past praying for, while the money was needed for the outer suburbs, where people now lived. From its earliest years, St Anne's House had to justify itself to the hilt for its very existence: And Dorothy found herself, as usual, in the forefront of the battle.

She had met Patrick McLaughlin some years earlier when he was vicar of Berden, a village in Essex not far from Witham; and a correspondence had begun between them after the Archbishop of York's Malvern Conference in January 1941, discussing among other things the writing of a simple book of Christian doctrine. "It's so silly", Dorothy wrote, "that after nearly two thousand years of theological writing, whose volumes bend the shelves of the British Museum, we cannot recommend to anybody a sensible book on the Christian Creeds. . . ."[11]

Both had also been members of various organizations concerned with the social aspects of Christianity, such as the Guild of St Alban and St Sergius, which included among its members the M.P. Tom Driberg.

It is not surprising that Dorothy was asked to contribute to the first course of lectures organized by St Anne's House. The course was run during the summer of 1943 and was called "Christian Faith and Contemporary Culture". It featured T. S. Eliot on literature; Dorothy's old ally, James Welch of the BBC, on broadcasting; her friend Lady Rhondda from *Time and Tide* on journalism; and the Director of the Victoria and Albert Museum on the visual arts.

Dorothy's subject was Drama; and this was the lecture at which the present writer first set eyes on Dorothy Sayers.

I was a young man, working at the Admiralty, with very little idea of what I wanted to do when – and if – the war ever ended; for it seemed endless, and there was always the off chance that one might not be there to see the end when it did come. An Anglican priest, chaplain to the Toc H Hostel where I was staying, had proposed the outing to several of us, and the idea of seeing the creator of Peter Wimsey in the flesh had stirred our curiosity just as he intended it should.

We sat in a hot, crowded, dusty room, with too few chairs – and almost immediately forgot our discomforts. Such was the force of Dorothy's enthusiasm, such her ability to communicate it, that the course of my life was changed. From that evening on, I knew what I wanted to do.

From the wardens' viewpoint, the lecture helped to launch St Anne's House with style and with much desirable publicity. Inevitably, they saw in Dorothy's name and talents an invaluable asset, and in November 1944 she agreed to join the Advisory Council of the House, becoming Chairman soon after.

She can have had little idea what she was letting herself in for. The differences in style and personality of the two wardens became ever more apparent, and the supporters of St Anne's became divided into two groups. Moreover neither of the wardens, for all their brilliance, had any great gift for organization; and the result all too often was that audiences arrived expecting to hear some distinguished philosopher or sociologist, only to discover that he was unable to come after all. So Dorothy found herself unwontedly cast in the role of peacemaker and diplomat, trying to reconcile the aims of the two wardens; and in addition forced to defend an imaginative but incoherent, not to say inefficient, organization against the attacks of the Diocesan Reorganization Committee, which, like most bureaucratic bodies, preferred efficiency, which it could recognize and assess, to imagination, which was intangible and indeed often rather disturbing. It must have been most uncomfortable for one who was such a champion of professionalism to have to fight a battle in which she was all too aware that, in matters of organization, her troops were amateur to a degree; and this adds an extra nobility to her faithfulness to the project.

The struggle to keep St Anne's alive and efficient was to last, like the translation of the *Commedia*, till the day of her death. The House saw many changes: the departure of Gilbert Shaw and the subsequent coming and going of various helpers, assistants, advisers and organizers – none of whom finally succeeded in mastering the multiple problems of personality, finance, organization, and the sheer intractability of the building and the area it was set in. Dorothy held on, attending long, tedious, recriminatory meetings, drafting memoranda, making speeches and writing letters to newspapers and Diocesan officials, as well as planning programmes and occasionally giving lectures herself; and in all this, harnessing her war-horse spirit to the tiresome details of day-by-day administration. There is little doubt that, but for her efforts, combined with the weight that her name still carried in the upper echelons of the Church of England, the St Anne's experiment would have perished much sooner than it actually did. A mark of its import-ance is that now, thirty years later, many of the ideas it promoted which seemed at the time to be wildly advanced are current practice in many parishes. Many of the seeds sown by Dorothy and Patrick McLaughlin with such weariness of spirit and against such opposition have come to fruition when the sowers are no longer able to enjoy the harvest.

There were compensations at the time – not least the excuse it gave Dorothy for getting out of that enclosed house in Witham and com-muning with kindred spirits. A few yards from St Anne's was the Moulin d'Or restaurant, where Dorothy had long had a running account and where, in the heady days when she had a play running in London, she would bring parties of friends and members of the cast for food, drink and loud conversation. It was good to be back, if only briefly, in the busy atmosphere of London which she had so enjoyed since 1920, when, hungry and anxious, she had struggled to prevent poverty driving her back to the tedious security of Christchurch.

Dorothy had not lost the habit of keeping the different areas of her life in separate compartments, and we at St Anne's (I was now working there in a secretarial capacity) knew nothing of her private life. Mac was a mystery and a myth; we knew that a husband existed, but we had no idea why he was never seen nor spoken of, and could only speculate what kind of strange relationship this could be; indeed what kind of man it could be who was mate to this large, dominating, wholly unfeminine female. Conventional comic images of the tiny henpecked husband alternated with more melodramatic visions of the mad monster chained in the attic. Slightly closer to the truth was the theory of the unpresentable alcoholic. But what seemed quite clear was that this was by no means what we in those days regarded as a normal marriage.

One of the very few people from Dorothy's public and professional life to penetrate that ménage was the artist and scenic designer, Norah Lambourne, who was responsible for the sets and costumes for *The Just Vengeance*. They had been brought together through Dorothy's habitual involvement with every part of the production, and also by a mutual love of cats; and when Norah was away from home on jobs, her cat Bramble joined the Witham household.

Dorothy's letters to Norah are mostly occasioned by various theatrical events – the possibility of a London production of *The Just Vengeance* (C. B. Cochran himself was rumoured to be interested at one time); a new production of *The Zeal of Thy House* at Canterbury in 1949; and Dorothy's last play, *The Emperor Constantine*, produced at Colchester in 1951. Norah did the designs for all three productions, and the friendship quickly ripened.

Though it has to be admitted that in Dorothy's letters to Norah the cats figure much more largely than poor Mac, we do learn something about him. One thing that becomes clear is that the marriage was by no means a total disaster. Despite the provocation he offered, she seems to have achieved an indulgent and affectionate humour about his weaknesses:

> My husband has no fixative, but has taken your drawing away with a view to fixing it in milk, which he says will be all right. He looked at it sourly, and said: "Who's that supposed to be?" "Man who played Christ for us," said I. "A most unpleasant looking person," said he; and I sensed the word "Dago" hovering at the back of his mind. So that if the milk turns in the fixing process I shall not put it down merely to the thunder![12]

The concern about Mac's health, too, is genuine if unsentimental:

> The doctor, when I saw him yesterday, took a rather poor view of his blood-pressure, and told me a number of things *I* could have told *him* years ago if I had had the opportunity. This was the first time he had ever happened actually to see Mac in that kind of giddy and unco-ordinated state. . . . The trouble, of course, with blood-pressurey people who have *uncontrolled tempers*, is that they may work themselves

up into a stroke at any moment. But one can't do anything about it, because nobody else can control their tempers for them.[13]

One of the few activities which Mac must have found congenial, and from which he was not excluded, was Dorothy's occasional foray into politics. In May 1947 she wrote a letter to the *Daily Telegraph* about the recent floods and blizzards in the Fens – or rather about public misapprehension as to what help and compensation could be expected from the Government:

> I think the time has come to protest against the use, whether in appeals or in Press and Radio announcements, of phrases like *the Government* have given £1,000,000", "*the Government* will give a £ for every £ subscribed" – as though "the Government" had any money of their own with which to make liberal gestures. The plain fact is that all the money comes from the tax-payers (including, incidentally, the flood-victims themselves) . . .[14]

And she followed this up in July with an article for the periodical *Tory Challenge*, entitled "You are the Treasury".

A Labour Government had come in on a landslide two years earlier, much to her consternation, for Dorothy considered socialist principles, however well-meaning, to be unrealistic and in the end an abrogation of individual responsibility. One aspect of socialism, she believed, was the growing tendency of people to assume that troubles could be thrown upon "the Government", who had endless money and a limitless responsibility to spend it on alleviating the lot of "the public". This was the sort of "muddled thinking" that always infuriated Dorothy:

> Some Governments take credit to themselves for being more lavish with the public purse than others; and lavishness may, indeed, be a Good Thing. But the fact remains that, whoever gets the credit, it is not the Government that provides the cash. You do that. A Government, of whatever complexion, has no money, except what it can beg, borrow or – that is, except what it can extract from you, me and the man in the street by loans or taxation.[15]

And she appended a short glossary of terms; for example:

> *Compulsory National Insurance.* This means that if any one of a particular set of disasters overtakes you, Lord Tomnoddy and Sir Gorgias Midas will be made to pay for it, whether they like it or not; it also means that

if a similar disaster overtakes Lord Tomnoddy or Sir G.M., you will have to pay for it, and so will the chimney-sweep, the factory-worker, and the down-and-out who likes his little bit of baccy. . . .
This service should be provided by the Nation. This means you want to pay for it yourself (and I highly commend you; but remember it will cost you something).[16]

One result of the *Tory Challenge* article was that Dorothy entered into correspondence with the Conservative Central Office, which seems to have thought that with a bit of luck it could make as good use of her as the Church of England had seven or eight years before. This, mercifully, was something into which she was not going to allow herself to be dragged. Salutary though her article may have been, she was well enough aware that, despite her consuming range of interests, the subjects on which she really knew what she was talking about were fairly limited; and they did not include politics or economics, except in a most general kind of way.

It is fortunate, for example, that she never gave public utterance to the sentiments she expressed in a letter to her old friend and ally James Welch, once of the BBC, now involved in the Groundnuts Scheme fiasco in Tanganyika:

I do wish somehow we could have let all these foreign peoples *alone*. A little Christianity would doubtless have done them no harm, if only it didn't have to be mixed up with things like industrialism, European institutions, party politics and the savage greed and waste of our kind of agriculture. If we go on like this much longer, there won't be a scrap of surface left on the earth anywhere. It *sounds* all right to heal the sick and preserve the lives of babies and so on, but if one goes on multiplying the population and destroying fertility, where does one end? We are doing away with all nature's safeguards (including the tsetse fly!), and as soon as we've broken down the defences of another bit of soil, we develop it until we develop it right away. I sometimes feel it would be an excellent thing if the native population murdered all the Europeans and proceeded to "let in the jungle".[17]

Dorothy's worries about dust-bowls, the population explosion and the Europeanization of Africa are valid enough; but it is extraordinary that she should have allowed herself to have any truck with the notion that nature knows best, and can be trusted to do best when left alone. Her own letter about the Fen floods had called for all possible help for the victims; the help most urgently needed being to get rid of the flood water that nature had deposited there. And even the most cursory examination of the African plight would have shown her that the jungle, however fertile, was totally useless for the production of food *until* it had been cleared and broken down.

One should not, of course, make too much of a tetchy paragraph or two in a private letter. Had Dorothy ever had to make a public statement on the subject, she would certainly have done her homework and changed her attitude. But it is an indication of the kind of mental bias to which she was susceptible, and which caused some people who met her to dismiss her as an arrant and arrogant reactionary.

Although her flirtation with the Conservative Central Office was short-lived, it may have had some connection with the fact that she was invited that same month, July 1947, to the Royal Garden Party at Buckingham Palace – an honour that she felt obliged to decline because of Mac's indisposition. Loyalist and traditionalist that she was, that sacrifice must have hurt her.

A couple of months later Mac was worse, and it was decided to send him to Guy's Hospital in London for observation; for his symptoms, though worrying, were vague and intermittent. Nothing very definite emerged from the examination, but he seemed better for a while on his return, thanks probably to his enforced abstemiousness in hospital and his efforts to practise a little self-denial when he got home. The improvement did not last long, and he soon relapsed into a very uncertain state of health, a constant misery to himself and a cause of constant anxiety to Dorothy.

Norah Lambourne was becoming a fairly regular house-guest, and her friendship was a comfort. And at the same time another friendship was developing, though more slowly than Norah's, from a professional to a personal relationship.

When the Society for Italian Studies emerged from its wartime hibernation in 1946, a young lecturer in Italian at Cambridge named Barbara Reynolds had been on the committee appointed to organize a Summer School; and it was largely due to her enthusiasm that an invitation had been sent to Dorothy to lecture at the Summer School on Dante – quite a long shot, for at that stage all that the committee knew of Dorothy's qualifications was that Penguins had announced her forthcoming translation of the *Commedia*.

Where Dante was concerned Dorothy couldn't say no, and she had lectured on Canto XXVI of the *Inferno*, where the Counsellors of Fraud walk, wrapped in flame, in the eighth Bolgia, and where Ulysses, in a passage of famous beauty, tells of his last voyage.

For Dorothy, that lecture had been "rather an ordeal", according to a letter she wrote soon after to Norah Lambourne:

. . . the audience was made up of (a) about 6 people who know *all* about Dante – sitting like sharks, just under the platform with their jaws wide open; (b) about 50 people who know more about Dante, and far more Italian, than I do; (c) about 400 people who (to judge by the looks of them) had never even *heard* of Dante! However, I did fairly well, because, the acoustics of Jesus Hall being bad, and most of the other lecturers academic gentlemen who mumbled serenely along with their noses in their papers, I turned out to be the only lecturer whom, so far, the audience had been able to hear properly. Thus I had an unfair advantage – merely because being no academic but a common popular soapbox lecturer, I didn't mind shouting at them in a loud and brassy voice, without regard for my own dignity or that of my subject.[18]

For Barbara Reynolds it was a revelation, exhilarating and enlightening. Dorothy had dressed up, as she always did for lectures, in the way that she knew suited her, for magnificence; that night it was a shimmering silver evening dress and long earrings. And her voice was not only louder than those of the other participants; it was more full of meaning. When she quoted from the Canto in Italian she did so with a rich appreciation of the poetry – unlike the professor, himself an Italian, who had read it out before the lecture, not only inaudibly but without feeling. And finally, she said things that Barbara had felt and half-felt, and said them well – things that the academics never said, based on the perception that Dante, from Dante's own point of view, was not a classic but a passionate, contemporary writer; and his poem was not a grammatical exercise but a statement of vital truth.

It was clear that such an approach could never command the allegiance of the nit-pickers and the chaff-chewers among the academic fraternity, to whom it was nothing but a threat; and indeed there were one or two professors to whom the name of Sayers rapidly became anathema. But for Barbara, an academic herself, there could be no question where the life and the truth lay. "I got so excited", she wrote later to Dorothy, "that I had to be held down by Lewis."[19] And she saw to it that Dorothy's Summer School lecture to the Society became something of an annual fixture.

Occasional letters were exchanged, and Dorothy would take tea with Barbara and her family – her husband, Lewis Thorpe, and their son Adrian – before the lectures. Gradually, confidence ripened. Something that began as admiration on the one side, and on the other gratitude for an appreciative ally, developed first into a full-scale professional relationship ("Now we're off!" Dorothy wrote in October 1947, in answer to a pertinent question from Barbara); and then began to grow, little by little, into something nearer to the relationship of a mother and daughter – or so at least Barbara felt.

Though Dorothy's mind was so happy in the historical past, so far as her own life was concerned she always preferred to look forward rather than back. "I thoroughly dislike all retrospect,"[20] she once wrote, and of all retrospect, the time she most wanted to forget was probably her schooldays. But there was one person from those days who had not been forgotten. Fräulein Fehmer, who had taught Dorothy the piano at Godolphin, had kept in touch with her in the years between the wars, writing to her about the Wimsey novels; and as each new book came out, Dorothy had sent her a copy. The war put a stop to the correspondence, but as the tide of battle swung against Germany and the great fleets of bombers had poured out over Essex, heading for Germany in columns that never seemed to end, she had written the poem "Target Area", from which a few lines have already been quoted:

The grim young men in the blue uniforms,
professionally laconic, charting, over the inter-com,
the soundings of the channel of death, have carried
another basket of eggs to Fräulein Fehmer –
I do not know, of course, whether she got them . . .

. . . There is a particular nocturne
that I cannot hear to this day without thinking of her;
when it is rendered
by celebrated musicians over the aether
I see the red-brick walls, the games trophies,
the rush-bottomed chairs, the row of aspidistras,
that garnished the edge of the platform, and Fräulein Fehmer,
gowned in an unbecoming dark-blue silk,
lifting the song from the strings with a squaring of her strong
    shoulders;
the notes on the wireless are only an imperfect echo
of that performance . . .

    When the great Lancasters,
roaring out of England, making the sky boil like a cauldron,
stooped at last upon Frankfurt from the blackness between the stars,
did the old, heartbreaking melody cry to you,
Poland's agony through the crashing anger of England?
Did we strike you, perhaps, quickly

tossing the soul out through the rent ribs or merciful
splitting of the skull? Or did you
find yourself suddenly awake at midnight,
peering from the blankets, fumbling for your glasses, to see,
by flare-light and fire-light,
the unexpected precipice by the bedside,
the piano shattered aslant, with all its music
coiling out of it in a tangle of metallic entrails,
dust, books, ashes, splintered wood, old photographs,
the sordid indecency of bathroom furniture
laid open to the sky? Or are you, I wonder,
still waiting the personal assault, the particular outrage,
expiating the world's sin in a passion of nightly expectation
till the unbearable is reiterated
and the promise fulfilled? . . .

    This I write
with the same hand that wrote the books I sent you,
knowing that we are responsible for what we do,
knowing that all men stand convicted of blood
in the High Court, the judge with the accused.
The solidarity of mankind is a solidarity in guilt,
and all our virtues stand in need of forgiveness,
being deadly . . .[21]

Dorothy, ever a borrower, was here borrowing her style from T. S. Eliot. But, that acknowledged, it is a poem of unusual tenderness and compassion, and the theological sententiousness which she seemed to find obligatory cannot outweigh the human perception and sympathy of it.

Now, in the aftermath of war, Germany was starving. Rations in England were by no means plentiful, and Dorothy herself had not bought a new coat and skirt since 1940; but there were organizations for sending parcels of food and clothing to Europe, and Dorothy went to a great deal of trouble to discover whether Fräulein Fehmer was still alive and, if so, where she was living; and having got in touch with her, she kept her supplied with basic requirements till the old lady's death at the end of 1948.

A revival of *The Zeal of Thy House* at Canterbury, planned but abandoned in 1940, at last took place in 1949, with Dorothy as closely involved as ever in such matters as the design and construction of the angels' wings. One of her letters to Norah Lambourne goes into the matter in some detail:

We shall try to get more volunteers tomorrow, because pleating eighty-eight yards of gold paper in half-inch pleats is No Joke. In the meantime, two art school girls laid gold paper on the eight "feather" sides of the wings, and I helped with the feathering, and we now have three "feather" sides complete except for the little narrow quill strips. We failed to find any means of keeping the glue heated, and so used Croid and Acrabond, which stick beautifully. . . .[22]

While this was going on, Dorothy was approached by the Bishop of Colchester to write a play for their Festival in 1951. And immediately she saw the opportunity to write a massive historical pageant which would culminate in the greatest theological debate in the Church's history; for one of the kings of Colchester was grandfather to the Roman Emperor Constantine, and Constantine presided over the Council of Nicaea, at which the Christian Creeds were hammered out, never to be altered since. "The play, if I did it," she wrote to Norah, "would be about Constantine and the Council of Nicaea – period 4th century – beginning at the court of King Coel (old King Cole to you), and proceeding to the court of Constantine at Rome, and afterwards to the Council (lots and lots of bishops and people in fantastic mitres and Constantine in full Imperial togs) . . . I should want you to do the costumes and decor; the bishop has readily agreed to my having a completely free hand with the production side. . . ."[23]

During that spring of 1949 Mac's health again began to give serious cause for worry, and he was examined by specialists. The fear was that there might be some growth in the intestinal tract, but no sign of this was found – nothing worse in the stomach than a rather high production of acid. There was, however, enlargement of the heart and "marked calcification of the aorta"[24] – though an electrocardiograph showed no evidence of coronary artery disease. Mac was advised to avoid physical and mental stress, and to reduce his consumption of alcohol and tobacco. He was not to overload the stomach, and was to stick to a regular life with eight to ten hours in bed daily.

In fact, he had not been drinking nearly so much in recent months, and he promised to cut down on the smoking. He was less enthusiastic, however, about the suggestion that he should take a quiet holiday somewhere. He was nearing seventy, and had long lost the habit of leaving home.

As on previous occasions, the regime had an effect, but it was inter-mittent. "Mac was better yesterday and the day before, but relapsed into gloom today. I think, though, he really is better, taking it all round . . .

They [his doctors] are still trying to find somewhere for him to go – but whatever they find they will have a job to get him really going!"[25]

The truth was, of course, that despite his hobbies of photography and portrait painting, from which he had sporadically tried to earn a little money, it was many years since Mac had had much to live for. In August he was back again in Guy's, sciatica adding to his troubles.

November at last saw the publication of the *Inferno*. Muriel St Clare Byrne wrote:

> Dearest Dorothy, I am really thrilled actually to possess the Dante at last, inscribed with your own hand! I re-read the Introduction last night, and am more convinced than ever that it's quite one of the most remarkable and powerful (and difficult) pieces of writing that you've ever done. . . . In fact, a major achievement, even for you. . . .[26]

And Barbara Reynolds wrote:

> *Greed* is the only word which describes my sessions with it; indeed it has thrown all my time-table out of joint. . . . I think that the key to you is that you do what you like. . . . You so obviously enjoy looking into Dante, and so the reader enjoys it with you. . . . The translation itself is most interesting. It startles sometimes, but it throws the original into relief and makes you look at it more closely. . . .[27]

The slight reservation about the translation, as distinct from the Introduction and Notes, is typical of many reactions. C. S. Lewis, for example, commented:

> You have got (what you most desired) the quality of an exciting story. On that side you may record almost complete success. Next; I think the metrical audacities are nearly all effective in their places, i.e. as things in *your* poem. How far they are like anything in Dante – I mean, "operate as Dante does" – is another matter. They have on me the effect of making Dante rather like Browning. That is certainly better than making him like Milton. I shd. say that they are everywhere doing more good than harm. . . . Every live rendering must sacrifice some things to achieve others. You have chosen to get in Dante the lively "scientifictionist" at all (reasonable) costs, and as all your predecessors chose to get in the *altissimo poeta* at *all* costs, this was the right thing to do. It is a strong, exciting view from one particular angle, and that is worth any number of timid, safe versions.

And he concludes; "Oh – best of all, it *frightens* me more than any translation I've seen . . . I'm ready for the "Purgatorio" as soon as you like. . . ."[28]

Dorothy's elucidation of the meaning and the background of the poem met with nothing but superlative praise. And she was well content with the reaction to the translation as well, having foreseen from the start that she could not possibly please everyone, or even herself, in every possible way. As she wrote later to Professor G. L. Bickersteth: "I think I can bear any amount of criticism or disagreement, provided the judgement ends up 'eppur si muove'!"[29] (which is what Galileo was supposed to have said after his recantation on the subject of the earth's rotation round the sun – "All the same, it does move!").

By now she was, of course, well into the translation of the *Purgatorio*, though this competed for her attention with the Colchester play. The two tasks went on side by side, with Dante rather the loser because of Dorothy's rash undertaking to look after the production side of the play; amateur shows, depending as they do on the goodwill of volunteers, suffer from all the ills that professional productions are heir to plus a host of others, as Dorothy was to discover. And in the background, all the while, was Mac's illness.

In April 1950 he was once again in Guy's, where he was visited, for the first time since his marriage to Dorothy, by his brother Edgar. This reunion seems to have come about through the efforts of a daughter by his first marriage, Ann, who had earlier attempted to get in touch with her father, but failed – owing, she believed, to opposition from Dorothy.

Whatever the rights and wrongs of this, the reunion seems to have meant a great deal to both brothers, and Dorothy too welcomed it, for it gave her someone with whom she could share the responsibility of Mac's increasing frailty.

The following month she had to go to Durham, to receive an Honorary Degree in Literature – the only Doctorate she ever received, and one of which she was extremely proud. But she cut her visit to the University as short as possible, for Mac was now back at home, and she did not want to be separated from him for any longer than was necessary.

Her concern was justified. On June 9 he had the stroke she had so long feared, and died instantly.

He had been ill, on and off, almost since their marriage – nearly a quarter of a century. And since their pre-war holidays in Scotland, he had rarely left the house. "It will seem very queer without Mac," she wrote to Muriel. "I shall miss having him to look after, and there will be no one to curse me and keep me up to the mark! I do hope you will be able to come down before long, so that I can have somebody to talk to and prevent me from relapsing into a kind of do-nothing stupor."[30] And to Una Ellis-Fermor: "It seems impossible there should be so many uninterrupted hours in the day."[31] Which was a sort of compensation, perhaps, but at the same time a desolation.

Edgar wrote to Ann, whose attitude towards Dorothy was one of deep suspicion and some bitterness, to assure her that he was satisfied that everything possible had been done to cure Mac; also that his death would not mean the end of the "voluntary allowance" which it appears Dorothy had been paying all this while to his first wife: Dorothy would continue this subsidy "as if Mac were still alive".[32]

Apart from a few personal effects, Dorothy inherited everything that Mac possessed – which was very little. "In reality," wrote Edgar, "I find that he hasn't any assets. . . . In fact he has been supported by his wife for many years."[33]

It is odd that Ann, in a recent biographical note about her father, should have made no mention of the allowance to her mother. Whatever her feelings about Dorothy – and a degree of resentment was natural enough – it was an item on the credit side that should not have been suppressed.

Mac was cremated at Ipswich. The doctor (a Scot himself) who had attended his last few years, was entrusted with the task of carrying out his last wishes and scattering the ashes in Mac's homeland of Scotland, in the churchyard at Biggar, historic home-town of the Fleming family since the twelfth century. The doctor, covertly performing his task after dusk, found it amusingly appropriate that the churchyard lay next door to a pub called "The Fleming Arms".

With Edgar's help, Dorothy went through "the poor old dear's litter of papers",[34] and sent his clothes to the Officers' Association in Belgrave Square, to be distributed among needy ex-Army officers. And then life went on.

CHAPTER TWENTY

DOROTHY WAS ALREADY hugely fat; and except for the occasions when she dressed up – for she still knew how to make herself superbly impressive for lectures and for meetings of the Detection Club, where she was now President – careless of her dress to the point of mild eccentricity. At the rehearsals for *The Just Vengeance* she had worn, as an accompaniment to her coat and skirt and sensible stockings, a pair of old gymshoes; and even at the first night, with the Queen present, had worn a knitted tam o' shanter with her fur coat. But while Mac was around, she made sure she did not let herself go altogether. Now that he was no longer there to keep his eye on her, she could indulge her love for food and drink without restraint, and could live in the kind of undergraduate style that suited her, with reference books, cats, pages of manuscript, letters and pots of marmalade scattered indiscriminately over all convenient flat surfaces.

She used to say that the great advantage of the pleasures of the mind was that they outlasted the pleasures of the body. If by the latter she meant the pleasures of physical fitness, it was certainly true of her, though it must be admitted that she had never done anything to promote or prolong these; but the physical pleasures of the table consoled her right to the end, and wider yet and wider spread her figure. "The elephant is crated", she once said to Muriel St Clare Byrne, when she had finally wedged herself into the back seat of Muriel's car; and the Corset Department at Marshall & Snelgrove had a good deal of difficulty in fitting her. "After about nine months' devoted labour on the part of all concerned a wearable garment has at last been achieved," she wrote, "and I am quite willing to settle the account. Please understand that I am in no way complaining of the assistants in the Corset Department, who have throughout displayed the utmost patience and good will. I am probably a very difficult person to fit. . . ."[1]

In other respects Mac's death caused little change in her life. Dante continued, and Dorothy must have wondered a little, as her translation took her up the terraces of Purgatory where the repentant souls gladly endured the cauterizing of their sins for the sake of the joy beyond, what exactly was happening to "poor, dear old Mac". It is a great lack in our understanding of Dorothy that there seems to be no indication anywhere in her writing that she was aware of any connection between the fate of those literary souls that she expounded so brilliantly, and that of this particular individual soul that she knew so well.

Intellectual irritation leapt out again when Professor Fred Hoyle, a popular scientist of the period, broadcast an attack on Christianity based on the belief that eternity meant the endless prolongation of time. This common misunderstanding, Dorothy felt, should not be voiced by a man who professed to be well-informed and intelligent; and she herself went on the air to point out that it meant, on the contrary, the annihilation of time, and that Hoyle's arguments were therefore hopelessly irrelevant.

Mac's death was followed, nine months later, by another. Dorothy had had only occasional contact with Ivy since Anthony had grown up and left home. For that matter, she had not been particularly close to Anthony himself, who was now twenty-seven years old and well established in an investment management company in the City of London. But Ivy's death brought them together for a while over the arrangements for her funeral and the disposal of her belongings.

The details of Ivy's estate were in fact handled by Anthony, at Dorothy's request. There have been some very odd speculations as to these details, which would hardly be worth mentioning but for the need to put the record straight.

Ivy died of broncho-pneumonia and measles, and myocardial degeneration, and she was neither a pauper nor a rich miser, as different versions of local gossip had it. She left about four thousand pounds, mostly in various types of conventional savings bonds. She had no jewelry of any value, and the cash found in the house amounted to six pounds ten shillings. She was buried at Banbury, in a grave space bought by Anthony.

Everything she had was left to Dorothy, who immediately handed it over to Anthony. Dorothy seems to have felt that she had no right to Ivy's money: Anthony had been closest to Ivy, and he had taken over the responsibility of winding up the estate. (Contrary to some reports, Dorothy had not contributed to Ivy's income, apart from Christmas presents, since the payments for Anthony's keep had come to an end.)

She was particularly pleased to be able to leave these matters in Anthony's hands, for Ivy's death occurred three months before the production of *The Emperor Constantine*, for which Dorothy had so rashly accepted responsibility. Her hopes of being able to avoid the usual shambles by organizing her own team had been steadily eroded by a combination of unpredictable crises and human fallibility ("it was a

fearful time . . . nobody did what they said they would"[2]); and even
Dante had had to be set aside while she struggled to hold the thing
together.

She had asked, it is true, rather a lot of the good people of Colchester.
The play has twenty-five scene changes, a cast of ninety-six, and a
running time approaching four hours. The finest professional stage-
management in the world, with a fully equipped stage, would have
found it a challenge. The fact that the show went on at all, and after a
fashion reached its end, is something of a tribute to Dorothy and her
team.

It received respectful, if exhausted, notices. The highlight of the
production was deemed to be the reconstruction of the passionate
debate about the nature of Christ which took place at Nicaea; the debate
out of which was forged the Nicene Creed. Nobody but Dorothy
could have made that into a *coup de théâtre*.

Powerful and effective, too, are the final scenes in which Constantine
is tricked into believing that his son is his wife's lover, and has him killed
before discovering, too late, that the accusation is false. Dorothy uses the
guilt provoked in Constantine by this dubious historical incident to lead
him towards his (genuinely historical) conversion to Christianity; so that
the story is yet again used as a peg on which to hang didactic scenes of
doctrinal instruction. But the powerful human situation, melodramatic
though it is, is convincing and moving, prompting again the wish that
she could have left God alone from time to time and concentrated on
human situations – allowing the audience (as indeed Jesus did in the
parables) to perceive for themselves what implications they could.

The chances are, though, that by the end of *The Emperor Constantine*
audiences were much too tired to perceive anything, however subtly or
overtly presented. Some cuts were made in performance, but a firm blue
pencil wielded by a good editor, such as she had spurned at the BBC,
might have helped the play considerably in achieving its full impact.

Constantine was the last of the major distractions from Dante, and the
last of Dorothy's plays of any note. A somewhat embarrassing little
playlet about Dante and his daughter Bice (short for Beatrice) was
broadcast by the BBC Schools programme in May 1952. It is chiefly of
interest for the fact that Richard Burton was cast as the young man,
Gino, whose love for Bice gives Dante the opportunity for some
elevating thoughts on human and divine love. In the event Burton failed
to turn up for the broadcast (which was live) thus creating a major panic
before a last-minute replacement was found.

Dorothy also started a novel about Dante and Bice, which exists in the
form of a rather fragmentary manuscript. The notion behind the story is

that it belatedly occurs to Dante, after he has written the *Commedia*, that the experience that meant so much to him might have been less significant to Beatrice – indeed that she might have found it amusing, if not mildly ridiculous. This causes an emotional crisis in Dante. The story is written in Dorothy's most impassioned style, harking back to her Musketeer days and oddly contradicting everything she admired about Dante's own writing – his coolness, his control, his lightness, his refusal to be bogged down in emotionalism. One cannot help contrasting Dorothy's attitude with that of Charles Williams, who regarded it as highly probable (and indeed quite proper, men and women being what they are) that had Beatrice lived she would have taken Dante's poetic passion with a sizeable pinch of salt.

In 1953 Dorothy went back to another of her abandoned styles. When the Detection Club was short of money and decided once again to put together a story written by various members in turn, Dorothy, as President, contributed the first episode. The story, *No Flowers by Request*, was published in the *Daily Sketch* that October. Dorothy's tale of the widow who decides that nowadays it is not the mistresses but the servants who have the whip hand, and who therefore applies for a job as a cook-housekeeper, has all the coolness, wit and style that the story of Dante and Bice lacks. Like many writers, Dorothy was at her best when the subject was not "important" – for she relaxed, letting her own natural talent flow freely; and there is no sense of straining to rise to the magnitude of her subject.

There were other moments of light relief, too, in her literary life. She wrote the words for a Christmas calendar – the kind with a little window to be opened for each of the days before Christmas – called "The Days of Christ's Coming". And this was so successful that she went on later to do an Easter calendar, and another Christmas one in 1955 based on Noah's Ark.

Lighter still were her *Pantheon Papers*. This delightful satirical series for *Punch* featured the saints and the celebrations of the secular society, served up in the mock scholarly manner which she did so well. Indeed, it imitated the ecclesiastical style so effectively that numerous earnest Christians saw the series as a satire on the Church, rather than on churchlessness, and took great offence.

I cannot resist reprinting here a couple of delightful saints, and an extract from the sermon for Cacophonytide:

ST LUKEWARM OF LAODICEA, MARTYR

St Lukewarm was a magistrate in the city of Laodicea under Claudius (Emp. A.D. 41–54). He was so broadminded as to offer

asylum and patronage to every kind of religious cult, however un-
orthodox or repulsive, saying in answer to all remonstrances: "There
is always some truth in everything." This liberality earned for him the
surname of "The Tolerator". At length he fell into the hands of a sect
of Anthropophagi (for whom he had erected a sacred kitchen and
cooking stove at the public expense), and was duly set on to stew with
appropriate ceremonies. By miraculous intervention, however, the
water continually went off the boil; and when he was finally served up,
his flesh was found to be so tough and tasteless that the Chief
Anthropophagus spat out the unpalatable morsel, exclaiming:
"Tolerator non tolerandus!" (A garbled Christian version of this
legend is preserved in Revelations 3:16.)

St Lukewarm is the patron saint of railway caterers and is usually
depicted holding a cooking pot.

ST SUPERCILIA

St Supercilia, born in Paris about the year 1400, was a maiden of
remarkable erudition, who steadfastly refused to marry anyone who
could not defeat her in open disputation. When the best scholars of all
the universities in Europe had tried and failed, her unworthy father
brutally commanded her to accept the hand of a man who, though
virtuous, sensible, and of a good estate, knew only six languages and
was weak in mathematics. At this, the outraged saint raised her
eyebrows so high that they lifted her right off her feet and out through
a top-storey window, whence she was last seen floating away in a
northerly direction.

St Supercilia is the patron of pedants. Her feast, Eyebrow Sunday,
falls in Cacophony, between Lowbrow Sunday and Derogation Day.[3]

A SERMON FOR CACOPHONYTIDE
(Reprinted from the Schisminster Perish Magazine)

My little Perishers:

Cacophony is the seedtime of the Polar Year. Not, of course, the
dilatory seedtime of conquered and discredited Nature! But as from
the refrigerator we cull fresh peas in December and ice cream in July,
so we may plant the seeds of enmity all the year round, but especially
in Cacophonytide. Scarcely is Wishmas over, with all its factitious
heartiness and family friction, before bills and income-tax demands
come in. Tempers are frayed, the weather is uniformly detestable;
spiritually and physically, the mud is ready – that rich unwholesome
mud in which the Polar seeds can germinate. Plant those seeds now.

Do not be discouraged if your opportunities appear limited. The smallest dispute, the most trifling misconception may, if sown with envy, watered with complaints, sprayed with clouds of verbiage and artificially heated with unrighteous indignation, grow into a lofty and isolated Pole, up which you may climb to look down upon your neighbours.[4]

This kind of learned jesting, leaping exuberantly off the page, gives us some idea of what her company meant to her chosen friends – why it is that they remember most vividly that being with her was fun.

Now that she was liberated from the somewhat philistine attitudes of Mac, (she had once had to turn down an invitation to a concert of classical music with dinner to follow, because she felt that however much Mac might have enjoyed the dinner his spirits could never survive the concert), one might have expected her to indulge in a spree of playgoing, travel and visiting friends. In fact, although she talked about going abroad immediately after his death, she actually did nothing very adventurous. Barbara Reynolds suggested a trip to Venice with the family, but Dorothy seems to have felt that she was too old and bulky to be good company for the younger people, and for all their protestations would not be budged. In 1953, however, Muriel St Clare Byrne did persuade her to go with her to Stratford upon Avon for a brief orgy of Shakespeare – "a nice change," wrote Dorothy, "after all this Dante";[5] and they saw *King Lear, Richard II* and *The Merchant of Venice* in three days. Not content with that, they took in *All's Well that Ends Well* in London on the way back.

And now, just when it might have seemed that Dorothy was finished with battles and sailing reasonably peacefully towards her end, with enough money, enough honour, enough friends, and the day-by-day stimulation of a long task which she adored, there came two challenges. Curiously they were the first challenges that Dorothy had really had to take seriously since she had stepped into the arena of religious controversy. One was public, somewhat unpleasant, but perfectly manageable. The other was private, damaging, but perhaps in the end a blessing.

The public one came in the form of a book by Kathleen Nott called *The Emperor's Clothes*, which appeared early in 1954. It set out to be an attack, in the name of science, upon what the author called "the return to dogmatic orthodoxy", as seen in the writings of various literary figures of the day; notably the Sayers–Williams–Lewis–Eliot group of Anglo-Catholics, but also the Roman Catholic Graham Greene.

Miss Nott was quite as aggressive, from her side, as Dorothy had ever been on hers, and in addition fairly rude, using such words about Dorothy herself as "vulgar", "stupid", "pin-headed", and "expressive of the soap box".

For a while, Dorothy and her friends preserved a dignified indifference towards the book, Dorothy rather ostentatiously not even bothering to read such scurrility. Unfortunately there was a sort of traitor in the St Anne's camp – someone who thought the book should be taken rather more seriously, and as a consequence launched the private, and much more threatening, attack.

John Wren-Lewis, the Honorary Secretary of the Society of St Anne, was an enfant terrible of a new generation of Christians. Brought up in the East End of London, he had shown such brilliance as a student of science that he was already Deputy Director of Research at I.C.I. in his early thirties. At the same time, having in his youth fallen under the spell of a rather exceptional clergyman, he was already becoming known as a writer and broadcaster on religious and philosophical subjects. His most passionate belief was that Christianity and science were complementary; not simply that there was no conflict between the two, but that the experimental method, which is the basis of all science, had for the first time given man the opportunity to move out of the dark ages of speculation, guesswork and superstition into the light of proven and unarguable truth; and that once man had learned to apply scientific method to the spiritual sphere, he might at last be ready to become what God had promised Adam he should be – a son of God and the inheritor of the earth.

This was not, of course, to say that all science was correct, much less that all scientists were right; only that the scientific method, used in conjunction with Christian understanding, must be allowed to supersede all previous attempts to understand the universe, and man himself as part of the universe: attempts which, however brilliant, were conditioned by the limitations of their own times, by images and ideas that had nothing to do either with science or even with Christianity. John Wren-Lewis had joined St Anne's because here, he felt, was perhaps the only organization in the Church of England where he might find people with enough breadth of mind to sympathize with his ideas and enough intelligence to help him to develop them.

Dorothy, for all her genuine respect for the scientist "in his proper place", had an instinctive dislike of the direction in which popular scientific thinking was leading the world. Her *Pantheon Papers* had included a "Creed of St Euthanasia", which ran thus:

I believe in man, maker of himself and inventor of all science. And in myself, his manifestation, and captain of my psyche; and that I should not suffer anything painful or unpleasant.

And in a vague, evolving deity, the future-begotten child of man; conceived by the spirit of progress, born of emergent variants; who shall kick down the ladder by which he rose and tell history to go to hell.

Who shall some day take off from earth and be jet-propelled into the heavens; and sit exalted above all worlds, man the master almighty.

And I believe in the spirit of progress, who spake by Shaw and the Fabians; and in a modern, administrative, ethical, and social organization; in the isolation of saints, the treatment of complexes, joy through health, and destruction of the body by cremation (with music while it burns), and then I've had it.[6]

Dorothy, in short, mistrusted science and thought it should be subject to theology. John mistrusted theology and thought it should be subject to science. The two attitudes could hardly co-exist peacefully for very long. And the issue was joined in the vestry of St Thomas's Church, Regent Street (the church which, since the bombing of St Anne's, had served both parishes), on the night of Maundy Thursday – the night when the Church solemnly commemorates the Last Supper and begins the all-night vigil that leads into Good Friday.

Exactly what was said there, we can only deduce from the letters which followed – some of which are missing. But the general terms of John's accusation are clear; and it is clear too that the attack was directed not only at Dorothy but at the other three in the group as well. The charge is the one that Charles Williams had put his finger on, years earlier – that the only aspect of Christianity that these writers really cared about was the dogmatic pattern. And John questioned whether this sort of emphasis was the best way to win over the hearts and minds of the intelligent agnostics and atheists that St Anne's professed to cater for. Kathleen Nott's book, he suggested, was an indication that such people were dissatisfied with Christianity at quite a different level.

At all events, Dorothy, perhaps aided by the sombre mood of that penitential period, took his remarks very seriously; and on Good Friday she sat down and wrote him a letter which in double-spaced typescript runs to seventeen pages.

I have found it difficult enough, in writing this book, to resist the temptation to quote long passages from Dorothy's remarkable letters. Of all those hundreds, perhaps thousands, of letters, this is surely the most important and the most interesting, for it is both a confession and a justification of what she has done and what she is; and it is expressed with a humility rare for Dorothy and a willingness to let down her defences that is even rarer. In fairness to her I feel I must give the reader enough of it to do justice to her case. Here then, considerably condensed but I hope not falsified, is Dorothy's Speech for the Defence in the case of Sayers v. Wren-Lewis:

Dear John, I have been thinking about what we were saying last night in the vestry. You are, of course, perfectly right. It is a thing that I have always known, and is the reason why I never speak or write *directly* about Christian faith or morals without a violent inner reluctance and a strong sense of guilt. I am not sure that every time I open my mouth on the subject, I am not falling into mortal sin. But I am not *sure*, and therefore I do not like to be altogether intransigent about it. The position of people like Eliot and Lewis and me is rather more complicated than people perhaps quite realize. So, if you can bear it, I ought – possibly – to try and explain it a little. Though I am afraid the "little" will work out rather long on paper.

I must begin with my own case, because that is the one I know about.

I am not a priest. . . . I am not by temperament an evangelist. . . . I am quite without the thing known as "inner light" or "spiritual experience". I have never undergone conversion. Neither God, nor (for that matter) angel, devil, ghost or anything else speaks to me out of the depths of my psyche. . . .

It follows naturally, perhaps, from this that I am quite incapable of "religious emotion". This has its good as well as its bad side. I am not seriously liable to mistake an aesthetic pleasure in ritual or architecture for moral virtue, or to suppose that shedding a few tears over the pathos of the Crucifixion is the same thing as crucifying the old man in myself. Nor can I readily dismiss religion as a "sublimation of sex", or anything of that kind, because I know perfectly well that it is nothing of the sort. But the lack of religious emotion in me makes me impatient of it in other people, and makes me appear cold and unsympathetic and impersonal. This is true. I am.

I have a moral sense. I am not sure that this derives from religious belief. . . . I do not enjoy it. If I ever do a disagreeable duty, it is in the spirit of the young man in the parable who said "I go not", but afterwards (probably in a detestable temper) went grumbling off and did the job. On consideration, I think that the existence and nature of the Christian God is the only rational sanction for the moral sense.

But moral sense by itself is not religion – or at any rate not Christianity.

Of all the presuppositions of Christianity, the only one I really have and can swear to from personal inward conviction is sin. About that I have no doubt whatever and never have had. Neither does any doctrine of determinism or psychological maladjustment convince me in the very least that when I do wrong it is not I who do it and that I could not, by some means or other, do better. . . . The point is that when anything speaks out of my interior it speaks in the out-moded terms of scholastic theology and faculty psychology, and I do not really know how to establish communication with people who have modern insides.

But since I cannot come at God through intuition, or through my emotions, or through my "inner light" (except in the unendearing form of judgement and conviction of sin) there is only the intellect left. And that is a very different matter. You said that I, and the rest of us, gave people the impression of caring only for a dogmatic pattern. That is quite true. I remember once saying to Charles Williams: "I do not know whether I believe in Christ or whether I am only in love with the pattern." And Charles said, with his usual prompt understanding, that he had exactly the same doubts about himself. But *this* you must try to accept: when we say "in love with the pattern", we mean *in love*. . . . Where the intellect is dominant it becomes the channel of all the other feelings. The "passionate intellect" is *really* passionate. It is the only point at which ecstasy can enter. I do not know whether we can be saved through the intellect, but I do know that I can be saved by nothing else. I know that, if there is judgement, I shall have to be able to say: "This alone, Lord, in Thee and in me, have I never betrayed, and may it suffice to know and love and choose Thee after this manner, for I have no other love, or knowledge, or choice in me."

Only we must be able to say that much. . . .[7]

From this point the letter goes on to a restatement of her "proper job" theory, and the distress she felt when dragged away from her proper job, by good church folk with the best possible intentions, to make utterances on the subject of the Christian faith. And here, for the first time, we can see her insistence on her "proper job" in the context of her problems and her personality; not, as she would have had it, because it was a genuine spiritual law, but because it was a psychological necessity for her. Lacking the "inner experience" of spiritual truth which would have enabled her to say with personal authority what the dogmatic pattern was *for*, she had nothing to cling to *except* the dogmatic pattern and the letter of the law. She could speak and write about the dogma because that was not hers, it was the Church's. She could acknowledge it and wholeheartedly admire it as a glorious intellectual construction; she could even translate it from the scholastic language in which it was formulated into vivid and vigorous modern speech, and sell it with all her considerable power. But more than that she could not do.

Never before had she conceded that her intellectual approach might be narrow or limited to its period. But now she was moved to write, towards the end of her letter: "It may be that our particular type of intellectual has had his day . . . I think it is very likely that the time has come that we ought to be superseded."

After this uncharacteristic moment of resignation, however, she puts in a very reasonable plea for recognition of what she and the others had in fact achieved:

I am not quite sure that we ought to be chastised by our even-Christians for not doing that which we are neither called nor fitted to do. I am not exactly asking for gratitude and appreciation – although, as I said, I do sometimes wish that the people who clamour for us to open their bazaars, address their ordinands, and allow them to perform our plays at derisory fees, would occasionally rally around when we are under fire. The C. of E.'s attitude to the "lay apostolate" is painfully like that of a government to a slightly disreputable secret agent: "Do your job; but remember, if you get into difficulties you must extricate yourself; His Majesty's Government cannot appear in the matter." But it would be nice not to be so chivvied. It would be nice not to be continually summoned from what one is doing to do something different and unsuitable. And it would be nice not to be continually pushed and pulled and coaxed and squeezed (always from the highest motives and in the name of the Incorruptible God) into corruption.

I am so sorry – the cat has trodden on the page!

I think it comes to this: that, however urgently a thing may be needed, it can only be rightly demanded of those who can rightly give it. . . .

Yours with apologies for going on and on about it.   D.L.S.[8]

The correspondence continued over several weeks. It ranged over a number of topics, but all were related to the main issue – the question as to which was the better way to approach intelligent non-Christians. Were they people on a wholly and fatally wrong path, who must be sternly warned of the fate in store for them? Or were they people in whose instincts and understanding there existed something of the divine, who must be gently shown the Christian significance of their experiences? John believed in "starting where they are"; Dorothy started with dogma – "I have nothing to give you but the Creeds."[9] And though Dorothy kept her end up with a will, she finally had to make an admission that seems to me fatal to her argument – she had to acknowledge that the Creeds are not in fact statements of ultimate and unalterable truth, but are the result of revisions, based on experience, of earlier drafts; and "there is no reason why there should not be other such revisions, except that the schism between East and West has deprived us of the means to call a General Synod."[10]

Dorothy was conceding, in effect, that only a historical accident had prevented the Creeds from being revised and up-dated. The experience of the church had continued, but the development of the Creeds had been arrested sixteen hundred years ago, after the Council of Nicaea. What is that but an admission that they no longer have the breath of life in them? And that being the case, what was Dorothy offering to our century after all?

The strange and sad thing is that though she believed that dogma was all she had to offer, it was not really true. As a person Dorothy often showed great kindness, thoughtfulness, patience, courage, generosity and humorous forbearance. As a writer she had a great deal of sympathetic understanding of human nature: it emerges in her letters, and in the Wimsey books. But something, some self-mistrust, prevented her from ever making the connection between the dogmatic and the personal. She might have offered more than the Creeds, yet she could not do it. And now she had admitted that the Creeds themselves could be questioned, they were subject to the laws of time and change.

She must have known, in her heart of hearts, what all this implied. And perhaps the reader will understand now why I find these letters so important and so moving. Dorothy had often said that the only business of the Christian, in the end, is to be crucified. And on that Good Friday, it seems to me, she did indeed offer up for crucifixion all that confidence, all that joy that she had always felt in battle and in victory. But there is this also to be said – that the humility and honesty with which she did it contradicts her claim that all she had to offer to her God was her intellect.

It was no good, however, expecting her to change. She was too old for that, she said. And when St Anne's House (which, after all, had been founded precisely to debate such issues as those raised by *The Emperor's Clothes*) organized an evening of debate between Dorothy and C. S. Lewis on the one side and Kathleen Nott on the other, Dorothy, it must be said, fairly unashamedly avoided the issues raised by John Wren-Lewis, and stuck to the kind of debating points that she understood.

Unfortunately, as so often happened at St Anne's, the debate was a good deal dampened by the fact that two out of the three debaters failed to appear. Dorothy's contribution thus became a solo speech, which enabled her to escape unscathed – and even with the appearance of having won the bout by default. Few, if any, of the audience who applauded her witty and confident speech knew of the very different thoughts she had expressed in her letters to John.

The work on Dante continued through these spiritual crises. Dorothy grew increasingly skilful at handling the terza rima, so that the translation of the *Purgatorio* flows with noticeably more ease and mastery than that of the *Inferno*. Dorothy's relationship with Barbara Reynolds was growing closer. At first she had simply been invited to tea, when visiting Cambridge; then she began staying overnight, and perhaps for the first time since her childhood actually experienced family life from the inside. Her self-proclaimed dislike of children was noticeably absent in her relationship with Barbara's family. She was patient and understanding with the children's questions, even if she never achieved the immediate warmth that makes children run to somebody's knees.

In June 1954 she took on a new responsibility. A group of out-of-work professional actors had the previous year founded a Theatre Centre, in which to practise their craft while out of work. They did experimental work and presented three public productions a year. One of their first shows was a production of *The Man Born to be King*, which was performed in April 1954. Dorothy went to see the production, and was astonished. These youngsters outstripped even the seasoned performers whom she had so trusted and admired in the early BBC productions. She was particularly impressed with Kenneth Mason, who played Christ. He had, she wrote, "both humour and authority, though only a kid and not particularly handsome; and could do, what none of them *ever* succeeded in doing – tell a parable as though he had just thought of it, and not *either* like a person in a pulpit, *or* Uncle Mac condescending to the Children's Hour."[11]

Muriel St Clare Byrne, who went to the show with Dorothy, was equally impressed; and the result was that she joined the Advisory Council of the Centre, while Dorothy, discovering that they were desperately under-financed, undertook to back them for a year and to join the founders, Brian Way and Margaret Faulkes, on the Management Committee.

That year Dorothy finished the *Purgatorio* – the original schedule of completion having been abandoned long since.

For nearly ten years now, Dorothy had lived with Dante and with the ringing of his triple rhyme scheme in her head. They had passed through purgatory together and now there was only paradise, the summit of bliss, to scale; but that, however blissful, was "by far the toughest nut of the three books".[12]

By way of a break Dorothy decided to go back to another poem, the eleventh-century *Chanson de Roland*, which she had first tried to translate from the French when she was at Somerville; and E. V. Rieu obligingly agreed to let her postpone the *Paradiso*, at the same time commissioning her *Song of Roland* for the Penguin Classics. So for the next two years Dante was laid aside, and the wars of Charlemagne and his court and the stirring rhythms of the anonymous mediaeval French poet rang in her ears as she went about her daily chores.

They were years of comparative peace, with enough congenial labour to keep her occupied and enough small crises and irritations at home, at the Detection Club and St Anne's to keep her from being bored. Norah Lambourne was still a frequent visitor, often consulting her about problems of period costume design; for Dorothy had by now amassed quite a collection of rare books – mostly for reference for her work on Dante, but some simply for their rarity and interest. Thanks to the efforts of Mr Seligman of Cecil Court she was beginning, rather late in life, to emulate her hero, Wimsey, with her collection of early and uncommon editions.

In the summer of 1955, her friend and correspondent Professor G. L. Bickersteth, of Aberdeen University, sent her his translation of the *Commedia*. He had been complimentary about her version, which he found "tingling with life",[13] and now she was able to return the compliment: "I have now read a great part of the Inferno, and must 'give you best' quite a lot. My chief error, I think, was to 'modernize' the terza rima. The moderns are wrong. They lose a strong effect, but gain nothing in exchange."[14]

To which he replied ". . . what I liked about your Inferno was that you weren't afraid of trying to make your English sound as *hellish* as Dante makes his Italian . . . I'm afraid I am much tamer."[15] It is a delight to find Dorothy so happily generous in the exchange of courtesies with a scholar and craftsman whom she can respect.

Early in 1957, however, the ever-rumbling situation at St Anne's suddenly flared up. The pressures on Patrick McLaughlin, some of them self-induced, had persuaded him that he could no longer go on, and his resignation obviously gave a wonderful opening to those who wanted to see St Anne's closed. His personality, imagination and vision had been central to the work of the House, and it was all too easy to argue that without him St Anne's was a spent force.

Dorothy was by now not only chairman of the council of St Anne's,

but also a churchwarden of St Thomas's, Regent Street. In both these
capacities, it fell to her to spearhead the faction that argued that St
Anne's was more than merely the brainchild of an advanced clergyman –
that it was indeed a centre for new thinking about the role of the Church
in society, and the Church could ill afford to lose it. Thinking boldly, the
council put forward a recommendation that on the vacant site of the
bombed church the diocese should build a new, multi-purpose structure which would house not only a chapel large enough to accom-
modate the shrunken Anglican population of Soho, but also conference
rooms, a theatre equipped for both plays and films, and perhaps a small
library – a place where a Christian way of living and thinking could be
explored and expressed in all its aspects.

The battle raged on throughout 1957, with the lobbying of bishops,
the issuing of circulars, the foregathering with lawyers and architects,
the holding of meetings, the confrontation of archdeacons; and in all
these activities it was Dorothy to whom we all turned for her weighty
presence, her shrewd counsel and her skill at writing, debating and
presentation.

Whether all this aroused her dormant belligerence, or whether it was
pure coincidence, suddenly she seemed to be engaging in other tussles as
well. She took extreme exception to derogatory remarks by Robert
Graves and A. E. Housman about the astronomy of Lucan, a Roman
epic poet of the time of Christ. And a touch of the old excess seemed to
show up in her reaction to a letter from Somerville which accompanied
an appeal from the Oxford Historical Buildings Fund. The Principal of
Somerville had the audacity (or so Dorothy saw it) to suggest that
possibly the need of Somerville for new buildings was just as great, or
greater, than the need of Oxford in general for the preservation of old
ones. Passionately Dorothy denounced this intervention as dishonest,
misguided, irrelevant and lacking perspective. In comparison with some
of her earlier battles, these causes hardly seem worthy of her steel.
Perhaps she just needed the exercise.

Christmas approached. The *Sunday Dispatch*, deciding that its readers
would still be interested in discovering "why Miss Sayers killed
Wimsey",[16] asked Val Gielgud to go to Witham and interview her – a
shrewd move, for one interviewer she would assuredly not turn away
with contumely was her old and beloved ally from the BBC. On
December 11 he took tea and "richly indigestible" cake with her, and
wrote two days later: "It was good to find you looking so well and in
your usual sparkling form." And he suggested renewing their collaboration on "a new and up-to-date version of the Dido-Aeneas situation. We
might even get into some hot water again, which would be fun!"[17]

He apologized for "what must have seemed an intolerable imposition",[18] but between them he and Dorothy managed to turn the interview into a puff for the recently published *Song of Roland*, and the article duly appeared on the Sunday as a full half-page with a big photograph.

Meantime, on Friday the 13th, she was in Cambridge. The occasion was, for her, an unusual one. She went there to become, it seems for the first time in her life, a godmother; and not to a child but to an adult.

For the past year or so Barbara Reynolds, influenced without doubt by Dorothy's constant assertions that the world of Dante was not simply a literary fantasy but expressed universal truth, had been moving towards her own acceptance of Christianity as an intellectual truth and a faith to live by. A few months earlier she had asked Dorothy if she would support her application for the Serena Professorship of Italian Studies at Oxford, and Dorothy had happily obliged; inevitably in the course of their correspondence about this and about Dante, Barbara had told Dorothy of her intention to be baptized.

Aware still, however, of the danger of seeming to exploit her older and more famous friend, she did not ask Dorothy to stand godmother. That was Dorothy's idea. And Barbara is probably not deceived in thinking that that Friday, a turning-point in her own life, was also important to Dorothy, to whom her godmotherhood seems to have given great delight. For the first time since her childhood she had a recognized place in a family. Not secretly, as with Anthony, but openly and in public she accepted and acknowledged a relationship, a mother and daughter bond. Simple human affection could for once be dragged out of its lifetime's hiding place and displayed without concealment.

Though she seemed tired, she insisted on buying Christmas presents for the children. And the following day, after visiting the Blake exhibition at the Fitzwilliam Museum, she heaved her great bulk into her hired car, and was driven off by her regular driver, Jack Lapwood.

The following Tuesday she went to London to do her normal Christmas shopping. Most of the gifts were left in the shops, with instructions for delivery; a few she carried with her.

She had arranged with Patrick McLaughlin to meet him that evening after her shopping, but she rang him from Liverpool Street Station to say that she had taken longer than she had expected and had been afraid that she might miss her train, so had taken a taxi to the station. She had a standing invitation to stay overnight at St Anne's if she wished, but she never took it up because, as she explained, she had to get back to feed the cats.

It seems that one of the things that delayed her was a promise to go to the Royal Institute Galleries at 195 Piccadilly, to look at the portrait of herself painted by Sir William Hutchison for that year's Exhibition of the Royal Society of Portrait Painters. (The portrait now hangs in the National Portrait Gallery.) Someone who saw and recognized her there, staring at her own likeness on the wall, noticed the contrast between the energy of the painted face and the tiredness of the real one.

The slow, rackety train took her back to Witham, and there she was met, as usual, by Jack Lapwood. He drove her the half-mile or so to No. 24 Newland Street, said goodnight, and left her at the door. She must have gone upstairs, for the upstairs lights had been switched on, and her coat and hat were on her bed. But she had had no time to feed the cats, and they were very hungry when the cleaner arrived at eight o'clock the next morning and found her at the foot of the stairs.

The doctor said that death was instantaneous; there was no evidence that she had fallen down stairs – it appeared to have been a simple sudden stroke, as unexpected as it was deadly.

If her spirit, en route for whatever was in store for it, hovered for a moment over the scene, no doubt it went on its way amused by the accuracy with which she had foretold it all long before in *Have His Carcase*: "Well, one day the usual thing happens. Blinds left down, no smoke from kitchen chimney, milk not taken in, cats yowling fit to break your heart."[19]

Many of us would say that this was the best way to go. Whether Dorothy would rather have had a few seconds in which to prepare herself to meet her Maker, who knows? She had once told Patrick McLaughlin, when he asked her whether she would give a lecture on dying, that this seemed extremely appropriate, not only because she was a specialist in fictional death but also because she was very much afraid of the real thing.[20] And on another occasion she had predicted that when she did have to abandon life, she would "probably do so with the greatest reluctance, protesting that there were still a great many things I had intended to do with it."[21]

And indeed there were a number of things left unfinished. Not only the *Paradiso*; not only the battle for St Anne's; a more immediate problem came to light when Dorothy's secretary phoned Muriel St Clare Byrne (with whom Dorothy was, as usual, to have spent Christmas), and Muriel hastened to Witham to help sort out her old friend's affairs.

The first thing was to find the will. Muriel had been given to understand in recent years that Dorothy had intended to make an up-to-date one; but though they hunted high and low, the only one they could find was dated 1939. Consultation with Laurence Harbottle, the solicitor who had drawn up the will in 1939, only confirmed that, so far as he at any rate was concerned, Dorothy had never brought it up to date. She had visited him on one or two occasions, and he had the impression that she wanted to talk to him about something important; but whatever it was she had never got around to it, and as she had never mentioned a new will, he had assumed that if there was one, it had been made with the aid of a local solicitor in Witham.

The will, of course, left everything to Mac; or in the event of his death to their "adopted son", John Anthony. In the event of *his* death, everything was to go to Ivy, with the exception of the houses in Witham, which went to Somerville College. The estate was valued for probate at about £35,000 – worth perhaps four times as much today.

Muriel, as she expected, was appointed Dorothy's literary executor. What she had not expected was Anthony. And even now she was only aware of him as an adopted son; although in retrospect some glimmering of suspicion had lingered in her mind since that winter night in 1933 when she and Dorothy had visited Ivy and her young charges in Westcott Barton.

Meanwhile Anthony had heard of Dorothy's death, and had contacted Laurence Harbottle independently. The following day he visited Muriel and declared his true relationship; at which she flung her arms around him and said "Thank God you've come", her dismay at his unexpected existence overcome by affection on behalf of her beloved friend and relief at having someone to help share her loss and her responsibilities.

The public at large, however, were still not let into the secret. For the Press, Anthony maintained the fiction that he was adopted. Interviewed for the *Daily Mail* by the diarist "Paul Tanfield", he was quoted as saying "Miss Sayers adopted me when I was ten. At that time I was being brought up by a cousin of hers, a maiden lady of small income . . . This lady felt for some reason that I might benefit by a good education and told her cousin so. One day I was told I was to regard Miss Sayers as my mother."[22]

And so the story remained, so far as the public at large was concerned, Dorothy figuring as the generous benefactor rather than the desperate mother. In fact, Dorothy had never legally adopted Anthony: it would have been impossible to do so, for the arrangements would have included a search into his actual parentage. It was only when the writer Janet Hitchman made such a search while researching her book about Dorothy sixteen years later, that the simple but noteworthy fact emerged that Anthony's birth certificate at Somerset House gave Dorothy herself as the mother, with the space for the father's name left blank.

To some of Dorothy's close friends, who met Anthony at Dorothy's

Memorial Service, Muriel broke the truth there and then, introducing him as "Dorothy's son". Others had to wait much longer. But whether they knew of Anthony as son or adopted son, it was a matter of some distress that Dorothy had never mentioned him in all their years of friendship.

It was not a cheerful Christmas for those friends. Their presents from Dorothy began arriving at about the same time that the obituaries came out in the newspapers. While the nation respectfully paid homage to a distinguished lady of letters, people who knew her were aware of a very large absence. Large of body, large of personality, loud of voice and loud of laughter, her death made a large gap in many lives.

She was cremated the following Monday, December 23, at Golders Green; and her ashes were taken to the little chapel that had been created in the base of the tower of St Anne's. But there was no plaque, no epitaph, for this was intended at the time to be only a temporary resting place. A plaque has recently been placed there by the Dorothy L. Sayers Historical and Literary Society, based at Witham, which reads: "In Memory of Dorothy Leigh Sayers, D.Litt., Scholar and Writer, Churchwarden of this Parish 1952–1957. Born 13th June, 1893. Died 17th December, 1957. Whose ashes lie beneath this tower. 'The only Christian work is good work well done.'"

That is respectful and dignified. But one cannot help feeling that her still young, still romantic soul might have preferred something on less formal lines – perhaps some echo of the lament she wrote when she said goodbye to her Musketeer comrades in Bluntisham and headed out into the large indifferent world:

> What say the wailing trumpets as they return from war?
> They say that he is fallen, brave Athos fights no more.

Dorothy stood – and knew that she stood – against a tide of history that has largely carried away all that she tried to defend – tradition, dogma, high standards of learning and literacy. The views of John Wren-Lewis have prevailed at least to this extent, that attempts now made to reach people with ideas about religion or culture nearly always begin "where they are".

What such attempts lack, in the absence of dogma, is any clear idea of where to go. As G. K. Chesterton pointed out, when people stop believing in God, they do not start believing in nothing; they start believing in anything. Whether or not Dorothy's dogmatism was right, whether or not the dogma she stood for was true, the flood of ill-informed and un-disciplined experimentation that has followed it has been little or no im-provement. It may be that the breaking down of the dykes was necessary for new fertilization and new spiritual growth, but so far the harvest has mostly been weeds. For Dorothy, nothing but disaster could follow the destruction of the dykes, and she put not merely her finger but her whole ample self into the hole to try to stop the flood.

The flood was too much for her, largely because it was a flood whose strength derived from the one thing that she lacked – personal experience. The twentieth century, with its expansion of travel, with the spread of information through the newspapers, radio and television, with the overthrowing of religious prohibitions and social taboos, with its unbelievable technological changes, has been a time of unprecedented enlargement of experience. After centuries and millennia when the experience of one generation varied little from that of the one before, suddenly the lust for experience has become an end in itself. Dorothy's greatest weakness was that she could never offer her own experience in answer to those other experiences that she believed to be spiritually useless or perhaps lethal. Direct spiritual experience was outside her range; and life robbed her of most of the ordinary human experiences of satisfactory emotional relationships, sexual and parental. No wonder she had to fall back on the intellect. No wonder she regarded the intellect as her salvation. No wonder Charles Williams and others warned her that perhaps it was not her salvation, but her temptation. And no wonder in the end it proved not to be enough.

The mysteries that Dorothy left behind her about the facts of her life are largely solved. The real mysteries remain insoluble: not what happened to her, but why. She often protested against the assumption that life could be treated as a series of problems with neat, discoverable solutions like detective stories. Her own life is a classic illustration of one of the deepest, least answerable questions of all – do we create the circumstances of our lives, or are we created by them? To what extent do we choose what we become?

By any reckoning Dorothy had a raw deal in a number of ways. Things would surely have been very different if her parents had not moved from the sociable milieu of Oxford to the isolation of Huntingdonshire; or if she had had brothers and sisters, or if she had gone to school earlier, or had been physically attractive and sure of herself in adolescence; or if, on top of all these other social handicaps, the First World War had not robbed her, and her generation, of the great majority of their potential mates.

These circumstances deprived her of many experiences that are common to the run of human kind, and no-one could pretend that she had any choice in them. But the child is mother to the woman, and Dorothy as a child did prefer her sunrise in books to the exhilarating but chilly reality; as a young woman she saw flirtation as a game, and could not take it seriously; during the First World War she decided to teach rather than to nurse; and when experience was thrust upon her and she found herself with a fatherless child, she elected to have him brought up in secret by another, rather than acknowledge him and thus acknowledge herself as no smarter than the "unfortunate" girl she had patronized a year or two before.

For all these decisions she had rational and convincing reasons, and she would certainly have accepted responsibility for them. But how much freedom did her early conditioning really allow her? Dorothy's whole nature demanded a disciplined, orderly, even conventional form for her life as well as for her thinking; and all her choices have this in common, that they are refusals to face the hazards of a reality that is unknown and incalculable. Others, after all, in like circumstances, have chosen differently.

On the other hand, she really did try, at least once, to break out. Once at least she admitted that she was vulnerably human, and wanted only to love and be loved. She did try to find her way into the world of plebeian pleasures, dancing at the Hammersmith Palais de Danse, mocking at over-refined voices, letting her less fine feelings have their fling.

That experiment failed. She cried every night for three years, and finished up terrified of emotion, fighting her way back to the safety of detachment and intellectual superiority.

What would have happened had things worked out differently, had she been enabled to trust her emotions, to enjoy and exploit them? What would have happened if the remorseless requirements of children had exercised on her the levelling effect they have exercised on so many others? These are questions that haunt me now as much as they did when I began this book.

But those moments passed, and she was left (as perhaps she might in her heart of hearts have preferred) with her books and her career, and with a marriage that was a means rather of stabilizing than of changing her life. For a while she was saved from choice by the brute necessity of earning a living, and during that time she expressed herself as never before or after. But once she was rid of financial necessity, she was free to return to her enslavement to the things that had dominated her first fifteen years – literature, theory, the need to be right, the need to be queen of the castle; and an indulgence in that "offensively dogmatic manner – you know that offensive manner of mine",[23] that she had confessed to, more in pride than regret, in a letter to Muriel Jaeger when she was still at Oxford.

The self-centredness and the habit of self-justification for which she castigated herself in *Cat o' Mary*, though she may have shaken them off while she was a working novelist and copywriter living in a busy city, crept back, as vices tend to do, as she grew older – not in her private life, where she showed patience and kindness and "those common human virtues which were to be attained in after years at so much cost and with such desperate difficulty"[24] – but in her professional dealings.

Her theory of the "proper job", for example, is a simple matter of professional integrity in so far as it is a refusal to stray outside the boundaries of her own understanding. But in the way she used the theory there was often a sort of self-importance and pomposity that is redolent of her young alter ego, Katherine Lammas. And it must be admitted that she did sometimes run close to deserving the charge levelled at her by C. S. Lewis, that she confused what she ought to be doing with what she felt like doing, and used the "proper job" as a rationalization for following her fancy.

The queen of a castle needs a castle to be queen of. Dorothy's castles were the established conventions and traditions of literature, religion and society. Despite her love of adventurous tales and her own superficial idiosyncrasies, Dorothy was deeply conventional, in the sense that she could only operate satisfactorily within the security of convention. All her writing was done within established forms and styles, and only in her detective stories did she forge a style of her own from the sources from which she borrowed. She lost John Cournos because his proposals to her did not include marriage and children. In politics, she accepted totally the stance of the rural Tory society in which she was brought up; and in religion, once having passed through the normal adolescent turmoil, she settled for a whole-hearted allegiance to the most traditional doctrine available.

From within these citadels of the mind she looked out at a generation that had abandoned citadels, and tried to remind it of what it had lost. But the world had decided that remaining in old citadels, however solid, was more dangerous than moving out into new country. It is true that they had forgotten what their forefathers had learnt, but they wanted to learn afresh, for themselves, and they didn't really care.

Had she not been what she was, she would not have produced the work that she did; and what she did produce was remarkable enough. For myself, I cannot help regretting, however uselessly, that the events of the early twenties worked out as they did for her; and that at a crucial stage in her life and career she was saddled with so much misery and with a life-long secret that cannot have failed to affect her. For her sake I cannot help wishing that she had had more happiness; for the world's sake, I cannot help thinking that without that guilty secret and with a more positive experience of life, she might have been able to trust herself to speak more freely, to break away from the detective convention into a full-scale novel, to use her religious understanding with more liberality and more personal authority.

This is ungrateful. Her "serious" work remains in print because the truths she reiterated are still true, the vitality of the writing still delights, its incisiveness still stimulates. A world that prefers experience to tradition will swing back again in due course, needing the ballast of ancient wisdom; they will find few who state more simply, more relevantly and more entertainingly what the wisdom of the Church has concluded about the condition of mankind.

Whether her Festival plays will survive is less sure. They were written for special occasions and special places, and are not easily transferable. In style, too, they are of their time; and they fall uneasily between the human and the divine.

The translations, almost by definition, will last only a limited time. They are successful, as Dorothy said, because they offer a version of the original that is suitable for their time. When the time passes, so will the suitability. But it will be a long time before the notes on Dante are surpassed.

Nor will *The Man Born to be King* easily find a successor. Its style dates a little already; but its story-telling strength, its scholarship and its imagination keep it vitally alive.

Into the essays Dorothy put some of the best of herself, and many of these deserve preservation for their vigour, wit and originality; though by their very nature most of them are concerned with matters of passing moment.

But however she might have resisted the notion, it is surely the detective novels that will last longest. And however proud she may have been of her scholarly, poetical, historical works, however she may have dismissed the Wimsey books as little more than a way of earning a living, she herself really knew better, as she showed in her lecture on "The Importance of Being Vulgar" in 1936: "Ben Jonson was a far more learned scholar than Shakespeare," she said, "but which is the greater poet? Which of them is now produced to the selected intelligentsia on Sunday afternoons, and which is uproariously applauded night after night in the New Cut?" Similarly we may ask, which of Dorothy's works are found, with luck, in second-hand bookshops, and which are to be seen in large numbers and gaudy paper-back covers on the popular bookstalls? How many ordinary households have well-thumbed copies of *The Just Vengeance* as compared with those that have tattered, backless copies of *Murder Must Advertise?*

In writing her classier works Dorothy enjoyed one immense advantage: she was virtually alone in the field. The detective novels were a very different matter. In 1928, when she was busy producing the Wimsey books, she wrote: "It is impossible to keep track of all the detective stories produced today. Book upon book, magazine upon magazine pour out from the press, crammed with murders, thefts, arsons, frauds, conspiracies, problems, puzzles, mysteries, thrills, maniacs, crooks, poisoners, forgers, garrotters, police, spies, secret service men, detectives until it seems that half of the world must be engaged in setting riddles for the other half to solve."[25] Against all that competition, Dorothy's twelve novels have survived effortlessly as some of the finest examples of their kind. In a genre in which most books exist only to be read once and then, the mystery revealed, thrown away or handed on to someone else, this is astonishing. Other writers have survived as much as anything by the sheer volume of their output. When one book is finished, another comes to hand. Dorothy's last Wimsey book appeared over forty years ago. Every keen reader of detective stories has learnt long ago who those twelve villains were. Yet still the books get published and read, and republished and re-read.

The stories are ingenious, certainly; but that's not the reason. Wimsey himself is an engaging chap, certainly; but that is not the whole reason either. The general air of literariness, the quotations that litter the books, are if anything a deterrent. What does draw readers back to these novels time and again? Surely it is Dorothy herself, communicating her energy, her amusement, her intelligence, her love of writing, her enthusiasm, her sense of fun. How fortunate we are that she was not able to stick exclusively to her poetry, her historical subjects, all the literary things she loved! We might never have known who she was.

APPENDIX

Statement of Aims for the proposed *Bridgehead* series of books

---

(1)

We believe that the chief trouble among the nations today is fear – the fear of death and especially the fear of life. Human life is "fear-conditioned": this is what depresses men's spirits and paralyses constructive effort. We believe that this fear can only be driven out by a strong awareness of the real value of life.[1]

Our aim is to give to the people of this country a constructive purpose worth living for and worth dying for.

(2)

A real value for life must be such as to satisfy man's nature as a whole. No value for life is real that involves the denial of any part of human personality.

(3)

We believe that absolute value cannot and must not be ascribed to any objective or authority within the framework of history. Any such ascription can only lead to an increasingly violent conflict of dialectical opposites.[2] When this happens, man sees himself as the helpless puppet of uncontrollable demonic forces, and loses the will to live.[3]

(4)

While, therefore, we do not deny, but strongly assert, the principle of

---

[1] The exaggerated fear of death appears to result directly from the fear of life, tending to diminish in the measure that a vigorous constructive hold on life is achieved.

[2] For instance: "absolute" individualism leads to social chaos, creating an intolerable situation, with a revolt into "absolute" collectivism, which leads to an individual slavery equally intolerable. Similarly, rationalism leads to the denial and suppression of the intuitions and emotions, provoking revolt into eroticism, racial mysticism, or other false absolutes, leading to the denial of reason. False absolutes are known by the fact that they give unconditioned validity to one side of man's nature at the expense of the whole.

[3] A conflict of dialectical opposites taking place in the political or economic sphere of activity leads inevitably to war. Where man's will to live is destroyed by a sense of his helplessness in the grip of uncontrollable forces, such wars are waged without heart and against the real desires of the people.

"relativity" in the spheres of physics, biology and psychology, we contend that this principle also, if erected into an absolute, displays man as a puppet of demonic forces, and either destroys his hold on life or causes him to revolt into some form of authoritarianism. The question "relative to what?" must be asked, and it can only be answered by reference to an absolute reality outside the "drift of becoming" and knowable at any moment in history. This absolute reality is the sole sanction for the sanctity and value of the individual personality.

(5)

We believe that peace and stability are not attainable if considered as static in their nature or pursued as ends in themselves. They are the by-products of a right balance between the individual and the community. This balance is attainable only by a ceaseless creative activity directed to a real standard of value.

(6)

We believe that liberty and equality are not attainable by considering the individual man as a unit in a limited scheme of society (e.g. "economic man", "political man", "the worker", etc.), but only by considering him as a complete personality, capable of self-discipline in a self-disciplined community; the aim of such discipline being the fulfilment of man's whole nature in relation to absolute reality.

(7)

We recognize that the past is irrevocable, and ought not to be otherwise. We shall not therefore advocate the return to outworn or discredited structures of society (e.g. feudalism, Marxist communism, etc.) or any programme that aims at "putting back the clock" (e.g. national isolation or the abolition of machinery). We realize that "the future can only be built upon the foundation of the real past." We shall not represent the present war, or any other human calamity, as an evil necessarily destructive of all civilized effort, but as an opportunity which, by breaking up false standards, opens the way to fresh creative effort. We believe that the only way to overcome evil is to transform it into a greater good.

(8)

We shall not primarily concern ourselves with methods – such as economic systems, or theories of government – though these will no doubt emerge. We shall try to quicken the creative spirit which enables man to build such systems in the light of his spiritual, intellectual and social needs. We aim at the Resurrection of Faith, the Revival of Learning and the Re-integration of Society.

We shall produce articles, pamphlets, books, lectures, etc., dealing with various branches of human activity, theoretical and practical: in everything we say or write we shall try deliberately to keep in view the beliefs we have expressed as to the true needs of society. Thus we shall endeavour, among other things:

To urge on creative activity, keep people interested in life, and combat lethargy, defeatism and depression of spirits.

To keep firmly before the minds of the people the true nature of man and the importance of the individual in the community and in the universe.

To remind people incessantly, while the War continues, of the spiritual aims for which it is waged and thus to prepare for a real energy of reconstruction in peace.

To explain to people, as well as we can, what is happening, why it is happening and how it concerns themselves, and to encourage them to form instructed opinions and act upon them.

To emphasize the value of active, individual thinking and feeling, and to do away with the prevalent reliance upon "spoon-feeding" and mental "dope".

To stimulate enjoyment in spiritual and mental exercise, and to correct the over-emphasis upon bodily comfort and "conspicuous waste" in the better-off sections of the population.

To lay stress, at the same time, on the necessity of a proper standard of physical well-being in all sections.

To open people's minds to the idea (a) that those whose work is interesting and stimulating should be given freedom to pursue it without crippling distractions, and (b) that those whose work is of necessity mechanical and uncreative should be given leisure for recreation.

To point the way to the proper employment of leisure (i.e. one which gives full play to creative energy – See note on Education below).

To recognize, encourage, and bring into action all the valuable qualities in which our nation is rich, and set them consciously working for the kind of society that shall be fully expressive of man's nature.

To examine into grievances, misunderstandings, etc., in the public mind (especially at the moment with regard to war aims and war restrictions) and to get those removed by the spread of correct information and the encouragement of a right spirit (whether in the public or in the governing bodies).

To observe and examine instances of social obstructiveness (e.g. contempt of the churches, resentment against intellectualism, readiness to cheat the government, etc.); to analyse the underlying causes (often unconscious) beneath their sometimes misleading expression; to discover and show how far such obstructiveness is justified by defects in the bodies concerned and how far an objection rightly made to those defects has been wrongly carried over to (e.g.) religion, learning and government as such; and to dispel, by explanation and argument, obstructiveness that arises from mere ignorance and misunderstanding of the facts.

To awaken the nation to a livelier understanding of the importance of the creative arts in the life of the community, and to secure for these a national and political recognition commensurate with their great actual and still greater potential influence.

To make the nation aware to how great an extent modern thought has been governed by scientific method, and, while strongly encouraging the application of scientific method to everything within its own sphere, to make it plain that this sphere is not unlimited.

To emphasize, in particular, that economics, though considered today as constituting the fundamental structure of society, was not always so considered, need not in the future be so considered, and has, in fact, been already found unworkable.

To explore suggestions for international settlement, bearing in mind the following considerations:

(a) While it is certainly at present impossible, and probably at any time undesirable, to abolish nationality or national feeling, nationalism must not be "deified" (i.e. regarded as an absolute).

(b) Treaties determining territorial boundaries must not be regarded as Divine Acts insusceptible to revision. An extreme rigidity in the administration of treaties or any other legal instrument ends inevitably in the opposite extreme of the denunciation of treaties, rebellion against law and an appeal to force.

(c) The establishment of international control (whether in such a form as the League of Nations or that of the suggested Federation of Europe) is bound to fail if the forms of justice and legality are or become, in fact, only a disguise for the forensic protection of vested interests.

(d) The existence of enormous world-resources of food and other materials (made available by science) side by side with extreme want among large numbers of the population has become a world scandal that is wholly intolerable. Means must be formed of distributing supplies to meet world needs even if this means a complete reconstruction of economic structure.

(e) A non-economic structure of the kind established in Russia and

Germany, which depends upon a low standard of living for whole populations, is wholly undesirable, and must be unnecessary in view of the world surplus in production.

To awaken the nation to the need for an entire overhaul of the aims and methods of education in this country. This is at present directed chiefly or wholly to the end of securing gainful employment, and is neither satisfactory in itself (i.e. in producing wise and happy citizens) nor even successful in its avowed purpose (i.e. it is powerless to check unemployment and does not fit people for the useful employment of leisure). The nation must be encouraged to take a very much wider view of the function of education, in better accordance with the needs of human nature and good citizenship, and to demand of its government that the necessary money for this better education shall be forthcoming. That is to say, that education which fits the citizen for peace must be taken at least as seriously as the armaments which fit him for war, and the necessary expenditure of thought and money cheerfully incurred.

NOTES

Chapter One

1 Letter to her parents dated July 16 1921
2 ibid.
3 Letter to her parents dated October 17 1921
4 Acts of the Apostles, ch. 21, verse 39
5 Letter to Ivy Shrimpton dated December 10 1928
6 Letter from Mrs H. Cross to M. L. Lord dated August 1977
7 *My Edwardian Childhood* – incomplete and unpublished MS.
8 Letter to Ivy dated February 1 1924
9 Letter to Winifred Pierce dated May 9 1944
10 *Cat o' Mary* – incomplete and unpublished MS.
11 *Rural England* by H. Rider Haggard, vol. 2, p. 3
12 ibid., vol. 2, p. 2
13 *Cat o' Mary*
14 ibid.
15 Letter from Mrs H. Cross to M. L. Lord dated August 1977

Chapter Two

1 *Cat o' Mary*
2 ibid.
3 ibid.
4 *My Edwardian Childhood*
5 ibid.
6 ibid.
7 *Cat o' Mary*
8 Rudyard Kipling, *The Sons of Martha*, 1907
9 *Cat o' Mary*
10 St Luke, ch. 10, verses 38–42
11 Letter to her mother dated February 1899
12 *Cat o' Mary*
13 ibid.
14 ibid.
15 ibid.
16 ibid.

17 ibid.
18 ibid.
19 Letter to Hilary Page dated August 16 1944
20 *Cat o' Mary*
21 ibid.
22 ibid.

Chapter Three

1 *Cat o' Mary*
2 ibid.
3 Letter to Ivy dated January 15 1907
4 ibid.
5 Letter to Ivy dated Good Friday [March 28] 1907
6 Letter to Ivy dated January 27 1907
7 Letter to Ivy dated February 7 1907
8 *Cat o' Mary*
9 Letter to Ivy dated June 19 1929
10 *Cat o' Mary*
11 ibid.
12 ibid.
13 ibid.
14 ibid.
15 Letter to Ivy dated September 3 1907
16 ibid.
17 *Cat o' Mary*
18 Letter to Ivy dated June 28 1908
19 ibid.
20 *Unpopular Opinions*, p. 24
21 *Cat o' Mary*
22 ibid.
23 Letter to Anthony Fleming dated December 1940
24 Letter to Ivy dated January 15 1907
25 Letter to Ivy dated February 23 1908
26 ibid.
27 ibid.
28 Letter to Ivy dated April 15 1908
29 Letter to Ivy dated June 28 1908
30 *Cat o' Mary*

Chapter Four

1 *Whose Body?*, p. 76
2 *Cat o' Mary*

3 Letter to Ivy dated November 6 1908

4 *Cat o' Mary*

5 ibid.

6 From "Target Area" printed in *The Fortnightly*, vol. 155, no. 927, March 1944, pp. 181–4. Also in *The Atlantic Monthly* March 1944, pp. 48–50

7 *Cat o' Mary*

8 ibid.

9 From the notes of Ann Shreurs, daughter of Dorothy's husband by his first wife – by courtesy of the Dorothy L. Sayers Historical and Literary Society, Witham, Essex

10 *Orthodoxy*, by G. K. Chesterton, p. 101

11 *Cat o' Mary*

12 Letter to Ivy dated April 15 1930

13 Letter to Ivy dated April 9 1910

14 Letter to her parents dated March 23 1910

15 *Cat o' Mary*

16 Letter to her parents dated June 27 1910

17 *Cat o' Mary*

18 ibid.

19 ibid.

20 ibid.

21 ibid.

22 ibid.

23 Letter to Mr K. M. Lewis dated April 28 1954

24 Letter to her parents dated October 29 1911

25 ibid.

Chapter Five

1 Marina Warner. Article in the *Guardian* June 27 1978

2 Letter to her parents dated March 2 1913

3 Letter to her parents dated March 8 1914

4 Letter to Muriel Jaeger dated July 30 1913

5 ibid.

6 Reply to an article on "Women at Oxford" in the *Daily News* of February 9 1927

7 Letter to Anthony dated January 15 1940

8 Letter to her parents dated June 7 1913

9 "Eros in Academe", printed in *The Oxford Outlook*, vol. 1, no. 2, June 1919

10 Letter to her parents dated Quinquagesima [February 22] 1914

11 Letter to her parents dated December 6 1911

12 *Cat o' Mary*
13 Letter to her parents dated March 8 1914
14 Letter to her parents dated May 10 1914
15 ibid.
16 Letter to Cyril Bailey dated September 23 1946
17 Letter to her parents dated May 1914
18 Letter to Cyril Bailey dated September 23 1946
19 Letter to her parents dated May 1914
20 ibid.
21 Undated letter to her parents
22 Letter to her parents dated July 1914
23 Letter to her parents dated August 11 1914
24 Letter to her parents dated January 24 1915
25 ibid.
26 Letter to her parents dated January 31 1915
27 Letter to her parents dated February 7 1915
28 ibid.
29 Letter to her parents dated May 16 1915
30 Undated letter to her parents June 1915
31 Letter to her parents dated June 6 1915
32 Report by Miss Mildred Pope, Michaelmas [Autumn] Term 1913, by courtesy of the Principal and Fellows of Somerville College, Oxford
33 Report by Miss Jourdain, Michaelmas [Autumn] Term 1913, by courtesy of the Principal and Fellows of Somerville College, Oxford
34 Report by M. Berthon, Hilary [Spring] Term 1914, by courtesy of the Principal and Fellows of Somerville College, Oxford
35 Report by M. Berthon, Michaelmas [Autumn] Term 1914, by courtesy of the Principal and Fellows of Somerville College, Oxford
36 Letter to her parents dated June 6 1915
37 Letter to her parents dated May 16 1915
38 Letter to her parents dated October 8 1911
39 Letter to her parents dated May 16 1915
40 Letter to her parents dated May 23 1915
41 Letter to her parents dated May 30 1915
42 Letter to her parents dated May 23 1915
43 Undated letter to her parents, September ? 1917

Chapter Six

1 Letter to Muriel Jaeger dated July 27 1915
2 ibid.
3 From "The Last Castle", one of the poems in *Op I*
4 Undated letter to her parents January 1916

5 Letter to Muriel Jaeger dated November 14 1916
6 Letter to her parents dated June 2 1916
7 Letter to Muriel Jaeger dated March 8 1917
8 Letter to her parents dated June 19 1917
9 Undated letter to her parents, July 1917
10 ibid.
11 *Cat o' Mary*
12 Letter to her parents dated June 14 1918
13 Letter to Muriel Jaeger dated October 2 1918
14 Letter to her parents dated October 28 1918
15 Letter to Muriel Jaeger dated October 6 1918
16 ibid.
17 Letter to Muriel Jaeger dated October 28 1918
18 Letter to Muriel Jaeger dated October 2 1918
19 Letter to Muriel Jaeger dated November 22 1918
20 Letter to Muriel Jaeger dated Epiphany [January 6] 1919
21 Letter to her parents dated May 2 1919
22 Eric Whelpton, *The Making of a European*, p. 126
23 Letter to her parents dated May 2 1919
24 Letter to Muriel Jaeger dated October 2 1918
25 Letter to her parents dated September 23 1918
26 From an uncompleted MS. short story, "The Tragical Comedy of the Automatic Call-Box", probably written about 1927–8
27 Letter to John Cournos dated October 27 1924
28 Letter to John Cournos dated August 25 1925
29 Letter to Leonard Green dated August 29 1919, by courtesy of the Humanities Research Center, University of Texas, Austin, Texas
30 Letter to her parents dated February 21 1919
31 Letter to Muriel Jaeger dated February 24 1919
32 Letter to Muriel Jaeger dated April 6 1919
33 Letter to her parents dated May 25 1919
34 Letter to her parents dated June 6 1919
35 ibid.

Chapter Seven

1 Eric Whelpton, *The Making of a European*, p. 138
2 Letter to Ivy dated December 23 1919
3 Letter to her parents dated November 23 1919
4 Letter to her parents dated November 2 1919
5 ibid.
6 Letter to her parents dated November 23 1919
7 ibid.

8 Letter to her parents dated December 7 1919
9 *Unnatural Death*, p. 183
10 Letter to her parents dated November 2 1919
11 Letter to her parents dated November 13 1919
12 Letter to her parents dated September 3 1920
13 Letter to her parents dated February 27 1920
14 ibid.
15 Letter to Muriel Jaeger dated March 8 1920
16 Letter to her parents dated April 24 1920

Chapter Eight

1 Letter to Muriel Jaeger dated September 1 1920
2 Letter to her parents dated December 9 1920
3 Letter to her parents dated February 19 1921
4 Letter to her parents dated July 1 1921
5 Letter to her parents dated October 17 1921
6 *Daily Express* dated February 28 1934
7 Letter to her parents dated January 22 1921
8 Letter to Ivy dated December 23 1921
9 Undated letter to her parents, November ? 1921
10 Letter to her parents dated November 8 1921
11 Letter to her parents dated Hallowmass Eve [October 31] 1921
12 Letter to her parents dated November 24 1921
13 Letter to her parents dated December 19 1921
14 ibid.

Chapter Nine

1 John Cournos, *Autobiography*
2 ibid.
3 ibid.
4 ibid.
5 Letter to her parents dated November 8 1921
6 John Cournos, *Autobiography*
7 Letter to her parents dated January 18 1922
8 Letter to her parents dated February 14 1922
9 Letter to her parents dated June 15 1922
10 Letter to her parents dated July 24 1922
11 Letter to John Cournos dated February 5 1925*
12 Letter to her parents dated November 23 1919
13 Letter to John Cournos dated December 4 1924*

* All quotations from letters to John Cournos by courtesy of Mr Alfred W. Satterthwaite and the Houghton Library, Harvard University, Cambridge, Mass.

14 Letter to John Cournos dated August 13 1925*
15 ibid.
16 ibid.
17 Letter to John Cournos dated December 4 1924*
18 Letter to John Cournos dated October 27 1924*
19 Letter to her parents dated November 8 1921
20 Letter to John Cournos dated December 4 1924*
21 Letter to John Cournos dated January 25 1925*
22 Letter to John Cournos dated December 4 1924*
23 ibid.
24 Letter to John Cournos dated February 25 1925*
25 Letter to John Cournos dated October 27 1924*
26 ibid.
27 Letter to John Cournos dated January 25 1925*
28 Letter to John Cournos dated February 5 1925*
29 ibid.
30 Letter to John Cournos dated August 22 1924*
31 Letter to John Cournos dated February 5 1925*
32 Letter to John Cournos dated August 13 1925*
33 ibid.
34 Letter to John Cournos dated December 4 1924*
35 Letter to John Cournos dated August 13 1925*
36 Letter to John Cournos dated December 4 1924*
37 Letter to her mother dated December 18 1922
38 Letter to John Cournos dated December 4 1924*
39 Letter to her parents dated February 15 1923
40 Undated letter to her parents November ? 1923
41 Letter to John Cournos dated January 25 1925*
42 *Clouds of Witness*, p. 197
43 Letter to John Cournos dated February 22 1925*
44 ibid.
45 Letter to Ivy dated February 6 1924
46 Letter to Ivy dated April 29 1924
47 Letter to Ivy dated May 2 1924
48 Letter to John Cournos dated December 4 1924*
49 *Clouds of Witness*, pp. 224–228

Chapter Ten

1 Letter to her father dated April 30 1924
2 Letter to Ivy dated June 18 1932

* All quotations from letters to John Cournos by courtesy of Mr Alfred W.
Satterthwaite and the Houghton Library, Harvard University, Cambridge, Mass.

3 Letter to John Cournos dated August 13 1925*
4 Letter to John Cournos dated January 25 1925*
5 Undated letter to John Cournos, end January 1925*
6 ibid.
7 Letter to Charles Williams dated October 18 1944
8 Letter to her parents dated April 8 1926
9 *How to See the Battlefields*, by Capt. Atherton Fleming, pub. Cassell & Company Ltd 1919 – pp. 44–45

Chapter Eleven

1 Letter to C. S. Lewis dated December 12 1955
2 *The Mind of the Maker*, p. 40
3 "Gaudy Night", article in *Titles to Fame*, ed. Denys Kilham Roberts, pub. Thomas Nelson & Sons – pp. 91–92
4 "How I Came to Invent the Character of Lord Peter", article in *Harcourt Brace News*, N.Y., vol. 1, July 15 1936 – pp. 1–2
5 *The Unpleasantness at the Bellona Club*, p. 12
6 Lecture given on February 12 1936 (? to the Red Cross)
7 *Gaudy Night*, p. 439
8 Letter to E. C. Bentley dated April 17 1936
9 *Clouds of Witness*, p. 48
10 Letter to Ivy dated December 31 1921, about *Whose Body?*
11 Letter to Ivy dated May 3 1927, about *Unnatural Death*
12 Letter to Ivy dated February 20 1933, about *Murder Must Advertise*
13 Letter to Victor Gollancz dated September 14 1932, about *Murder Must Advertise*
14 Letter to Ivy dated September 9 1935, about *Gaudy Night*
15 Lecture given on February 12 1936 (? to the Red Cross)
16 Letter from Dr Eustace Barton (pen name Robert Eustace) dated May 24 1928
17 Letter from Dr Eustace Barton dated November 17 1932
18 *Strong Poison*, p. 50

Chapter Twelve

1 Letter to Ivy dated April 15 1925
2 Letter to Ivy dated March 15 1926
3 Letter to the *Evening Standard*, November 19 1928
4 Letter to her parents dated June 1 1922
5 "The Psychology of Advertising" – article in the *Spectator*, November 19 1937

---

* All quotations from letters to John Cournos by courtesy of Mr Alfred W. Satterthwaite and the Houghton Library, Harvard University, Cambridge, Mass.

6 *The Poetry of Search and the Poetry of Statement*, p. 97
7 Letter to Ivy dated July 5 1928
8 Letter to Ivy dated September 6 1928
9 Letter to Ivy dated May 13 1927
10 Letter to Ivy dated September 24 1928
11 Letter to her mother dated October 10 1928
12 ibid.
13 Letter to Ivy dated December 10 1928
14 Letter to Ivy dated April 15 1930

Chapter Thirteen

1 Letter to John Cournos dated August 13 1925, by courtesy of Mr Alfred W. Satterthwaite and the Houghton Library, Harvard University, Cambridge, Massachusetts
2 Letter to Victor Gollancz dated September 14 1932
3 "The Case of Miss Dorothy Sayers" – article by Q. D. Leavis in *Scrutiny*, issue of December 1937
4 ibid.
5 ibid.
6 Letter to Peter Haddon dated November 1 1935
7 ibid.
8 Letter to Muriel St Clare Byrne dated March 6 1935
9 ibid.

Chapter Fourteen

1 Letter to G. R. Collinge dated March 25 1955
2 Letter to Anthony Fleming dated January 2 1940
3 ibid.
4 From the Preface by Laurence Irving to *The Zeal of Thy House*. (Mr Irving designed the set)
5 *The Zeal of Thy House*, Act III
6 Letter from "Anglican Priest, Guildford" quoted in publicity leaflet
7 Letter from "R.C., Kent" quoted in publicity leaflet
8 Letter from "B.G., London WC.1" quoted in publicity leaflet
9 Letter from "K.G.H., London WC.1" quoted in publicity leaflet
10 Letter to John Wren-Lewis dated Good Friday [April 16] 1954
11 "The Greatest Drama Ever Staged is the Official Creed of Christendom" – article in the *Sunday Times*, April 3 1938
12 Letter to Frederick Muller dated January 3 1938
13 ibid.
14 Letter to Messrs Longmans dated May 13 1938
15 Letter to the author from Bartlett Mullins dated December 5 1979

16 ibid.
17 Letter to Ivy dated May 18 1938
18 *The Times*, leader, November 21 1938
19 Letter to *The Times* dated November 22 1938
20 Letter from "Booth, Dublin", quoted in publicity leaflet
21 Letter from "Hardisty, Huddersfield" quoted in publicity leaflet
22 Letter from John Rhode, Kent, quoted in publicity leaflet
23 Letter to Ivy dated August 21 1934
24 Letter from A. P. Waterfield dated July 22 1939
25 Letter to Mrs MacLoughlin (pen name Eileen Wincroft) dated September 27 1939

Chapter Fifteen

1 Wimsey Papers I, the *Spectator*, November 17 1939
2 Wimsey Papers XI, the *Spectator,* January 26 1940
3 Letter to Muriel St Clare Byrne dated November 23 1939
4 Publicity material for "Methuen's Coming Books" 1941
5 ibid.
6 *Love All* (MS) Act II
7 *Love All* (MS.) Act III
8 ibid.
9 *The Times*, April 10 1940
10 *Time & Tide*, April 13 1940
11 "They Tried to be Good", first published in *World Review* 1943. Reprinted in *Unpopular Opinions*, see pp. 103–104
12 Letter to Anthony dated June 23 1940
13 "The English War", first printed in *The Times Literary Supplement*, no. 2014, 7 September 1940, p. 445
14 Letter to Graham Greene at the Ministry of Information dated July 26 1940
15 Letter to Sir Richard Maconochie, Controller of Home Broadcasting at the BBC, dated 14 July 1940
16 Undated letter to W. G. Williams, autumn 1940
17 ibid.
18 Letter from Dr J. H. Oldham dated December 28 1939, quoting the Archbishop of York

Chapter Sixteen

1 Letter from Miss May E. Jenkin dated November 19 1940
2 ibid.
3 ibid.
4 Letter to Miss Jenkin dated November 22 1940

5   ibid.
6   Letter from Derek McCulloch dated November 26 1940
7   Letter to Derek McCulloch dated November 28 1940
8   ibid.
9   ibid.
10 Letter to Dr James Welch dated November 28 1940
11 ibid.
12 Letter to Dr Welch dated December 7 1940
13 Letter from Miss Jenkin dated December 19 1940
14 ibid.
15 ibid.
16 ibid.
17 ibid.
18 ibid.
19 Letter from Dr Welch dated December 30 1940
20 Letter to Dr Welch dated January 2 1941
21 ibid.
22 ibid.
23 Introduction to *The Man Born to be King*, p. 19
24 Letter to Dr Welch dated July 23 1941
25 Letter to William Temple, Archbishop of York, dated August 30 1941
26 Mr H. H. Martin, quoted in the *Sunday Dispatch*, December 28 1941
27 *Daily Mail*, December 11 1941
28 *The Man Born to be King*, play 4, "The Heirs to the Kingdom"
29 *The Mind of the Maker*, Chapter V, p. 60

Chapter Seventeen

1   Letter to Muriel St Clare Byrne dated November 16 1941
2   Letter to Muriel St Clare Byrne dated October 25 1942
3   Letter from Alice M. Long dated September 29 1941
4   Unpublished MS.
5   "Letter to the People of America" – unpublished
6   Letter to Herbert Agar dated August 20 1941
7   ibid.
8   "The Feast of St Verb", article in the *Sunday Times*, March 24 1940
9   Letter to the Rev. G. H. Crosland dated May 18 1943
10 Letter to the Rev. G. H. Crosland dated June 16 1943
11 Letter to Helen Waddell dated September 2 1942
12 Letter from William Temple, Archbishop of Canterbury, dated September 4 1943

13 Letter from William Temple, Archbishop of Canterbury, dated September 10 1943

14 Letter from William Temple, Archbishop of Canterbury, dated September 15 1943

15 Letter from William Temple, Archbishop of Canterbury, dated September 22 1943

16 Letter from William Temple, Archbishop of Canterbury, dated September 30 1943

17 From "Are Women Human?", published in *Unpopular Opinions*, p. 108

18 Letter to Sir Wyndham Deedes dated April 16 1943

19 ibid.

20 Letter to J. J. Lynx dated June 28 1943

21 Letter to J. J. Lynx dated July 12 1943

22 Letter to J. J. Lynx dated August 1943

23 Letter to Messrs Lindsay Drummond, publishers, dated July 5 1944

24 Letter to Maurice Reckitt dated October 30 1945

25 ibid.

26 ibid.

27 "Aerial Reconnaissance", published in *The Fortnightly*, vol. 154, no. 922, October 1943, pp. 268–270

28 Letter to Michael Powell dated February 19 1947

Chapter Eighteen

1 Letter to Miss Sheila Cudahy dated August 20 1948

2 *New York Times Book Review*, August 21 1949

3 *The Figure of Beatrice* by Charles Williams, p. 176

4 Article by Anne Ridler, in *The New English Weekly*, May 31 1945

5 Letter to Professor G. L. Bickersteth dated June 12 1957

6 Letter from Victor Gollancz quoting Charles Williams, dated December 29 1933

7 Letter to Margaret Babington dated February 26 1937

8 Letter from Charles Williams dated August 13 1943

9 Letter from Charles Williams dated June 1 1944

10 Letter to Charles Williams dated August 16 1944

11 ibid.

12 ibid.

13 Letter to Professor G. L. Bickersteth dated November 24 1954

14 Letter to Charles Williams dated August 31 1944

15 Undated letter to Charles Williams, August 1944

16 ibid.

17 ibid.

18 ibid.
19 Letter to Charles Williams dated August 31 1944
20 Letter to Charles Williams dated September 26 1944
21 Letter from Charles Williams dated September 7 1944
22 Published posthumously in *Nottingham Mediaeval Studies*, no. IX, 1965
23 Letter to E. V. Rieu dated March 23 1945
24 ibid.
25 Letter from E. V. Rieu dated March 8 1945
26 Letter from E. V. Rieu dated April 8 1945

Chapter Nineteen

1 Letter from C. S. Lewis dated October 23 1945
2 Letter from C. S. Lewis dated December 14 1945
3 Letter from C. S. Lewis dated July 23 1946
4 Letter from C. S. Lewis dated July 29 1946
5 Letter from C. S. Lewis dated August 8 1946
6 Letter to Muriel St Clare Byrne dated March 2 1946
7 ibid.
8 Letter to Phyllis Potter dated December 6 1937
9 ibid.
10 Letter to Muriel St Clare Byrne dated March 2 1946
11 Letter to Patrick McLaughlin dated March 12 1941
12 Letter to Norah Lambourne dated July 5 1946
13 Letter to Norah Lambourne dated April 26 1947
14 Letter to the *Daily Telegraph* dated May 1 1947
15 "You Are the Treasury", published in *Tory Challenge*, July 1947
16 ibid.
17 Letter to Dr James Welch dated March 31 1949
18 Letter to Norah Lambourne dated August 27 1946
19 Letter from Dr Barbara Reynolds dated June 4 1949
20 Letter to Charis Frankenberg dated March 5 1929
21 "Target Area", printed in *The Fortnightly*, vol. 155, no. 927, March 1944, pp. 181–184. Also in *The Atlantic Monthly*, March 1944, pp. 48–50
22 Letter to Norah Lambourne dated June 10 1949
23 Letter to Norah Lambourne dated May 14 1949
24 Letter from Dr J. G. Benjamin dated May 11 1949
25 Letter to Norah Lambourne dated July 20 1949
26 Letter from Muriel St Clare Byrne dated November, 1949
27 Letter from Dr Barbara Reynolds dated November 15 1949
28 Letter from C. S. Lewis dated November 11 1949

29 Undated letter to Professor G. L. Bickersteth, 1950
30 Letter to Muriel St Clare Byrne dated June 12 1950
31 Letter to Una Ellis-Fermor dated June 12 1950
32 Letter from Edgar Fleming to Ann Fleming dated June 13 1950
33 ibid.
34 Letter to Muriel St Clare Byrne dated June 12 1950

Chapter Twenty

 1 Letter to Messrs Marshall & Snelgrove dated March 8 1954
 2 Letter to Dr Barbara Reynolds dated November 1 1951
 3 *Punch*, November 2 1953
 4 *Punch*, January 20 1954
 5 Letter to Norah Lambourne dated September 21 1953
 6 *Punch*, January 13 1954
 7 Letter to John Wren-Lewis dated "Good Friday" [April 15] 1954
 8 ibid.
 9 ibid.
10 Letter to John Wren-Lewis dated June 18 1954
11 Letter to Norah Lambourne dated June 11 1954
12 Letter to E. V. Rieu dated August 24 1956
13 Undated letter to Prof. G. L. Bickersteth, quoting his to her, 1950
14 Undated letter to Prof. G. L. Bickersteth, July 1955
15 Letter from Prof. G. L. Bickersteth dated July 19 1955
16 *Sunday Dispatch*, December 15 1957
17 Letter from Val Gielgud dated December 13 1957
18 ibid.
19 *Have His Carcase*, Chapter XI
20 Letter to Patrick McLaughlin dated August 22 1940
21 Letter to Kenneth Robinson dated November 4 1949
22 *Daily Mail*, December 24 1957
23 Letter to Muriel Jaeger July 30 1913
24 *Cat o' Mary*
25 Introduction to *Great Short Stories of Detection, Mystery & Horror, Part I*,
     p. 31

SELECT BIBLIOGRAPHY

Two excellent bibliographies of Dorothy L. Sayers' works already exist. They run to 286 and 263 pages respectively – such was Dorothy's creative fertility; and since I have read almost every item mentioned therein, and one or two more besides, an exhaustive list of my sources would only duplicate the work done by more thorough scholars than myself, delay the publication of this book by several months and double its length.

For those, however, who would be interested in something a little less overwhelming, I append a list of Dorothy's principal works, and from among her numberless lectures and articles I have tried to select those which appear to me to summarize an attitude, to signal a change of direction or in some way to have special interest or importance. These are in chronological order.

I have also listed the unpublished works that I have been lucky enough to see; and a selection of works by other authors that are relevant to her life and her output.

The bulk of my work has been among her letters, and the tiny proportion of these that I have actually quoted are individually itemized in the endnotes.

BIBLIOGRAPHIES

An Annotated Guide to the Works of Dorothy L. Sayers, by Robert B. Harmon and Margaret A. Burger, Garland Publishing Inc., New York and London 1977.
A Bibliography of the Works of Dorothy L. Sayers, by Colleen B. Gilbert, Macmillan Press Ltd., London 1978.

SELECTED PUBLISHED WORKS OF DOROTHY L. SAYERS
IN CHRONOLOGICAL ORDER

Poems and articles in *Godolphin Gazette* (School Magazine) 1909–1911.
Op I, book of poems, B. H. Blackwell, Oxford, 1916.
Catholic Tales and Christian Songs, book of poems, B. H. Blackwell, Oxford, 1918.
Various poems in *The Fritillary*, 1915–1916.
Various poems in *The Oxford Magazine*, 1915–1916, including "To Members of the Bach Choir on Active Service", February 18 1916.
"Thomas Angulo's Death", poem in *Saturday Westminster Gazette*, May 20 1916, written under the pseudonym of H. P. Rallentando.

"Who Calls the Tune", short story in *Blue Moon*, published for the Mutual Admiration Society, 1917.

Various poems in *The New Witness, Oxford Outlook, Oxford Chronicle, Oxford Journal Illustrated*, 1918–1920.

"The Tristan of Thomas – A Verse Translation", in *Modern Languages*, June and August 1920.

Various poems in *The London Mercury*, 1921.

Various poems in *The New Decameron*, Basil Blackwell, Oxford, 1920–1925.

Whose Body?, detective novel, Boni and Liveright, New York and T. Fisher Unwin, London, 1923.

Clouds of Witness, detective novel, T. Fisher Unwin, London, 1926 and Lincoln McVeagh, New York, 1927.

Unnatural Death, detective novel, Ernest Benn, London, 1927 and Lincoln McVeagh, New York, 1928.

The Unpleasantness at the Bellona Club, detective novel, Ernest Benn, London and Payson and Clarke, New York, 1928.

Introduction to *Great Short Stories of Detection, Mystery and Horror*, Gollancz, London, 1928 and Payson and Clarke, New York, (retitled *The Omnibus of Crime*), 1929.

Lord Peter Views the Body, collection of short stories, Gollancz, 1928 and Payson and Clarke, New York, 1929.

Tristan in Brittany, translation, Ernest Benn, London and Payson and Clarke, New York, 1929.

The Documents in the Case, detective novel, with Robert Eustace, Ernest Benn, London and Brewer and Warren, New York, 1930.

"Behind the Screen", part 3, contribution to radio serial by members of the Detection Club, printed in *The Listener*, July 2 1930.

Strong Poison, detective novel, Gollancz, London and Brewer and Warren, New York, 1930.

"The Present Status of the Mystery Story", article in *The London Mercury*, November 1930.

"The Scoop", parts 1 and 12, contribution to radio serial by members of the Detection Club, printed in *The Listener*, February 11 and April 8 1931.

The Five Red Herrings, detective novel, Gollancz, London and Brewer, Warren and Putnam, New York, (retitled *Suspicious Characters*), 1931.

Introduction to *Great Short Stories of Detection, Mystery and Horror, Second Series*, Gollancz, London, 1931 and Coward-McCann, New York, (retitled *The Second Omnibus of Crime*), 1932.

The Floating Admiral – Introduction and Solution, contributions to detective novel written by members of the Detection Club, Hodder and Stoughton, London, 1931 and Doubleday, Doran, New York, 1932.

Have His Carcase, detective novel, Gollancz, London and Brewer, Warren and Putnam, New York, 1932.

Murder Must Advertise, detective novel, Gollancz, London and Harcourt Brace, New York, 1933.

"The Conclusions of Roger Sheringham", contribution to *Ask a Policeman*, written by various authors, Arthur Barker, London and William Morrow, New York, 1933.

Hangman's Holiday, collection of short stories, Gollancz, London and Harcourt Brace, New York, 1933.

The Nine Tailors, detective novel, Gollancz, London and Harcourt Brace, New York, 1934.

Introduction to *Great Short Stories of Detection, Mystery and Horror, Third Series*, Gollancz, London, 1934 and Coward-McCann, New York, (retitled *The Third Omnibus of Crime*), 1935.

"What is Right with Oxford?", a speech at Somerville College Gaudy, 1934, printed in *Oxford*, Summer 1935.

Gaudy Night, detective novel, Gollancz, London, 1935 and Harcourt Brace, New York, 1936.

"The Importance of Being Vulgar", speech given on February 12 1936, possibly to the Red Cross.

Introduction to *Tales of Detection*, J. M. Dent, Everyman's Library, 1936.

"Aristotle on Detective Fiction", speech given in Oxford on March 5 1936, printed in *English: the Magazine of the English Association*, vol. 1 no 1, 1936.

"How I Came to Invent the Character of Lord Peter", *Harcourt Brace News*, New York, July 15 1936.

"The Murder of Julia Wallace", study of a real-life murder contributed to *The Anatomy of Murder*, written by several members of the Detection Club, John Lane, The Bodley Head, 1936 and Macmillan, New York, 1938.

Busman's Honeymoon, play, with Muriel St Clare Byrne, Gollancz, London, 1937 and Dramatists' Play Service, New York, 1939.

Papers Relating to the Family of Wimsey, with C. W. Scott-Giles, privately printed, Westminster Press, 1936.

Busman's Honeymoon, detective novel, Harcourt Brace, New York and Gollancz, London, 1937.

"The Fen Floods – Fiction and Fact", article in the *Spectator*, April 2 1937.

The Zeal of Thy House, play for Canterbury Cathedral, Gollancz, London and Harcourt Brace, New York, 1937.

"Gaudy Night," article in *Titles to Fame*, ed. Denys Kilham Roberts, Nelson, London and New York, 1937.

"The Psychology of Advertising", article in the *Spectator*, November 19 1937.

"An Account of Lord Mortimer Wimsey, Hermit of the Wash", spoof memoir privately printed as a Christmas present for her friends, Oxford University Press, 1937.

"The Greatest Drama Ever Staged", article in *The Sunday Times*, April 3 1938, later published by Hodder and Stoughton, 1938.

Double Death, part 1, contribution to a murder story by several authors, Gollancz, London, 1939.

The Devil to Pay, play for Canterbury Cathedral, Gollancz, London and Harcourt Brace, New York, 1939.

In the Teeth of the Evidence, collection of short stories, Gollancz, London, 1939 and Harcourt Brace, New York, 1940.

He That Should Come, nativity play for radio, Gollancz, 1939.

"Wimsey Papers", articles in the *Spectator*, November 1939 – January 1940.

Begin Here, a war-time essay, Gollancz, London, 1940; Harcourt Brace, New York, 1941.

Love All, play, unpublished but performed at the Torch Theatre, April 1940.

"The English War", poem, *The Times Literary Supplement*, September 7 1940.

"The Church's Responsibility", address given at the Archbishop of York's Conference on "The Life of the Church and the Order of Society", January 1941. Published by Longmans Green, 1942.

The Mind of the Maker, Methuen, London and Harcourt Brace, New York, 1941.

The Man Born to be King, series of plays for radio on the life of Christ, first broadcast December 1941–October 1942. Published by Gollancz, London, 1943 and Harper, New York, 1949.

"The Human-Not-Quite-Human", article on the situation of women, *Christendom*, September 1941.

The Other Six Deadly Sins, address to the Public Morality Council, Methuen, 1943.

"Church and Theatre", address given at St Anne's House, June 1943.

"Aerial Reconnaissance", poem, *The Fortnightly*, October 1943.

"Target Area", poem, *The Fortnightly*, March 1944.

Even the Parrot – Exemplary Conversations for Enlightened Children, Methuen, 1944.

Introduction to *The Moonstone* by Wilkie Collins, Dent, London and Dutton, New York, 1944.

Introduction to *A Time is Born* by Garet Garrett, Blackwell, Oxford, 1945.

The Just Vengeance, Lichfield Festival Play for 1946, Gollancz, 1946.

Unpopular Opinions, collection of articles and addresses on various subjects, Gollancz, London, 1946 and Harcourt Brace, New York, 1947.

Creed or Chaos, collection of essays in popular theology, Methuen, London, 1947 and Harcourt Brace, New York, 1949.

"You Are The Treasury", article in *Tory Challenge*, July 1947.

The Comedy of Dante Alighieri the Florentine. Cantica I: Hell, translation, Penguin Classics, 1949.

The Emperor Constantine, Colchester Festival play, Gollancz, London and Harper, New York, 1951.

"The Days of Christ's Coming", Christmas Calendar card, painted by Fritz Wegner, Hamish Hamilton, London, 1953.

"Pantheon Papers", *Punch*, November 1953 – January 1954.

Introductory Papers on Dante, collection of eight essays, Methuen, London, 1954 and Harper, New York, 1955.

The Comedy of Dante Alighieri the Florentine. Cantica II: Purgatory, Penguin Classics, 1955.

Further Papers on Dante, collection of eight essays, Methuen, London and Harper, New York, 1957

The Song of Roland, translation, Penguin Classics, 1957.

The Comedy of Dante Alighieri the Florentine. Cantica III: Paradise, translation with Barbara Reynolds, published posthumously, Penguin Classics, 1962.

The Poetry of Search and the Poetry of Statement, twelve essays on various subjects, published posthumously, Gollancz, 1963.

"The Art of Translating Dante" and "The 'Terrible' Ode", articles published posthumously in *Nottingham Mediaeval Studies*, vol. IX, 1965.

"Talboys", short story about Wimsey written in 1942, published posthumously, Harper, 1972.

Striding Folly, three Wimsey short stories, including "Talboys", published posthumously, New English Library, 1973.

Wilkie Collins, uncompleted critical and biographical study, edited by E. R. Gregory and published by the Friends of the University of Toledo Libraries, 1977.

UNPUBLISHED WORKS OF DOROTHY L. SAYERS

Early Poems.

The Matador, screenplay based on the novel *Blood and Sand*, 1920.

"The Adventure of the Piccadilly Flat", fragment of short story, probably the first appearance of Lord Peter Wimsey.

The Mousehole. A Detective Fantasia in Three Flats, fragment of play featuring Lord Peter Wimsey.

"The Tragical Comedy of the Automatic Call-Box", fragment of a short story featuring Lord Peter Wimsey, about 1927.

My Edwardian Childhood, fragment of an autobiography, 33 pages, about 1932.

Cat o' Mary, fragment of a novel with autobiographical content, 209 pages, about 1934.

Thrones, Dominations, fragment of a murder novel featuring Lord Peter Wimsey and Harriet Vane after their marriage, 6 chapters.

Admiral Darlan, fragment of a verse play, about 1943.

Playlet for radio about Dante and his daughter Bice, May 1952.

Untitled novel about Dante and his daughter Bice, fragment, about 1952.

Speech given at St Anne's House in answer to *The Emperor's Clothes*, autumn 1954.

WORKS OF CAPTAIN ATHERTON FLEMING

How to See the Battlefields, Cassell & Co, 1919.

The Gourmet's Book of Food and Drink, John Lane, The Bodley Head, London, 1933.

The Craft of the Short Story (under the pen-name Donald Maconochie), Pitman, 1936.

Articles in *News of the World*, March 6, 13, 20, 1927.

WORKS BY OTHER AUTHORS

Joan Ross Acocella, "The Cult of Language: A Study of Two Modern Translations of Dante", *Modern Language Quarterly*, June 1974.

Jacques Barzun, with Wendell Taylor, *A Catalogue of Crime*, Harper, New York, 1971.

John Cournos, *Autobiography*, Liveright, New York, 1935. *The Devil is an English Gentleman*, Liveright, New York, 1932.

Alzina Stone Dale, *Maker and Craftsman*, a junior biography of D. L. S., Eerdmans, Grand Rapids, Michigan, 1978.

Charis U. Frankenberg, *Not Old, Madam-Vintage*, Galaxy Books, Lavenham, Suffolk, 1975.

Martin Green, "The Detection of a Snob", article in the *Listener*, March 14, 1963.

Carolyn G. Heilbrun, "Sayers, Lord Peter and God", *The American Scholar*, vol. 37, Spring 1968.

Janet Hitchman, *Such a Strange Lady – An Introduction to Dorothy L. Sayers*, New English Library, 1975.

Ralph E. Hone, *Dorothy L. Sayers, a Literary Biography*, Kent State University Press, 1979.

Q. D. Leavis, "The Case of Miss Dorothy Sayers", *Scrutiny*, vol. 6, December 1937.

G. A. Lee, *The Wimsey Saga – A Chronology*, 1980, obtainable from the Dorothy L. Sayers Historical and Literary Society, Witham, Essex.

Kathleen Nott, *The Emperor's Clothes*, Chapter IX, "Lord Peter Views the Soul", Heinemann, London, 1954.

Barbara Reynolds, "The Origin of Lord Peter Wimsey", address given to the Dorothy L. Sayers Historical and Literary Society, June 1976, printed in *The Times Literary Supplement*, April 22 1977. "Dorothy L. Sayers, Interpreter of Dante", address given to the Dorothy L. Sayers Historical and Literary Society, July 1978.

H. P. Rickman, "From Detection to Theology (The Work of Dorothy L. Sayers)", *Hibbert Journal*, July 1962.

Eric Routley, *The Puritan Pleasures of the Detective Story*, Gollancz, 1972.

C. W. Scott-Giles, *The Wimsey Family*, an account based on his correspondence with D.L.S. about the fictional family, Gollancz, 1977.

Ann Schreurs, *Memoir* of her father, Capt. Fleming (Mac), circulated by the Dorothy L. Sayers Historical and Literary Society, July 1976.

Helen Simpson, "Mary Wimsey's Household Book", presented to the Confraternitas Historica of Sidney Sussex College, Cambridge, with other papers by D.L.S., Muriel St Clare Byrne and C. W. Scott-Giles, March 7 1937.

Rosamund Kent Sprague, *A Matter of Eternity – Selections from the Writings of Dorothy L. Sayers*, Eerdmans, Grand Rapids, Michigan and Mowbrays, Oxford, 1973.

Frank A. Swinnerton, *The Georgian Literary Scene*, Chapter 15, "A Post-War Symptom; Edgar Wallace and Others", Heinemann, London, 1935.

Julian Symons, *Bloody Murder: From the Detective Story to the Crime Novel; a History*, Faber & Faber, London, 1972.

John Thurmer, "The Theology of Dorothy L. Sayers", *Church Quarterly Review*, October–December 1969.

Colin Watson, *Snobbery with Violence – Crime Stories and their Audience*, Eyre and Spottiswoode, London, 1971.

Eric Whelpton, *The Making of a European*, Johnson, London, 1974.

Edmund Wilson, *A Literary Chronicle: 1920–1950*, Doubleday Anchor Books, New York, 1956.

INDEX

DLS = Dorothy L. Sayers   * denotes a character in a work by DLS

Affirmation of Images (Charles Williams), 224, 229, 238
Agar, Herbert, 211
Allen, Sir Hugh Percy, 50–1, 52, 54–5, 56, 70
Arundell, Denis, 156
Authors' Planning Committee (Ministry of Information), 175–6

Babington, Margaret, 160, 169
Barber, Marjorie, 228, 232
Barnett, Charis, 44, 53
Barton, Dr Eustace, 130–1
BBC, 18, 183, 187–8; making *The Man Born to be King*, 192–200. *See also* Children's Hour
Behind the Screen (radio serial) (Detection Club), 143
Beith, Ian Hay, 175
Bell, Bishop George, 160
Benn, Ernest, 139
Benson's Advertising Agency, 91, 92, 108, 134
Bentley, E. C., 125, 143
Berkeley, Anthony, 143
Bibliographies of DLS, 291
Bickersteth, Professor G. L., 267
"Bill", 97–100, 105
Blackwell, Basil, 60–3, 70, 75
Blake, Sexton, 122–3, 126
Bluntisham, 7–9
Bond, James, 121
Brabant, Frank, 70
Brabazon, James, first sight of DLS, 159, 241
Bridgeheads (series of books), 183–4, 278–82
Brown, Denis, 184
Bunter*, 120, 121

Burton, Richard, 256
Byrne, Muriel St Clare, 44, 48, 111, 151, 154, 155, 160, 183, 184, 209, 228, 251, 259, 271

Canterbury Festival, 160, 164, 169, 237
Chanson de Roland, 267, 269
Chapman, John and Annie, 11–12
Chesterton, G. K., 51
Children's Hour (BBC), 18, 191–2, 197–8, 200
Christianity *see* Religion
Christie, Agatha, 128, 138, 143
Climpson, Miss*, 128–9
Colchester Festival, 250
Collins, Wilkie, 129; *The Moonstone*, 129; Biography of by DLS, 139
Cournos, John, 89–96, 175, 275
Creativity, DLS' view of, 162–3, 206–7
Crofts, Freeman Wills, 143
Crossman, R. H. S., 175

Dakers, Andrew, 91
Dane, Clemence, 143
Deedes, General Sir Wyndham, 216
Delagardie, Uncle Paul*, 77
Denver, Duchess of*, 123–4
Denver, Duke of*, 106
Detection Club, The, 143–5, 181, 239
Diocesan Reorganization Committee, 240, 241–2
Divine Comedy, The (Dante), 224, 227–9; DLS' translation of, 231–4, 266
Dixey, Giles, 44, 70
Douglas, Miss, 33, 38
Driberg, Tom, 241

Durham University, Honorary degree, 215, 252

École des Roches (Verneuil sur Avre), 76–7, 185
Economics, DLS' interest in, 219–21
Egg, Montague*, 157
Eliot, T. S., 223, 235, 241
Ellis-Fermor, Una, 184
Eustace, Robert, 130–1

Faulkes, Margaret, 266
Fehmer, Fräulein, 248–9
Figure of Beatrice (Charles Williams), 223, 225
Fleming, Anthony (DLS' son), 97, 173–4, 181, 271–2; his birth, 102; with Ivy Shrimpton, 102–5, 133, 140–1, 145–6; "adoption" by DLS, 151, 255. *See also* "Bill"
Fleming, Edgar, 252–3
Fleming, Oswald Atherton, ("Mac"), 113–18, 134, 139–40, 145, 146–7, 174, 242–4, 246, 250–1, 252; his death, 252–3
Floating Admiral, The (Detection Club), 143
Foster, Basil, 168

Gielgud, Val, 171, 192, 195, 200, 268–9
Gietch, Eleanor, 70
Gilroy, John, 135–7
Glendinning, Ethel, 168
Godolphin School, Salisbury, 31–41
Gollancz, Victor, 139, 177, 225

Haggard, H. Rider, 7, 9
Harbottle, Laurence, 270, 271
Hay, Ian, 175
Herbert, A. P., 175
Higham, David, 142
Hilton, Professor John, 175, 176
Hitchman, Janet, 271
Hodgson, Leonard, 62–3
Horlicks Malted Milk (advertisement), 170–1

How to See the Battlefields (O. A. Fleming), 114–15
Hoyle, Professor Fred, 255

"Inklings, The", 235

Jaeger, Jim (Muriel), 1–2, 46–7, 69, 86
Jenkin, May E., 192, 197
Jews, DLS' attitude towards, 216–19
Judas*, 201

Kensit, J. A., 202

Lambeth Degree, 214–15
Lambourne, Norah, 243, 246, 267
Lammas, Katherine*, *see* DLS' childhood, and *Cat o' Mary* (under DLS' works)
Lapwood, Jack, 269, 270
Leavis, Q. D., 153–4
Leigh, Helen, *see* Sayers, Helen
Leigh, Johanna (DLS" pseudonym), xvii
Leigh, Percival, 5
Levy, Sir Reuben*, 124
Lewis, C. S., 28, 223, 235–6, 251
Livingstone, Miss L. M., 216, 218
Lord's Day Observance Society, 202–3, 204
Lynx, J. J., 217–18

"Mac" *see* Fleming, O. A.
Macaulay, Rose, 168
Maconochie, Sir Richard, 188
Mannering, Mr, 84
Martin, Rev. H. A., 202, 204
Mason, Kenneth, 266
McCulloch, Derek, 193–7
McKinnon, Donald, 188
McLaughlin, Patrick, 183, 240–1, 267, 269
Ministry of Information, 175–6, 187
Ministry of Supply, 180
Moulin d'Or (restaurant), 242
Mullins, Bartlett, 170
Mustard Club, The, 135–8
Mutual Admiration Society (Oxford), 44–5, 111

Norton, Sybil, 93
Nott, Kathleen, 259–60

Ordination of women, 215–6
Oxford, DLS at, 42–55
Oxford Bach Choir, 50–1

Pailthorpe, Dr G. W., 184
Parker, Charles*, 106
Penrose, Miss, 48, 62, 68
Personality cult of DLS, 212
Peters, A. D., 175
Politics, DLS and, 244–5
Protestant Truth Society, 202, 204

Reed, Janet*, 185–6
Religion, DLS and, 23–4, 29–30, 35,
    67–8, 69–70, 166–9, 177–9, 183–4,
    189, 201, 262–5
Religious Drama Society, 184
Reynolds, Barbara, 234, 246–8, 251,
    259, 266, 269
Rhondda, Lady, 241
Richardson, Samuel, 129; *Sir Charles
    Grandison*, 129
Ridler, Anne, 224
Ridley, Roy, 155–6
Rieu, E. V., 183, 233–4, 267
Roches, École des, 76–7, 185
Rowe, Dorothy, 42, 44, 56, 102

St Anne's House, 239–42, 267–8
St Clare Byrne, Muriel, *see under* Byrne
Sassoon, Siegfried, 70
Sayers, Dorothy L. LIFE: her birth, 2;
    her father, 2, 4, 10–11, 141; family
    background, 3–4, 5; her mother,
    4–5, 11, 133, 141–2; professional
    name, 5–6; childhood, 6–7, 9–10,
    11, 13–21, 22–30; relations, 9; self-
    knowledge, 14, 36; education, 18,
    31–41; and religion, 23–4, 29–30,
    35, 67–8, 69–70, 166–9, 177–9,
    183–4, 189, 201, 262–5; and Ivy
    Shrimpton, 22–3, 25, 28–9, 101–4,
    133, 140–1, 145–6, 255; dislike of
    publicity, 27; appearance, 39–40,
48–9, 254; at Oxford, 42–55; in
First World War, 52–4; teaching at
Hull, 59–61; working at
Blackwell's, 62, 75; her sexuality,
58, 60, 71–4, 111–12; working for
Whelpton in France, 76–83;
interest in detective stories, 82;
graduation, 84–5; in London,
85–8; and John Cournos, 89–96;
work for Benson's, 92, 108, 135–8;
and "Bill", 97–100, 105;
pregnancy, 99–102; birth of
Anthony, 102; Anthony's
childhood, 102–5, 108; and
"Mac", 113–18, 134, 139–40, 145,
146–7, 174, 209, 213, 242–4, 246;
method of inventing characters,
117–18; as writer, 117–32, 148–58;
her vulgarity, 127–8; and Victor
Gollancz, 139, 177, 225; death of
parents, 141–2; in Witham, 142–3;
and the theatre, 159–65; view of
creativity, 162–3, 206–7; and
Canterbury Festival, 160, 164, 169;
in Second World War, 175–7,
180–3, 187–90, 209–10; as lecturer,
188–90, 211–12; and the BBC,
187–8, 192–200; attitude towards
Jews, 216–19; and Charles
Williams, 223–31, 238; reading
Dante, 227–31; translating Dante,
231–4, 266; and St Anne's House,
239–42, 267–8; last works, 255–9;
her death, 270; summary of life,
273–7

WORKS: *Begin Here*, 177–8; *Blood and
Sand* (scenario), 84; *Busman's Honeymoon* (novel), 125, 155, 157; (play),
161, 168; *Cat o' Mary*, xvii–xviii, 12,
13, 14–17, 37, 39, 106, 152; *Catholic
Tales and Christian Songs* (poems),
66–7, 165; *Clouds of Witness*, 104,
106, 109, 120, 127, 134; *Devil to Pay,
The* (play), 172–3; *Documents in the
Case, The*, 129–32; *Emperor Constantine, The*, 243, 250, 255–6; "Eros
in Academe" (article), 74; *Five
Red Herrings, The*, 140, 148; *Gaudy*

Sayers, Dorothy L.: WORKS—cont.
  Night, xvii, 48, 124, 127–8, 152–4;
  Great Short Stories of Detection, Mystery
  and Horror (ed.), 139; "Greatest
  Drama Ever Staged" (article), 165;
  Hangman's Holiday, 151; Have His
  Carcase, 149, 270; He That Should
  Come (radio play), 171–2, 191;
  Inferno (translation), 251–2; Just
  Vengeance, The (play), 237–8;
  Juvenalia, xi, 19–20; Lord Peter
  Views the Body, 139; Love All (play),
  184–6; Man Born to be King, The, 171,
  183, 190, 200–2, 205, reception of,
  202–4; Mind of the Maker, The, 190,
  199, 205–8; Mouse Hole, The (play),
  155; Murder Must Advertise, 150–1;
  My Edwardian Childhood, xvii, 2, 13,
  151–2, 207; Nine Tailors, The, 8, 11,
  149–50; No Flowers by Request, 257;
  Pantheon Papers, 257–9, 260–1;
  Pied Pipings (play: DLS co-author),
  56–7; Poems, 58–9, 60, 66;
  "Problem of Uncle Meleager's
  Will" (story), 109; Silent Passenger,
  The (film), 154; Song of Roland
  (translation), 267, 269; Strong
  Poison, 85, 131–2, 148; Thrones,
  Dominations (unfinished), 157;
  Tristan in Brittany (translation), 64,
  139; Unnatural Death, 97, 127, 128,
  130; Unpleasantness at the Bellona
  Club, The, 122, 139, 147; "Who
  Calls the Tune?" (story), 65–6, 173;
  Whose Body?, 2, 87, 109, 124, 125;
  Zeal of Thy House, The (play), 160–9,
  191, 249–50
Sayers, Helen Mary, 4, 5, 11, 133,
  141–2
Sayers, Henry, 2, 4, 10–11, 141
Schreurs, Ann, 113, 252–3
Scoop, The (radio serial) (Detection
  Club), 143
Seligman, E., 234, 267
Shaw, Rev. Gilbert, 240, 242
Shrimpton, Ivy, xi, 22–3, 25, 101–4,
  133, 140–1, 255. See also Fleming,
  Anthony

Sidelings, The, 140–1
Simpson, Helen, 183
Sitwells, 70
Socialism, DLS' view of, 244
Society for Italian Studies, 246–7
Somerville College, Oxford, 43–4,
  154, 268
Song of Roland, 267, 269
Strong, L. A. G., 175

Temple, Archbishop William, 188,
  214–15
Theology see Religion
Thomas, Parry, 138
Tolkien, J. R. R., 235
Turleigh, Veronica, 156

Underwood, Eric, 211

Vane, Harriet*, 72, 85, 122, 131–2,
  148–9, 152

Waddell, Helen, 213
Wallace, Doreen, 70, 71
War, First World, 51–2; Oxford in,
  52–3
War, Second World, 175–6, 180–3,
  187–90, 209–10
Way, Brian, 266
Welch, Dr J. W., 183, 195–6, 198–9,
  202, 241, 245
Whelpton, Eric, 70–1, 76–82, 86. See
  also École des Roches
Whitelock, Mr, 63, 64
Williams, Charles, 160, 223–31, 235,
  237, 238, 257; The Figure of Beatrice,
  223, 225
Wimsey, Lord Peter*, 2, 72, 86–7,
  109, 119–26, 131–2, 148–9, 152,
  157–8, 180, 277
Winchester, Bishop of, 203, 204
Women, ordination of, 215–16
Wooster, Bertie, 121, 125
Workers' Educational Association
  (WEA), 180
Wren-Lewis, John, 260–5, 272